Expanded Second Edition

ALPHA-THETA NEUROFEEDBACK IN THE 21ST CENTURY:
A HANDBOOK FOR CLINICIANS AND RESEARCHERS

Edited by

ANTONIO MARTINS-MOURAO

AND

CYNTHIA KERSON

Foundation for Neurofeedback and Neuromodulation Research

Copyright © 2017 by the Foundation for Neurofeedback and Neuromodulation Research.

All rights reserved. No part of this publication may be reproduced, distributed or transmitted in any form or by any means, including photocopying, recording, or other electronic or mechanical methods, without the prior written permission of the publisher, except in the case of brief quotations embodied in critical reviews and certain other noncommercial uses permitted by copyright law. For permission requests, write to the publisher at the address below.

Foundation for Neurofeedback and Neuromodulation Research
1715-K S. Rutherford Blvd. #200
Murfreesboro, TN 37130
www.theFNNR.org

Publisher's Note: The content of this book does not reflect the official opinion of the Foundation for Neurofeedback and Neuromodulation Research. No responsibility is assumed by the publisher for any injury/or damage to persons or property as a matter of product liability, negligence or otherwise, or from any use or operation of any methods, products, instructions or ideas contained in the material herein. Because of rapid advances in the health sciences, in particular, independent verification of diagnoses should be made.

Layout Design & Graphics: Cynthia Powers
Copy Editors: Jon Frederick and Cynthia Powers
Cover Art: Ana Tiburtius
Correspondence: a.martins-mourao@londonscientificneurotherapy.com

Alpha Theta Neurofeedback in the 21st Century: A Handbook for Clinicians and Researchers, Expanded 2nd Edition

ISBN: 978-0-9978194-3-4

Dedications

For Ana
—AMM

For Perry
—CK

Contents

Contributors	ix
Acknowledgments	xix
Foreword *Joe Kamiya*	xxi
Introduction	xxxi
1 Neurofeedback, Brainwaves, and Alpha/Theta Neurofeedback Training *Antonio Martins-Mourao*	1
2 How It All Began *Patricia Norris*	53
3 Experiences With Alpha Theta: Its Origins in Studies of Meditation *David L. Trudeau*	75
4 Alpha/Theta Training as a "State Access" Process *John Nash*	107
5 The Neurophysiology of Trauma: Effects on the Individual, the Body, and the Brain *Cynthia Kerson*	123
6 The Therapeutic Crossover in A/T Training Neurofeedback: Temporal and Spectral Components of Access to Levels of Consciousness *Mark Johnson and Eugenia Bodenhamer-Davis*	141

7	Alpha/Theta Training and Phenotypes *Jay Gunkelman*	173
8	Two Case Studies in Outpatient A/T Training for Trauma *Richard Davis and Eugenia Bodenhamer-Davis*	185
9	Alpha-Theta Training in the Treatment of Dissociative Identity Disorder *Dan Chartier*	206
10	Peniston Protocol as an Integrated, Stand-Alone Therapeutic Modality *Nancy White and Leonard Richards*	223
11	Lessons Learned From Peniston's Brainwave Training Protocol *Estate (Tato) Sokhadze*	245
12	Alpha/Theta Training Applied to Substance Abuse and Post-Traumatic Stress Disorder *William Scott*	281
13	Evolution of Alpha-Theta Training Over a Quarter Century *Siegfried Othmer and Susan F. Othmer*	317
14	The Integration of the Peniston Protocol: A Tool for Neurotherapists and Psychotherapists *Antonio Martins-Mourao*	345
15	Equipment, Training and Ethical Issues *Antonio Martins-Mourao and Cynthia Kerson*	373

Afterword	383
Index	385

Contributors

Eugenia (Genie) Bodenhamer-Davis, PhD is a licensed psychologist and board certified in neurofeedback. She is a professor emeritus of disability and addictions rehabilitation at the University of North Texas (UNT) where she taught courses in biofeedback, neurofeedback, rehabilitation counseling, and health psychology until her retirement in 2013. As founder and director of the UNT Neurotherapy Lab from 1992 to 2013, she supervised graduate-level clinical training and research in EEG and general biofeedback. Her published research focuses primarily on physical rehabilitation and addictions applications of bio/neurofeedback. Dr. Davis has received several awards from the International Society for Neurofeedback and Research (ISNR) recognizing her contributions to neurofeedback education. She currently serves on the board of directors of the Biofeedback Certification International Alliance (BCIA) and chairs its task force on the review of EEG biofeedback certification examination and training standards.

Dan Chartier, PhD, QEEGD is a licensed psychologist and health service provider in Raleigh, NC. He is a founding member of SNR (now ISNR) and served as president in 1999. Dr. Chartier is a founding member of SABA (Society for the Advancement of Brain Analysis) and the QEEG Certification Board, serving as board chairperson for 2016. He is also a member of the board of the Southeastern Biofeedback and Clinical Neuroscience Association. In 1990 as an early adopter of QEEG assessment and neurofeedback training, Dr. Chartier extended his biofeedback and psychotherapy practice to include these modalities. His previous academic experience includes a clinical associate professorship in the Psychiatry Department, UNC-CH School of Medicine. He continues to provide annual lectures on

QEEG and neurofeedback for the UNC-CH School of Medicine Complementary and Alternative Medicine Program.

Richard E. Davis, MS, LPC, BCN is a licensed professional counselor in private practice in Denton, Texas. He has specialized in neurofeedback and QEEG for the last 18 years, and his practice has included neurofeedback services for patients of the Sante Center for Healing, a private residential addiction treatment facility in Argyle, Texas. He was a regular consultant to and a member of the training staff of the former UNT Neurotherapy Lab and has co-authored papers on neurofeedback clinical topics. He is a past president and former treasurer of the International Society for Neurofeedback and Research (ISNR), former treasurer for the ISNR Research Foundation (now FNNR), and a former board member of the Neurofeedback Section of the Association for Applied Psychophysiology and Biofeedback (AAPB).

Jay Gunkelman, QEEGD is recognized as one of the top leaders in the field of EEG and QEEG and has processed over 500,000 EEGs since 1972. He has served as president of the International Society for Neurofeedback and Research (ISNR), as well as a board member and treasurer of the Association for Applied Psychophysiology and Biofeedback (AAPB) and is a past-president of the Biofeedback Society of California. Jay was the first EEG technologist to be certified in QEEG (1996) and was granted diplomate status in 2002. He has conducted, published or participated in hundreds of research papers, articles, books and meetings internationally. He has co-authored the textbook on EEG artifacting (2001). Jay remains busy with current projects and publications related to his seminal paper on EEG endophenotypes (2005, *Clinical Electroencephalography*). He is co-founder and chief science officer of Brain Science International and is a popular lecturer worldwide on the topic of QEEG and phenotype identification of neurological disorders.

Mark Johnson, PhD, BCN received his PhD in clinical health psychology and behavioral medicine at the University of North Texas where he served as assistant clinical coordinator in the UNT Neurotherapy Lab and developed strong interests in clinical applications of QEEG and neurofeedback. Dr. Johnson went on to complete his doctoral residency in the medical psychology track at Duke University Medical Center, Department of Psychiatry, in North Carolina. He is currently a licensed psychologist specializing in multi-modal interventions for chronic pain, addiction, PTSD and other disorders. Mark's research publications focus on clinical topics in neurofeedback, including alpha-theta crossovers and QEEG-guided neurofeedback.

Joe Kamiya, PhD was born in 1925 in a Central California community of Japanese immigrant farmers. He attended local public elementary and high schools where at least one-third of students were of Japanese descent. He took courses in agriculture in high school and developed the ambition to become the owner of the largest chicken farm in the state. The war against Japan and racism prevented all hopes of the realization of this dream. All persons of Japanese descent, American citizens or not, living in California, Oregon, and Washington were forced into confinement in U.S. concentration camps ("relocation centers") during much of the war. Joe graduated from high school in a camp in southeastern Colorado.

After the war, Dr. Kamiya enrolled at UC Berkeley in psychology and earned his PhD in 1953. He began teaching and research in the Psychology Department at the University of Chicago where he developed interests in psychophysiology, especially about how the electroencephalogram (EEG) was related to states of consciousness. Dr. Kamiya discovered humans could be taught to discern the difference in subjective state associated with the presence vs. absence of alpha activity in their EEGs. He also found that with the aid of an auditory signal that tracked the fluctuations in alpha amplitude of their EEGs, they could learn to control them. In 1962, Dr. Kamiya returned to California, joining the Department of Psychiatry and the Langley Porter Clinic at the University of California at San Francisco. With federal grant support, he established a laboratory and confirmed and extended earlier results. He was president of AAPB in 1975. Dr. Kamiya retired as a Professor in Residence in 1992.

Cynthia Kerson, PhD, QEEGD, BCN, BCB, co-editor, is currently the founder and director of education for APEd (Applied Psychophysiology Education), the clinical director of Marin Biofeedback in San Rafael, California, and adjunct professor at Saybrook University Department of Clinical Psychology. She is BCIA certified in biofeedback and neurofeedback, holds certification as a diplomate in QEEG and mentors for both. Dr. Kerson is also on the Board of Directors for the Behavioral Medicine Foundation and AAPB, served as president of the AAPB Neurofeedback Section, vice president of FNNR (formerly the ISNR-Research Foundation), and is two times past president of the Biofeedback Society of California.

Antonio Martins-Mourao, PhD, Clin Psych., AFBPsS, FHEA, co-editor, is a chartered member of the clinical division of the British Psychological Society (BPS) and has lectured on psychophysiology and mental health in several universities in Europe, the UK and Brazil, including the Open University (UK), where he also founded the QEEG & Brain Research Lab, dedicated to the research of EEG-phenotypes for Obsessive Compulsive Disorder (OCD) and Post-Traumatic Stress Disorder (PTSD). He is the clinical director at London Scientific Neurotherapy in

London's Harley Street and serves on the board of FNNR (formerly the ISNR-Research Foundation). Dr. Martins-Mourao is a regular presenter of specialized QEEG workshops in the UK, Italy (BFE), Spain and Brazil and is also a regular presenter at international conferences on the theme of biomarkers for mental health. Some of his other interests include theology, comparative religion, and screenwriting.

John K. Nash, PhD is a licensed psychologist in the state of Minnesota. He received a BSc degree in biology and biochemistry from Princeton University in 1968, a master's degree at the Institute for Neurological Science at the University of Pennsylvania, and a PhD in psychology from the University of California, Santa Barbara, where his dissertation involved human EEG research on attention and perception. Dr. Nash has worked with psychological, emotional and physical problems for over 25 years, in a large multi-specialty medical practice in the Twin Cities, using cognitive behavior therapy and biofeedback. He was also clinical director of a community mental health center, has consulted on human EEG and biofeedback research for NASA, while operating his own private practice in the Twin Cities since 1987. He also helped found the Society for the Study of Neuronal Regulation (now the International Society for Neurofeedback and Research, ISNR) and was its president in 2000. He has published on neurotherapy and EEG in peer-reviewed journals including *Clinical Electrophysiology*, *Journal of Adult Development*, *Memory and Cognition*, and *Psychophysiology*, was the consulting editor for the *Journal of Neurotherapy*, and has extensive experience speaking and consulting with management and professional groups.

Patricia Norris, PhD is professor of transpersonal psychology at Holos University Graduate Seminary. From 1993 to 2005, she was clinical director at Life Sciences Institute of Mind-Body

Health. Prior to that she was clinical director of the Center for Applied Psychophysiology and Biofeedback at the Menninger Clinic. Her work emphasizes integrating body, emotions, mind, and spirit using biofeedback-assisted psychophysiological self-regulation, psychosynthesis and visualization/ imagery. Dr. Norris has specialized in psychoneuroimmunology since 1978, working with clients with cancer, autoimmune disorders such as multiple sclerosis and rheumatoid arthritis, and AIDS. Her research and treatment interests include A/T training and Psychosynthesis in addictive disorders, energy medicine, and states of consciousness. Dr. Norris is past president of the Association for Applied Psychophysiology and Biofeedback (AAPB) and of the International Society for the Study of Subtle Energy and Energy Medicine (ISSSEEM). She served as a faculty member of the Karl Menninger School of Psychiatry 1979–1995; she is an adjunct professor of psychology at Union Graduate School and serves on the boards of the International School for Psychotherapy, Counseling and Group Leadership, the Gladys Taylor McGarey Medical Foundation, True North Center for Integral Medicine, and served on Health World On-Line. Current interests include community rights, prison reform, meditation and Oneness in the planetary field of mind.

Siegfried Othmer, PhD, BCIAC is the chief scientist at the EEG Institute. Since 1985 Siegfried Othmer has been engaged in the development of research-grade instrumentation for EEG feedback, and since 1987 has been involved in the research of clinical applications utilizing that instrumentation. Currently he is chief scientist at the EEG Institute in Woodland Hills, CA. From 1987 to 2000, he was president of EEG Spectrum, and until 2002 served as chief scientist of EEG Spectrum International. Dr. Othmer provides training for professionals in EEG biofeedback, and presents research findings in professional forums.

Dr. Othmer was president of the Neurofeedback Division of the Association for Applied Psychophysiology and Biofeedback over the two-year period of 2011–2013. Presently he is a member of the board of the Western Association of Biofeedback and Neuroscience (formerly the Biofeedback Society of California).

Susan Othmer, BA, BCIAC is clinical director of the EEG Institute. She has been involved in clinical research and the development of neurofeedback protocols since 1988. She teaches professional training courses in neurofeedback, and presents clinical research findings in professional forums.

Leonard M. Richards, MBA, ThD is a clinical associate with Unique Mindcare treating post-traumatic stress and autism using brain-body protocols involving neurofeedback and neuro-stimulation. Dr. Richards is a principal of Lenan Partners, a consultancy that incorporates brain-body fitness into its executive coaching curriculum. In that capacity, he also mentors several young entrepreneurs. Before changing careers to pursue a doctorate in counseling, he and various associates built and managed several high-functioning financial services organizations well-known for their rigorous qualitative and quantitative research, an approach he still uses in his clinical, coaching and research work. Dr. Richards has been active in community affairs and has sat on a number of corporate and charitable boards.

William C. Scott, BSW originally educated as a social worker, has worked in the field of EEG biofeedback for over 20 years, lecturing and publishing numerous times. His work at UCLA and with Dr. Eugene Peniston included a large randomized controlled study using neurofeedback for substance abuse and one that showed 79% success rate with Native American alcoholics. Bill has taught more than 4,000 neurofeedback practitioners around the globe since 1995. He continues his research and innovative developments in the field of EEG biofeedback as CEO of BrainPaint®. He is currently participating in BrainPaint® studies with researchers at Harvard Medical School, UNCW, UNC Chapel Hill, UCLA, UC San Diego and Fort Bliss.

Estate (Tato) Sokhadze, PhD received his degree in human physiology in 1988 (Novosibirsk, Russia). He completed a post-doctoral fellowship in psychopharmacology at Wake Forest University in 2001–2003, and post-doctoral training in cognitive neuroscience at Rice University in 2004. Dr. Sokhadze worked as an associate professor of psychiatry and behavioral sciences at the University of Louisville and director of the Evoked Potential Lab for more than 10 years. Currently, he is a professor of biomedical sciences at the University of South Carolina in Greenville. His research interests include the application of dense-array EEG/ERP-based brain mapping, neurofeedback, TMS, and other applied psychophysiological techniques in psychiatric research. Specific psychopathology areas of interest are autism, ADHD, substance abuse, PTSD, and comorbid mental conditions. He is the recipient of numerous awards from AAPB and ISNR. Dr. Sokhadze currently is the president of the FNNR.

David L. Trudeau, MD was the editor of the *Journal of Neurotherapy*. Dr. Trudeau was the chair of the ISNR Research Committee for 4 years and then served as president of the ISNR Research Foundation (now FNNR) until 2014. He directed the Neurofeedback Lab in the Department of Psychiatry at Minneapolis Veterans Affairs Medical Center for 10 years, prior to his retirement in 2000. Dr. Trudeau has served as assistant professor and adjunct associate professor in the Department of Family Practice and Community Health in the Academic Health Center at the University of Minnesota and as assistant professor in the Department of Psychiatry at the University of Kansas-Wichita. He is a career addictionist and has been the recipient of grants from the Center for Addiction and Alternative Medicine Research under the Office of Alternative Medicine, NIH. He has been active in the teaching of medical students, psychiatry and family practice residents and addiction fellows in addiction medicine and brain wave biofeedback. He has authored 48 scientific articles, book chapters and commentaries in the fields of neurofeedback, QEEG, and addiction medicine. He has co-chaired annual national scientific meetings of ISNR and has served on the board of directors.

Nancy E. White, PhD, LPC, LMFT, AADC serves as clinical director of Unique MindCare in Houston, Texas, a clinical practice focusing on neurobehavioral wellness. Dr. White has practiced in the field of neurofeedback and neuromodulation for more than 25 years and has trained many other practitioners in its modalities. She is BCIA certified as a senior fellow in neurofeedback (BCN), a diplomate in quantitative EEG (QEEGD) and is vice chair of the QEEG Certification Board. Dr. White is a senior fellow of the International Society for Neurofeedback and Research (ISNR), has served as secretary on its board of directors, as a former president of that organization and as a consulting editor of its peer-reviewed journal *NeuroRegulation*. Dr. White has presented at conferences internationally and has published in academic books and peer-reviewed journals on ways to enhance brain function and the brain-body relationship.

Acknowledgments

The idea for this book stemmed, in great part, from a conversation I had with David Trudeau, then President of the ISNR-RF (now FNNR), when I first joined the foundation's board. We talked at length about A/T training and the need to disseminate this powerful technique to psychotherapists, as a way to help a growing number of patients with emotional trauma and addictive behaviors around the world. Thank you, David, for sharing your insights on this theme. I would like to thank Tato Sokhadze, the FNNR's current president, for supporting this project, and the all participating authors who patiently engaged in the rather innovative internal peer-reviewing process used for each chapter included in the book. We wanted authors to talk and learn from each other. My thanks also go to Cynthia Powers and Jon Frederick for their outstanding collaborative effort towards the completion of our expanded 2nd edition. Thank you, Ana Tiburtius for donating the cover Art to this book. Finally, I would like to thank Elizabeth St John, a student of Maxwell Cade, a 1970's British bio- and neuro-feedback pioneer, mentioned in this book by David Trudeau. Elizabeth introduced me to the field of bio- and neuro-self-regulation, thus changing the course of my professional life.

—AMM

Thank you, Tato Sokhadze, for your efforts as president of FNNR and your sincere interest in seeing this book to its completion.

—CK

Foreword

This book, *Alpha Theta Neurofeedback in the 21st Century*, brings to the public some interesting and important news about a component of psychotherapy that has been rather successful for over 15 years in treating clients seeking relief from stress-related problems, including stress suffered early in life, and post-traumatic stress. The component is neurofeedback training of voluntary, conscious control of the abundance of alpha and theta activity in the electroencephalogram (EEG).

The chapters of this book are not only a clear demonstration of the power of alpha-theta training in psychotherapy, but they also seem important for the future science of human life. They suggest that additional studies of technologically-aided introspective exploration of the mind-brain interface could be fruitful.

For those readers for whom the words used in this field—or the procedures used in training—are unfamiliar, it may be helpful to imagine that you have arrived at the neurofeedback office on the first day of your training to learn to control the alpha and theta frequencies of your EEG. You sit in a comfortable chair with small speakers placed near you. The trainer has just finished placing tiny silver disks filled with conductive paste on various locations on your scalp. These conduct the microvolt to millivolt fluctuations detected at your scalp via thin wires to amplifiers and signal processors in the EEG electronic system. The trainer has turned on the electronics, and when you are ready, can send you two tones that fluctuate exactly as the selected features of your EEG fluctuate. For theta frequencies (4–7 Hz) the tone could have a pitch at middle C; for alpha frequencies (8–12 Hz) the tone could be an octave higher to be clearly discernible from theta frequencies. The volume of each tone will be controlled by the half-second moving average size (amplitudes) of their respective EEG waves. These are the feedback signals that you will be learning to control by trial and error, learning of the states of mind most effective at turning them on. False signal sources from muscle activity such as jaw clenching or head and neck movement cause the feedback tones to stop and activate a warning signal to sound. You are asked to close your eyes while a baseline assessment of alpha and theta activity is conducted. The results help the trainer to set optimal threshold values for alpha and theta amplitudes, above which you will the hear feedback tones.

Neurofeedback training of clients to achieve control of specific features of their EEG is an effective tool for treating certain disorders, and so long as it works, one need not know how or why. My experience is limited mostly to training persons to control alpha abundance, as will be discussed later. But I believe that most persons learn the skill of theta amplitude control better when, during breaks in the training, they are encouraged to talk about what they have been trying. I think this helps them to code their successes and failures in their cognitive maps, helping them to recall from memory an essentially non-verbal task.

Neurofeedback is a technological aid to improve our naturally evolved trait to reflect and recall by introspection our own private world of awareness or consciousness.

Academic psychology was born in the Western world with its central focus on consciousness as its subject matter, with introspection being the central method of observation. Neurofeedback owes part of its origins to an academic interest in consciousness and introspection. Introspection was the tool with which experimental psychology was launched in the 19th century. The aim of the science then was the use of disciplined introspective search of the irreducible primary dimensions of sensory experience, led by Wilhelm Wundt and Edward B. Titchener. Because of unresolvable disagreements among different schools over what those dimensions were, the effort was abandoned, and Behaviorism, led by J.B. Watson and later by B.F. Skinner, became the new science of the 20th century.

The change seemed promising. Behavior can be seen and measured, while sensations, perceptions, thoughts, and feelings cannot, and all too often require inferences that are too difficult to become the basis of solid science. However, people do have experiences like emotions, wishes, and dreams. Verbal behavior was certainly observable, and the behavior used to describe dreams were the words the dreamer used to describe them. Verbal report became the data of private experience. But verbal reports are less-than-perfect indicators of private experience because of their ambiguities, our selective memory, regional language habits, and wishful thinking.

Verbal behavior is a product of evolution. The naming of internal states like hunger, anger, fear, sleep, dreaming, has without doubt been aided substantially in precision by technology which points to their biological concomitants. Neurofeedback is a technological aid to improve our naturally evolved trait to reflect and recall by introspection one's own private world of awareness or consciousness.

The middle of the 20th century brought forth new opportunities to develop the science of private experience. Psychophysiology became an important ally of both psychology as well as physiology. It demonstrated that the experience of embarrassment, for example, was quite reliably indicated by increased electrical conductivity of the skin at the palms and, of course, by blushing, at least in persons with fair skin.

Sleep onset was invariably indicated by the EEG sleep spindle. Dreaming during sleep is accompanied by many physiological indicators, of which eye movements were among the most interesting.

Johann Stoyva and I published in 1958 an article in the Psychological Review in which we examined the logic of indicators of dreaming sleep. The central concept of the article is that all indicators of private experience like dreaming, including the verbal reports of the dreamer, coordinated eye movements and accelerated heart rate are less than perfect individually, but together they converge in strong support of the presumed event in nature.

I was fortunate to be allowed the use of the sleep laboratory of Professor Nathaniel Kleitman, who had completed a distinguished research career and was about to retire. With help from his student, William Dement and the aid of a research grant from the National Institutes of Mental Health, I started studying other physiological indicators of sleep and dreaming.

The work in the sleep laboratory was interesting in that it was an opportunity to study additional, physiological correlates of dreaming, but I became interested in another psychophysiological matter concerning the awake person. The EEG alpha rhythm intrigued me. In most persons, its trains of 10 Hz waves did not usually last for more than a few seconds and its absent periods were also fairly brief. They varied widely in duration among different individuals. Some individuals showed alpha activity as much as 80% of the time, while others might show as little as five percent. I became curious about what was the significance of the rhythm.

When the EEG alpha rhythm was present in the brief moments in the record of an awake person whose eyes were closed, was it accompanied by some subjective quality that differed from the brief moments when it was absent? The pursuit of this question led me to devote most of my attention to it and away from sleep research.

To answer the question of a possible subjective difference between the presence of alpha and its absence I decided to see if they could learn to discern any difference with the method of discrimination training.

I chose college students who had clear trains of alpha of at least one second in duration about one-third to one-half the time. I had them prepared for EEG recording, sitting alone with eyes closed in a darkened room, and instructed them to listen for a single ding of a bell I would ring about two or three times each minute. About half the time I would ring the bell when they were showing EEG alpha, and the other times when they were showing no alpha. Each ding of the bell would be a prompt for them to report their guess as to whether it was pattern A or B. I would immediately indicate if their guess was right or wrong by giving two quick dings if their guess was correct and only one ding if their guess was wrong. "A" was correct for alpha present, and "B" was correct for alpha absent.

Most subjects learned to make significant progress within one or two sessions. Some achieved 100% correct labeling of A and B. within four sessions. The subject who achieved the most accurate discrimination of alpha from its absence was able, without any further training, to produce at my command nearly continuous streams of alpha for as long as 20 seconds on several occasions. The more accurate subjects were at discriminating alpha, the more adept they seemed to be at controlling it. Clearly, learning to discriminate alpha from its absence seemed to contribute to the ability to control its presence. In 1956 I tried testing this idea by what I believe to be the first experiment to train the control of alpha abundance using feedback of alpha amplitude as an aid. With some circuitry including a voltage detector, I arranged a tone to be sounded whenever the subject's alpha amplitude exceeded a threshold that I set. I asked the subject to try whatever mental state that would work to increase the proportion of time the tone was on.

After an initial drop, nearly all subjects showed an increase in alpha production. As expected, individuals previously trained in alpha discrimination learned more quickly to increase alpha than individuals who had not been trained.

When asked to describe the difference in subjective quality between A and B, or tone on from off, even the most accurate performers did not have clear descriptions. There was a trend toward words like "calm," "alert," and "relaxed" for alpha's presence but ambiguities in the language were apparent. This problem has led me to explore the development of ways of mapping for each person the principal components underlying his or her judgments of similarity of several EEG and other trained physiological variables to each other. I would expect that this method would significantly reduce the wide individual differences seen in ordinary verbal descriptions. The underlying assumption is the sense of the differences among the different measures should be less than the words used to describe them.

Among the first clinical applications of neurofeedback (then called operant conditioning of the EEG) was one by Barry Sterman. Around 1965 he told me in a conversation that having heard me present my work on feedback trained increases of alpha abundance at a scientific conference, he tried the method to train increases in the sensory motor rhythm in epileptic patients because he had earlier observed the rhythm was relatively absent in epileptic patients. He was pleased that this non-pharmacological method was successful with his patients. Seizures were either stopped altogether or dramatically reduced.

A second successful application of neurofeedback was developed by Elmer Green and his wife, Alyce Green. Elmer heard a presentation I gave on my work with alpha in the Department of Psychology when he was a graduate student there. I did not know him then because he was a student in the Biopsychology section of my Psychology Department. I believe Elmer came to me after I had finished my presentation and indicated he enjoyed it. After completing his studies and earning his PhD at Chicago, Elmer and Alyce traveled to the Menninger Foundation in Kansas and developed a Volunteer Controls Laboratory. They had developed an interest in meditation and its EEG correlates, especially the alpha and theta frequencies. They traveled to India and set up the EEG Neurofeedback Training Project which included training of theta amplitude increases simultaneously with training of alpha amplitude increases.

Alpha-Theta Training

Five steps are involved in the training:

A part of the total electrical activity of the trainee's brain, detected at the scalp at a selected region of the head, usually the occiput, is amplified.

The amplified signal is processed online to extract one or more features, such as the amplitude of the signal after it has passed through a band pass filter that mostly rejects all frequency components above or below the 8 to 12 Hz band., which is the frequency range of the EEG alpha rhythm. If the filter band pass limits were 4 to 7 Hz, its output would be the theta rhythm.

A signal (a tone or light) is sent to the trainee whenever the extracted feature meets a preset requirement, such as exceeding a preset amplitude threshold, thus informing the trainee what worked and what did not in controlling the feedback signal.

The trainee is instructed to increase the total on time of the signal, by learning through trial and error what states of mind increase the likelihood of increased duration of the signal.

During breaks in each training session, the trainee is encouraged to discuss his or her experience with the feedback signal.

When the training session starts, two tones of varying duration are presented: one for alpha waves (8–12 Hz) which exceed a threshold amplitude, the other for theta waves which exceed a threshold amplitude in the frequency range of 4–7 Hz. Once above these thresholds, the tones continue to increase in volume. As performance improves, the thresholds are adjusted without the trainee's knowledge.

In this book, several authors review their experience with using neurofeedback training for enhancing the central neural control of responses to stress with training to increase the amplitude of alpha and theta frequencies. They provide a wide range of experience in clinical settings, including treatment of disorders of memory, post-traumatic stress, multiple personalities, and substance abuse. There appears to be agreement among most authors that when theta increases, especially when alpha amplitude does not increase as much, or even decreases, the quality of what the trainee experiences begins to change toward a hypnagogic one, in which spontaneous images come and go in a dream-like sequence. Further, as the theta becomes more dominant, clients often report more emotional content. This may contribute to the therapeutic utility of theta neurofeedback.

Looking back at the growth of neurofeedback training, it

seems clear to me that the field will continue to grow, both in clinical settings and in a new kind of self-education. It seems reasonable to expect that people of all ages can use neurofeedback for acquiring knowledge of who we are—the thinking, feeling, and emotional selves that we are, based on what we are as biological creatures whose existence depended upon our capacity to function as members of a social system which required complex brains to survive. We ought to be able to understand more of this organ by developing systems that monitor it in action and thereby learn to communicate with it, to learn what kind of creatures we are. One hopes this technology can be further developed in the 21st century.

Joe Kamiya, PhD
San Francisco, CA, USA
April 11, 2016

Introduction

This volume focuses on how neuromodulation, namely alpha/theta neurofeedback training (henceforth A/T training), may be useful to assist and treat deep emotional trauma. Thus, it is dedicated to all health professionals interested in emotional rehabilitation, including neurofeedback practitioners, clinical psychologists, psychotherapists, psychiatrists and many other mental health professionals with an active interest in this area of work. The list is certainly too long to be included here, but all are welcome to immerse themselves in this fascinating field.

In nearly 30 years after the publication of Peniston and Kulkosky's seminal work of 1989 this is the first attempt at bringing together some of the best experts in the field to initiate a fresh conversation about A/T training, and how this technique may be useful to current and future generations of neurofeedback practitioners, psychotherapists and many other mental health professionals interested in emotional rehabilitation.

This handbook, now on its expanded 2nd edition, has three main aims. On the one hand, to ensure the dissemination of what are currently regarded as best practices in A/T training. Secondly, to initiate a much-needed discussion about the various methodological aspects of A/T training for the benefit of all and future practitioners. Finally, this book aims at presenting this innovative and promising technique to other mental health professionals new to the field of.

We have the privilege of including a preface by Joe Kamiya, the originator of the field of neurofeedback. In **Chapter 1**, Antonio Martins-Mourao (co-editor), presents a brief introduction to neurofeedback, EEG brainwaves and the essence of A/T training to readers new to the field. The chapter defines basic concepts, such as neurofeedback, differences between brainwave frequencies, recent developments in neurofeedback practice, and provides a quick guide to the alpha/theta training method.

In **Chapter 2**, Pat Norris reminds readers how the alpha-theta movement began at the Menninger Clinic in Topeka in the mid-1970s under the leadership of Elmer and Alyce Green. Eugene Peniston, then working with alcoholics in a conventional addiction treatment program at the state prison at Fort Lyons, Colorado, began attending Menninger's biofeedback workshops and soon became interested in the group's experience in alpha training to help alcoholics overcome their need to self-medicate. We were saddened by Elmer Green's departure following a brilliant career that enabled the emergence of A/T training and its clinical applications.

In **Chapter 3**, David Trudeau offers a personal experience while being introduced to A/T training as a meditator, who was also working in addiction therapy. David reminds readers about the technical limitations of the early neurofeedback devices, addresses the issue of skepticism and differences in outcomes by different practitioners. He also highlights how differences in outcomes experienced by different practitioners might lie in the intensity of the psychotherapy accompanying the alpha-theta sessions, returns to the importance of alpha-theta in organizing experience into a narrative—both issues also covered in chapter 14—and speculates about the value of LORETA (low resolution electromagnetic tomography analysis) imaging in measuring parahippocampal changes during episodes of alpha-theta crossover.

In **Chapter 4**, John Nash describes his direct experience with Peniston's alpha-theta protocol and Eugene Peniston himself, as a pioneering workshop facilitator working at the Menninger

Foundation Voluntary Controls Program, in the early 1990s. He also reflects on the clinical scope of the A/T training, what this method does and why it does it, and discusses relevant psycho-analytically-oriented literature that may have been neglected by modern clinicians.

In **Chapter 5,** co-editor Cynthia Kerson focuses on the neurophysiology of emotional trauma, including recent evidence of suggesting close interconnections between reward circuits and the brain's default mode network (DMN), both playing an essential role in trauma rehabilitation. She also discusses some emotion theories and ties them to how and why A/T training works when we are simply putting one sensor at the back of the head.

In **Chapter 6,** Mark Johnson and Eugenia Bodenhamer-Davis present recent evidence-based advances in the alpha-theta method, focusing on the role of the elevation of the beta frequencies (13–26 Hz) as a third factor that may increase subject recall of content emerging during the so-called therapeutic crossover. Their study developed a categorization of types of imagery reported as abstract, biographical, perinatal and transpersonal which then provided a further framework for examining relationships between neurofeedback session graph configurations, brainwave frequency ratios, and different types of subjective reports. Sufficient beta amplitude was found to be associated with the best improvements on post-treatment assessment measures for the subjects in the study.

In **Chapter 7,** Jay Gunkelman focuses on the relevance of EEG-phenotypes in the preliminary assessment of A/T training candidates, suggesting that overarousal of the CNS may present with phenotypes (patterns of EEG that are consistently found in the EEG) other than the classic "low voltage fast," with direct implications for treatment success. The chapter also discusses other EEG phenotypes for overarousal, one of them involving anterior cingulate issues, that usually cannot be addressed by A/T training, thus making a case for the usefulness of EEG-guided interventions prior to alpha-theta interventions.

In **Chapter 8**, Richard Davis and Eugenia Bodenhamer-Davis present two case studies. The first one discusses a successful example of outpatient treatment for adulthood trauma using a slightly modified version of the original Peniston protocol. The second one details complications and setbacks that can be encountered when offering outpatient treatment for individuals subjected to multiple early life traumas.

In **Chapter 9**, Dan Chartier presents a case study focusing on the treatment of dissociative identity disorder (DID) and how the patient developed a sense of integration of the self and a deeper understanding of her trauma history, leading to greater insight about the parent responsible for her early trauma. The case also illustrates some of the obstacles raised by patient resistance before more positive health outcomes are achieved.

In **Chapter 10**, Nancy White and Leonard Richards discuss the recovery of an alcoholic patient and offer a more speculative interpretation about the potential reasons for the success of A/T training. The chapter also discusses the role of the therapist as a facilitator and the several components of the A/T protocol.

In **Chapter 11**, Tato Sokhadze presents a review of the literature on the lessons learned from Peniston's alpha-theta protocol. The chapter includes the definition of alpha-theta's levels of clinical efficacy and issues of comorbidity, and the role of dual diagnoses. It also discusses the combination of interventions in outpatients, presenting a conceptual approach to treatment and a rationale for a suggested adjunct neurofeedback therapy for opiate addicts in a treatment using Suboxone, a partial agonist opioid receptor modulator used for the treatment of opioid addiction.

In **Chapter 12**, Bill Scott highlights A/T training efficacy through a comparative discussion between the original Peniston protocol and the Scott & Kaiser modification to the original protocol. The chapter also covers recent literature formulating the mechanisms of change with this intervention and the evidence of successful knowledge transfer of this technique to 699 clients from 39 different clinical settings. The chapter ends with a detailed description on how the author conducts A/T training sessions with an evidence-based methodology that has been used in research and clinical practice since 2001.

In **Chapter 13**, Siegfried and Susan Othmer introduce a comprehensive neurofeedback strategy that incorporates A/T training as a key element, combined with frequency ranges below 0.1 Hz, also known as the infra-low frequency (ILF) region. Experience has led them to evolve from the early temperature training used by Eugene Peniston, on to heart rate variability training and, finally, to ILF to help reduce states of sympathetic over arousal typically found in clients with emotional trauma, before they successfully engage in A/T training.

In **Chapter 14**, Antonio Martins-Mourao (co-editor) addresses issues of theoretical jurisdiction that may explain the unexpected historical isolation of A/T training in relation to its allied disciplines of clinical neuroscience and psychotherapy, as well as some silent theoretical divisions found amongst alpha-theta practitioners. The chapter also reviews some recent and fundamental progress in the neuroscience of memory reconsolidation, which now reframes the relevance of the A/T training to psychotherapists and other mental health professional groups interested in emotional rehabilitation.

In **Chapter 15**, Antonio Martins-Mourao (co-editor) and Cynthia Kerson (co-editor) highlight issues related to choice of equipment, training requirements, ethical principles, standards of care, client engagement and informed consent while offering A/T training to clients.

1

Neurofeedback, Brainwaves, and Alpha/Theta Neurofeedback Training

Antonio Martins-Mourao, PhD

Alpha/theta neurofeedback training—henceforth A/T training—is a powerful psychotherapeutic technique that enables clients and skilled therapists to access and reprocess *unconscious* emotional memories known to affect individual decision-making processes and behaviors. A/T training, like all neurofeedback, uses the modulation of specific individual brainwaves. A/T training, in particular, addresses the theta frequencies known to modulate individual emotional memories situated deep in the brain, in the limbic-related areas.

Conceptually, A/T training sits between psychodynamic theories and the modern clinical neurosciences thus offering a powerful and innovative psychotherapeutic and research tool for both groups, including psychotherapists interested in neuroscience, as described by Cozolino (2017).

A/T training is also likely to attract interest from clinicians and researchers working in neuropsychoanalysis, an emerging field that seeks to understand the human mind from a first-person experience (Panksepp & Solms, 2012; Ramus, 2013; Salone et al., 2016). Methodologically, however, rather than using the traditional talk-therapy approach, A/T training uses advanced EEG-based techniques to monitor precise brainwave shifts known to support a state of *reverie* that can facilitate direct access to the individual's *traumatic* footprint. Details about this technique are further explored in this and other chapters in this book.

In a nutshell, and as Freud (1954) put it well over a century ago, in 1895, in his unpublished "project for a scientific psychology," such technique would one day address the "heart of the matter" in therapeutic terms. A/T training practitioners will argue that "that" moment has arrived, perhaps illustrating the magnitude of Eugene Peniston's contribution to the field of mental health.

Many of our readers won't be new to neurofeedback and A/T training, but for those who are, this chapter will offer a summary introduction to neurofeedback and brainwave frequencies, its history and theoretical underpinnings. It will also discuss the quantitative electroencephalography (QEEG) and will outline the essence of A/T training, and how it differs from the more "classic" neurofeedback practice. It should be noted, however, that the term "classic" neurofeedback does not exist in the literature. It is only used on this occasion to distinguish the well-known neurofeedback practice from A/T training, from which it emerged and separated at the end of the 1980s, following the Peniston and Kulkosky (1989) study, remaining as a separate discipline within the field. We elaborate further on this issue in chapter 14 of this volume. For now, we will briefly introduce neurofeedback, as a technique.

What is Neurofeedback?

Neurofeedback—also known as EEG-biofeedback or neurotherapy—is a psychophysiological procedure that uses real-time information about individual EEG brainwave activity to teach clients to self-regulate their brain functions. Learning control over specific neural substrates has been shown to change specific behaviors thus providing a novel approach to investigate brain function and neuroplasticity (Sitaram et al., 2011). So, as an example, a client may learn how to increase the power in the 8 to 10 Hz frequency range at the back of their head, over a number of neurofeedback sessions, to reduce her symptoms of anxiety.

Hans Berger recorded the first human EEG (electroencephalogram) in the late 1920s (Berger, 1929). Berger was a psychiatrist who saw the potential of the brainwave measurement for the investigation of mental illness and set a research agenda to match his aims. Only 10 years later, however, neurologists progressively adopted the technique after studies began to suggest the EEG as an effective technique for the detection of epilepsy (Gibbs et al., 1937; Gibbs, Gibbs, & Lennox, 1943, among others). Interestingly, it is perhaps a little-known fact that neurofeedback saw its dawn at around the same time, as discussed later in a section dedicated to the history of neurofeedback.

During a typical neurofeedback training session, the clients will sit comfortably in front of a computer monitor while sensors are placed on their scalp to measure subtle electrical activity in their brain (step 1 in Figure 1.1). Training is based on precise guidelines, or *protocols*, that contain information about the relevant *frequency* bands being trained and the specific scalp *locations* for the application of the sensors. Protocol design is based on a variety of sources and methodologies, including an expanding research literature, as will be discussed later in the chapter.

During a session, clients will use the biological feedback provided by the software (step 2 in Figure 1.1) to modify their cognitive and emotional response via a combination of video, sound and (often) tactile feedback, which provides positive feedback (or reward) for desired brain activity, and negative feedback for brain activity that is undesirable. For example, a lapse of concentration can produce undesired brain activity, which will trigger a negative feedback signal.

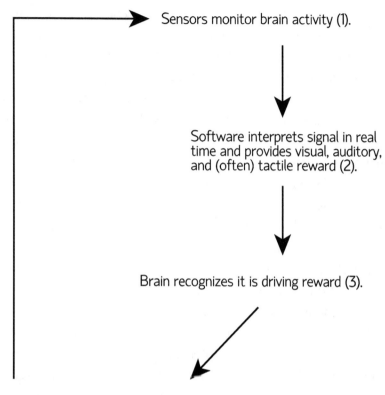

Figure 1.1. Summary description of the neurofeedback loop during a typical session.

Positive feedback may be conveyed as an increasingly sharper video image and sound or a faster-moving object, whereas negative feedback may be presented as a progressively foggier and/or shrinking video image, or a slower-moving object. In time, the brain will recognize its role in driving the reward (step 3 in Figure 1.1) and this learning process will eventually translate into new neural connections and self-awareness (step 4 in Figure 1.1), leading to altered behavior and the remission of key symptoms.

This technique has several strengths. The brain thrives on change, so neurofeedback draws upon the brain's ability to learn, self-regulate and adapt. It is also a *drug-free*, safe and non-invasive technique that both children and adults find non-threatening. On average, clients are recommended a course of at least 30 sessions until a learning curve is established, and the results obtained may become stable and permanent. The number of sessions will vary depending on the condition being treated and the therapist's skills.

Neurofeedback practitioners are required to interpret different brainwave frequencies and make clinical judgments about their functional meaning, according to their locations in the cortex. Before we engage with this complex issue, we will first briefly define the various brainwave frequencies and some of their functional meanings in the next section.

Brainwave Frequencies

Brainwaves can be broadly defined according to three main parameters: *frequency*, *amplitude* (or *power*) and *phase*. **Frequency** is the speed of an oscillation—or rhythm—defined in Hertz (Hz), which refers to the number of cycles, or oscillations, per second. This is similar to heart beats per minute, or BPM. To illustrate this concept, four handclaps within a second will define the theta frequency of 4 Hz. Ten claps within a second would define an alpha frequency of 10 Hz, and so on. The brain oscillations recorded in the human EEG have been *conventionally* divided into five main frequencies ranging typically from 0.1 to 80 Hz, to include the *delta* (0.1–4 Hz), *theta* (4–8 Hz), *alpha* (8–12 Hz), *beta* (13–30 Hz) and *gamma* (> 30 Hz) frequencies.

Amplitude is the intensity of the wave, proportional to its height when represented in a graphic display. Amplitude is measured in volts. It should be noted, however, that the skull and tissue layers surrounding the brain significantly attenuate the signal, so when measured at the scalp, the EEG displays significantly reduced amplitude seen on the scale of 1–100 microvolts (μV). **Power** is a related measure that refers to the amount of energy in a frequency band, usually expressed as squared amplitude; the words power and amplitude are sometimes used interchangeably in the EEG literature.

The amplitude or power of a sound wave is a useful analogy. When the power of synchronized applauding in a soccer stadium increases it also produces a signal with more power. A higher power in the alpha frequency, for example, will reflect a greater number of *neurons* firing at that frequency, or more fans clapping in a stadium. So more power will also mean higher amplitude in the relevant frequency. In general, the higher the frequency (more cycles per second), the lower the amplitudes will tend to be.

Phase is the amount of synchronization across different generators (neurons, people, or other). Everyone clapping in unison will result in perfect phase alignment. Conversely, if everyone claps independently, there will be zero phase alignment and significantly less power. In terms of brain activity, researchers have developed theories on how external stimuli may induce changes in the internal synchronization patterns. Using a soccer match as an example, a "goal" (external stimulus) will initiate an explosion of synchronized applause by the fans, just as virtually all noise in the stadium might fade seconds before a penalty kick.

The brain is an exceedingly noisy place considering that its 100+ billion neurons are being driven at different frequencies and in complex patterns. Yet, there seems to be relative coherence in apparent chaos, all forming an orchestrated symphony with important clinical and behavioral meaning.

The neural oscillations that can be measured with EEG are always a mixture of several underlying base frequencies thought to reflect a range of cognitive, and affective states.

The following frequency band definitions are presented as a brief introduction to the theme and are based on reputed sources such as *Niedermeyer's Electroencephalography: Basic Principles, Clinical Applications, and Related Fields* (Schomer & Lopes da Silva, 2011) and other benchmark publications such as Steriade, Gloor, Llinas, Lopes da Silva, and Mesulam (1990). We encourage all neurofeedback practitioners to consider the review of these important sources to further their understanding of this complex issue.

Delta rhythms (1–4 Hz) are usually largest in infants as well as young children; see Figure 1.2, showing a 1-second segment of EEG recording. Traditionally, delta oscillations have been largely associated with slow-wave, anesthesia and the brain's repairing cycles when no conscious function was thought to take place during these states (Achermann & Borbely, 1997; Niedermeyer, 2005). Recent data, however, has suggested that the slow wave delta-band oscillations could reflect important neural activity between distant—and large scale—cortical networks during decision-making (Nácher, Ledberg, Deco, & Romo, 2013). Delta also seems to be involved in the formation and internal arrangement of biographical memory as well as acquired skills and learned information (Harmony, 2013), so further research is likely to change the role of the delta frequency in brain functioning. When recorded in awake subjects, the finding of delta may suggest brain lesions or important structural issues and pathology (Sharbrough, 2005).

Delta rhythms may become larger in subjects during meditation or while entering trance states. At an optimal level, delta waves may reflect balanced immune function and restorative

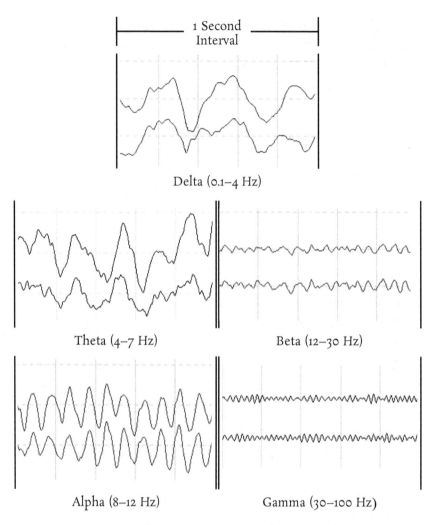

Figure 1.2. Brainwave frequencies seen in the typical human EEG.

sleep. Much remains to be understood regarding the lower and infra low frequencies (or ILF), as discussed in chapter 13, by authors Siegfried and Susan Othmer.

The delta frequencies can often be confounded with movement *artifacts* such as eye blinks and lateral eye-movements, head, body, pulse pressure waves, heart rate, or even tongue movements. Muscle tension (electromyographic or EMG) artifact can easily be mistaken for gamma, beta or even alpha activity, because EMG has a very wide power spectrum from about 10–400 Hz. To get a competent EEG recording the client must be shown the effect of some of the above-mentioned artifacts and taught to remain relatively still and to relax the face, jaw and neck muscles. In some cases, clients need to be pre-trained to relax to avoid muscle artifacts.

Artifacts do not reflect neural activity and may appear for a number reasons in various frequencies, which won't be detailed in this chapter. It suffices, however, to say that EEG analysis and interpretation typically begins with the filtering or de-artifacting of the raw data, which requires competent training (Hammond & Gunkelman, 2011). Neurofeedback protocols often include extra filters to inhibit the reward signal when an artifact is detected. For instance, eye blinks and movements are often detected by high amplitude excursions in the delta band, and muscle tension will be seen as high amplitude in the high beta and gamma range.

Research in the area of EEG de-artifacting is quite active and one recent important finding in terms of "hard-to-identify" artifacts in the delta range has been described by Ulrich, Schlosser, and Juckel (2016), as the arterial pulse impedance artifact (APIA). Untypically, the APIA cannot be detected in the raw EEG data thus requiring more elaborate methods of EEG analysis.

Theta rhythms (4–8 Hz), shown in Figure 1.2, can be detected in the frontal lobes in normal subjects and has been found to correlate with the difficulty of mental operations such as focused attention and information processing and learning. These frequencies tend to become more prominent with increasing task difficulty, leading to its association with brain processes underlying mental workload or working memory (Klimesch, 1996, 1999;

O'Keefe & Burgess, 1999; Schack, Klimesch, & Sauseng, 2005). Other studies have suggested the involvement of theta frequencies in a wide-ranging network involving medial prefrontal areas, central, parietal (back) and medial temporal cortices (sides), connecting cognitive processing across distant brain regions (Mizuhara et al., 2004).

Longer theta bursts may signal reverie states, such as those found during A/T training, or sleep onset. Prolonged theta periods during wakefulness may suggest daydreaming, typical of ADHD, for example. Excessive theta frequencies, on the other hand, may indicate cortical slowing often with clinical consequences (Kropotov, 2016). At an optimal level, theta waves may reflect creativity, emotional connection, intuition, and relaxation. Finally, the theta frequencies play a fundamental role in A/T training by enabling states of reverie and access to implicit memories with positive therapeutic consequences, as discussed throughout this book.

Moving upwards, the **alpha rhythms** (8–12 Hz), shown in Figure 1.2, were the first oscillation reported by Hans Berger in 1929, hence named as alpha. Alpha is usually generated at the back of the head, including the occipital, parietal and posterior temporal brain regions. Alpha power typically increases during mental and physical relaxation with eyes closed, and reduces during mental or bodily activity with eyes open (Hardt & Kamiya, 1978). The increase in eyes closed alpha power correlates with lack of visual stimulation and the expected idleness in the occipital cortex.

Further, alpha waves have several functional correlates reflecting sensory, motor and memory functions (Klimesch, 1996, 1999, 2012; Schomer & Lopes da Silva, 2011). The increase and suppression of alpha power constitute an important biomarker for states of mental activity and engagement, for example during focused attention towards external stimuli (Hanslmayr et al., 2005; Klimesch, 2012; Pfurtscheller & Aranibar, 1977). Meditators are known to increase their alpha power resulting in states of focus and alertness (Davidson & Begley, 2012; van Lutterveld et al., 2017). Some anxious individuals may not show alpha in their eyes closed EEGs, while others may show excessive eyes closed alpha. Interestingly, the interpretation of these biological differences has initiated the study of the so-called EEG-phenotypes (Johnstone, Gunkelman, & Lunt, 2005), which may inform the design of neurofeedback protocols (see chapter 7).

The alpha frequencies are seen as a thalamo-cortical rhythm that oscillates between the *thalamus* and the *cortex* in a continuous motion (Lopes da Silva, Vos, Mooibroek, & van Rotterdam, 1980). The thalamus acts as a sensory gateway, continually relaying sensory information to the cortex, thus explaining why alpha *suppresses* while the brain is processing sensory information and coordinating attentional resources in a particular moment (Hanslmayr et al., 2005; Hanslmayr, Gross, Klimesch, & Shapiro, 2011). Clinically, alpha tends to be the first port of call during EEG analysis. John Nash, an author in this book, describes alpha to his clients as "a pause, a momentary inhibited state, like the period at the end of a sentence or the space at the end of a paragraph."

As it will become clearer throughout most of the remaining chapters in this book, the alpha frequency plays a fundamental role in informing about the subjects' arousal levels (Dongier, McCallum, Torres, & Vogel, 1976). Over-aroused subjects are unlikely to engage in A/T training so they may need to engage in relaxation procedures before they initiate their training. This subject is further explored in chapter 7, authored by Jay Gunkelman.

Beta rhythms designate the frequencies ranging between 12 and 30 Hz (see Figure 1.2). Beta activity, mainly above 15 Hz, reflects intra-cortical connections, as opposed to the thalamo-cortical rhythms seen in the alpha frequencies, as discussed above (Steriade et al., 1990). Beta waves are known as high-frequency low-amplitude brain waves that are commonly observed during wakefulness. They are typically involved in conscious thought, logical thinking and tend to have a stimulating effect. So, active concentration and busy, anxious thinking are generally known to correlate with higher beta power (Schomer & Lopes da Silva, 2011). Beta waves are conventionally split into three sections: low beta, ranging from 12 to 15 Hz; beta 2 waves, ranging from 15 to 20 Hz, and high beta waves, ranging from 20 to 30 Hz.

Beta states associated with normal waking consciousness and cognitive activity are typically found between 15 to 20 Hz, depending on individual differences. Beta activity above 20 Hz, in the beta 3 range, is usually associated with cortical irritability and stress, although they may also be associated with muscle activity (i.e., muscular artifacts). An important biomarker related to the beta frequencies are their excessive amplitude, which above 20 microvolts (μV), is regarded as beta spindling, suggesting anxiety, hyperarousal, and often ruminative thinking. Yet, at an optimal level beta activity reflects cognitive engagement, conscious focus and active problem solving.

Finally, **gamma rhythms** range from 30 to 80 Hz (see Figure 1.2). These frequencies are involved in higher processing tasks as well as cognitive functioning and so are relevant and important for learning, memory and information processing. Some authors claim that the 40 Hz gamma wave is important for the binding of our perceptions and are involved in learning new material (e.g., Crick & Koch, 2003; Engel, Fries, Koenig, Brecht, & Singer, 1999; Lehmann et al., 2001). However, the clinical use and interpretation of the gamma frequencies is still in its infancy, although some authors have studies the role of gamma waves in neuropsychiatric disorders (Herrmann & Demiralp, 2005). At an optimal level, the gamma frequencies are thought to enhance cognition, information processing, and REM sleep.

Following a brief introduction of the various brainwave frequencies, we now turn to the history of neurofeedback.

Brief History of Neurofeedback

Neurofeedback, as a science, emerged 80 years ago when human *voluntary* control of brainwaves was demonstrated. Preliminary research in the mid-1930s had suggested that individual brain oscillations could be *affected* by different mental states and external stimuli (Durup & Fessard, 1935; Travis & Egan, 1938a). Then came evidence that the eyes closed alpha blocking response could be classically conditioned using *involuntary* associations between lights, sounds and changes in the EEG (Loomis, Harvey & Hobart, 1936; Travis & Egan, 1938b). Other experiments later confirmed that the blocking response responded to several types of classical Pavlovian techniques (Jasper & Shagass, 1941a; Knott & Henry, 1941).

The key moment, however, came when Jasper and Shagass (1941b) showed that subjects could gain *voluntary* control over their alpha blocking response by pairing the light onset to a subvocal command ("block") rather than to an auditory tone. This experiment can be considered the first basic demonstration of a neurofeedback loop, involving *operant* (i.e., voluntary) control over the EEG based on basic learning principles. Further variants of voluntary control over the alpha frequencies were also confirmed using voluntary fist clenching (Shagass, 1942) and subject expectations (Shagass & Johnson, 1943). This was a time when psychologists were at the center of EEG research.

In its more modern form, however, neurofeedback emerged out of Joe Kamiya's Lab at the University of Chicago in the early 1960's (Kamiya, 1969, 1971; Hardt & Kamiya, 1978), when he began teaching subjects to identify and gain voluntary control of their alpha power and alpha peak frequency, resulting in enhanced relaxation states (see details in Joe Kamiya's preface). Similar studies focusing on the conditioning of alpha rhythms in humans include Albino and Burnand (1964).

Almost simultaneously, Barbara Brown, chief psychologist at the Experiential Physiology Research Department at the Veterans Administration Hospital in Sepulveda, California, published a series of peer-reviewed studies on core EEG-related research and bio- and neurofeedback techniques (Brown, 1968, 1970a, 1970b; Brown & Shryne, 1964). As an experienced bio- and neurofeedback clinician, Brown suggested early on that doctor-patient relations should change to accommodate a "working partnership," famously writing that the "person is no longer the object of treatment, the patient *is* the treatment" (Brown, 1977; see also Brown, 1974).

In the UK, in the early 1970s, Maxwell Cade, a British scientist and physicist interested in the use of biofeedback equipment for the development of higher consciousness, introduced the "Mind Mirror," (co-developed with Geoff Blundell) to research the brain's physiological properties of creativity and how the mind influenced individual health patterns (Cade & Coxhead, 1979). Cade also trained Anna Wise, a well-known author in peak-performance, creativity and A/T training who taught at the Esalen Institute in Big Sur, California (Wise, 1996, 2002).

The next studies extended the demonstration of operant conditioning to other brain responses. A study reported by Irwin, Knott, McAdam, & Rebert (1966), suggested that contingent negative variation (CNV), a long-latency EEG index of cortical arousal with cognitive and motor components observed during response anticipation (Nagai et al., 2004), could involve motivational factors, thus becoming an important index of "expectancy." The same research group also demonstrated that subjects could be taught to control CNV amplitude at will (McAdam, Irwin, Rebert, & Knott, 1966).

Barry Sterman's lab demonstrated that operant conditioning of sensory motor rhythm (SMR) activity in cats had anticonvulsant properties (Sterman, 2000; Sterman & Friar, 1972; Sterman, LoPresti, & Fairchild, 1969, 2010; Wyrwicka & Sterman, 1968), thus paving the way to clinical applications of operant conditioning of the EEG. Only a few years later, Joel Lubar and colleagues showed results suggesting the effectiveness of neurofeedback for the treatment of attention deficit hyperactivity disorder (ADHD; Lubar, Swartwood, Swartwood, & O'Donnell, 1995) a claim later verified by Arns, Heinrich, and Strehl (2014) and many other authors.

Over the last 15 years, neurofeedback has attracted the interest of many other academic research groups and labs, and the result has translated into a remarkable growth in studies supporting its effectiveness. Since Kamiya's, Sterman's, and Brown's initial studies, the number of publications has steadily grown to now include nearly a thousand articles published in peer-reviewed journals, as shown in Figure 1.3. At the time of writing, a study search on the pubmed.com search engine using "neurofeedback" as a key word in the "title/abstract" field has revealed 971 scientific articles published in peer-reviewed journals since the early 1990s. The use of "EEG-biofeedback" as a keyword will list studies published as far back as 1973.

Taken together, the weight of the evidence suggests that neurofeedback can be used to successfully modulate specific functional networks (deBettencourt, Cohen, Norman,

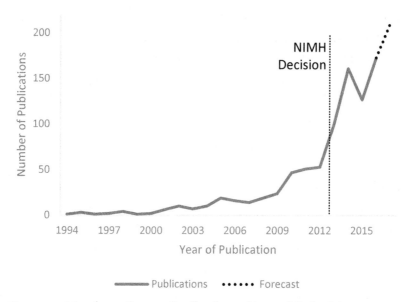

Figure 1.3. Number of neurofeedback studies published in peer-reviewed journal by year, including NIMH's decision to abandon funding for DSM-based research in 2013.

& Turk-Browne, 2015; Shibata, Watanabe, Sasaki, & Kawato, 2011), thus facilitating neuroplasticity in humans (Ranganatha, et al., 2017; Ros, Munneke, Ruge, Gruzelier, & Rothwell, 2010; Sitaram et al., 2011). Specifically, neurofeedback is reported to offer a reliable and effective therapy for conditions such as attention deficit and hyperactivity disorder, ADHD (Albrecht, Sandersleben, Gevensleben, & Rothenberger, 2015; Arns et al., 2017; Mayer, Wyckoff, Fallgatter, Ehlis, & Strehl, 2015; Strehl et al., 2017) stroke rehabilitation (Ramos-Murguialday et al. 2015), epilepsy (Monderer, Harrison, & Haut, 2002; Sterman, 2000; Sterman & Egner, 2006; Sterman & Friar, 1972; Tan et al., 2009), autism (Christoffersen & Schachtman, 2016; Friedrich et al., 2015; Wang et al., 2016), PTSD (van der Kolk et al., 2016) and many other conditions (Heinrich, Gevensleben, & Strehl, 2007;

Micoulaud-Franchi et al., 2015).

Unfortunately, however, neurofeedback research hasn't perhaps received due credit for its early (as well as modern) role in unveiling some of the essential neuro- and electrophysiological aspects underpinning animal and human neuroplasticity. This is a story worth telling. Following William James' initial speculations about the brain's capacity to change itself (James, 1890), Donald Hebb's suggestion that behavioral experience could alter neuronal structure, leading to strengthened connection and ultimately learning (Hebb, 1949), and Paul Bach-y-Rita's concept of sensory substitution (Bach-y-Rita, Collins, Sauders, White, & Scadden, 1969), the first lab-based evidence of cellular changes related to neuroplasticity was reported by Ladislav Tauc in 1965 (Bruner & Tauc, 1965; for an English translation published in the journal *Nature*, see Bruner & Tauc, 1966).

Tauc, a Czech-born French biophysicist and neurophysiologist, introduced the "simplified" brain (or the *Aplysia* nervous system) to study the cellular and molecular basis of organized neuronal interaction. *Aplysia* are large sea slugs with brains containing about 20,000 neurons. Incidentally, Tauc mentored Eric Kandel who went on to develop the application of the of *Aplysia* nervous system to the neuroscience of behavior. Raisman (1969) later reported evidence of neuroplastic processes in rats.

As we will see in the next section, it is often ignored that neurofeedback researchers were already making fundamental contributions describing the electrophysiology of neuroplasticity using animal studies at that time.

Learning Theory and Other Emerging Theoretical Underpinnings

Neurofeedback uses a learning paradigm that links electrophysiological changes observed in the brain with behavior. The first report uncovering such in-depth changes in the brain of mammals was published by Clemente, Sterman, and Wyrwicka (1964), a year before Tauc's pioneering work on the *Aplysia* nervous system.

Since the early alpha voluntary conditioning studies in the late 1930s and 1940s, many neurobehavioral researchers had meanwhile abandoned the traditional EEG in favor of more tangible in depth single-unit recordings, or evoked neuroelectric response (Sterman, Wyrwicka, & Roth, 1969), with important consequences for the future of neurofeedback research. Earlier in this chapter (see section titled Brainwave Frequencies), we had introduced the notion that the skull and tissue layers surrounding the brain significantly attenuate EEG signals recorded on scalp. The use of in-depth single unit recording attempted to solve this limitation.

So by using single-unit recordings to "zoom-in" into the epiphenomena of brainwave at brain tissue level, Clemente et al. (1964) were able to describe a crucial electrophysiological event known as "post-reinforcement [EEG] synchronization," or PRS. PRS refers to distinct alpha-like synchronization (or increase) observed in the posterior areas of the brain of cats *immediately* upon receiving food (reward).

Further studies confirmed that PRS could be trained via operant response (Poschel & Ho, 1972) and correlated positively with learning outcomes in animals (Marczynski, 1972; Marczynski, Harris, & Livezey, 1981) and humans (Hallschmid, Mölle, Fischer, & Born, 2002). Stemming from this research, Barry Sterman famously showed that the operant conditioning of sensory motor rhythm (SMR) activity in cats had anticonvulsant properties (Sterman, LoPresti, et al., 1969; Wyrwicka & Sterman, 1968) as discussed earlier. Marczynski et al. (1981), as another example, demonstrated a significant positive correlation between greater

PRS indices and faster learning in 25 of 27 cats trained to receive 1 ml of milk after pressing a lever.

Put together, these studies described a fundamental learning paradigm on which future clinical applications of neurofeedback would be tested, as demonstrated by later studies suggesting functional relations between alpha and theta activity during learning processes (Doppelmayr, Klimesch, Pachinger, & Ripper, 1998; Klimesch, 1999).

What Happens in the Clinic?

In clinical settings, the neurofeedback loop is established when the clients associate their spontaneous electromagnetic signal with the sensory information being fed through the feedback modality. We will now draw directly from a milestone review publication explaining this process within the context of learning theory (Sherlin et al., 2011), which we encourage our readers to become acquainted with.

Historically, and since Jasper and Shagass (1941b) and Kamiya's (1971) initial studies, EEG brain activity has been demonstrated to be responsive to operant and classical conditioning, thus finding its theoretical basis in Skinner's (1958) operant learning principles. This will require the review of some basic concepts. As recapped by Sherlin et al. (2011), operant conditioning can increase a *preferred* behavior and *decrease* an undesired behavior by providing a reward or punishment (Skinner, 1948). Accordingly, a reward is any event (presentation of food, tones, etc.) that follows a specified and desirable response that is intended to promote the specified response to occur again under the same conditions.

To illustrate the above concept, consider a girl that is learning to reduce her elevated frontal theta waves, being recorded at the front of her head, as typically seen in some cases of ADHD. As she watches a computer game, every time her theta power decreases, she will be reinforced positively with a faster-moving (and louder) airplane shown on the computer monitor in front of her. Another pleasant event will be an increased score. Getting more points and getting a fun (and liked) movie or game running will make the behavior that just happened more frequent, while changes in her brain are occurring.

In practice, most current neurofeedback implementations should use a *continuous* fixed ratio reinforcement schedule followed by variable ratio to enable the girl in our example to reach the final representation of a response by reinforcing successive approximations of the desired response; i.e., the reduction of fronto-central theta, a process termed *shaping* (Skinner, 1958).

This means that the neurofeedback loop should specifically inform the girl whether her brain's response was desirable or not and to what extent her brain signal may have changed (Sherlin et al., 2011). Additionally, the *timing* of the reinforcement during a session is critical to learning because delays as small as a fraction of a second can decrease the strength of the conditioning (Skinner, 1958). In other words, the contingent relationship between the behavior and the reinforcement must become evident to the girl within the shortest delay possible. Based on Felsinger and Gladstone (1947) and Grice (1948), Sherlin et al. (2011) suggest that the latency for the response should not exceed 250 to 350 ms.

Learning theory has been extremely useful to explain the impact of neurofeedback on learners by illustrating how and why clients remain engaged during a neurofeedback session, independently of their awareness of the changes happening in their brains. The post-reinforcement synchronization (PRS) paradigm has added compelling evidence about specific electrophysiological changes associated with learning. However, other biomarker-based explanations are beginning to emerge, which have contributed to the reframing of neurofeedback as a clinical and research tool within the wider field of neuroscience.

Subtler Brain Processes: Endogenous Control of Dopamine Production?

Neuroscience is now starting to uncover the influence of this technique on much processes. Recent studies have, for example, suggested that the neurofeedback loop can help individuals learn a non-invasive strategy for endogenous control of dopamine production. This *extraordinary* claim, awaiting replication, would be possible by gaining voluntary control of the so-called substantia nigra and ventral tegmental nuclei of the basal ganglia, thereby potentially enhancing dopamine release to target brain regions (Sulzer et al., 2013). The substantia nigra and ventral tegmental nuclei are brain structures involved in the reward circuitry in the brain.

Neurofeedback-related research is expanding fast, as shown in Figure 1.3. The results reviewed earlier suggest that the explanatory power associated with neurofeedback is quickly increasing and new causal connections between self-regulation and specific biomarkers, such as dopamine production, are being reported. We are thus getting a step closer to explaining how experience and changes in awareness may change our biology, as initially suggested by Conrad Waddington who proposed that genome expression could be affected by environmental factors (e.g., Waddington, 1942a, 1942b, 1953; see also Hebb, 1949). This concept has recently become a very active area of research known as epigenetics (Berger, Kouzarides, Shiekhattar, & Shilatifard, 2009).

Crucially, however, progress in neurofeedback-related

research is also being influenced in perhaps previously unpredictable ways by one of the most important paradigmatic shifts seen in mental health since Kraepelin's work in the 19th century: the abandonment of the DSM. We turn to this discussion in the next section.

Recent Technological Developments and the Post-DSM Era

Mental health care is currently undergoing a paradigmatic shift that is reframing the relevance of this field as a technique for neuroscience research and, as therapeutic tool psychotherapists interested in neuroscience, as described by Cozolino (2017).

This shift has two important aspects. On the one hand, a growing number of neurofeedback practitioners have become interested in biomarker-based diagnostic methodologies, such as the quantitative EEG or QEEG. Earlier in the chapter, we described the EEG as the measurement and recording of electrical brain activity commonly referred to as "brainwaves." The QEEG is the transformation of the digitized EEG data acquired by 19-channel amplifiers into color maps of brain functioning (often called "brain maps"), created by comparing the individual's EEG to a carefully developed normative database. Usually, these maps correspond to positive and negative standard deviations from the mean of a normative database (also known as z-scores), allowing the detection of functional abnormalities, where large deviations are often associated with disordered functioning.

It should be noted that the use of the QEEG in mental health, also known as psychiatric EEG, differs from the conventional analysis and interpretation competently made by neurologists since the early 1940s, which has traditionally focused on the investigation of epilepsy, tumors and other organic brain lesions in the brain (Hughes & John, 1999). The psychiatric EEG, on the other hand, has developed from suggestions that nearly 70% of EEGs in psychiatric patients could provide evidence of pathophysiology, thus having additional utility beyond the task of ruling out organic brain lesions (Coburn et al., 2006; Hughes, 1995; Hughes & John, 1999; Small, 1993). The clinical scope of the psychiatric EEG would include distinguishing between dementia and depression, schizophrenia and mood disorders, assessing cognitive, attentional or developmental disorders and evaluating substance abuse, amongst other conditions (Hughes & John, 1999). Both, the American Electroencephalographic Society (1987) and the American Academy of Neurology and the American Clinical Neurophysiology Society (Nuwer, 1997) have endorsed this new discipline. Like the neurological EEG, the psychiatric EEG does not rely on normative database comparisons.

Neurometrics

This *other* concept for QEEG analysis and interpretation, involving the comparison of clinical EEG data with normative databases, is known as "neurometrics." The term was coined by E. Roy John, an American neurobiologist based at the University of New York. Akin to the concept of psychometrics, used by psychologists to measure on constructs such as intelligence, personality, motivation and so on, neurometrics offers a method of quantitative EEG to provide "a precise, reproducible estimate of the *deviation of an individual record from normal.* This computer analysis makes it possible to detect and quantify abnormal brain organization, to give a quantitative definition of the severity of brain disease, and to identify sub-groups of pathophysiological abnormalities within groups of patients with similar clinical symptoms" (John, 1990, emphasis added; see also John, 1977).

Neurometrics has been applied to the evaluation of cognitive dysfunctions and neurological disorders in children (John et al., 1983), to computer-assisted differential diagnosis of brain dysfunctions (John, Prichep, Fridman, & Easton, 1988) and the diagnosis of psychiatric and neurological disorders (John, 1989), amongst many other examples.

Several commercial neurometrics software systems have been registered since the 1980s, including the Neurometric Analysis System, in 1988, based on the normative data collected at the University of New York and published by John (1977), followed in 2004 by the NeuroGuide Analysis System, based on the normative data published at University of Maryland (Collura, Thatcher, Smith, Lambos, & Stark, 2009; Thatcher, 1998; Thatcher, North, & Biver, 2005). A year later, BRC Software Products, registered their platform including normative data collected internationally in several laboratories, published by Gordon, Cooper, Rennie, Hermens, and Williams (2006). Another example is the HBimed database recorded and developed in Switzerland by Tereshchenko, Ponomarev, Müller, and Kropotov (2010).

Neurometrics contributed significantly to progress in the field and a shift towards research of EEG-phenotypes—or biomarkers—for the *diagnosis* and *modulation* of brain dysfunctions (Collura et al. 2009; Kropotov, Pąchalska, & Muller, 2014), helping thousands of clients worldwide. Yet, new statistical procedures are currently bringing yet another quantum leap in the field of QEEG analysis and interpretation. One such novelty enables the estimation of source localization from surface EEG recordings enabling a better understanding of the possible contributions of activity with subcortical structures and potential neuronal networks associated with these structures (Cantor, 2009; Sherlin, 2009), as discussed in the next section.

Independent Component Analysis, ICA

Recently, the analytical capability of QEEG-related software has been significantly extended by a sophisticated statistical procedure known as independent component analysis, or ICA (Comon, 1994; Hyvärinen, Karhunen, & Oja, 2001; Makeig, Bell, Jung, & Sejnowski, 1996; Makeig, Jung, Bell, Ghahremani, & Sejnowski, 1997; Stone, 2002). ICA has mitigated an old limitation of the EEG: spatial resolution. Compared to fMRI, EEG technology has outstanding temporal resolution but poor spatial resolution, resulting from the dispersion of electrical signals that propagate in all directions in the human cortex. The brain is a busy and noisy place so it often happens that electrical activity seen in the frontal cortex, for example, may affect signals being recorded in other areas of the scalp, as well. For this reason, the functional interpretation of electrical signal *directly under* a particular electrode should be taken with caution (Kropotov, 2016).

Alternatively, ICA extracts essential features of the raw EEG by decomposing the data as a linear combination of statistical independent components, which means that the raw EEG data can be *separated* into maximally independent components that may isolate *individual* signal generators (Makeig et al., 1996). Put simply, ICA is a new method used for the discovery of different sets of brain regions that may work together as *networks*. Examples of relevant brain networks currently being researched include the brain default network, for example (Beckmann, DeLuca, Devlin & Smith, 2005; Buckner, Andrews-Hanna, & Schacter, 2008; Chen, Ros & Gruzelier, 2013; Luckhoo et al., 2012; Raichle et al., 2001).

ICA is seen as a robust procedure that has been validated for both, EEG artifact filtering and correction (Jorge, Grouiller, Gruetter, Van Der Zwaag, & Figueiredo, 2015; Mayeli, Zotev, Refai, & Bodurka, 2016; McMenamin et al., 2010; Zhou &

Gotman, 2004) and for enhanced objectivity in the imaging of human EEG dynamics (Beckmann et al., 2005; Bugli & Lambert, 2006; Hsu, Mullen, Jung, & Cauwenberghs, 2016; Jonmohamadi, Poudel, Innes, & Jones, 2014; Onton, Westerfield, Townsend, & Makeig, 2006; Wessel, 2016; Wessel & Ullsperger, 2011).

How does ICA work? ICA is currently expanding the neurofeedback practitioner toolset by enabling in-depth analysis of brain function and functional interpretation of bio- and neuromarkers in mental health, without the need to rely uniquely on normative database comparisons. ICA is also likely to further expand the training requirements for neurotherapy practitioners.

For pedagogical purposes, Figure 1.4 shows a simplified version (i.e., fewer components) of the ICA process. The resting state EEG recording—Figure 1.4(a)—is decomposed by the ICA algorithm into 19 independent components, although only three brain topographies of the components are shown—Figure 1.4(b). The ICA-derived calculations are then plotted using LORETA—or low resolution electromagnetic tomography; Figure 1.4(c). It should be noted that the EEG measures electrical while LORETA method estimates current densities at deeper cortical levels (Pascual-Marqui et al., 1994; see also Pasqual-Marqui, 2002, for an explanation of sLORETA tomographies).

Whereas the first generation of practitioners relied on their client's subjective reports about DSM-based symptoms, which were then matched with a range of standard neurofeedback protocols (Crane, 2007; Evans & Rubi, 2007), neurometrics and ICA have provided, for the first time, the necessary high-definition required to obtain a global view of brain dynamics. ICA, in particular, holds the promise of informing the design of personalized neurofeedback protocols.

After briefly discussing some of the important technological developments that have affected neurofeedback practice, we now turn to a crucial decision taken by the National Institute of Mental Health (NIMH), in 2013. The NIMH is perhaps the most powerful funding agency for mental health research in the United States. As discussed in the next section, this decision has had the merit of spurring a historic paradigm shift in mental health research; something we hadn't seen since Kraepelin's objective classification of mental diseases at the end of the 19th century. Interestingly it has also (and arguably) become the most important *external* influence the field of neurofeedback has had since its early days in the 1940s.

NIMH Decides to Abandon Funding of DSM-Based Research

Simultaneously to the technological developments discussed in the previous section, the National Institute for Mental Health (NIMH), a world-leading research-funding agency recently announced, in 2013, that it would no longer fund symptom-based (or DSM-based) research projects in favor of biomarker research, known in the field as research domain criteria (RDoC). The DSM, or Diagnostic and Statistical Manual of Mental Disorders, has been described as the "bible" of diagnostic categories for the field of psychopathology since the 1950s. Following the NIMH announcement, however, the research funding effort will now focus on the understanding of how genetic, imaging, neurophysiologic and cognitive data—not just the symptoms—cluster and how these clusters may relate to treatment response (Insel, 2013). This shift arguably gives neurofeedback practice and research a new empirical platform for clinical use and scientific validation, as explained below.

DSM had always been seen as validity-deficient. To illustrate this point, the DSM-I (first edition) published in 1952, included 106 diagnostic categories. However, by the time the DSM

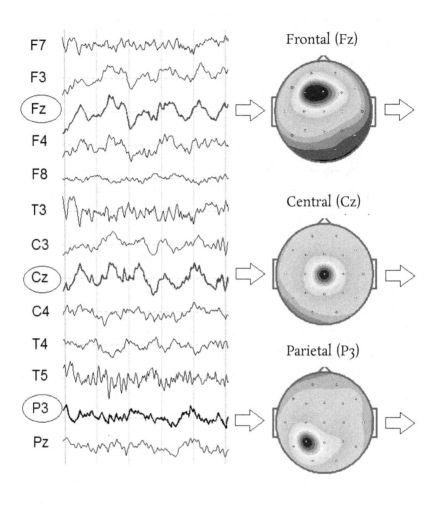

(a) Raw EEG (b) ICA: components, topographies

Figure 1.4. Decomposition of 19-channel EEG into independent components. A fragment of a 10-minute resting state EEG at (a) is decomposed by the WinEEG algorithm (Mitsar) of independent component analysis into 19 components (3 of them are shown for
(continued)

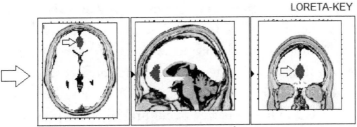
Subcortical source: anterior cingulate; BA 32

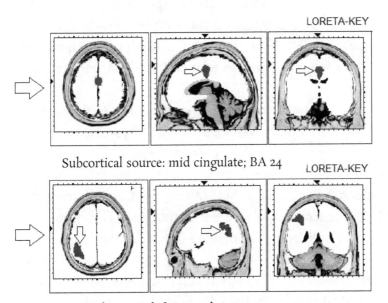
Subcortical source: mid cingulate; BA 24

Cortical source: left parietal; BA 39

(c) LORETA: tomographies

Figure 1.4. (continued)
pedagogical purposes); (b) brain topographies of the components; and (c) LORETA tomographies showing their estimated sources (Pascual-Marqui, Michel, & Lehman, 1994).

reached its fourth revised edition, published in the year 2000, its already counted 297 diagnostic categories leading to several challenges to its reputed validity (Craddock & Owen, 2010; Kandel, 1998; Kapur, Phillips, & Insel, 2012; Rosenhan, 1973). On the other hand, the use of diagnostic categories does not predict success in treatment interventions (Gunkelman, 2006). Finally, the DSM was also reported to have an array of cultural and peer-pressure biases that further affect its validity (Martins-Mourao, 2011).

David Rosenhan in particular (see Rosenhan, 1973), famously challenged the medical establishment with the now infamous "pseudo-patient" and the "impostor" experiments, which we encourage our readers to research further due to our limited space in this chapter.

The NIMH announcement has been beneficial to the neurofeedback field, which may now contribute and participate in the research of biomarkers, or EEG-phenotypes for the *diagnosis* and *modulation* of brain dysfunctions (Gunkelman, 2006; Kropotov, 2016; Kropotov, Pąchalska, & Muller, 2014). In fact, following the NIMH's announcement in 2013, the scientific interest in this technique, as indexed by the number of publications in peer-reviewed studies in neurofeedback, has grown exponentially, as shown in Figure 1.3 (see growth in published research studies after the NIMH announcement). Further, this methodology-driven shift is likely to have an impact in the training of future neurofeedback practitioners in many ways, although this debate should be continued elsewhere.

Neuromodulation and Mental Health v3.0

Looking back, the alternative offered by the first-generation neurofeedback practitioners could be named as "neuromodulation and mental health v1.0," for the hope they offered to thousands of patients dissatisfied with the one-size-fits all approach of conventional medicine. Later, the quantum leap brought by neurometrics, and the early days of biomarker research could be identified as "neuromodulation and mental health v2.0." Currently, following the paradigmatic shift facilitated by the NIMH'S abandonment of traditional DSM-based assessments, the consolidation of research domain criteria (RDoC) and the use of ICA and event-related potentials (ERP), amongst other techniques, neurofeedback is likely to have inaugurated a new phase in health care known as "neuromodulation and mental health v3.0."

We now turn to the last segment in this chapter, to discuss the main differences between neurofeedback and A/T training.

Differences Between Neurofeedback and A/T Training

On the surface, both neurofeedback and A/T training use real-time information about individual brainwave patterns to teach clients to self-regulate their brain functions. Yet, the

Table 1.1
Main Difference Between Neurofeedback and A/T Training

	Neurofeedback	A/T training
Training type	Eyes open and eyes closed	Eyes closed
Frequencies modulated	All brainwave frequencies	Theta and alpha
Processes targeted	Cognitive processes	Emotional processes
Examples of conditions treated	ADHD, autism, epilepsy	Emotional trauma, addictions

impact of each technique on brain optimization is very different, with crucial implications in terms of psychotherapeutic scope and relevance to emotional rehabilitation. Table 1.1 summarizes the main differences between neurofeedback and A/T training.

Neurofeedback training focuses on the brain's cortical (or surface) activity using the full range of brainwave frequencies—in the eyes open or eyes closed conditions—depending on the therapeutic objectives of the relevant protocol. A/T training, on the other hand, focuses exclusively on the *slower* frequency ranges, including theta and alpha, and training is done with eyes closed, using auditory feedback to induced states of relaxation. Interestingly, Mark Johnson and Genie Bodenhamer-Davis (see chapter 6) suggest that the additional co-modulation of the beta frequencies may have a relevant impact on A/T's therapeutic outcomes.

Crucially, neurofeedback training typically targets the rehabilitation of *cognitive* processes (e.g., ADHD, autism, and epilepsy), whereas A/T training focuses on the rehabilitation of *emotional* processes (e.g., emotional trauma, PTSD, and addictions)—which neuroscience today recognizes—are processed in different and distant areas of the brain, with clear consequences in psychotherapeutic terms.

Developmentally speaking, there is a clear time lag between the child's early emotional processing (and learning), and the emergence of analytical thought. Whereas emotional development starts early on and is modulated by the slower "memory forming" theta frequencies found in the limbic system (Aftanas, Varlamov, Pavlov, Makhnev, & Reva, 2001; Kugler & Laub, 1971; Sammler, Grigutsch, Fritz, & Koelsch, 2007), cognition and analytical thinking are modulated by the faster beta frequencies that are only expected to develop after age 12 (Garsche, 1956, cited by Niedermeyer, 2005), mainly in the frontal lobes, thus marking the formal operational stage and the development of the child's ability to think logically about abstract concepts (Piaget, 1997; Piaget & Cook, 1952). It is therefore hypothesized that in cases of early emotional trauma, especially before age 12, the brain is not yet *equipped* with the analytical tools required to process such *overwhelming* experiences. The child—or the adult—is, for this reason, likely to seek distance from the traumatic events via the development of defense mechanisms; otherwise known as avoidance strategies to reduces anxiety arising from unacceptable or painful thoughts and memories (Freud, 1937).

This partially explains why the access to traumatic content via the "analytical mind," although useful in psychotherapeutic terms, has proven insufficient to release traumatic memories and their associated unprocessed negative emotions that remain, for this reason, stored in the body (van der Kolk, 2014) as a subjective experience of central nervous system overarousal.

As discussed in several of the chapters in this book, A/T training will have the therapeutic merit of calming the beta-driven frontal lobes, thus reducing the "analytical critic," so that emotional contents may express consciously, while being witnessed by the analytical mind and re-integrated in the client's narrative. This process is thought to enable clients to reprocess traumatic memories from a new perspective, which may facilitate unprecedented insights about root emotional issues.

The steps involved in A/T training will be covered in greater detail and from different perspectives in the following chapters included in this book, so here is a brief summary:

1. Basic pre-training for a relaxed state is done using skin temperature, heart rate variability or other autonomic biofeedback, often with the self-suggestions of autogenic training.
2. The global electrical activity of the client's brain is

detected, amplified and measured at the scalp, usually at the back of the head, in the occipital or the central parietal areas.

3. The amplified signal is processed using dedicated software to extract one or more features, such as the amplitude of the signal after it has passed through a band pass filter. This filter mostly rejects all other frequency components above or below the 4 to 7 Hz and 8 to 12 Hz bands, which are the frequency ranges of the EEG theta and alpha rhythms, respectively.
4. The clients develop their own healing imagery and alcohol/drug rejection scenarios (in cases of substance abuse).
5. The patient is instructed to "tell your unconscious to eliminate the urge to drink," or "tell your unconscious to resolve the conflicts that cause your symptoms."
6. A signal (a tone or sound) is sent to the trainee whenever the extracted feature meets a preset requirement, such as exceeding a preset amplitude threshold for the alpha and theta frequency bands, thus informing the trainee what worked and what did not in controlling the feedback signal.
7. The trainee is instructed to increase the power of the signal, by learning through trial and error what states of mind increase the likelihood of increased duration of the signal.
8. As the trainee begins to relax into the session, activity in the alpha band is likely to reduce in power, signaling stage 1 sleep, and the theta band is likely to increase typically inducing a state of reverie. The client is told to go with it, "just let go, sink down."
9. Whenever the theta amplitude climbs above the alpha amplitude, the trainee is likely to experience the therapeutic

cross-over, which may lead to the emergence of conflict-related imagery.
10. After each training session, the trainee is encouraged to discuss his or her experience with the feedback signal and share and re-interpret any content that may have emerged during the crossover period.
11. During this conversation the therapist must pay attention not to influence responses in the client. Famously, Eugene Peniston instructed therapists to simply use the question, "What is _____?" to invite the client to make a first-person interpretation of any images they had the session.

Advantages and Contraindications of A/T Training

Traditionally, psychotherapeutic techniques could only be discussed at the conceptual and theoretical levels due to the fact that their direct applicability was known to depend on individual variability. This could be contrasted with the reputed—although often criticized—objectivity of psychometrics. Interestingly however, and perhaps for the first time in the history of mental health, A/T training has the potential to offer a *standard* technique, that may be utilized therapeutically with anyone undergoing the A/T process. It should be noted that we used the word "potentially" to signal some caution. One of the objectives of this book has been to initiate a broader discussion about the standardization of electrode locations used during A/T sessions. Eugene Peniston recommended the left occipital (O1) and later modifications of the protocol have recommended a centro-parietal location (Pz). Other practitioners have used other locations in the scalp.

Each location is likely to have specific advantages that should be carefully described and documented for the benefit of all practitioners in the field. Nineteen channel QEEG data is also likely to continue to bring new light to this debate, as discussed by David Trudeau in chapter 3. We can now speculate that the use of the 19-channel QEEG to inform the design of neurofeedback protocols is also expected to influence pre- and post-assessment research about the effects of A/T training.

A/T training also has contraindications and caution should be exercised when dealing with psychotic patients. A/T enhances theta frequencies but in some cases the power of theta may already be high which is likely to have adverse effects. The same applies to patients with brain injury, which are likely to have increased theta frequencies. This, again justifies the use of a QEEG pre-assessment to provide essential information about the trainee's brainwave patterns.

To sum up, the alpha-theta methodology clearly emerged ahead of its time and, unfortunately, Eugene Peniston's work attracted little interest outside the field of neurofeedback practice, following his initial publications. However, the neurosciences have caught up and significantly more is now known and understood about the brain processes involved in emotional processes. Such important progress has, in turn, reframed the relevance of A/T training for modern psychotherapy and mental health in general. This is probably what Freud, Jung, and several generations of psychotherapists after them may have wished for as they devised techniques to reprocess unconscious content.

References

Achermann, P., & Borbely, A. A. (1997). Low-frequency (< 1 Hz) oscillations in the human sleep electroencephalogram. *Neuroscience, 81*, 213–222.

Aftanas, L., Varlamov, A., Pavlov, S., Makhnev, V., & Reva, N. (2001). Event-related synchronization and desynchronization during affective processing: Emergence of valence-related time-dependent hemispheric asymmetries in theta and upper alpha band. *International Journal of Neuroscience, 110*, 197–219.

Albino, R., & Burnand, G. (1964). Conditioning of the alpha rhythm in man. *Journal of Experimental Psychology, 67*(6), 539.

Albrecht, B., Sandersleben, H., Gevensleben, H., & Rothenberger A. (2015). Pathophysiology of ADHD, comorbid disorders and associated problems—Starting points for Neurofeedback interventions? *Frontiers in Human Neuroscience, 9*, 359. 10. 3389/fnhum. 2015. 00359

American Electroencephalographic Society (1987). Statement on clinical use of quantitative EEG. *Journal of Clinical Neurophysiology, 4*, 75.

Arns, M., Batail, J. M., Bioulac, S., Congedo, M., Daudet, C., Drapier, D., ... & Mehler, D. (2017). Neurofeedback: One of today's techniques in psychiatry? *L'Encéphale, 43*(2):135–145.

Arns, M., Heinrich, H., & Strehl, U. (2014). Evaluation of neurofeedback in ADHD: The long and winding road. *Biological Psychology, 95*, 108–115.

Bach-y-Rita, P., Collins, C. C., Sauders, F. A., White, B., & Scadden, L. (1969). Vision substitution by tactile image projection. *Nature, 221*, 963–964. doi:10. 1038/221963a0

Beckmann, C. F., DeLuca, M., Devlin, J. T., & Smith, S. M. (2005). Investigations into resting-state connectivity using independent component analysis. *Philosophical Transactions of the Royal Society of London B: Biological Sciences, 360*(1457), 1001-1013. doi: 10. 1098/rstb. 2005. 1634

Berger, H. (1929). Über das elektrenkephalogramm des menschen. 1st report. *Arch Psychiat Nervenkr, 87*, 527–570.

Berger, H. (1929). Über das elektrenkephalogramm des menschen. *European Archives of Psychiatry and Clinical Neuroscience, 87*(1), 527-570.

Berger, S. L., Kouzarides, T., Shiekhattar, R., & Shilatifard, A. (2009). An operational definition of epigenetics. *Genes & Development, 23*(7), 781-3.

Brown, B. B. (1968). Some characteristic EEG differences between heavy smoker and non-smoker subjects. *Neuropsychologia, 6*(4), 381–388.

Brown, B. B. (1970a). Recognition of aspects of consciousness through association with EEG alpha activity represented by a light signal. *Psychophysiology, 6,* 442–452. doi: 10. 1111/j. 1469-8986. 1970. tb01754. x

Brown, B. B. (1970b). Awareness of EEG-subjective activity relationships detected within a closed feedback system. *Psychophysiology, 7*(3), 451–464.

Brown, B. B. (1974). *New mind, new body: Bio feedback: New directions for the mind.* New York, Harper & Row.

Brown, B. B. (1977). *Stress and the art of biofeedback.* New York, Harper & Row.

Brown, B. B., & Shryne Jr., J. E. (1964). EEG theta activity and fast activity sleep in cats as related to behavioral traits. *Neuropsychologia, 2*(4), 311–326.

Bruner, J. & Tauc, L. (1965). Synaptic plasticity involved in the habituation process in Aplysia. *Journal de physiologie, 57,* 230–1.

Bruner, J. & Tauc, L. (1966). Habituation at the synaptic level in Aplysia. *Nature, 210,* 37–39.

Buckner, R. L., Andrews-Hanna, J. R., & Schacter, D. L. (2008). The brain's default network: Anatomy, function and relevance to disease. *Annals of the New York Academy of Sciences, 1124,* 1–38. doi: 10. 1196/annals. 1440. 011

Bugli, C., & Lambert, P. (2006). Comparison between principal component analysis and independent component analysis in electroencephalograms modeling. *Biometrical Journal, 48*(5), 1–16.

Cade, M., & Coxhead, N. (1979). *The awakened mind: Biofeedback and the development of higher states of awareness.* Element Books.

Cantor, D. S. (2009). Applying advanced methods in clinical practice. In T. Budzynski, H. Budzynski, Evans, J. R., & A. Abarbanel (Eds.), *Introduction to QEEG and neurofeedback: Advanced theory and applications* (2nd ed.). New York: Elsevier.

Chen, J. L., Ros, T., & Gruzelier, J. H. (2013). Dynamic changes of ICA-derived EEG functional connectivity in the resting state. *Human Brain Mapping, 34,* 852–868. doi: 10. 1002/hbm. 21475

Clemente, C. D., Sterman, M. B., & Wyrwicka, W. (1964). Post-reinforcement EEG synchronization during alimentary behavior. *Electroencephalography and Clinical Neurophysiology, 16*(4), 355–365.

Coburn, K. L., Lauterbach, E. C., Boutros, N. N., Black, K. J., Arciniegas, D. B., & Coffey, C. E. (2006). The value of quantitative electroencephalography in clinical psychiatry: A report by the committee on research of the American Neuropsychiatric Association. *Journal of Neuropsychiatry and Clinical Neurosciences 18*(4), 460–500.

Collura, T. F., Thatcher, R. W., Smith, T. F., Lambos, W. A., & Stark, C. R. (2009). EEG biofeedback training using Z-scores and a normative database. In T. Budzynski, H. Budzynski, J. R. Evans, & A. Abarbanel (Eds.), *Introduction to QEEG and neurofeedback: Advanced theory and applications* (2nd ed.). New York: Elsevier.

Comon, P. (1994). Independent component analysis, a new concept? *Signal Processing, 36,* 287–314.

Cozolino, L. (2017). *The neuroscience of psychotherapy, healing the social brain.* New York: WW Norton & Company.

Craddock, N., & Owen, M. J. (2010). The Kraepelinian dichotomy—going, going. . . but still not gone. *British Journal of Psychiatry, 196*(2) 92–95.

Crane, R. (2007). Infinite potential: A neurofeedback pioneer looks back and ahead. In J. R. Evans (Ed.), *Handbook of neurofeedback: Dynamics and clinical applications.* The Hawworth Medical Press: New York.

Crick, F., & Koch, C. (2003). Framework for consciousness. *Nature Neuroscience, 6*(2), 119–26.

Christoffersen, G. R., & Schachtman, T. R. (2016). Electrophysiological CNS-processes related to associative learning in humans. *Behavioural Brain Research, 296,* 211–232.

Davidson, R., & Begley, S. (2012). *The emotional life of your brain.* New York: Penguin.

deBettencourt, M. T., Cohen, J. D., Norman, K. A., & Turk-Browne (2015). Closed-loop training of attention with real-time brain imaging. *Nature Neuroscience, 18,* 470–475.

Dongier, M., McCallum, W. C., Torres, F., & Vogel (1976). Psychological and psychophysiological states. In A. Rémond, (Ed.), *Handbook of electroencephalography and clinical neurophysiology, Vol 16A*, 195–256. Amsterdam: Elsevier.

Doppelmayr, M. M., Klimesch, W., Pachinger, T., & Ripper, B. (1998). The functional significance of absolute power with respect to event-related desynchronization. *Brain Topography, 11*, 133–140.

Durup, G., & Fessard, A. I. (1935). L'électrencéphalogramme de l'homme. Observations psycho-physiologiques relatives à l'action des stimuli visuels et auditifs. *L'année Psychologique. 36*, 1–32.

Engel, A. K., Fries, P., Koenig, P., Brecht, M. & Singer, W. (1999). Temporal binding, binocular rivalry, and consciousness. *Consciousness and Cognition, 8*(2), 128–151.

Evans, J. R., & Rubi, M. C. M. (2007). Ours is to reason why and how. In J. R. Evans (Ed.), *Handbook of neurofeedback: Dynamics and clinical applications*. The Hawworth Medical Press: New York.

Felsinger, J. M., & Gladstone, A. I. (1947). Reaction latency (StR) as a function of the number of reinforcements (N). *Journal of Experimental Psychology, 37*, 214–228.

Friedrich, E. V., Sivanathan, A., Lim, T., Suttie, N., Louchart, S., Pillen, S., Pineda, J. A., (2015). An effective neurofeedback intervention to improve social interactions in children with autism spectrum disorder. *Journal of Autism and Developmental Disorders, 45*(12), 4084–4100.

Freud, A. (1937). *The ego and the mechanisms of defence*. London: Hogarth Press and Institute of Psycho-Analysis. (Revised edition in the UK in 1968).

Freud, S. (1954). Project for a scientific psychology. In *The origins of psycho-analysis* (1895). Edited by Bonaparte, M., Freud, A., Kris, E; translated by Mosbacher, E., Strachey, J. London: Imago.

Gibbs, F., Gibbs, E., & Lennox, W. (1937). Epilepsy: A paroxysmal cerebral dysrhythmia. *Brain, 60*, 377–388.

Gibbs, F., Gibbs, E. L., & Lennox, W. G. (1943). EEG classification of epileptic patients and control subjects. *Archives of Neurology & Psychiatry, 50*,111–128.

Gordon, E., Cooper, N., Rennie, C., Hermens, D., & Williams, L. M. (2006). Integrative neuroscience: The role of a standardized database. *Clinical Electroencephalography and Neuroscience, 6*, 64–75.

Grice, G. R. (1948). The relation of secondary reinforcement to delayed reward in visual discrimination learning. *Journal of Experimental Psychology, 38*(1), 1–16.

Gunkelman, J. (2006). Transcend the DSM using phenotypes. *Biofeedback, 34*(3), 95–98.

Hallschmid, M., Mölle, M., Fischer, S., & Born, J. (2002). EEG synchronization upon reward in man. *Clinical Neurophysiology, 113*, 1059–1065. doi: 10. 1016/s1388-2457(02)00142-6

Hammond, D. C., & Gunkelman, J. (2011). *The art of artifacting.* San Rafael, CA: ISNR Research Foundation.

Harmony, T. (2013). The functional significance of delta oscillations in cognitive processing. *Frontiers in Integrative Neuroscience, 7*, 83. doi: 10. 3389/fnint. 2013. 00083

Hanslmayr, S., Gross, J., Klimesch, W., & Shapiro, K. L. (2011). The role of alpha oscillations in temporal attention. *Brain Research Reviews, 67*(1–2), 331–43.

Hanslmayr, S., Klimesch, W., Sauseng, P., Gruber, W., Doppelmayr, M., Freunberger, R., & Pecherstorfer, T. (2005). Visual discrimination performance is related to decreased alpha amplitude but increased phase locking. *Neuroscience Letters, 375*(1), 64–8.

Hardt, J. V., Kamiya, J. (1978). Anxiety change through electroencephalographic alpha feedback seen only in high anxiety subjects. *Science, 201*(4350), 79–81.

Hebb, D. O. (1949). *The organization of behavior.* New York: Wiley & Sons.

Heinrich, H., Gevensleben, H, & Strehl, U. (2007). Annotation: Neurofeedback—Train your brain to train behavior. *Journal of Child Psychology and Psychiatry, 48*(1), 3–16.

Herrmann, C. S., & Demiralp, T. (2005). Human EEG

gamma oscillations in neuropsychiatric disorders. *Clinical Neurophysiology, 116*, 2719–2733.

Hughes, J. R. (1995). The EEG in psychiatry: An outline with summarized points and references. *Clinical Electroencephalography, 26*, 92–101.

Hughes, J. R., & John, R. (1999). Conventional and quantitative electroencephalography in psychiatry. *Journal of Neuropsychiatry and Clinical Neurosciences, 11*(2), 190–208.

Hsu, S., Mullen, T. R., Jung, T., & Cauwenberghs, G. (2016). Real-time adaptive EEG source separation using online recursive independent component analysis. *IEEE Transactions on Neural Systems and Rehabilitation Engineering, 24*, 309–319.

Hyvärinen, A., Karhunen, J., & Oja, E. (2001). *Independent component analysis*, Wiley, New-York.

Insel, T. (2013). *Transforming diagnosis*. Source: https://www.nimh.nih.gov/about/directors/thomas-insel/blog/2013/transforming-diagnosis.shtml

Irwin, D. A., Knott, J. R., McAdam, D. W., & Rebert, C. S. (1966). Motivational determinants of the "contingent negative variation. *Electroencephalography and Clinical Neurophysiology, 21*(6), 538–543.

Jasper, H., & Shagass, C. (1941a). Conditioning of the occipital alpha rhythm in man. *Journal of Experimental Psychology, 28*(5), 373–388.

Jasper, H., & Shagass, C. (1941b). Conscious time judgments related to conditioned time intervals and voluntary control of the alpha rhythm. *Journal of Experimental Psychology, 28*, 503–508.

James, W. (1890). *The principles of psychology*. New York: Holt.

John, E. R. (1977). *Neurometrics: Clinical applications of quantitative electrophysiology*. New Jersey: Lawrence Erlbaum Associates.

John, E. R. (1989). The role of quantitative EEG topographic mapping or "neurometrics" in the diagnosis of psychiatric and neurological disorders: The pros. *Electroencephalography and Clinical Neurophysiology, 73*, 2–4.

John, E. R. (1990). Principles of neurometrics. *American Journal of EEG Technology, 30*, 251–266.

John, E. R., Prichep L., Ahn H., Easton P., Fridman J., Kaye H. (1983). Neurometric evaluation of cognitive dysfunctions and neurological disorders in children. *Progress in Neurobiology*, 21, 239–90.

John, E. R., Prichep LS., Fridman J., Easton P. (1988). Neurometrics: Computer-assisted differential diagnosis of brain dysfunctions. *Science*, 239, 162–9.

Johnstone, J., Gunkelman, J., & Lunt, J. (2005). Clinical database development: Characterization of EEG phenotypes, *Clinical EEG and Neuroscience*, 36(2), 99–107.

Jonmohamadi, Y., Poudel, G., Innes, C., & Jones, R. (2014). Source-space ICA for EEG source separation, localization and time-course reconstruction. *Neuroimage*, 101, 720–737. doi: 10. 1016/j. neuroimage. 2014. 07. 052

Jorge, J., Grouiller, F., Gruetter, R., Van Der Zwaag, W., Figueiredo, P. (2015). Towards high-quality simultaneous EEG-fMRI at 7 T: Detection and reduction of EEG artifacts due to head motion. *Neuroimage*, 120, 143–153.

Kamiya, J. (1969). Operant control of the EEG alpha rhythm and some of its reported effects on consciousness. In C. Tart (Ed.), *Altered states of consciousness*. New York: Wiley.

Kamiya, J. (1971). Operant control of the EEG alpha rhythm and some of its reported effects on consciousness. *Biofeedback and self-control: An Aldine reader on the regulation of bodily processes and consciousness*.

Kandel, E. R. (1998). A new intellectual framework for psychiatry. *American Journal of Psychiatry*, 155(4), 457–469.

Kapur, S., Phillips, A. G., Insel, T. R. (2012). Why has it taken so long for biological psychiatry to develop clinical tests and what to do about it? *Molecular Psychiatry*, 17(12), 1174–9.

Klimesch, W. (1996). Memory processes, brain oscillations and EEG synchronization. *International Journal of Psychophysiology*, 24(1–2), 61–100.

Klimesch, W. (1999). EEG alpha and theta oscillations reflect cognitive and memory performance: A review and analysis. *Brain Research Reviews*, 29(2–3), 169–95.

Klimesch, W. (2012). Alpha-band oscillations, attention, and controlled access to stored information. *Trends in Cognitive Sciences, 16*(12), 606–617.

Knott, J. R., & Henry, C. E. (1941). The conditioning of the blocking of the alpha rhythm of the human electroencephalogram. *Journal of Experimental Psychology, 28*(2), 134.

Kropotov, J. (2016). *Functional neuromarkers for psychiatry: Applications for diagnosis and treatment*. London: Elsevier.

Kropotov, J., Pąchalska, M., & Muller, A. (2014). Neurotechnologies for the diagnosis and modulation of brain dysfunctions. *Health Psychology Report, 2*(2), 73–82.

Kugler, J., & Laub, M. (1971). "Puppet show" theta rhythm. *Electroencephalography and Clinical Neurophysiology, 31*, 532–533.

Lehmann, D., Faber, P. L., Achermann, P., Jeanmonod, D., Gianotti, L. R. R., & Pizzagalli, D. (2001). Brain sources of EEG gamma frequency during volitionally meditation-induced, altered states of consciousness, and experience of the self. *Psychiatry Research: Neuroimaging Section, 108*, 111–121.

Loomis, A. L., Harvey, E. N., & Hobart, G. (1936). Electrical potentials of the human brain. *Journal of Experimental Psychology, 19*(3), 249–279.

Lopes da Silva, F. H., Vos, J. E., Mooibroek, J, & van Rotterdam, A. (1980). Relative contributions of intra-cortical and thalamo-cortical processes in the generation of alpha rhythms, revealed by partial coherence analysis. *Electroencephalography and Clinical Neurophysiology, 50*(5–6), 449–456.

Lubar, J. F., Swartwood, M. O., Swartwood, J. N., & O'Donnell, P. H. (1995). Evaluation of the effectiveness of EEG neurofeedback training for ADHD in a clinical setting as measured by changes in TOVA scores, behavioral ratings, and WISC-R performance. *Applied Psychophysiology and Biofeedback, 20*(1), 83–99.

Luckhoo, H., Hale, J. R., Stokes, M. G., Nobre, A. C., Morris, P. G., Brookes, M. J., & Woolrich, M. W. (2012). Inferring task-related networks using independent component analysis in magnetoencephalography. *Neuroimage, 62*, 530–541. doi: 10.1016/j. neuroimage. 2012. 04. 046

Makeig, S., Bell, A. J., Jung, T. P., & Sejnowski, T. J. (1996). Independent component analysis of electroencephalographic data. *Advances in Neural Information Processing Systems, 8*, 145–151.

Makeig, S., Jung, T. P., Bell, A. J., Ghahremani, D., & Sejnowski, T. J. (1997). Blind separation of auditory event-related brain responses into independent components. *Proceedings of the National Academy of Sciences, 94*, 10979–10984.

Marczynski, T. J. (1972). Electrophysiological correlates of positive reinforcement: Post-reinforcement synchronization, modulation of sensory input, and steady potentials. In A. G. Karczmar, & J. C. Eccles (Eds.), *Brain and human behavior*. Springer-Verlag.

Marczynski, T. J., Harris, C. M., & Livezey, G. T. (1981). The magnitude of post-reinforcement EEG synchronization (PRS) in cats reflects learning ability. *Brain Research, 204*, 214–219. doi: 10. 1016/0006-8993(81)90667-3

Martins-Mourao, A. (2010). Diagnosing mental illness. In C. Rostron (Ed.), *The science of the mind: Investigating mental health*. Milton Keynes: The Open University Press.

Mayeli, A., Zotev, V., Refai, H., & Bodurka, J. (2016). Real-time EEG artifact correction during fMRI using ICA. *Journal of Neuroscience Methods, 274*, 27–37.

Mayer, K., Wyckoff, S. N., Fallgatter, A. J., Ehlis, A. C., & Strehl, U. (2015). Neurofeedback as a nonpharmacological treatment for adults with attention-deficit/hyperactivity disorder (ADHD): Study protocol for a randomized controlled trial. *Trials, 16*, 174.

McAdam D. W., Irwin D. A., Rebert C. S., Knott J. R. (1966). Conative control of the contingent negative variation. *Electroencephalography and Clinical Neurophysiology, 21*, 194–195.

McMenamin, B. W., Shackman, A. J., Maxwell, J. S., Bachhuber, D. R. W., Koppenhaver, A. M., Greischar, L. L., Davidson, R. J. (2010). Validation of ICA-based myogenic artifact correction for scalp and source-localized EEG. *Neuroimage, 49*, 2416–2432.

Micoulaud-Franchi, J. A., McGonigal, A., Lopez, R., Daudet, C., Kotwas, I., & Bartolomei, F. (2015). Electroencephalographic neurofeedback: Level of evidence in mental and brain disorders and suggestions for good clinical practice. *Neurophysiologie Clinique/Clinical Neurophysiology, 45*(6), 423–433.

Mizuhara, H., Wang, L. Q., Kobayashi, K., & Yamaguchi, Y. (2004). A long-range cortical network emerging with theta oscillation in a mental task. *Neuroreport, 15*(8), 1233.

Monderer, R. S., Harrison, D. M., & Haut, S. R. (2002). Neurofeedback and epilepsy. *Epilepsy & Behavior, 3*(3), 214–218.

Nácher, V., Ledberg, A., Deco, G., & Romo, R. (2013). Coherent delta-band oscillations between cortical areas correlate with decision making. *Proceedings of the National Academy of Sciences, 110*(37), 15085–90.

Nagai, Y., Critchley, H. D., Featherstone, E., Fenwick, P. B., Trimble, M. R., & Dolan, R. J. (2004). Brain activity relating to the contingent negative variation: An fMRI investigation. *Neuroimage, 21*(4), 1232–41.

Niedermeyer, E. (2005). Maturation of the EEG: Development of waking and sleep patterns (chapter 5). In E. Niedermeyer, & F. Lopes da Silva (Eds.) *Electroencephalography: Basic principles, clinical applications, and related fields* (5th ed.). Lippincott Williams & Wilkins.

Nuwer, M. (1997). Assessment of digital EEG, quantitative EEG and EEG brain mapping: Report of the American Academy of Neurology and the American Clinical Neurophysiology Society, *Neurology, 49*, 277–292.

Onton, J., Westerfield, M., Townsend, J., & Makeig, S. (2006). Imaging human EEG dynamics using independent component analysis. *Neuroscience & Biobehavioral Reviews, 30*, 808–822.

O'Keefe, J., & Burgess, N. (1999). Theta activity, virtual navigation and the human hippocampus. *Trends in Cognitive Sciences, 3*(11), 403–406.

Panksepp, J., & Solms, M. (2012). What is neuropsychoanalysis? Clinically relevant studies of the minded brain. *Trends in Cognitive Sciences, 16*(1), 6–8.

Pascual-Marqui, R. D. (2002) Standardized low-resolution brain electromagnetic tomography (sLORETA): Technical details. *Methods and Findings in Experimental and Clinical Pharmacology,*

24(Suppl D), 5–12.

Pascual-Marqui, R. D., Michel, C. M., Lehmann, D. (1994). Low resolution electromagnetic tomography: a new method for localizing electrical activity in the brain. *International Journal of Psychophysiology, 18,* 49–65.

Peniston, E., & Kulkosky, P. (1989). Brainwave training and b-endorphin levels in alcoholics. *Alcoholism: Clinical and Experimental Research, 13*(2), 271–279.

Piaget J. (1997). Development and learning. In: Gauvain M. & Cole G. M. (eds.) *Readings on the development of children* (2nd ed.). W. H. Freeman, New York: 19–28.

Piaget, J., & Cook, M. T. (1952). *The origins of intelligence in children.* New York, NY: International University Press.

Poschel, B. P., & Ho, P. M. (1972). Post-reinforcement EEG synchronization depends on the operant response. *Electroencephalography and Clinical Neurophysiology, 32,* 563–567. doi: 10. 1016/0013-4694(72)90067-3

Pfurtscheller, G., & Aranibar, A. (1977). Event-related cortical desynchronization detected by power measurements of scalp EEG. *Electroencephalography and Clinical Neurophysiology, 42*(6), 817–826.

Raichle, M. E., MacLeod, A. M., Snyder, A. Z., Powers, W. J., Gusnard, D. A., & Shulman, G. L. (2001). A default mode of brain function. *Proceedings of the National Academy of Sciences, 98,* 676–682.

Raisman, G. (1969). Neuronal plasticity in the septal nuclei of the adult rat. *Brain Research, 14*(1), 25–48.

Ramos-Murguialday, A., Broetz, D., Rea, M., Läer, L., Yilmaz, Ö., Brasil, F. L., ... & Cho, W. (2013). Brain–machine interface in chronic stroke rehabilitation: A controlled study. *Annals of Neurology, 74*(1), 100–108.

Ramus, F. (2013). What's the point of neuropsychoanalysis? *British Journal of Psychiatry, 203*(3), 170–171.

Ranganatha, S., Ros, T., Stoeckel, L., Haller, S., Scharnowski, F., Lewis-Peacock, J., ... & Sulzer, J. (2017). Closed-loop brain training: The science of neurofeedback. *Nature Reviews*

Neuroscience 18, 86–100.

Ros T., Munneke M. A. M., Ruge D., Gruzelier J. H., Rothwell J. C. (2010). Endogenous control of waking brain rhythms induces neuroplasticity in humans. *European Journal of Neuroscience*, 31(4), 770–778.

Rosenhan, D. (1973). On being sane in insane places, *Science*, 179(4070), 250–258.

Salone, A., Di Giacinto, A., Lai, C., De Berardis, D., Iasevoli, F., Fornaro, M., ... & Di Giannantonio, M. (2016). The interface between neuroscience and neuro-psychoanalysis: Focus on brain connectivity. *Frontiers in Human Neuroscience, 10*. https://doi.org/10.3389/fnhum.2016.00020

Sammler, D., Grigutsch, M., Fritz, T., & Koelsch, S. (2007). Music and emotion: Electrophysiological correlates of the processing of pleasant and unpleasant music. *Psychophysiology, 44*, 293–304.

Schack, B., Klimesch, W., & Sauseng, P. (2005). Phase synchronization between theta and upper alpha oscillations in a working memory task. *International Journal of Psychophysiology*, 57(2), 105–114.

Schomer, D., & Lopes da Silva, F. (Eds.). (2011). *Niedermeyer's Electroencephalography: Basic Principles, clinical applications, and related fields*. Lippincott Williams & Wilkins.

Shagass, C. (1942). Conditioning the human occipital alpha rhythm to a voluntary stimulus. A quantitative study. *Journal of Experimental Psychology*, 31(5), 367.

Shagass, C., & Johnson, E. P. (1943). The course of acquisition of a conditioned response of the occipital alpha rhythm. *Journal of Experimental Psychology* 33(3), 201.

Sharbrough, F. W. (2005). Nonspecific abnormal EEG patterns. In E. Niedermeyer, & F. Lopes da Silva (Eds.), *Electroencephalography: Basic principles, clinical applications, and related fields* (5th ed.). Lippincott Williams & Wilkins.

Sherlin, L. H. (2009). Diagnosing and treating brain function through the use of low resolution brain electromagnetic tomography (LORETA). In T. Budzynski, H. Budzynski, J. R. Evans, & A. Abarbanel (Eds.), *Introduction to QEEG and* neurofeedback: Advanced theory and applications (2nd ed.). New York: Elsevier.

Sherlin, L., Arns, M., Lubar, J., Heinrich, H., Kerson, C., Strehl, U., & Sterman, B. (2011). Neurofeedback and basic learning theory: Implications for research and practice. *Journal of Neurotherapy, 15*, 292–304,

Shibata, K., Watanabe, T., Sasaki, Y., & Kawato, M. (2011). Perceptual learning incepted by decoded fMRI neurofeedback without stimulus presentation. *Science, 334*(6061), 1413–1415.

Sitaram, R., Lee, S., Ruiz, S., Rana, M., Veit, R., & Birbaumer, N. (2011). Real-time support vector classification and feedback of multiple emotional brain states. *Neuroimage, 56*(2), 753–765.

Skinner, B. F. (1948). "Superstition" in pigeons. *Journal of Experimental Psychology, 38*, 168–172.

Skinner, B. F. (1958). Reinforcement today. *American Psychologist, 13*, 94–99.

Small, J. G. (1993). Psychiatric disorders and EEG. In E. Niedermeyer, & F. Lopes da Silva (Eds.), *Electroencephalography: Basic principles, clinical applications, and related fields*. Baltimore: Williams and Wilkins, 581–596.

Steriade, M., Gloor, P., Llinas, R. R., Lopes da Silva, F. H., Mesulam, M. M. (1990). Basic mechanisms of cerebral rhythmic activities. *Electroencephalography and Clinical Neurophysiology, 76*(6), 481–508.

Sterman, M. B. (2000). Basic concepts and clinical findings in the treatment of seizure disorders with EEG operant conditioning. *Clinical Electroencephalography, 31*(1), 45–55.

Sterman, M. B., & Egner, T. (2006). Foundation and practice of neurofeedback for the treatment of epilepsy. *Applied Psychophysiology and Biofeedback, 31*(1), 21–35.

Sterman, M. B., & Friar, L. (1972). Suppression of seizures in an epileptic following sensorimotor EEG feedback training. *Electroencephalography and Clinical Neurophysiology, 33*(1), 89–95.

Sterman, M. B., LoPresti, R. W., & Fairchild, M. D. (1969). *Electroencephalographic and behavioral studies of monomethylhydrazine toxicity in the cat*. Alexandria, VA: Storming

Media.

Sterman, M. B., LoPresti, R. W., & Fairchild, M. D. (2010). Electroencephalographic and behavioral studies of monomethylhydrazine toxicity in the cat. *Journal of Neurotherapy*, 14, 293–300.

Sterman, M. B., Wyrwicka, W., & Roth, S. (1969). Electrophysiological correlates and neural substrates of alimentary behavior in the cat. *Annals of the New York Academy of Sciences*, 157, 723–739.

Stone, J. V. (2002) Independent component analysis: An introduction. *Trends in Cognitive Sciences*, 6, 59–64. doi:10. 1016/ S1364-6613(00)01813-1

Strehl, U., Aggensteiner, P., Wachtlin, D., Brandeis, D., Albrecht, B., Arana, M., ... & Freitag, C. M. (2017). Neurofeedback of slow cortical potentials in children with attention-deficit/hyperactivity disorder: a multicenter randomized trial controlling for unspecific effects. *Frontiers in Human Neuroscience*, 11. https://doi. org/10. 3389/fnhum. 2017. 00135

Sulzer, J., Haller, S., Scharnowski, F., Weiskopf, N., Birbaumer, N., Blefari, M. L., ... & Herwig, U. (2013). Real-time fMRI neurofeedback: Progress and challenges. *Neuroimage*, 76C, 386–399. 10. 1016/j. neuroimage. 2013. 03. 033

Tan, G., Thornby, J., Hammond, H. C., Strehl, U., Canady, B., Arnemann, K., & Kaiser, D. A. (2009). Meta-analysis of EEG biofeedback in treating epilepsy. *Clinical EEG and Neuroscience*, 40(3), 173–179.

Tereshchenko, E. P., Ponomarev, V. A., Müller, A., & Kropotov, J. D. (2010). Normative EEG spectral characteristics in healthy subjects aged 7 to 89 years. *Human Physiology*, 36(1), 1–12.

Thatcher, R. W. (1998). EEG normative databases and EEG biofeedback. *Journal of Neurotherapy*, 2, 8–39.

Thatcher, R. W., North, D., & Biver, C. (2005). Evaluation and validity of a LORETA normative EEG database. *Clinical EEG and Neuroscience*, 36(2), 116–22.

Travis, L. E., & Egan, J. P. (1938a). Increase in frequency of the alpha rhythm by verbal stimulation. *Journal of Experimental*

Psychology, 23(4), 384.

Travis, L. E., & Egan, J. P. (1938b). Conditioning of the electrical response of the cortex. *Journal of Experimental Psychology, 22*(6), 524.

Ulrich, G., Schlosser, W., & Juckel, G. (2016). The impact of arterial pulse impedance artifact (APIA) on test-retest reliability of quantitative EEG. *Neuropsychiatric Electrophysiology, 2,* 5. https://doi. org/10. 1186/s40810-016-0019-y.

van der Kolk, B. (2014). *The body keeps the score: Brain, mind, and body in the healing of trauma.* Viking Press.

van der Kolk, B. A., Hodgdon, H., Gapen, M., Musicaro, R., Suvak, M. K., Hamlin, E., & Spinazzola, J. (2016). A randomized controlled study of neurofeedback for chronic PTSD. *PLoS ONE, 11*(12), e0166752. https://doi. org/10. 1371/journal. pone. 0166752

van Lutterveld, R., van Dellen, E., Pal, P, Yang, H., Stam, C. J., & Brewer, J. (2017). Meditation is associated with increased brain network integration. *Neuroimage, 158,* 18–25. doi: 10. 1016/j. neuroimage. 2017. 06. 071.

Waddington, C. H. (1942a). Canalization of development and the inheritance of acquired characters. *Nature, 150*(3811), 563–565.

Waddington C. H. (1942b). The epigenotype. *Endeavour, 1,* 18.

Waddington, C. H. (1953). Epigenetics and evolution. *Symposia of the Society for Experimental Biology, 7,* 186–199.

Wang, Y., Sokhadze, E. M., El-Baz, A. S., Li, X., Sears, L., Casanova, M. F., Tasman, A. (2016). Relative power of specific EEG bands and their ratios during neurofeedback training in children with autism spectrum disorder. *Frontiers in Human Neuroscience, 14*(9). doi: 10. 3389/fnhum. 2015. 00723

Wessel, J. R. (2016). Testing multiple psychological processes for common neural mechanisms using EEG and independent component analysis. *Brain Topography,* 1–11. doi 10.1007/s10548-016-0483-5

Wessel J. R., & Ullsperger M. (2011). Selection of independent components representing event-related brain potentials: A data-driven approach for greater objectivity. *Neuroimage, 54,*

2105–2115. doi:10. 1016/j. neuroimage. 2010. 10. 033

Wise, A. (1996). *The high-performance mind: Mastering brainwaves for insight, healing and creativity.* Putnam.

Wise, A. (2002). *Awakening the mind: A guide to harnessing the power of your brainwaves.* Penguin Random House.

Wyrwicka, W., & Sterman, M. B. (1968). Instrumental conditioning of sensorimotor cortex EEG spindles in the waking cat. *Physiology & Behavior, 3*(5), 703–707.

Zhou, W., & Gotman, J. (2004). Removal of EMG and ECG artifacts from EEG based on wavelet transform and ICA. *IEEE Engineering in Medicine and Biology Society,* 392–395.

2
How It All Began

Patricia A. Norris, PhD

Triple Training Project

In 1968, the Menninger Voluntary Controls Group undertook a research project to train subjects in three major indices of relaxation with a grant from the National Institutes of Health (NIH). This was the first NIH-funded study of biofeedback. The name Triple Training refers to thermal feedback, muscle feedback, and alpha brain rhythm feedback, with the aim of eliciting a quiet body, quiet emotions, and a quiet mind. At the time, exciting developments were taking place in the area of self-regulation and voluntary control. Elmer Green, the founder of the Menninger program, had shown that subjects and clients who had been trained to raise the temperature of their fingers could stop and prevent headaches. John Basmajian had demonstrated that subjects could influence single motor units, and Joe Kamiya had taught students to recognize the presence and increase the amplitude of alpha brainwaves. Brainwave control and intentional changes in hand temperature and muscle tension are primarily the physiological results of psychological processes. The control generally comes from the central nervous system, and the peripheral nervous system responds.

Awareness of any part of the body activates the relevant efferent and afferent pathways. To explain the observed voluntary control, Green articulated the Psychophysiological Principle, which affirms, "every change in the physiological state is accompanied by an appropriate change in the mental-emotional state, conscious or unconscious and, conversely, every change in the mental-emotional state, conscious or unconscious, is accompanied by an appropriate change in the physiological state" (Green, in Rose, 1969; Green & Green, 1977). However, one of the important methodological discoveries from this study was that it is easier for subjects to attend to one parameter at a time, which enhanced their ability to control their physiology.

Elmer and Alyce Green were interested in studying creativity via theta training, since Alyce, while studying creativity at the University of Chicago Laboratory Schools, noted that all the famous instances of creative insight had occurred during a state of deep reverie, which seemed to correlate with the theta brainwave. To investigate this hypothesis, they undertook a series of research projects together with their colleague Dale Walters, the first of which was the Triple Training Project. In 1966 they built a large laboratory brainwave analyzer that could feed back information of the three brainwave states of beta, alpha, and theta simultaneously. A different tone was produced for each frequency from 8 to 13 that centered around 10 Hz. By now the normal adult peak alpha frequency has been abundantly published as between 9.5 and 10.5 Hz, and at the time we found for most people the range centered around 10 Hz, therefore producing most of the tones between 9 and 11 with a bell curve between 8 and 13.

I did my first personal brainwave training on this instrument, and the tones were very beautiful and enchanting. The highest tones, beta, soon diminished and faded away as I turned my attention within. I could feel, think, intend this downward movement on the scale, which sounded like flutes gradually singing down the scale, but with all tones occasionally appearing. This instrument was demonstrated at the first Council Grove Conference on the Voluntary Control of Internal States in 1969.

The audience included many physicians and psychologists, as well as other participants interested in voluntary control, and the interest generated resulted in the decision to start a new organization, which met the following fall and resulted in the formation of the Biofeedback Research Society (now the Association for Applied Psychophysiology and Biofeedback—AAPB) in late 1969.

During the next few years, meditators and professionals alike were studied individually in the Menninger Voluntary Controls Laboratory. One goal was to investigate whether subjects could intentionally produce a "theta state" of consciousness, and, ultimately, whether achieving and maintaining theta could be learned. Ten medical doctors and psychologists took part in this initial exploration, in which I was a participant, and it was found that the production of theta could be influenced and enhanced with feedback.

Brainwave Training for Creativity Study

Meanwhile, a formal research proposal was being developed to study creativity in college students using theta brainwave training. At the same time, portable brainwave instruments were designed and developed that produced different pleasant musical tones for beta, alpha, and theta frequencies, sounding simultaneously when each frequency was present. These brainwave biofeedback instruments ended up being the workhorses during many following years of training and research at the Menninger Foundation, hospital, and clinic, and later at the Life Sciences Institute of Mind-Body Health in Topeka, Kansas.

The subjects of this study were 26 male students in their junior and senior years at Washburn University. Included in the training sessions were autogenic training exercises to achieve relaxation of the body and emotions, and a quiet, inwardly-turned state of mind conducive to theta reverie. Breathing exercises were also included, as a way to start each session, including hyperventilation to stimulate the nervous system, followed by breathing exercises to still body functions and focus attention.

The students practiced daily for 10 weeks during the semester. Washburn University had provided three small rooms for the exclusive use of students in the study, and they signed up for the times they wished to train. Every other week students had a session in the Voluntary Controls Laboratory, at which time, in addition to measuring brainwaves, skin temperature, and blood flow in the hands, heart rate, breathing rate, galvanic skin response, and skin potential were measured. Students practiced for about an hour every day that school was in session. Each student kept a notebook, recording images, experiences, and also the durations that alpha and theta were present. In the last 5 weeks, students were asked to pay special attention to and record hypnagogic imagery, which is imagery that comes suddenly, rising spontaneously from the unconscious into consciousness. Hypnagogic imagery was known to be present in creativity, including creative solutions to problems being worked on over a period of time, such as Kekule's famous hypnagogic image that solved the chemical basis of organic chemistry. Kekule, and others with these spontaneous "ah-ha" solutions, described being in a state of reverie, an almost-sleep, when the insights, the breakthroughs, occurred. Since what they described was not descriptive of beta, alpha, or delta, it seemed safe to assume, initially, that this creativity occurred in the theta state of consciousness. These were assumptions at the time; nothing previous had been done, and there are no earlier references.

Most significantly, students reported many integrative experiences in their notebooks. Reports included increased feelings of well-being, of having things in hand, and increased dreaming. Many images were archetypal; a tunnel filled with light, staircases and climbing up or down, a single eye, a wise old man, and a book of knowledge were all reported by many of the students. Students reported feeling calmer, feeling sharper, on top of their game: "I feel good inside, I feel I can get things done," "I worry less, if there is something I need to do, I just do it," "I feel more relaxed in my everyday life, I feel more inner peace."

Creative problem solving centered mainly on interpersonal relations, insights for dealing with a spouse, girlfriend, a teacher or boss, as well as intrapersonal problems such as feelings of guilt and insecurity, and feelings associated with self-image and self-identity. The creativity that was encountered was focused not on major academic and scientific problems, but on what was uppermost in the students' minds and where they were emotionally invested, such as the problems of daily life. These creative, integrative experiences were often so significant and so helpful that the students made major adjustments in the ways they functioned and related to others. These findings led to the next research project undertaken, a theta training program for hospitalized mental patients at the Menninger Clinic, described next.

Brainwave Training for Mental Health

Pilot work with a few of the hospitalized patients at Menninger had already demonstrated positive indications of integrative experiences, with accompanying benefits in functioning. In proceeding with the more formal research study, our basic hypothesis was, "If psychiatric patients are trained to attain theta reverie, using insofar as possible the same training technique used with college students, they will tend to have the same kinds of integrative experiences that college students have." Over a period of several years, patients were trained substantially with this protocol.

All of the patients came to the Voluntary Controls Lab for their training, and all the people providing the training were therapists and researchers on the Voluntary Controls staff. As with the students in the Theta Brainwave Training for Creativity study, patients were trained first toward a quiet body, quiet emotions, and quiet mind by means of autogenic training and yogic breathing, which they then used briefly to initiate each session. Improved functioning, improved relations, and improved inner comfort were reported by both patients and their hospital staff.

Although patients were asked to report on images, their reports differed to some extent from those of the college students. Emphasis in this study was placed on objective, measurable outcomes of the training. Each subject completed the Minnesota Multiphasic Personality Inventory (MMPI) at the outset of training, at the end of the 30 sessions of training, and at a follow-up conducted 3 months after completion. The first three scales (Hypochondriasis, Depression, Hysteria) changed very little, although there was a specific trend toward improvement in depression. Essentially no changes were noted in Psychopathic Deviate or Masculinity/Femininity scales. One participant remarked, "I like myself more now."

Most surprising, the three scales (Paranoia, Psychasthenia, and Schizophrenia) changed in all the participants immediately after completing the training, in many dramatically, by as much as two standard deviations from their initial testing. At the follow-up testing 3 months later, there was some reversion back toward their original scores; however, almost all patients retained a clinically significant gain, generally about one standard deviation improvement.

One interesting and informative case was that of a young man who suffered from severe obsessive thoughts and compulsive behavior. He described himself as always engaged with these symptoms, and as always exhausted. He actually fell asleep while predominantly in beta and no alpha in his measured occipital (O1) brainwave record. This phenomenon persisted whether he was awake or asleep, whether his eyes were open or closed. This went on for several weeks, and then I decided to give him some relief by leading him in guided imagery. The aim was to attempt to move him away from constant reiteration of his obsessive thoughts. It was simple imagery, but as multi-sensory as I could devise. Walking down a path, everything green and bright, feeling warmth of sun on back, smelling the air, hearing birds, and before long, there was onset of alpha, the first ever recorded from his brain during the training sessions.

Greater and greater amounts of alpha were generated, with growing amplitude, and then this sleep-deprived man fell asleep with more normal brain rhythms, for a short while, before awakening with a start. I continued guided imagery in subsequent sessions, and he had moderate improvement in his functioning and in his inner comfort. I made him a guided imagery tape that he could use; mostly he only used it to fall asleep. He was afraid to relinquish his obsessive thoughts, believing that some terrible punishment awaited him.

Under the umbrella of brainwave training for mental health, we undertook another small but significant study to train subjects specifically to control the brainwave being measured. Participants were trained in either theta (4–8 Hz) or beta (13–26 Hz), in a random and single-blind manner assigned by the flip of a coin. When the first 10 patients flipped a coin to see which group they would be in (Group "A" or Group "B"), it seemed to us that the results were undesirable: although at the time we were interested in what theta could do, the results of their coin flipping placed eight out of 10 in the beta training group. However, this turned out to be fortuitous, for reasons that follow.

Training was conducted as follows. In each session, participants were given training with feedback in the selected brainwave (either beta or theta). All patients received alpha feedback, so that turning beta off resulted in an increase in alpha, and turning theta off also resulted in an increase in alpha. After 20 minutes of training in the selected brainwave state, they were asked about their experience and then asked to keep the feedback tones on for 2 minutes, followed by 2 minutes of reducing the state (instruction: keep the tone off), followed by 2 more minutes of keeping the tones on.

Participants were not told whether the tones represented increases in beta or theta, and the machines were modified so that identical low tones could provide feedback for either beta or theta, and were coded so that the therapist doing the training could select the appropriate instrument, a beta machine or a theta machine, depending on the group to which the patient had been randomly assigned.

We used the on-off-on protocol right from the beginning, reassuring the participants that this method was part of the learning process. Over the period of time, most became quite good at doing this. For example, in the "keep the tone on" condition, it might be on 60% of the time, and in the "keep the tone off" condition, only present 10–15% of the time.

As it turned out, the beta training was very helpful to almost all of the mental health patients, regardless of their diagnostic condition. They reported that the brainwave training experience was helping them to remain more in the present, to be in the here-and-now instead of being anxious about the past or the future. The ability to be in a beta state of consciousness and to be in the present is illustrated in the following case.

A year or so after learning to achieve and maintain beta, one patient with whom I was working had a serious breakdown. He was at the point of leaving the hospital and entering college when this occurred, at a time when I was out of town. When I returned, he was in the hospital and he was not contained at all. As he described it, his "mind was all over the hospital." He claimed he was having more or less continuous ESP experiences and was telling hospital staff members what was going on with them. He told the nurse in his section that she had a mark on her shoulder that was making her very anxious. This really frightened her, because she had a mark of the size and at the location he described, and it made her feel invaded. He told patients and staff alike about their fears and desires that he was picking up on. Everyone on the unit was afraid of him, and he was the most scared of all. He was terrified and lost in these experiences.

I brought an EEG machine to his room, one of our standard machines that provided beta, alpha, and theta channels, and began beta feedback sessions with him. Because he had learned this skill before, he was able almost immediately to be back in the present. And once reminded of it, he was able to maintain voluntary control over the state without the need for feedback. He was highly motivated to maintain this control, which he described as being able to pull all the scattered parts of himself back into his brain. Unfortunately, I do not have follow-up data on this, because after only 2 or 3 weeks, the Menninger Hospital sent him to another mental hospital.

Biofeedback Workshops for Health Professionals

While these studies were going on, the Voluntary Controls

group received many visits and requests for information. As a result, and eager to share information, the group initiated a 2-day clinical training workshop for professional practitioners who wanted to include biofeedback applications into their own practices. The workshop covered background/rationale, thermal training and demonstration and experience of deep diaphragmatic breathing and their clinical applications, galvanic skin response (GSR), deep muscle relaxation, experience with electromyography (EMG) feedback, and discussion of corresponding clinical applications.

Brainwave feedback with the portable EEG systems we had built, and discussion of experiences and clinical applications, took up the afternoon of the second day. There were myriad illustrations to share in all these domains. These workshops were in such demand that we scheduled them every Monday and Tuesday except for holiday weekends, and registration was backed up for several weeks. Literature was sought and collected from all the publications we could find on biofeedback and self-regulation topics, and eventually the Voluntary Controls library contained thousands of articles and references. Health care practitioners, physicians, psychologists, nurses, and teachers came from all over the United States, and some international attendees came as well, especially from Japan and China.

A/T Training for Substance Use Disorders (SUDs)

Brainwave training for SUDs was an early focus of our clinical work, and studies and treatment work in this area continued for the next 20 years. Initially we had requests from individuals caught in substance abuse to see whether they could be helped with biofeedback. Dale Walters was treating a patient with alcoholism who was temporarily hospitalized at the Menninger Clinic, and I was treating an individual who wanted help in eliminating his cocaine addiction. Because of our many positive experiences with theta training for various subject/patient populations with diverse conditions, we made this the center of our treatment. Walters was looking for literature on alcoholism and discovered a number of studies, most of which were connected with Alcoholics Anonymous work.

Seminal work was being conducted at the Missouri Research Institute with a very in-depth study of alcoholism. Subjects were brought into the hospital and were withdrawn from alcohol so that a number of physiological functions could be studied without the inebriating effects of drink. Electroencephalographic data were collected, and it was observed that these patients showed virtually no alpha when their brains were not under the influence of alcohol.

We later learned that these same individuals, once they were able to get alcohol, showed almost continuous alpha rhythms, and we speculated, from our earlier experiences with creativity studies and with patients, that they were drinking to achieve the alpha experience—or self-medicating. This observation was later corroborated in many cases, as will be seen in the various research studies we and others performed and investigated, many of them cited throughout this handbook.

The Brainwave for Health Professionals workshop participants were very excited about the possibilities of brainwave training and wanted to learn more. We then designed a 2-day workshop focused entirely on brainwave training, with more intensive training and experience. We presented the history of theta brainwave training and all our experiences with it in diverse studies, and expressed our conviction that theta was extremely useful.

These workshops were very popular. (For the record, we soon had 2-day workshops devoted to the treatment of pain and to cancer treatment, and later a 2-day workshop on the treatment of hypertension. It was an exciting time, and it felt as if we were among the forerunners.)

Eugene Peniston was working with clients with alcoholism in a conventional SUD treatment program at the state prison at Fort Lyons, Colorado, when he attended the biofeedback overview workshop provided by the Voluntary Controls Research group at Menninger. He was very interested in hearing about the studies of the brain functions being conducted at the Midwest Research Institute, and intrigued by our suggestion that alpha training might help people with alcoholism overcome their need to self-medicate. Thus, A/T training was added to his protocol. Peniston then returned for the 2-day brainwave training workshop, and during the experiential part, designed the broad outlines of the training program he was soon to develop at Fort Lyons.

This program included A/T training and was provided by Peniston to 10 individuals with alcoholism who were to be discharged from the prison by the end of treatment. A control group of individuals who received only conventional addiction treatment and who were also soon to be discharged served as a comparison group.

Both groups were followed while on parole, and these results were reported at the end of the first year in charts and talks at conferences and workshops (unfortunately, these were not published at the time). As sometimes happens with the advent of a new paradigm in treatment, the results were spectacular, giving a big impetus to the furtherance of this work. It had been demonstrated in all our earlier work with individuals and in groups, as in the creativity study with students, that theta was a doorway to personal problem solving and to deeper inner work with transformative potential. Peniston was familiar with our experiences, our work, and the rationale for theta's importance. He followed the Menninger treatment protocol as closely as possible.

The results of Peniston's study spoke for the efficacy of the A/T training paradigm. In the control group, relapse occurred for three participants within the first 3 months; by the end of the year, all but one had relapsed. In the group who learned alpha-theta production, eight of the 10 participants had no use of their substance of choice whatsoever (and were healthier and happier than before, according to self-report). One participant became abstinent from alcohol, but died before the year was up from cirrhosis of the liver engendered by years of heavy drinking. The tenth participant did not want to give up drinking; he tried to drink but got sick, and after a couple of tries in the first 3 months of follow-up, decided that he had to limit himself to one drink a day, and did so successfully for the remainder of the time.

Two officials from the Kansas Department of Corrections (KDOC) also participated in the 2-day brainwave training workshop. Roger Werholtz was the director of programs at the Department of Corrections, soon to become director of KDOC, and Warren Berry directed the alcoholism division.

During one of his A/T training sessions, Berry had a strong experience of vividly reliving an occurrence that he had repressed for a long time. It was one of those "being there in every detail" experiences, and it affected him profoundly. He was convinced of the potential power of brainwave training for addicted subjects, and he in turn then convinced Werholtz that it would be a worthwhile endeavor. These events signified the beginning of our A/T training for substance use disorders in the prisons, although it was to take time before we actually got started.

Over the years at the Menninger Foundation and the Menninger Clinic, there were many changes in the organi-

Background

In the early 1970s, I was working at the Kansas Reception and Diagnostic Center (KRDC), a facility devoted to intake and assessment of newly arrested persons prior to sentencing. A team consisting of a social worker, a psychologist or psychiatrist, a substance abuse expert, and a chaplain met with the inmate to make a considered recommendation to the court for either probation or parole, or for sentencing guidelines. Among other considerations, all were evaluated to determine the need for substance abuse treatment prior to assignment to prison. As a clinical psychologist on a team, I tested and interviewed many inmates, read their records, met with other team members, and participated in recommendations to the court.

During this time, I became acutely aware of many aspects of the incarceration system, and of the men themselves, that I had had no conception of before taking this job. I expected to see crooks, hardened men deliberately preying on society (as they are so often portrayed in the popular press). Instead, I found frightened and angry, guilt-ridden and impulsive people who felt inadequate and had very low self-esteem. At KRDC all professional staff were expected to run some kind of a training program for the inmates while they were there. Most chose traditional topics, but my favorite was a psychologist doing assertiveness training, which appalled most of our colleagues. I decided to do groups focused on empowerment and self-image change, and this became the foundation of my PhD dissertation; after 1 to 3 years of follow-up after release from prison, 12.9% percent remained successfully out of prison, a powerful result.

A basic premise of self-image change is that we do not and cannot act outside of the image we hold of ourselves. With the six counselors being trained for the program at Ellsworth state prison, we presented this didactically and with illustrations, and laid the groundwork for their own self-image change. They also experienced the same psychophysiological self-mastery techniques they would be teaching to the inmate population.

zation, and also in the Voluntary Controls staff, and the organization was eventually renamed the Center for Applied Psychophysiology and Biofeedback. We did a lot of our early work in the treatment of patients with SUDs from this center, and also worked with the Menninger Alcoholism Treatment program, organized along conventional addiction treatment lines.

In 1993, six of us (your author, Steven Fahrion, Carol Snarr, Jeff Nichols, Hugh Boeving, and Deb Carter from the Center for Applied Psychophysiology and Biofeedback) left the Menninger Clinic and formed the Life Sciences Institute of Mind-Body Health (LSI), from which we conducted all of the workshops, clinical treatments, and professional workshops that we formerly provided at Menninger. LSI signed a contract with the Kansas Department of Corrections for a 3-year randomized controlled evaluation of A/T training to be conducted at Ellsworth State Prison, which included a 2-year follow-up after release. State parole officers provided the follow-up of all participants after completion of treatment and release from prison.

In the beginning, we hired six counselors who had never worked in SUD programs to provide the training under supervision of the LSI staff. We were well aware that it would be difficult to change the perspective of conventional addiction counselors to the holistic and self-regulation model we planned to use with the brainwave training. Ellsworth required that inmates assigned to any program, including SUD treatment, participate in a 6-hour-a-day, Monday through Friday, 9-week, 45-day module, and we accommodated our program to that schedule. We gave the six new counselors the exact same training that we were planning for the research participants.

The self-regulation one acquires by means of biofeedback affects self-image, sometimes profoundly, as the individual realizes this is something within his or her body and life that can be regulated. Temperature biofeedback, which was performed first in our model of AT training, is associated with emotional control, with the ability to lower arousal. As one young person put it, "I can now keep myself from getting mad, I can think about it instead and have time to decide." Breathing exercises were also taught at the beginning of training. Participants began each session for the entire 9 weeks with breathing and hand warming, regardless of group. The non-biofeedback group received an extra small-group experience in place of the A/T training.

The initial intent for the research protocol was that an A/T training group would be compared with a conventional addiction training group. After many considerations, the final protocol was that all the training was identical for all participants with the exception of the brainwave sessions themselves.

Participants randomly assigned to the alpha-theta condition had one brainwave session every day; those assigned to the non-brainwave condition had an extra "small-group" treatment instead. The neurofeedback training placement was O1 and we trained theta (4–8 Hz) and alpha (8–12 Hz) with tone feedback. We suggested that they keep the tones low. Both the brainwave sessions and the small group (control) sessions had eight participants at a time; sessions for both groups began with a few minutes of hand warming and breathing exercises to calm the participant by decreasing sympathetic arousal and bring him or her to present. It is important to note that the two trainings were virtually identical, except for the absence of A/T training in the control group. Therefore we were easily able to compare the effects of the EEG training to the lack of training in the small group control group. And what we ended up with was an as-close-to-pure-as-possible measure of the effects of brainwave training alone. Brainwave sessions and small group sessions were cited most frequently as the best liked and the most helpful in program evaluations completed by the participants.

Drinking alcohol produces almost continuous, high amplitude alpha activity in both alcoholic and non-alcoholic individuals. At the Midwest Research Center we found that hospitalized alcoholics withdrawn from alcohol had little or no alpha production; it can be surmised that drinking is a way that alcoholics can get the experience of alpha, experiencing pleasure and reward. We used to quip to the alcoholic individuals, "Well, they don't call alcohol 'spirits' for nothing." Deficient alpha is part of a pattern that has been labeled reward deficiency syndrome associated with discomfort, anxiety, and anger (Blum, Cull, Braverman & Comings, 1996). With brainwave training, individuals can learn to increase, often markedly, the presence of alpha and theta brainwaves, correcting the deficit and increasing satisfactions and pleasure from everyday life.

Demographics

The research design was a 5-year randomized study of incarcerated individuals with SUDs and 2-year follow-up after release from prison. The 35 participants in the study were convicted felons, ranging in age from 18 to 62 (n = 35). The groups were racially mixed, with Blacks (51%) and Whites (42%) predominating. Drug of choice was primarily alcohol (38%), marijuana (31%) or cocaine (23%).

In addition to 35 A/T sessions (daily except Saturday and Sunday), all participants were given some standard SUD treatment elements such as presentations and exercises on relapse prevention, shame and guilt, family dynamics, and one-on-one counseling. Didactic presentations on philosophical and psychodynamic aspects of self were also featured. An example is a presentation and exercise centered on life determinants, which we titled "Every Acorn is a Perfect Oak Tree." The premise is that this is true in the seedling stage, and then life happens. Does the budding tree fall on rich or dry soil, get nurturance or scarcity, get ravaged by winds and storms or perhaps nibbled on by a passing animal? The oak tree and each human being are determined by an accumulation of life events. Participants are invited to think of their own lives in these terms. What conditions did they fall into at birth? We are each a product of what has occurred in our life up to now. Lots of personal experiences were shared. So if so much of who we are is determined, where does free will come in? Free will exists only in the present, where we have the freedom of making a choice, and then we become a product of all that has occurred, including this choice.

Core values were explored in many ways, with exercises from psychosynthesis, founded by Roberto Assagioli (1971). The most basic precept of psychosynthesis is that we are a center of consciousness and will, capable of observing, directing, and harmonizing all the psychological processes and the physical body.

Change, learning, and transformation are brought about by awareness and volition, consciousness and will, step-by-step as we go through our lives. These concepts were inspiring to the participants and had a lasting value for as long as we were able to follow them. Biofeedback and psychosynthesis are perfect companions in basic conceptions. Self-regulation and mastery via biofeedback is a process of awareness and volition.

Results and Follow-up

Beyond all the statistics below, and beyond any outcome measures, there was an unseen factor that played a very significant role in the results. Insofar as possible in the prison setting, we treated the participants with deference, respect, and compassion. We asked our fellow professionals to run the program exactly the way we would if the participants were university professors.

At the end of every 45-day session, we had a ceremony, like a graduation, and participants would share what it meant to them, what it might mean for their future, what they visualized as happening, and so forth. One participant said, "You all may find this hard to believe, but these many days have been the happiest days of my life!" He felt listened to, respected, and cared about quite possibly for the first time in his life. It had intense meaning for him, and for his self-image, a whole new platform on which to stand.

Upon release and after completion of the study, participants were followed for at least 2 years by state parole officers who submitted monthly reports (we have follow-up data for 2 years only). Supervision was tight, and included frequent random urine tests. At the conclusion of the 2-year follow-up for each individual, survival analyses were conducted on the outcome for the participant as a whole.

Survival analysis was chosen as the outcome measure to determine effects of the treatments over time. "Survival" represents the time a participant succeeded in compliance with parole requirements. Failure was signified by SUD relapse, absconding, committing a new offense, and/or technical violations that resulted in a return to prison. Survival status was determined every 2 months for each participant, providing 12 data points in the 2 years, so we could pinpoint the timing of failure instances as precisely as possible.

The primary result, most important for guidelines and for determining cost effectiveness, was that half or more of the treated inmates succeeded at 2-year follow-up, despite the more stringent measures of occurrences that would constitute failure. It is generally recognized that typical SUD programs in prisons have a success rate of 10 to 20% because the chronic nature of addiction generally requires multiple treatments before lasting results are achieved.

When we compared A/T training vs. control groups (which, remember, received identical treatment except for the substitution of an extra small-group session instead of brainwave training), the difference in survival was marginal, not quite reaching statistical significance. At the end of 1 year, the brainwave-trained group had a 78% survival rate, and the control group had a 75% survival rate; at the end of 2 years of follow-up, the survival rate was 69% for those who received the brainwave training, and the control group had a 64% survival rate. These figures are remarkable, and show how durable this training was. Some significant and important factors and comparisons were examined.

Both treatments were more effective with younger patients than with older ones, divided at the median age of 35, and this was significantly more in the case with the brainwave treatment. For the younger subjects, at the 12-month point, the survival rate was 72% for the brainwave cohort, and 54% for the control cohort; at the 24-month point, the brainwave treated had a 60% success rate, and the control group was at 46% success.

Both treatments were effective with White participants, but brainwave training was significantly more effective for the non-White participants, who were mostly Black with Hispanic and Asian persons also represented. After 1 year, at the 12-month point, 70% non-Whites who received A/T treatment were successful, and 55% of the control cohort were succeeding; at the end of 2 years, 48% of the brainwave trained group were still successful, and 40% of the control group remained successful. The differences between 1 year and 2 years led us to believe that short booster sessions after 1 year may prove very helpful. In private practice, boosters were very useful for patients in preventing relapse of all kinds.

Comparisons between drug of choice and success were also

made. Overall, treatment was least effective for cocaine users. For the users of cocaine who did not receive brainwave training, 75% did not succeed, whereas 25% remained successful. For cocaine users who did receive the brainwave training, 54% had problems, but 46% remained successful. This was not statistically significant, but I think it suggests considerable clinical significance.

For participants whose drug of choice was alcohol, those who did not receive brainwave training had a 56% failure rate, with 44% remaining successful, whereas for those who did receive brainwave training, 32% had further problems, and 68% remained successful at the end of 2 years. For marijuana users, 59% of those who did not receive brainwave treatments failed, with 41% remaining successful, and these figures were reversed for those who received brainwave training: 59% remained successful after 2 years. These represent real differences in people's lives.

This success led to expansion of our treatment program to people with SUDs in the Lansing State Prison; in the state prison at Hutchinson; at El Dorado State Prison in the special hospital section for those diagnosed with mental illness in addition to SUDs; and in a program at the state prison for women in Topeka. At the time, it was our hope and vision that if this treatment proved successful, it could become the model for the whole state and for the nation.

Conclusion

This chapter describes the evolution of a new paradigm. The theories and research provided herein demonstrate a series of stepping stones that determined much of how brainwave biofeedback developed, and were instrumental in moving the field forward. Although this handbook is about A/T training as practiced today, the field of biofeedback has covered many other parameters of health and well-being. Real change, lasting change, depends on these intrapersonal factors: self-regulation and self-mastery, self-efficacy and self-esteem, empowerment, and self-image change. These are the most essential factors, the foundations of real and lasting change.

Our SUD work in prisons proved entirely affirmative. We did not ask participants to attest to anything they did not believe, and discouraged them from saying things because they thought that was what we wanted to hear. Our intention was to operate with mutual love and respect, with unconditional positive regard, with a belief in participants' human potential to grow, change, gain control, and transform. Our goal was to give each client a glimpse into an enlarged potential, to help clients gain genuine self-esteem, recognize their innate value and personal worth, feel the joy of connectedness, hope, and empowerment, and believe in themselves.

It is this author's hope and intention that some researchers reading this will be stimulated to continue the SUD work that we began, which holds so much promise. In the world that we are living in at present, self-regulation and self-image change hold keys to a future that may be more compassionate, more caring, or at least, more benign.

References

Assagioli, R. (1971). *Psychosynthesis: A manual of principles and techniques.* New York: Viking Compass.

Blum, K., Cull, J. G., Braverman, E. R., & Comings, D. E. (1996). Reward deficiency syndrome. *American Scientist,* 84(2), 132–145.

Green, E., & Green, A. (1977). *Beyond biofeedback.* San Francisco, CA: Delacorte.

Rose, J. (Ed.). (1970). *Progress of cybernetics: Proceedings of the First International Congress of Cybernetics, London, 1969.* Gordon and Breach Science Publishers, Inc.

3

Experiences With Alpha Theta: Its Origins in Studies of Meditation

David L. Trudeau, MD

Today while perusing my daily mail I came across a web article that reexamines the use of hallucinogens in psychiatry (Stetka & Nutt, 2013). These drugs have been used to promote recall of suppressed traumatic events, to treat PTSD and addictive disorders, and to promote insight and transformational changes in self-motivation and self-belief (Grof, 1976)—much the same focus as A/T training. However, the scientific study of hallucinogens has been largely abandoned for the last three decades due to their DEA schedule 1 status (Drug Enforcement Agency controlled substance), probably inspired by the epidemic of counter-culture psychedelic drug abuse that occurred in the late sixties and early seventies.

Aside from mind-expanding drugs, the "Woodstock Era" also led to an increased interest in more traditional (non-neurotoxin) forms of mind expansion, such as meditation. Richard Alpert, a colleague of Timothy Leary, became Baba Ram Dass and a proponent of drug-free mind expansion (Dass, 1971). The Beatles, who got by with a little help from their friends ("their friends are Mary Jane and Bennie," said Spiro Agnew), sought out the Maharishi Mahesh Yogi to "transcendentalize." Moreover, at the Menninger Clinic in Topeka, Kansas, Elmer Green studied gifted healers, gifted meditators, and ordinary people with brain wave analysis and electric fields (Green & Green, 1977; Norris, 2000, chapter 2). There was a convergence of interest of exploring mental phenomena that went beyond everyday consciousness into realms of spirituality, personal transformation, and the study of subtle energies. Largely because of the work at Menninger by Elmer and Alyce Green, Dale Walters, Patricia Norris, and Steve Fahrion, there was an attempt to quantify the trancelike, meditation-like states induced by alpha-theta neurofeedback. These states potentially unlock creativity, transform treatment-resistant alcoholics, and release unprocessed traumatic memories (Green, Green, & Walters, 1974; Norris, 2000, chapter 2).

At the same time of the work by the Menninger group, Maxwell Cade, in the United Kingdom, was studying meditators and healers, developing brain wave biofeedback methods intended to mimic the electroencephalographic activity occurring in gifted meditators (Cade & Coxhead, 1989).

The idea of all this work was that if one could reproduce what was seen with analog processing of single-lead EEG taken during meditation in gifted meditators, then one could become a better meditator. By changing brain electrophysiology voluntarily through biofeedback, one could open the mind to new awareness and the possibilities of change. A/T training could become an important adjunct to psychotherapy and personal transformation.

Beta Trainers and Alpha-Theta Trainers

I recall my early days in attending the initial meetings of the Society for the Study of Neuronal Regulation (SSNR—the forerunner of today's International Society for Neurofeedback and Research—ISNR). There seemed to be two distinct camps—those interested in attention deficit and TBI remediation with higher bandwidth EEG biofeedback, and those interested in achieving hypnagogic states with lower bandwidth EEG biofeedback. Eugene Peniston, with what some called evangelistic fervor, created huge attention and some controversy as he presented his work on A/T training in post-combat PTSD and alcoholism to entranced audiences at the SSNR and AAPB (Association for Applied Psychophysiology and Biofeedback) conferences (Peniston & Kulkosky, 1989, 1990, 1991).

The main point is that A/T training came about because of studies on meditators and began as an attempt to reproduce meditational states like the ones seen in the EEG signal produced by meditators in trance-like states. At the time A/T training was being developed, there may have been substantially more interest in meditation, altered states of consciousness, and transformational states, than in mental health conditions. Perhaps over time some of that interest and emphasis has shifted as pharmacological interventions have often replaced psychotherapy in behavioral health, and perhaps the psychedelia of the sixties is seen as passé. However, I would argue that A/T training is an important tool and that there is still much to be learned about it. Many of the clinical conditions for which A/T training has been used—addiction, PTSD, anxiety—are complex. These therapies are transformational and based on personal growth and change.

In this chapter, I would first like to relate my personal experiences in my introduction to A/T training, because in my conversations with others interested in A/T training, I am impressed that what motivates their interest (as well as mine) is personal experience. In the early days of neurofeedback, there seemed to be little dialogue—or mutual respect for that matter—between these two groups of beta trainers and alpha-theta trainers.

As I will explain, I was largely interested in A/T training and roundly ignored what was being done with SMR (sensory motor rhythm) and beta feedback. I suspect many others had the same bias, one way or another, and I also suspect they may continue with that perspective today. Then I would like to look at why I think the almost evangelical enthusiasm for A/T training that was present in the 1990s gradually waned. Finally, I would like to make a case for a renaissance of interest in studying what is going on in A/T training vs. meditation, hypnosis, traumatic recall, and self-realization vis-à-vis brain electrophysiology and emerging knowledge of neural networks.

I am convinced that the early studies on meditators using crude equipment, while laying an important groundwork, need to be revisited with twenty-first century technology. The whole premise of A/T training is that it can be used to achieve the types of self-actualization, optimization, and personal transformation sought by practitioners of yoga and Zen, by using neurofeedback as a shortcut mechanism to achieve these states. While the reader may not be particularly interested in meditation, it is in fact where the whole premise of A/T training lies. Thus, the utilization of A/T training is grounded in studies of meditators.

My approaches in this chapter will be largely narrative and anecdotal. I have participated in reviews that look at A/T training in depth in substance use (i.e., Sokhadze, Cannon, & Trudeau, 2008a, 2008b; Trudeau, 2000, 2005a) and several book chapters (Sokhadze, Trudeau, & Cannon, 2013; Trudeau, Sokhadze, & Cannon, 2009) that summarize the extensive literature on A/T training in addictions. I refer the reader to those for a more scholarly discussion of the emergence and criticisms of A/T training.

Early Experiences in A/T Training

My introduction to A/T training occurred in 1991, well after the important groundwork had been established. I had recently come to the Veteran's Affairs Medical Center in Minneapolis as medical director of the inpatient alcohol and drug rehab program. An old friend, a treatment center executive I had worked with, called me one day to ask about "this new kind of brain therapy that's got everything beat." I did not know what he was talking about but got the name of a VA psychologist at Fort Lyons VA in Colorado—a fellow named Gene Peniston. I called Gene, and he sent me reprints of his papers, which I read, and I was immediately anxious to learn more about his technique of A/T training for addictions. Then I made the happy discovery that a colleague at the Minneapolis VA had begun to use A/T training in PTSD and most importantly had acquired some equipment and lab space in the PTSD department. This colleague—a psychiatrist who specialized in PTSD—had an early model biofeedback device, an easy-to-use but primitive device that provided set auditory tones for predefined bandwidths of analog processed EEG when arbitrary thresholds were met. I was told the device had been developed in concert with Elmer Green at Menninger.

While revolutionary by 1980s standards, this equipment is quite inadequate by today's standards, which require exacting measurement of EEG and digitized processing with displays and recording. The analog device could be easily overridden with any signal a little stronger than the one of interest, for instance by clenching one's jaws to create some louder EMG signal. There were no measures of impedance. So the subject, given the instruction to "close your eyes and sink down and be guided by the sounds" could easily be waylaid into a session of jaw clenching feedback or sounds coming from a loose electrode.

There were three choices of bandwidth—"alpha," "theta," and "beta"—and three accompanying preset tones and three dials to select a squelch point for the selected signals. There appeared to be a fair amount of spillover from one defined bandwidth to the other and no way of seeing or recording the actual analog or digitized EEG. (This is the DEI mentioned in Norris, chapter 2. —Ed)

Nevertheless, having read Peniston's papers on A/T training in the treatment of addiction and PTSD, I was eager to experience just what this feedback was supposed to be like. Moreover, I also referenced a much earlier experience in the early 1970s with a medical student (whom I had precepted, and who was interested in brain research). He had a mail order device that attached to the head and produced sounds that were supposedly representative of alpha and theta activity beneath the scalp and could be used as a training tool to practice deep meditation. I do not think I got much beyond some relaxation, but I did become interested in learning more about the technique of meditation and its physiology as a result of this experience.

Peniston—in his papers and also in many conversations we had—described striking changes in alcoholics as a result of alpha-theta experiences, including a complete loss of tolerance to alcohol ("the Peniston flu") and rather dramatic psychometric changes of personality as well as long-standing abstinence in his subjects, chronic repeaters recruited from a VA alcohol treatment program. I was especially impressed because I had an inexhaustible supply of such patients. Gene also described spontaneous recall of repressed traumatic memories in subjects who had received absolutely no prompting to do so while undergoing A/T training, which he then processed in brief psychotherapy sessions following the feedback.

So, being something of a meditator, and curious about alpha/theta applications for addiction, I underwent the first of many A/T training sessions, reclining comfortably on a couch in my colleague's basement. Ear clips on and an electrode attached to

Experiences With Alpha Theta: Its Origins in Studies of Meditation

my occiput, I listened to tones generated by a little black box which set thresholds for alpha and theta feedback as I closed my eyes and sank down into a relaxed, meditative state.

I was absolutely amazed at the experience. Guided by the tones, I entered a state where I was aware of sounds and voices in my vicinity but unaware of the passage of time, and found myself freely associating with no effort, with vivid imagery. When the 30-minute session ended (I did not know if it was hours or minutes—it felt like half the afternoon), I had the surprising realization that some of my self-behaviors were pretty toxic.

This insight came to me as a visual and auditory image of me barking at my wife, taking out some of my job frustrations on her. Somewhat later and with this insight, I apologized to her. She was obviously deeply affected, and she said something to the effect that I was no fun to live with, and she was glad I could finally see it. During the session, which was unforgettable, I was impressed with the ease with which I entered what I gauged as an excellent meditational experience. Of course, I had been primed with positive expectations, and the induction script I got from my colleague was pretty suggestive. From courses in hypnotism I took, I learned I was suggestible and could enter a trance without much difficulty. But, qualitatively, the alpha-theta guided experience was far different from anything I had experienced.

This experience was the beginning of a career of personally and professionally exploring A/T training, both as a research subject and as a therapeutic technique. In my conversations with others who have become very interested in studying A/T training, they said that they also were impressed with their personal experience of it. When I went to Menninger for A/T training courses with Dale Walters and Steve Fahrion, having the experience as a subject of A/T training was part of the process, using the same DEI equipment. As soon as I could, we purchased Lexicor (Lexicor, Boulder, CO, USA) equipment that would display and record actual EEG in a reliable way, and used that for A/T training. The experience seemed the same. Experiencing A/T training (or meditation, for that matter) seems very much like eating ice cream. One can read the ingredients on an ice cream carton and see an ice cream factory in operation and still have no idea what the experience of eating ice cream really is. Ah, but taste it! For the next 10 years, from 1991 to 2001, I organized and directed the neurofeedback lab at the Minneapolis VAMC in addition to my many clinical duties.

The Foundations of A/T Training

A/T training involves the simultaneous measurement of occipital alpha (8–13 Hz) and theta (4–8 Hz) and feedback by separate auditory tones for each frequency band representing amplitudes greater than preset thresholds. The participant is encouraged to relax and to increase the amount of time they hear the signal, that is, to increase the amount of time that the amplitude of each defined bandwidth exceeds the threshold. A variety of equipment and software has been used to acquire, process, and filter these signals, and there are differences in technique inherent with each type of equipment and software (see chapter 15).

In 1968, Joe Kamiya, while working at the University of Chicago, demonstrated that the alpha rhythm in humans could be operantly conditioned. He published an influential article in *Psychology Today* that same year summarizing research showing that subjects could learn to discriminate when alpha was present or absent and that they could use feedback to voluntarily generate alpha. Almost half of his subjects reported experiencing a

Experiences With Alpha Theta: Its Origins in Studies of Meditation

pleasant "alpha state" characterized as an "alert calmness." He also studied the EEG correlates of meditative states (Kamiya, 1969; Nowlis & Kamiya, 1970).

A/T training was first employed and described by Elmer Green and colleagues (Green, Green, & Walters, 1974) at the Menninger Clinic. This method, based on Green's observations

JOE KAMIYA

In the 1950s and 60s, Joe Kamiya (author of the Foreword) was a psychologist and professor at the University of Chicago. In 1958, he began experiments on brain wave frequencies. Observing the posterior region with surface EEG electrodes, Kamiya studied whether, when a tone sounded, the subject could guess whether he was in predominantly alpha power. Kamiya was watching the EEG signal and could determine whether the subjects (college students) were correct in their subjective sense.

Through these experiments, Kamiya concluded that people could regulate brain waves, previously thought to be involuntary brain mechanisms. Kamiya published his findings in *Psychology Today* (1968). He continued to develop a style of "first person science" in which he looks at very personalized teachings and trainings, observing the subjective experience of the subject while conducting objective modalities.

of single-lead EEG during meditative states in practiced meditators, resulted in the theta-alpha crossover (see Johnson & Bodenhamer-Davis, chapter 6), an initial increase in alpha amplitude followed by an increase in theta amplitude and then a drop-off of alpha amplitude. When participants received the feedback signal, they reported states of profound relaxation and reverie. The method was seen as useful in augmenting psychotherapy and promoting individual insight. It could be seen as a use of brain wave signal feedback to enable a participant to maintain a particular state of consciousness similar to a meditative or hypnotic relaxed state over a 30- or 40-minute feedback session that may have enabled access to previously unconscious (or sub-conscious?) contents.

The Menninger Foundation was founded in 1919 by the Menninger family in Topeka, Kansas and it operated independently there until 2003, when it merged with the Baylor School of Medicine and moved to Houston, Texas. Elmer Green is a co-founder of both the AAPB and the International Society for the Study of Subtle Energies and Energy Medicine (ISSEEM). His background as a physicist in WWII plus his broad interest in human spirituality led to studies in biopsychology at the University of Chicago, where he obtained his PhD in 1962.

In 1964 he established the Psychophysiology Research Laboratory at the Menninger Clinic in Topeka, Kansas. There, over the next three decades, Elmer Green, his wife and colleague Alyce Green, his colleague Dale Walters, and his daughter and colleague Patricia Norris and her spouse Steve Fahrion devoted their studies to somatic biofeedback, brain wave biofeedback, and alpha-theta biofeedback. They were joined there by a number of clinicians from the Topeka VA, the Menninger Foundation, and others who became the first to use A/T training.

The interest in brainwave states that accompanied paranormal phenomena and meditation was part of a larger interest that Green and his colleagues had in studies of physiological states of meditators and healers (Green & Green, 1977). Elmer Green constructed a copper-walled room in which he was able to study the discharges of direct current states of gifted healers when they felt the transmission of healing energy to their subjects, whether in the same room or at a distance. He also studied meditators and reproduced and described Tibetan monastery practices of having students meditate while seated in front of a copper wall with a crystal suspended over their heads at the vertex (Green & Green, 1977).

During the 1970s, Maxwell Cade in the United Kingdom (see the box on the next page for a discussion of Cade's early work) and Elmer and Alyce Green in the United States studied experienced meditators with EEG during meditation and developed the alpha-theta hypothesis (Green & Green, 1977). During early states of relaxation and meditation with eyes closed, they noted large amplitude alpha, and as meditation proceeded, theta emerged as a dominant frequency (the "idle frequency" found in the posterior regions of the brain with eyes closed, associated with the resting state of the brain). The measurement of these changes was largely analog, and performed with single-lead measurements that were not recorded, but rather described. There were no standards developed for impedance or other technical specifications and band pass filters were largely analog; much of this equipment was developed at Menninger by the Greens in collaboration with an engineer as a proprietary device, the DEI.

The Greens brought portable biofeedback equipment to India and monitored yoga practitioners as they demonstrated self-regulation. The film, "Biofeedback: The Yoga of the West" (1974), contained footage of their investigation. Using their

MAXWELL CADE

Maxwell Cade, a British scientist and physicist, was a strong proponent and user of hypnotherapy and meditation as well as other approaches in the development of higher consciousness.

His interests, which included his belief that all things functioned in light, sound or other frequency domain, lead to his collaboration with bioengineers to develop biofeedback machines. With the first, an ESR (electrodermal skin response) sensor, he found one could discern physiological correlates to meditation and hypnotic state by looking at arousal level. When the assumed state was in fact not authentic, he used this information to help develop more authentic states.

His seminal book, The Awakened Mind: Biofeedback and the Development of Higher States of Awareness (1979) introduced the "Mind Mirror," his second physiological measuring device (co-developed with Geoff Blundell). With it, he investigated the brain's physiological properties of creativity, how the mind influenced health, healer/healee relationships and Zen Buddhism by observing the amplitude of its rhythms.

Cade is an important figure in the foundations of biofeedback, consciousness and creativity. His insight to the relationship between mind and body embodies our current beliefs and along with other important forefathers jump started the field of applied psychophysiology as is currently stands.

observations of many meditators and yoga masters as a foundation, they developed A/T training at the Menninger Foundation from the 1960s to the 1990s. They hypothesized that theta states allow access to unconscious memories and increase the impact of prepared images or suggestions. Their alpha-theta research fostered the development of an alpha-theta addiction protocol by several investigators at the Topeka and Fort Collins VAs (Goslinga, 1975; Peniston & Kulkosky, 1989; Twemlow & Bowen, 1976; Twemlow, Bowen, & Sizemore, 1977).

In addition to its applications in addiction, A/T training has also been employed in the field of creativity, peak performance (Gruzelier, 2009), and anxiety disorders (Moore, 2000). It has also been employed in PTSD for traumatic recall as described in the first papers about PTSD published by Peniston (Peniston & Kulkosky, 1991; Peniston, Marrinan, Deming, & Kulkosky, 1993).

Skepticism and Differences in Outcomes by Different Practitioners

As noted above, in the early days of SSNR the meetings were clearly divided into two groups of interest. One group was interested primarily in techniques to increase alertness and attention with higher frequency brain wave feedback to remediate ADHD and TBI. The other group's objective was to use A/T training to coach the brain into relaxed, reverie-like hypnagogic states. The two groups had little to say to one another.

The A/T training camp was largely focused on psychotherapy experiences and perhaps had a little evangelical fervor which largely turned off the ADHD camp. Having the experience of co-chairing three of the early SSNR–ISNR meetings with Jay Gunkelman and then having the experience of editing the *Journal of Neurotherapy* (Taylor and Francis, publishers) through 6 years, I was very impressed by how the anecdotal experiences of neurotherapy were related in both the meetings and submitted papers. "True believers" prevailed, with clinical nuggets and case experience abounding, and the atmosphere was geared—in my estimation—as much to marketing as to science, if not more so. Many of the best papers submitted to the conferences and the Journal on my watches were those done by the students during that time, some of whom are now prominent practitioners in the field.

Several good replication studies of Peniston's work with alcoholics treated by A/T training were done. Saxby and Peniston (1995) reported on 14 chronically alcohol dependent and depressed outpatients using this same protocol of alpha-theta brainwave biofeedback. Following treatment, participants showed substantial decreases in depression and psychopathology as measured by standard instruments. The 21-month follow-up data indicated sustained abstinence from alcohol confirmed by collateral report. These male and female outpatients received twenty 40-minute sessions of feedback. Eleanor (I know her as "Ellen") Saxby (personal communication) said that she felt the purpose of the A/T training was to open the door to psychotherapy and stated that much more time was spent doing psychotherapy than doing A/T training in her series. In the mid-1990s, I discussed this issue with Ken Graap who said he had done many A/T training sessions with PTSD subjects who liked the sessions but failed to improve in any meaningful way. He was unable to see the changes in personality testing that Peniston had reported which was my experience also. Graap went on to dissect Peniston's papers and published an in-depth critique of the data reported, the methods used, and the overlap of data points that suggested several subjects were repeatedly reported in papers relating to A/T training efficacy in alcoholism and PTSD.

Also, the differences in outcomes experienced by different practitioners might lie in the intensity of psychotherapy accompanying the alpha-theta sessions, and that was part of the critique of Graap and Freides (1998) of Peniston's reports. In an in-depth critical analysis of the original Peniston papers, Graap and Freides raised serious issues about the reporting of original samples and procedures in these studies. In their analyses, the results may have been due as much to the intense therapies accompanying the biofeedback as to the biofeedback itself. One issue raised by Graap and Freides is that the participants may have been comorbid with a number of conditions, which were not clearly reported, particularly PTSD, and PTSD may have been the focus of the accompanying psychotherapy treatment. In his reply to these criticisms, Peniston (1998) acknowledged that it "remains unknown whether the temperature training, the visualizations, the ATBWNT (alpha-theta brain wave neurotherapy), the therapist, the placebo, or the Hawthorne effects are responsible for the beneficial results." Many of the clinical studies on A/T training and addictions are difficult to compare and analyze because of the lack of control for comorbid conditions and the variability among practitioners' interactions accompanying the A/T training sessions in which recovered memories and intense personal imagery would come up. These issues are discussed in depth elsewhere (i.e., Sokhadze, Cannon, & Trudeau, 2008a, 2008b; Trudeau, 2000, 2005a) and two book chapters (Sokhadze, Trudeau, & Cannon, 2013; Trudeau, Sokhadze, & Cannon, 2009).

Several controlled studies of the Peniston protocol for addictions suggest that alpha-theta training for addictions may be nonspecific in terms of effect when compared to suggestion, sham or controlled treatment, or meditational techniques (Lowe, 1999a, 1999b; Moore & Trudeau, 1998; Taub & Rosenfeld, 1994; Taub, Steiner, Weingarten, & Walton, 1994). So it remains unclear if A/T training itself is responsible for the reported benefits, or if they are due to something else. Does A/T training synergize with psychotherapy to produce an effect? Another question is, does A/T training significantly differ from meditation as a therapeutic tool in addiction, PTSD, or other psychotherapy applications?

In another, more scientifically rigorous replication, Callaway and Bodenhamer-Davis (2008) reported a clinical trial with 16 chemically dependent outpatients, 10 of whom were probationers classified as being at high risk for re-arrest. Participants completed an average of 31 A/T training sessions. Psychometrics demonstrated improvements in personality and mood. Follow-up at 74 to 98 months indicated 81.3% of the treatment participants were abstinent. Re-arrest rates and probation revocations for the probation treatment group were lower than those for a probation-only comparison group (40% vs. 79%).

One of the largest studies of A/T training in addiction remains relatively unreported, largely because the outcomes were surprisingly weak. Fahrion (1995) gave a preliminary report (n = 119) on a large randomized study of alpha-theta training for addiction in the Kansas Prison System using group-training equipment. A report of the completed study (n = 520; Fahrion, 2002) showed little difference between the two groups overall at the 2-year outcome. However, analyzing results for age, race, and drug of choice, suggested neurofeedback was a more efficacious treatment for younger, non-white, non-stimulant abusing participants (see Norris, Chapter 2, for more details). In commenting on these studies, Norris (2000) notes that A/T training was an add-on to a standard treatment that she and Fahrion had developed for the Kansas prison system that incorporated meditation techniques as well.

Several issues clouded this study. One is that the analog and non-calibrated feedback equipment used was highly subject to EMG-generated noise interference from movement and jaw clenching. Another is that the A/T training sessions were unaccompanied by intense and prolonged psychotherapy sessions that may have been used by Peniston and Saxby (Steve Fahrion, personal communication). Another potential confound is that meditation was possibly included in the control group as well and it may be that adding A/T training to meditation does little to improve the outcome, although I was not completely clear about this in my discussion with Steve Fahrion.

Another issue in evaluating A/T training in addictive disorders is that addictive disorders are associated with a variety of EEG anomalies, associated either with the effects of drugs of abuse (Prichep et al., 2002) or with other underlying conditions. This has been reviewed and discussed extensively (Sokhadze, Cannon, & Trudeau, 2008a, 2008b; Trudeau, 2000, 2005a). There are several reports of using other EEG biofeedback approaches to address comorbid or underlying conditions prior to employing A/T training (Scott, chapter 12; Gunkelman & Cripe, 2008; Gurnee, 2004; Scott, Kaiser, Othmer, & Sideroff, 2005; Burkett, Cummins, Dickson, & Skolnick, 2005). My impression from round table and workshop discussions is that most clinicians who currently use A/T training to treat addictive disorders often screen with QEEG and pre-treat EEG anomalies associated with other conditions or phenotypes prior to A/T training. One of the confounds not addressed in Peniston's work and subsequent attempts to replicate it, including Fahrion's large prison study, is the issue of identifying comorbid ADHD and other EEG anomalies that may influence the clinical response to A/T training. For instance, the high frontal theta/beta subtype of ADHD may be worsened by theta reinforcement, although to my knowledge this has not been methodically studied. It is interesting that

Scott and Kaiser (1998) used feedback to remedy high frontal theta/beta ratios before doing A/T training.

In 2008, Sokhadze, Trudeau, and Cannon reported that "based on published clinical studies and employing efficacy criteria adapted by the AAPB and ISNR, alpha-theta training, either alone for alcoholism or in combination with beta training for stimulant and mixed substance abuse and combined with residential treatment programs is probably efficacious" (p 274). Despite that pronouncement, there are probably not enough reported data on A/T training in addiction to do a meta-analysis of efficacy. There are clearly not enough published data on A/T training in anxiety disorder or psychotherapy to do any analysis at all. Still, it remains a very effective tool in the hands of those clinicians who use it regularly, correctly, and appropriately (White, 2008).

More to Learn About How A/T Training Affects the Brain

Given that there were inconsistencies in the widely popularized original reports by Peniston of A/T training success, and that much of the early work used analog equipment that was largely descriptive rather than quantitative, is there a place for revisiting A/T training today? Those who work with A/T training, or who have experienced it, remain convinced of its unique ability to aid in traumatic recall and to empower personal change. Are the states produced by A/T training like those produced through hypnosis? Are they like meditational states? Are they unique or different from these states in terms of things that can be measured and quantified in the brain? This topic probably deserves a separate chapter at the end of this book, but forgoing that, I would like to offer a few sketchy ideas about some future research in what A/T training does. I realize this is speculative.

The perennial interest in meditation is germane to A/T training; A/T training emerged from studies of meditators. The work by Cade and Green in the 1970s used observation based on unrecorded analog signal using single-lead techniques. The signal was simply described and not really recorded and quantified or analyzed in any way, except by recorded summaries of time exceeding bandwidth thresholds. Since those early days of single-lead analog devices there has been a quantum leap to new digitized EEG technologies including QEEG, LORETA (low resolution electromagnetic tomography), MEG (magnetoencephalogram), and ERP (event related potential) analysis, plus the use of imaging studies to correlate with EEG findings (Ghaziri, et al., 2013; Cannon, Kerson, & Hampshire, 2012).

The focus of research has expanded due to improved technologies for doing controlled clinical trials, and more importantly to huge leaps forward in measuring physiologic outcomes of A/T training (and other neurofeedback interventions). I am impressed with the interest today in researching the neurophysiology of meditation after doing a perusal of the literature and reviewing in depth some papers submitted for publication. The methods being used to study the neurophysiology of meditation with QEEG and ERP (Cahn & Polich, 2006) could be applied to studies of A/T training. The early investigators such as Green and Cade suggested that A/T training could lead to a state like meditation because they observed alpha amplitude increase followed by theta amplitude increase in the meditators they studied. However, the possibility exists that meditational states are also defined by changes in other frequencies and changes in phase and coherence, as well as amplitudes at many EEG sites, beyond O1 and O2. Is A/T training the end-all of EEG feedback to promote meditation-like states?

If indeed A/T training produces the high alpha/theta states seen in meditators, does it also produce the other types of performance enhancement and neurophysiologic changes seen in meditation?

With new interest in mindfulness meditation and performance enhancement using visualization, and with the panoply of techniques to study brain electrophysiology available today, I think it is time to look at the literature on meditation and see if the same results can be obtained studying A/T training. For instance, it is quite feasible to do evoked auditory potential (EAP) studies on meditators in meditational states because the EAP does not interfere with the eyes-closed state or with concentration/awareness (Telles, Raghavendra, Naveen, Manjunath, & Subramanya, 2012).

Other recent studies of brain physiology in meditative states may be germane to understanding A/T training. Baijal and Srinivasan (2010) studied frontal theta generated by accomplished meditators vs. neophytes. Amishi Jha, at the University of Miami's Contemplative Neuroscience, Mindfulness Research, and Practice Initiative, has been researching the effects of mindfulness meditation on cognitive performance showing improved working memory capacity and less emotional reactivity as the result of mediation training (Jha, Stanley, Kiyonaga, Wong, & Gelfand, 2010).

Broadly, meditational techniques can be described as mantra- or mindfulness-based. Approximately 10% of the population in the U.S. practices meditation and there is a growing body of evidence on effectiveness. Given that A/T training has something to do with reproducing brain states found in meditation, any studies of A/T training compared to meditation must take into account the heterogeneity of meditational techniques, ranging from classic yoga techniques described thousands of years ago, classical Zen techniques, and modern adaptations of various techniques (Goyal et al., 2014). A review of meditation and EEG is well beyond the scope of this chapter, but these few examples are given here of how A/T training can be studied anew with an eye toward the advances made in the study of brain physiology in meditation.

The Importance of Organizing Experience Into a Narrative

In addition to reinvestigating A/T training as compared to meditation, the issue of what is happening in the brain during A/T training also begs investigation using contemporary technology. Imagery and recall have been impressive to practitioners of A/T training from Walters and Green going forward. A/T training is understood as transformational in some way and integrated with other transformational approaches such as psychotherapy. What is happening in the amygdaloid complex during episodes of theta/alpha crossover-associated visualization? Are we sure that A/T training-associated insights and visualization are indeed associated with theta/alpha crossover, as Peniston suggested, or is something else happening?

I have often wondered if the model of subprimate theta dreaming for memory processing in sleep may somehow be related to unprocessed, highly visceral memories in humans. My clinical experience with A/T training sessions in postcombat PTSD victims who were flooded with autonomic recall as they came out of a session reinforced this notion. The fragments of recall, it seemed, were highly emotional and could not be put into a narrative. But when they did become part of a narrative, they were controllable. Much of the technique that Peniston used with PTSD (personal communication) involved placing subjects in A/T training with pre-suggestions and then debriefing them about recalled sensory experiences during their sessions, putting that experience recall into a narrative.

Some work exploring deeper structures during A/T training is being done by Rex Cannon, who is looking at the precuneus as one of the possible targets of occipital alpha feedback (Cannon, et al., 2014). Using LORETA as well as radiologic imaging (Volkow, Fowler, & Wang, 2004) as measures of outcome for A/T training combined with other EEG biofeedback pretreatment as an intervention for substance abuse is likely possible and could yield substantial information.

Alpha-Theta and Shifts in Parahippocampal Activity

With the advent of LORETA, is it possible to measure amygdaloid complex or parahippocampal changes during episodes of alpha-theta crossover? Recalls of memories associated with increases of theta (as well as beta) amplitude during A/T training (Johnson & Bodenhamer-Davis, 2009) are observed, but it is not understood how they are generated. Is it possible to use LNFB (LORETA neurofeedback) as a tool to target memory-recall areas and at the same time monitor alpha and theta activity to see if there is any relationship between alpha and theta frontal amplitude increase (and other parameters)? Is it possible to link imaging of suppressed memory recall to A/T training states in some way? The physical interference of fMRI during A/T training feedback is a barrier, but there has been interest in SPECT scanning techniques during neurofeedback. And as previously mentioned, auditory evoked potential study is feasible and could lead to understandings of brain electrophysiology differences in A/T training states as compared to baseline, aside from any implications for meditation similarities.

Green and Cade were limited by equipment that displayed

only easily measurable dominant frequencies, but what about gamma frequencies in states of A/T training high focus/high relaxation? Maxwell Cade looked at bihemispheric comparisons, and Adam Crane looked at quadrant comparisons (Crane & Soutar, 2000) and felt that there were states of balance or synchrony that reflected higher brain states of awareness. Many of their comparisons seemed naïve when QEEG became more accessible, but I am not aware that their thinking about increases in coherence and phase in A/T training and meditation were ever developed more with contemporary QEEG analysis. Does some measure of similarity of brain electrical activity at distant 10-20 sites mean anything in terms of meditative states? Or in terms of A/T training states? Easily accessible normative databases and LORETA analyses should be more able to answer those queries.

How do we know that A/T training is the best way to achieve meditation-like hypnagogic states of human transformation? Perhaps a more specific approach remains to be discovered with studies that revisit what is happening in the brain during the recall of visualized, unprocessed memories. Is there an EEG difference between focused, intentional healing and mindfulness or other meditation? Do these observations correlate with our understanding of functional brain circuits and the default mode network? Does functional MRI have a role to play in understanding the EEG descriptors of meditational, hypnotic, healing, and traumatic recall states? Much of the focus in the past has been on devising experiments based on the drug model of clinical trials—difficult work when attempting to design a convincing double-blind placebo condition for an active operant condition, basically a training paradigm. Aside from efficacy studies, showing how A/T training operates to change the brain physiology is an equally convincing approach to research. Peniston tried to show that resting single-lead bandwidth amplitudes changed over time as a result of training. Perhaps this is so, but that does not seem to be the meaningful question to answer in today's world of in-depth analysis of surface EEG with LORETA, evoked potential analysis, direct current or very slow wave analysis, and correlations with imaging blood flow techniques.

Summary and Conclusion

In this chapter I have focused much primarily on my personal experiences in A/T training as related to meditation and as employed in addiction therapy. A/T training has been effective in addictive disorders, especially when combined with other neurotherapy techniques, and has been used in PTSD, psychotherapies, anxiety disorders, and performance enhancement. Reviews have been written and efficacy assessed, but it is difficult to assess the efficacy of A/T training further because of comorbidities as well as the highly individualized therapies with which it has been integrated. It began as an attempt to give feedback for EEG dominant rhythms that were seen in meditators.

After a flurry of activity and reviews, interest in A/T training has diminished, and I am not aware of newer studies. Part of this problem may lie in an understanding of meditation and psychotherapy as non-objective approaches that defy mainstream science. However, newer technologies and studies of meditation that show changes in processing speed, retention, memory, and concentration associated with meditation make it important to revisit A/T training as it relates to EEG, LORETA, MEG, fMRI, auditory evoked potentials, and whatever other tools the future may hold. The point is that it is probably much more important to visit A/T training by looking at what can be described and measured in terms of brain physiology than to attempt more clinical trials of efficacy.

Many of the other authors in this volume can be relied on to give a more informed and documented scholarly discussion of issues than I have presented here. I have mixed anecdote and speculation with a little science and history, but have done so because I sincerely believe this is an abandoned area that deserves new interest and energy. To those who work clinically with A/T training, I suspect there is no need for more "proof of the pudding," you are already willing eaters of that pudding—or ice cream—and true believers in what works well for you and your clients.

To those who would like to step out from the limitations of the past and continue exploring the phenomenology of the mind of timelessness and healing, I wish you inventive curiosity and most importantly, fundability to do your work.

References

Baijal, S., & Srinivasan, N. (2010). Theta activity and meditative states: Spectral changes during concentrative meditation. *Cognitive Processing*, 11(1), 31–38. https://doi.org/10.1007/s10339-009-0272-0

Burkett, V. S., Cummins, J. M., Dickson, R. M., & Skolnick, M. (2005). An open clinical trial utilizing real-time EEG operant conditioning as an adjunctive therapy in the treatment of crack cocaine dependence. *Journal of Neurotherapy*, 9(2), 27–47. https://doi.org/10.1300/J184v09n02_03

Cade, C. M., & Coxhead, N. (1989). *The awakened mind: biofeedback and the development of higher states of awareness*. Shaftesbury: Element.

Cahn, B. R., & Polich, J. (2006). Meditation states and traits: EEG, ERP, and neuroimaging studies. *Psychological Bulletin*, 132(2), 180–211. https://doi.org/10.1037/0033-2909.132.2.180

Callaway, T. G., & Bodenhamer-Davis, E. (2008). Long-term

follow-up of a clinical replication of the Peniston protocol for chemical dependency. *Journal of Neurotherapy*, 12(4), 243–259. https://doi.org/10.1080/10874200802502060

Cannon, R., Kerson, C., Hampshire, A., & Garner, C. L. (2012). Pilot data assessing the functional integrity of the default network in adult ADHD with fMRI and sLORETA. *Journal of Neurotherapy*, 16(4), 246–263.

Cannon, R. L., Baldwin, D. R., Diloreto, D. J., Phillips, S. T., Shaw, T. L., & Levy, J. J. (2014). LORETA Neurofeedback in the precuneus: Operant conditioning in basic mechanisms of self-regulation. *Clinical EEG and Neuroscience*, 1550059413512796. https://doi.org/10.1177/1550059413512796

Cannon, R., Lubar, J., Sokhadze, E., & Baldwin, D. (2008). LORETA neurofeedback for addiction and the possible neurophysiology of psychological processes influenced: A case study and region of interest analysis of LORETA neurofeedback in right anterior cingulate cortex. *Journal of Neurotherapy*, 12(4), 227–241. https://doi.org/10.1080/10874200802501948

Crane, A., & Soutar, R. (2000). *MindFitness Training: The Process of Enhancing Profound Attention Using Neurofeedback* (First Edition edition). San Jose Calif.: iUniverse.

Dass, R. (2010). *Be Here Now*. New York, NY: Crown Publishing.

deBeus, R., Prinzel, H., Ryder-Cook, A., & Allen, L. (2002). QEEG-based versus research-based EEG biofeedback treatment with chemically dependent outpatients: Preliminary results. *Journal of Neurotherapy*, 6(1), 64–66.

Fahrion, S. L. (1995). Human potential and personal transformation. *Subtle Energies & Energy Medicine*, 6(1).

Fahrion, S. L. (2002). Group biobehavioral treatment of addiction. Presented at the 4th Meeting on the Neurobiology of Criminal and Violent Behavior, Scottsdale AZ.

Fahrion, S. L., Walters, E. D., Coyne, L., & Allen, T. (1992). Alterations in EEG amplitude, personality factors, and brain electrical mapping after alpha-theta brainwave training: A controlled case study of an alcoholic in recovery. *Alcoholism: Clinical and Experimental Research*, 16(3), 547–552. https://doi.

org/10.1111/j.1530-0277.1992.tb01415.x

Ghaziri, J., Tucholka, A., Larue, V., Blanchette-Sylvestre, M., Reyburn, G., Gilbert, G., ... Beauregard, M. (2013). Neurofeedback training induces changes in white and gray matter. *Clinical EEG and Neuroscience, 44*(4), 265–272.

Goslinga, J. J. (1975). Biofeedback for chemical problem patients: A developmental process. *Journal of Biofeedback, 2,* 17–27.

Goyal, M., Singh, S., Sibinga, E. M., Gould, N. F., Rowland-Seymour, A., Sharma, R., ... Haythornthwaite, J. A. (2014). *Meditation programs for psychological stress and well-being.* Rockville (MD): Agency for Healthcare Research and Quality (US). Retrieved from http://www.ncbi.nlm.nih.gov/books/NBK180102/

Graap, K., & Freides, D. (1998). Regarding the database for the Peniston alpha-theta EEG biofeedback protocol. *Applied Psychophysiology & Biofeedback, 23*(4), 265–272.

Green, E. E., Green, A. M., & Walters, E. D. (1974). Alpha-theta biofeedback training. *Journal of Biofeedback, 2*(7–13).

Green, E., & Green, A. (1977). *Beyond biofeedback.* San Francisco, CA: Delacorte.

Grof, S. (1976). *Realms of the human unconscious: Observations from LSD research.* New York: Dutton.

Gruzelier, J. (2009). A theory of alpha/theta neurofeedback, creative performance enhancement, long distance functional connectivity and psychological integration. *Cognitive Processing, 10*(1), 101–109. https://doi.org/10.1007/s10339-008-0248-5

Gunkelman, J., & Cripe, C. (2008). Clinical outcomes in addiction: A neurofeedback case series. *Biofeedback, 36*(4), 152–156.

Gurnee, R. (2004). Subtypes of alcoholism and CNS depressant abuse. Presented at the Winter Brain, Optimal Functioning, and Positive Psychology Meeting, Palm Springs, CA.

Herning, R. I., Glover, B. J., Koeppl, B., Phillips, R. L., & London, E. D. (1994). Cocaine-induced increases in EEG alpha and beta activity: Evidence for reduced cortical processing. *Neuropsychopharmacology, 11*(1), 1–9.

Jha, A. P., Stanley, E. A., Kiyonaga, A., Wong, L., & Gelfand, L.

(2010). Examining the protective effects of mindfulness training on working memory capacity and affective experience. *Emotion*, 10(1), 54.

Johnson, M., & Bodenhamer-Davis, E. (2009). Relationship of alpha-theta amplitude crossover during neurofeedback to emergence of spontaneous imagery and biographical memories. Presented at the International Society for Neurofeedback & Research Annual Conference, Indianapolis, IN.

Jones, F. W., & Holmes, D. S. (1976). Alcoholism, alpha production, and biofeedback. *Journal of Consulting and Clinical Psychology*, 44(2), 224–228.

Kaiser, D. A., & Othmer, S. (2000). Effect of neurofeedback on variables of attention in a large multi-center trial. *Journal of Neurotherapy*, 4(1), 5–15.

Kamiya, J. (1968). Conscious control of brain waves. *Psychology Today*, 1, 57–60.

Kamiya, J. (1969). Operant control of the EEG alpha rhythm and some of its reported effects on consciousness. In C. T. Tart (Ed.), *Altered States of Consciousness: A Book of Readings* (1st edition, pp. 507–556). New York: John Wiley & Sons.

Lowe, F. (1999a). Does alpha-theta EEG biofeedback for substance dependence cure or enhance outcomes? Presented at the 30th Annual Meeting of the Association for Applied Psychophysiology and Biofeedback, Vancouver, B.C. Canada.

Lowe, F. (1999b). How essential is the EEG component of the Peniston and Kulkosky protocol? Presented at the 30th Annual Meeting of the Association for Applied Psychophysiology and Biofeedback, Vancouver, B.C. Canada.

Moore, J. P., & Trudeau, D. L. (1998). Alpha theta brainwave biofeedback is not specific to the production of theta/alpha crossover and visualizations. *Journal of Neurotherapy*, 3(1), 63.

Moore, N. C. (2000). A review of EEG biofeedback treatment of anxiety disorders. *Clinical EEG and Neuroscience*, 31(1), 1–6.

Norris, P. (2000). Clinical work on the new frontier using elements of the map. *Bridges*, 11(4), 1–5.

Nowlis, D. P., & Kamiya, J. (1970). The control of electroencephalographic alpha rhythms through auditory feedback and the associated mental activity. *Psychophysiology*, 6(4), 476–484.

Peniston, E. G. (1998). Comments by Peniston. *Applied Psychophysiology and Biofeedback*, 23(4), 273–275. https://doi.org/10.1023/A:1022217900096

Peniston, E. G., & Kulkosky, P. J. (1989). α-θ brainwave training and β-endorphin levels in alcoholics. *Alcoholism: Clinical and Experimental Research*, 13(2), 271–279.

Peniston, E. G., & Kulkosky, P. J. (1990). Alcoholic personality and alpha-theta brainwave training. *Medical Psychotherapy*, 3, 37–55.

Peniston, E. G., & Kulkosky, P. J. (1991). Alpha-theta brainwave neurofeedback for Vietnam veterans with combat-related post-traumatic stress disorder. *Medical Psychotherapy*, 4(1), 47–60.

Peniston, E. G., Marrinan, D. A., Deming, W. A., & Kulkosky, P. J. (1993). EEG alpha-theta synchronization in Vietnam theater veterans with combat-related PTSD and alcohol abuse. *Medical Psychotherapy*, 6, 37–50.

Prichep, L. S., Alper, K. R., Sverdlov, L., Kowalik, S. C., John, E. R., Merkin, H., ... Rosenthal, M. S. (2002). Outcome related electrophysiological subtypes of cocaine dependence. *Clinical EEG and Neuroscience*, 33(1), 8–20.

Saxby, E., & Peniston, E. G. (1995). Alpha-theta brainwave neurofeedback training: An effective treatment for male and female alcoholics with depressive symptoms. *Journal of Clinical Psychology*, 51(5), 685–693.

Scott, W. C., Brod, T. M., Sideroff, S., Kaiser, D., & Sagan, M. (2002). Type-specific EEG biofeedback improves residential substance abuse treatment. In *American Psychiatric Association Annual Meeting*.

Scott, W. C., Kaiser, D., Othmer, S., & Sideroff, S. I. (2005). Effects of an EEG biofeedback protocol on a mixed substance abusing population. *The American Journal of Drug and Alcohol Abuse*, 31(3), 455–469.

Scott, W., & Kaiser, D. (1998). Augmenting chemical dependency treatment with neurofeedback training. *Journal of Neurotherapy*, 3(1), 66.

Sokhadze, E. M., Trudeau, D. L., & Cannon, R. L. (2013). Treating addiction disorders in clinical neurotherapy—Applications of techniques for treatment. In Cantor, D., & Evans J. (Eds.), *Clinical Neurotherapy*. San Diego: Elsevier.

Sokhadze, E., Singh, S., Stewart, C., Hollifield, M., El-Baz, A., & Tasman, A. (2008). Attentional bias to drug-and stress-related pictorial cues in cocaine addiction comorbid with posttraumatic stress disorder. *Journal of Neurotherapy*, 12(4), 205–225.

Sokhadze, E., Stewart, C., Sokhadze, G., Hollifield, M., & Tasman, A. (2009). Neurofeedback and motivational interviewing based bio-behavioral treatment in cocaine addiction. *Journal of Neurotherapy*, 13(1), 84–86.

Sokhadze, T. M., Cannon, R. L., & Trudeau, D. L. (2008a). EEG biofeedback as a treatment for substance use disorders: Review, rating of efficacy, and recommendations for further research. *Applied Psychophysiology and Biofeedback*, 33(1), 1–28. https://doi.org/10.1007/s10484-007-9047-5

Sokhadze, T. M., Cannon, R. L., & Trudeau, D. L. (2008b). EEG biofeedback as a treatment for substance use disorders: Review, rating of efficacy and recommendations for further research. *Journal of Neurotherapy*, 12(1), 5–43. https://doi.org/10.1080/10874200802219855

Sokhadze, T. M., Stewart, C. M., & Hollifield, M. (2007). Integrating cognitive neuroscience research and cognitive behavioral treatment with neurofeedback therapy in drug addiction comorbid with posttraumatic stress disorder: A conceptual review. *Journal of Neurotherapy*, 11(2), 13–44.

Stetka, B. S., & Nutt, D. J. (2013, December 13). Psychedelic medicine: Worth the trip? Retrieved from http://www.medscape.com/features/slideshow/psychedelic-drugs

Taub, E., & Rosenfeld, J. P. (1994). Is alpha/theta training the effective component of the alpha/theta therapy package for the treatment of alcoholism. *Biofeedback*, 22(3), 12–14.

Taub, E., Steiner, S. S., Weingarten, E., & Walton, K. G. (1994). Effectiveness of broad spectrum approaches to relapse prevention in severe alcoholism: A long-term, randomized, controlled trial of transcendental meditation, EMG biofeedback and electronic neurotherapy. *Alcoholism Treatment Quarterly*, 11(1–2), 187–220.

Telles, S., Raghavendra, B. R., Naveen, K. V., Manjunath, N. K., & Subramanya, P. (2012). Mid-latency auditory evoked potentials in 2 meditative states. *Clinical EEG and Neuroscience*, 43(2), 154–160.

Trudeau, D. L. (2000). The treatment of addictive disorders by brain wave biofeedback: A review and suggestions for future research. *Clinical EEG and Neuroscience*, 31(1), 13–22.

Trudeau, D. L. (2005a). Applicability of brain wave biofeedback to substance use disorder in adolescents. *Child and Adolescent Psychiatric Clinics of North America*, 14(1), 125–136.

Trudeau, D. L. (2005b). EEG biofeedback for addictive disorders—The state of the art in 2004. *Journal of Adult Development*, 12(2–3), 139–146.

Trudeau, D. L., Sokhadze, T. M., & Cannon, R. L. (2009). Neurofeedback in alcohol and drug dependency. In T. H. Budzynski, H. K. Budzynski, J. R. Evans, & A. Abarbanel (Eds.), *Introduction to quantitative EEG and neurofeedback: Advanced theory and applications* (2nd Edition, pp. 241–268). Amsterdam: Academic Press.

Twemlow, S. W., & Bowen, W. T. (1976). EEG biofeedback induced self-actualization in alcoholics. *Journal of Biofeedback*, 3, 20–25.

Twemlow, S. W., & Bowen, W. T. (1977). Sociocultural predictors of self-actualization in EEG-biofeedback-treated alcoholics. *Psychological Reports*, 40(2), 591–598.

Twemlow, S. W., Bowen, W. T., & Sizemore, D. G. (1977). Biofeedback induced energy redistribution in the alcoholic EEG. *Journal of Biofeedback*, 3, 14–19.

Volkow, N. D., Fowler, J. S., & Wang, G.-J. (2003). The addicted human brain: Insights from imaging studies. *The Journal of Clinical Investigation*, 111(10), 1444–1451.

Volkow, N. D., Fowler, J. S., & Wang, G.-J. (2004). The addicted human brain viewed in the light of imaging studies: Brain circuits and treatment strategies. *Neuropharmacology, 47,* 3–13.

White, N. E. (2008). The transformational power of the Peniston protocol: A therapist's experiences. *Journal of Neurotherapy, 12*(4), 261–265.

4

Alpha/Theta Training as a "State Access" Process

John K. Nash, PhD

In this chapter I will describe my experience with Peniston's alpha-theta protocol and put forth my ideas about what this neurotherapy method does and why it does it. I will discuss some psychoanalytically-oriented literature that appears to me to be all too neglected by modern clinicians. This is not intended to be a complete scholarly treatise, simply my own thoughts, my necessarily anecdotal experience, recollections and working hypotheses. Note that I used the term "neurotherapy." I consider neurofeedback to be simply the name we chose for the technology that allows feedback of essentially real-time information about the EEG to the client. Neurotherapy refers to the process of using neurofeedback toward therapeutic ends, and includes all the necessary elements of any competent therapy, e.g., establishing rapport and a therapeutic alliance, having what Rogers so elegantly termed "accurate empathy" (knowing the person's feelings, identifying them during the interaction and knowing the difference between those empathically felt emotions and your own emotional reaction to the interchange), operant conditioning, cognitive behavior therapy, etc. In point of fact, neurotherapy is cognitive behavior therapy. Neurofeedback (and biofeedback, more generally) is a technology, no different conceptually from assertiveness skills training, communication skills training, or other specific, goal oriented behavioral methodologies that involve systematic applications of the principles of learning in the service of a patient's interests.

I learned the Peniston methods from Eugene Peniston in 1991 during several visits to the Menninger Foundation Voluntary Controls Program for workshops by Eugene Peniston, Dale Walters and Steve Fahrion. I decided something important was going on when I had my first alpha-theta training and experienced an intense A/T "cross-over" image: I am moving fast across a wide beach, toward the ocean. Next to me, running at full tilt, is a German shepherd dog. And next to the dog, a white horse with no saddle is galloping, the three of us, moving fast toward the ocean. When I learned Eugene's method of debriefing, what I think of as the simple question, "What is... [the image, e.g. a white horse with no saddle]...?" the meaning of the image became very clear. What is a white horse with no saddle? For me, a symbol of freedom and power. And what is a German shepherd dog? For me, loyalty and protection. And what is a beach? The edge of the world. And what is the ocean? It is deep, it is unknowable, the Unconscious. And there I was approaching it rapidly, in the company of my friends, the dog and the horse. I have had many German shepherds; I love them. And I have a photograph I took a long time ago of a white horse with no saddle, a wild horse in the foothills above Santa Barbara, who came running up to me, stopped 20 feet away, whinnied, looked me in the eye and said, "You have business on my mountain???" before galloping away just after I caught the moment of him looking at me on film. These things happen very occasionally. So this alpha-theta imagery that was evoked spontaneously—I hadn't thought of these images at all deliberately—was beautifully and completely connected to the context of the session, an approach to the Unconscious (the ocean) with the companionship of my

Alpha/Theta Training as a "State Access" Process

loyal friend and protector and the horse I've always called No Man's Horse, powerful and free.

The other event that happened after that first alpha-theta training was a comment from an older Indian Yogi—I don't remember his name—who was in my training group. After 30 minutes of alpha-theta, we all opened our eyes and looked around, back in the world. He smiled broadly and in a delicious Indian accent announced "Just like Yoga—only faster!" I thought this constituted a very high level professional recommendation of the technology. Even at the level of the technology at that time, analog devices that simply beeped or buzzed one note for alpha, one for theta, the process of feeding back alpha and theta amplitudes above a certain threshold had caused a remarkable experience in my mind and caused a Yogi to make such a comparison with Yoga, his life's dedication. I determined to pursue this "alpha-theta brain wave training" as Eugene called it. My experiences at Menninger added to my conviction that this feedback technology would be a part of my practice, ongoing. That conviction had at that point largely been shaped by the results Joel Lubar had produced with kids carrying the ADHD diagnosis and by Barry Sterman's (Sterman & House, 1980) stunning demonstration that he could use neurofeedback not only to help control epileptic seizures, but that importantly he showed contingency-specific normalization of the abnormal background EEG (less high and very low frequency power), even while patients were asleep. Sterman demonstrated that the learning was not simply giving the patient a cool self-management skill; it was clearly changing their underlying brain biology. I've since worked with chronically alcoholic patients and those with severe trauma from war and from physical and sexual abuse.

Methodology

I normally follow the same process that Eugene described, including skin temperature training, imagery of the Self succeeding in some important way, e.g. rejecting alcohol, being a more relaxed person, etc., and directives to the Unconscious. I do alpha-theta training at O1, single channel, which is the way Eugene did it. Finger temperature training (thermal blood flow plus autogenic phrases) comes first, until they can reach 94 degrees F, then O1 alpha/theta, adjusting the thresholds so that the patient gets 60–70% above alpha threshold, 40% above theta threshold after a 2-minute baseline. This has been very successful for my patients. I should note that Eugene worked in-patient and trained his patients twice a day. I did the same working with in-patients in a 30-day treatment program and in my office outpatient whenever possible. Insurers will not always support such frequency, so I make the best of it with 2–3 sessions a week at times. I also encourage people to make their own autogenic recording, saying a phrase from a script, breathing slowly 3–4 times, and then saying the next phrase. I ask them then to listen to the recording daily, "circulating" the phrase (mentally repeating it slowly) until they hear themselves say the next phrase. This is very relaxing "homework" for most. I also have them get a $22 "stress thermometer" on Amazon to practice letting go to the point their skin temperature goes to around 94 degrees Fahrenheit. The process seems to work well enough outpatient, although the results are much faster in the twice daily inpatient format.

Electrode Placement

There has never been any systematic experimenting done with scalp placements; clinicians just seem to decide to do it the way they do it, sometimes at O2, sometimes Pz. I think it may matter. O1 is over the visual association regions of the left hemisphere. I suspect one thing that may be going on is that the left brain getting some alpha training (alpha is "idling") and even being "asked" to drop into theta, which might simply be getting the logical analytic process out of the way long enough for the image processing right brain to put something into consciousness without the left brain immediately jabbering about it. It is significant and worth noting here that there is a normal asymmetry in alpha power in posterior regions, with the right side having somewhat larger alpha. Alpha is an "idling state." So alpha training on the left side might be allowing the right brain more of an opportunity to "speak" in its wordless way.

Conceptualization

I explain the Unconscious—to the patient and to myself—as the process that "knows more about you than you do, and certainly than I (the therapist) can ever know!" "It's what makes up our dreams, and provides our intuition if we listen." I suggest to the person that "the Unconscious can act independent of you, like when it creates your dreams, but it can also be addressed, even directed to do tasks." That leads in to Peniston's idea of giving a "directive" to the Unconscious: "Eliminate the urge to drink" or "Resolve the conflicts that are causing these PTSD symptoms." This is an update on Freud's (and others) observation that "day residue" can be incorporated into dreams, and psychoanalyst Ernst Kris' concept of "regression in the service of the ego" (Kris, 1936). Kris recognized that the conscious, analytic verbal "secondary process" can pull important, creative material from the pre-analytic, nonverbal "primary process," something that would be called "regression" in the classical Freudian model.

There is a strong relationship of accessing this spontaneous, alogical, non-verbal material with the art process. Discussing the "regression" that occurs during inspiration in the creation of art, Knafo (2002) describes something that sounds very much like the results of effective alpha/theta training:

Lichtenberg-Ettinger's description of her creative process attests to a disinhibition that takes place at least during the inspirational phase of her work. For her, and many other artists, this disinhibition allows for low levels of arousal, defocused attention, and primary process thinking that is more associative and tolerant of a number of simultaneous representations. Past, present, and future merge and become undifferentiated (pp. 37–38).

Knafo makes a cogent argument that the term "regression" has a negative connotation and that the process should be understood more broadly. There is pathological regression, but there is also regression that accesses a more spontaneous, primary and non-verbal, non-analytic reality, a temporary abandoning of identity and separation. This type of regression is the source of creativity in the artist and something like it is also required of the viewer of the art if they are to make a vital connection with the art piece.

I think alpha-theta training is—or can be used as—something like an electronically-guided rapid form of psychoanalysis, without the interference of the therapist's learned interpretations of what is produced. The productions are also intensely artful in the truest sense. The patients themselves are asked to make the interpretation of the images, while the therapist simply facilitates, giving voice—verbal language—to the unconsciously produced images. I think classical analysis may induce alpha-theta crossover states when it is successful. Lying down on a comfortable couch, even covered with a blanket (find a picture of Freud's actual therapy room in the Freud museum in London), little or no interaction with the therapist, and the instruction "Just say whatever comes to mind..." it is easy to imagine this would eventually lead at least some people to fall asleep—or halfway asleep. In that "in between state" the normal controls of the ego are relaxed, allowing unconscious material to emerge in its raw form. The alpha/theta images I have experienced and heard from my patients are extraordinarily variable, but most commonly are rich with deeply personal and individually meaningful images. The key feature of all of them is that they come unbidden, they are not "thought up" by the conscious self (ego). The interested reader should see Charles Tart's remarkable book "Altered States of Consciousness" (Tart, 1969) for many interesting discussions of dreams, regression and other altered states.

Alpha (and beta) power gradually diminishes during normal sleep onset. Some people, those with greater ego strength (less fear of being "out of control"), more "openness to experience" and less defensiveness will routinely experience images during sleep onset (Fitzgerald, 1966). This has been called the "hypnagogic" period of sleep onset. In a review of the literature on the hypnagogic state Schacter (1976) pointed out that it was even then "fairly well documented" that slowing of the EEG frequency and diminished amplitudes, coupled with slow eye movement is characteristic of the hypnagogic state. In the morning when one is not quite awake, a "hypnopompic" state with similar dream-like images may also occur. Accessing this hypnogogic state allows access to what has classically been called "primary process," the precognitive, pre-intellectual state that exists in all of us, before we learn high levels of symbolic verbal representation and abstract reasoning. Easy access to this state fades gradually by around the age of 8, except perhaps in artists, who seem to have a looser doorway to this state (Knafo, 2002). I have seen a trained, professional artist slip into and out of moderate amplitude runs of theta with her eyes open while drawing, with strong activation—beta elevation—in between. When I asked her about her experience, she described "unconsciously" responding to what was on the paper, then examining what she did critically (ego state), then again responding unconsciously, spontaneously. This alternating between conscious and "unconscious" seems common during the art process. When doing alpha/theta training with certain tightly defended patients, I have seen them "hang out" in alpha for many sessions, sustaining very low theta amplitudes for the entire 30 minutes and reporting no spontaneous imagery, just "thoughts." When alpha is present, you are awake, conscious, and you can think "I am sitting here, I am thinking, etc." Hence I think of alpha as reflecting the resting ego state. When alpha (and beta) lose enough amplitude and theta begins to increase, you loosen the ego boundaries and eventually the self-conscious sense of "I" disappears, although an "observer self" remains—if beta remains at high enough amplitude. If beta goes very low and theta gets very large (perhaps > 20–25 μV at O_1 in an adult), you are likely to see sleep spindles and the person will simply have fallen asleep.

I think alpha-theta "training" is not much about operant conditioning of particular amplitudes of brainwaves, but mostly about teaching a person to become comfortable accessing this state during therapy sessions. If you believe the story, Napoleon may have used a mechanical neurofeedback device to access the same creative unconscious state. He would sit in his chair holding a light cannonball, thinking about his battle plans—"How can I win this?—then he would fall toward sleep, finally dropping the cannonball and waking himself up. Then he would repeat this and eventually capture creative ideas on how to proceed. There are many such anecdotes of creative people utilizing this "cross-over" state to come up with problems they couldn't solve consciously.

The Alpha/Theta Experience

Subjectively, the alpha-theta experience is this: there is a period during which you think "I'm getting pretty relaxed... Oh that's nice, the alpha tone is on... I'm going to imagine this or that (alcohol rejection, being relaxed and kind with so-and-so," or whatever you've decided to work on consciously. Later, something else happens. You've kind of almost fallen asleep. A movie has run, a stream of imagery has happened. In the deep background of your awareness, you notice the alpha tone is gone, replaced by this deeper tone. Then "Oh! I'm in theta, that's a theta-dream." And as soon as you can think such a thing, the theta tone stops, the alpha tone resumes and you are again back in a conscious ego-state characterized by alpha amplitudes higher than theta. Alpha is a definitive sign of being awake (except for the pathological condition of "alpha coma") and when alpha is above theta the spontaneous imagery stops. Because you have been getting feedback the whole time, you don't go deep asleep and you retain what Eugene (and others) referred to as the "Observer." That is, you are still "there" enough to remember what went on, but your ego (conscious self that has this sense of "I") had got out of the way enough for the Unconscious (primary process, image based, no language) to communicate with you. Those communications carry extraordinary power. I will illustrate this with a few examples in the following pages.

Case 1

The man was in a 30-day inpatient chemical dependency treatment for I think the sixth time for chronic alcoholism. He was of the First Nations people in far northern Minnesota. His family carried the tradition of the medicine man, the healer. This was what he was trained to become, but he fell into alcoholism and his younger brother took over the role. Hank was his name and he gave me written permission to use his name; he wanted others to know what he experienced. He, like many others in the program was offered alpha-theta neurofeedback to supplement the traditional 12 Step program offered by the center. At the time I was clinical director of a three-county community mental health center that had kindly purchased quantitative EEG and neurofeedback equipment and sent me to Menninger Foundation for training. Over the course of 30 neurofeedback sessions, done twice daily, Hank reported a series of remarkable images. He found himself in a large teepee, with a fire burning in the middle. There he met his Grandfathers, elders from the past. The Eagle spirit appeared. At another time, the healing Turtle Spirit appeared. Once he took a diversion: a hurricane was approaching North Carolina, where he had some family in the path of the storm. He experienced talking with the Hurricane Spirit and asked it to veer away from the coast. We always did the training with the windows of my office slightly open. He normally placed some tobacco on the window ledge as an offering to the spirits; the window needed to be open to allow their entry. I had stayed in the room for some reason that day—normally I followed Eugene's procedure of leaving the room once the thresholds were set, returning 30 minutes later. After that session, Hank asked if I'd felt the Hurricane Spirit; he said it had come in the room and went around three times. I realized I had felt a slight breeze pass me during the session, three times. Coincidence, I suppose.

    Hank lost any desire to drink again. He said the alpha-theta work was the equivalent of a Vision Quest. I was stunned at this comment regarding a computerized technology wielded by a White psychologist, me. At the end of his treatment

Alpha/Theta Training as a "State Access" Process

Hank brought a large number of people from his family to the Recovery Center and did a Drum Ceremony, the family being keepers of the Sacred Drum, a very large, very old drum. The drum was pounded and we all—including the staff of the Center—danced around the drum. Hank blessed the various computer systems we had, placing Arbor Vitae branches on them.

The take home point I learned in these early years of doing alpha-theta training is that people had spontaneous, unbidden experiences that were intensely and specifically tuned to their needs, sometimes blissfully beautiful, sometimes terrifying, in ways that no one could possibly have known.

Case 2

One man had an image of ice skating on freshly frozen, crystal clear ice. And what is skating on crystal clear ice? "I could see right through it, I could see the plants and some small fish. I'm skating around the sacred island in the middle of the reservation where I grew up." And what is skating around the sacred island? "I'm 10 years old—and I'm innocent, before all this crap started." He rediscovered his innocence, and lost all interest and urges to drink.

Case 3

Another man, also very chronically alcoholic, was very pale and visibly shaken when I came back in the room after about his 20th session. What was your experience? Any images this time? "My dead friend was here. He showed up at his sister's in International Falls in the middle of last winter, drunk again. She wouldn't let him in. He sat down on her porch and froze to death. He was here. He looked at me and put his frozen cold hand on my shoulder and said, 'You have to stop drinking.'" This man stopped drinking. Reportedly all three of these men remained abstinent after 3 years.

Case 4

I treated a Vietnam veteran—a Marine. He had been in either a psychiatric hospital or chemical dependency treatment approximately annually for 15 years since returning from Vietnam. He lived far out in the countryside with his wife, who reported that he continued to have nightmares and would wake up screaming in Vietnamese. Sometimes he would grab a rifle and run into the backyard in the middle of the night and empty a clip into the shadows. Very little happened for many, many sessions. Sometimes he would just report colors. What are colors? "Life." I took this as promising progress. Then, at about 25 sessions, he appeared somewhat shaken and puzzled at the end of the 30-minute training. What was your experience? "I was in the middle of a battle, firing, emptying my weapon. But I couldn't see past the muzzle flash, it was just a wall of white." Nothing more that session, nothing the next session, but he felt cold. His skin temperature was down. Eugene taught that this is a sign that something's coming. And then it did. What was your experience? "I was firing again, in the middle of battle, smoke, gunfire, rockets; and then I could see past my weapon. A Vietnamese was running toward me, screaming, part of his arm was missing, I unloaded my weapon into him. But this was a South Vietnamese soldier, he was running to me for help. The man had saved my life, my own life, twice before in other battles." Tears came with this remembering, many tears. A couple weeks later, his wife said, "the black cloud has lifted." The nightmares stopped, the drinking stopped. The conflict that had been buried, repressed, had been revealed. Marines don't kill soldiers who saved their life. But this happened. Once it returned to consciousness, he could grieve, cry, talk about it and finally accept that this had happened—it was done.

Case 5

Another man, a soldier, also with chronic alcoholism and PTSD reported after a session, "I'm digging a hole." And what is digging a hole? "I'm digging and—there's a human heart at the bottom of the hole—a beating, living human heart." I would say this man recovered his heart. He opened up about things he had never spoken, horrors he had committed accidentally. This is the kind of imagery one finds when it is needed and facilitated by alpha-theta state access training.

I should note that some people have talked about the possibility of negative emotional "abreactions" resulting from alpha-theta training, the sudden and overwhelming accessing of traumatic memories and feelings. I have not seen this in my own practice, although I saw it happen once as an observer with another provider who was using EEG-driven neurofeedback (a method in which the dominant EEG frequency was used to drive a sound and light stimulator at slightly above or below the dominant frequency of the EEG at each moment) and going way, way too fast. The experiences I described above were not uncontrolled; perhaps trained psychoanalyst would think of them as such, but I experienced these moments with these people as deep, powerful, emotional yet not in any way out of control and certainly not harmful. The people left even those breakthrough experiences feeling stronger and more connected with themselves than they had felt in years, if ever. I think if you create an atmosphere of trust and confidence, and rely on the very passive therapist position of simply asking the "what is" question about the imagery, you allow the person and their Unconscious to "pace" the process in a way that is tolerable and healing. I have seen little bits and pieces come out across many sessions. It appears to me as if the Unconscious process is assessing just how much calm and equanimity the person has developed. The defenses don't drop quickly—and they shouldn't. But drop they do, once the deep calm state is accessed. I think the "alpha" part of the alpha-theta training is the beginning, the quieting of the analytic, verbal mind. The "theta" part is the opening of the access to the Unconscious' commentary and response to the directive—the focused wish expressed by the patient—in the form of the images that come, not entirely unbidden.

It is worth considering that many cases of post-traumatic stress disorder are sustained by an unspoken, unconscious conflict. That is why Dr. Peniston used the directive "Tell your Unconscious to resolve the conflicts that are causing your symptoms." I think an important part of trauma is the conflict between your deepest knowledge or belief about how the world is versus the way the world actually turned out to be, or the conflict between how you know yourself to be, your values, your deepest beliefs about yourself—and how you actually acted, deliberately or accidentally. A Marine can't possibly kill a soldier who saved his life in battle. A survivor of rape may have conflicts between rage at the attacker and rage at herself. A survivor of incest can have deep conflicts between rage at the perpetrator and love for the perpetrator, and between feeling harmed and exploited but having also felt sexual arousal. These are delicate matters requiring clinical skill to approach, with or without neurotherapy. I have found adding neurotherapy as part of the mix to be most useful.

References

Fitzgerald, E. T. (1966). Measurement of openness to experience: A study of regression in the service of the ego. *Journal of Personality and Social Psychology, 4,* 655–663. http://dx.doi.org/10.1037/h0023980

Knafo, D. (2002). Revisiting Ernst Kris's concept of regression in the service of the ego in art. *Psychoanalytic Psychology, 19,* 24–49. http://dx.doi.org/10.1037/0736-9735.19.1.24

Kris, E. (1952). The psychology of caricature. In *Psychoanalytic explorations in art* (pp. 173–188). New York: International Universities Press.

Schacter, D. L. (1976). The hypnagogic state: A critical review of the literature. *Psychological Bulletin, 83,* 452–48. http://dx.doi.org/10.1037/0033-2909.83.3.452

Sterman M. B. & House M. N. (1980). Quantitative analysis of training, sleep EEG and clinical response to EEG operant conditioning in epileptics. *EEG & Clinical Neurophysiology, 49,* 558–576. https://doi.org/10.1016/0013-4694(80)90397-1

Tart, C. T. (1969). *Altered states of consciousness.* Wiley, NY Oxford, England: Doubleday.

5

The Neurophysiology of Trauma:
Effects on the Individual, the Body, and the Brain

Cynthia Kerson, PhD

This chapter will discuss and provide theoretical bases for the systems, circuits, and networks that A/T training affects. Organisms achieve homeostatic balance naturally and incredibly efficiently. They rely upon prediction, expectation and subsequent learning when responding to internal and external stimuli. The brain and peripheral systems work closely together to accommodate and regulate responses to changes in their environment.

The brain relies upon memory systems to reduce uncertainty of the future, predicting the best action to achieve the best outcome, based upon experience. This is very important to survival (De Ridder, 2013). When given the choice, we respond in familiar ways that we consider to be safe. While the CNS (central nervous system) houses the majority of the systems to facilitate these processes, the human response is whole-body, made up of many subsystems that work collectively, at the right time and in concert.

Superstition, prediction, and instinct facilitate desired behavioral outcomes and dysregulation curtails this highly efficient process. Faulty predictions accumulate from traumatic events, behaviorally-learned misconceptions, and misinformation. The body cannot function optimally when its constant demand is to orchestrate responses to these faulty and/or conflicting internal predictions, and may present as a panic response to a fairly insignificant event. Its many checks and balances fail. Now, the remarkable efficiency of homeostatic balance becomes inefficient and drives the organism to undesired outcomes, such as panic, disinhibition and/or poor decisions. The more profound the anxiety or other disorder, the more skewed the responses.

Stress-regulating systems are meant for acute activation; they're designed to turn on (sympathetic arousal) in order to resolve the emergency and then drive the body back to homeostasis (parasympathetic arousal). This works efficiently in a perfect and simple world where the desired outcome might simply be resolution of hunger or thirst.

Yet even when the goals are this limited, optimally functioning organisms lose efficiency over time. This is seen in slower, older animals that cannot run, charge or predate as well as they used to. Thus they may miss hunting opportunities, resulting in higher levels of central and autonomic vigilance and frustration. More expeditious to aging, enhanced hypervigilance may result from severe traumatic events such as births, deaths, wars, accidents, divorce, etc. It then derails prediction, expectation and learning mechanisms more quickly than the aging process, leading to disorders such as anxiety, PTSD, and substance abuse.

Theories of Emotion

William James and James Lange had conflicting perspectives with Walter Cannon and Phillip Bard as to how we react emotionally to environmental events. In the 1920s, James and Lange believed emotions resulted from physiological reactions. Cannon and Bard later posited that physiological reactions were the resolution of emotional salience.

The James-Lange theory suggests that an emotional event

stimulates the thalamus, which then transmits to the limbic system, and finally, after the response and within the cortex, designates the emotional reaction.

Cannon and Bard, on the other hand, stated that once the message was received in the thalamus, it was simultaneously transmitted to both the cortex and limbic structures. Thus at the time of the reaction, the emotion is fully and cognitively articulated.

In the mid-1990s, Joseph LeDoux (1996) discussed two brain circuits leading to emotional responses, most specifically fear: "rapid" and "slower." In the rapid, or reflex, system, there is no cognitive process. The event occurs, the signals go through the thalamus and amygdala, and then the motor response occurs in a classically conditioned pattern. Of course, after the reflex, we cognize and say, "Ouch, that was hot," a mechanism that helps us to predict that stoves are hot and avoid touching them in the future.

Alternatively, the slower emotional response adds frontal cognitive processes, creating an operant conditioning opportunity that gives time for cognitive evaluation and expression prior to the emotional response.

LeDoux's rapid and slower theories run somewhat parallel with those of James-Lange and Cannon-Bard (respectively); however, he was able to demonstrate and validate his theories with modern neuroscientific measures. These two routes set the scene nicely for A/T training, by helping the client shift from the first, rapid (limbic) reflex to the second, slower response (engagement of the pre-frontal cortex).

Emotion theory aside, in her song, *People's Parties*, Joni Mitchell said, "Laughter and crying, you know it's the same release." It is clearly observable that on an individual basis, physiological responses to all emotions, whether positive or negative, are essentially the same.

Whether it be heart palpitations, brain ache or fog, muscle constriction, excessive sweat or trembling, one's physiological reaction is essentially consistent regardless of context and emotional meaning. The brain mechanisms that construct sudden or measured reaction to stimuli are efficient and thus a limited and individualized repertoire.

As we will see a bit further along in this section, this emotion/cognition brain-networking marvel includes pathways through the parietal and frontal areas that are affected by A/T training. A/T training not only affects one's cognitive relationship to emotion, whether faulty or constructive, it also is intimately connected to the mechanisms that regulate emotional undertone, reaction, reflex, state, and trait.

Cognitive Influence on Trauma

A current central understanding of stress is that it is what you make of it. Recent studies have shown that one's "attachment" to the stressors in one's life dictates the influence of those stressors, which is resonant to the concept of pain as a subjective measure. Individual responses to life-threatening, traumatic, and/or emotionally negative events become the basis for the next time a reaction of this nature is sought and becomes the etiology of stress diseases as well as of habituated and heightened stress reactions and their modulations. To add to this, while the stress response can be narrowed down to only a few physiological phenomena, the same stress will yield differing responses in each individual.

The HPA Axis

The HPA axis was identified in the mid-1930s by Hans Selye

(Selye, 1950), an Australian-Canadian endocrinologist, who became interested in unspecific reflexes to stress such as heart palpitations or sweaty palms. He named stress as the body's way of combating disturbance to it, citing that a normal, acute reaction is healthy. However, when chronic or excessive stressors persist, the body loses its ability to respond healthfully and I will add efficiently.

Selye described three stages of the stress response: (a) alarm (fear for survival), (b) resistance (management of the stressor), and (c) exhaustion (mismanagement and dysregulation when the response becomes overwhelming) and named this phenomenon the general adaptation syndrome (GAS). Of these stages, exhaustion, the final stage, is the one in which most prospective A/T training candidates exist. They have exhausted all means of healthy regulation and it is in this stage that the HPA is in chronic effort.

During the first stage (alarm), which is the response to any physical or psychological concern to survival or well-being, whether perceived or real, the hypothalamus releases corticotropin-releasing factor (CRF). Once the HPA axis is stimulated, a cascade of events occurs. The CRF binds to specific pituitary receptors, triggering the release of adrenocorticotropic hormone (ACTH). ACTH then leaves the central nervous system, heading to the adrenal glands, located just atop the kidneys. These glands then manufacture and release cortisol—the main stress-diminishing hormone. The purpose of cortisol is to induce the body back from the sympathetic, flight/fight state to the parasympathetic, homeostatic state when the organism has determined that survival is no longer threatened, and to bring the body to the second stage: resistance.

The adrenal glands manufacture and release epinephrine, norepinephrine, aldosterone, androgens, and cortisol. All of these hormones play important roles in homeostatic balance. Cortisol, the hormone released during the final stage of the activation of the HPA, assists in maintaining blood sugar, immune suppression, and regulating metabolism. Its task is generally short-lived and flows with circadian rhythm, normally highest in the morning (to motivate waking).

The pituitary gland, as small as a pea and situated below the hypothalamus, manufactures and releases many hormones indicated in homeostatic and stress systems. These "trophins," such as human growth hormone (HGH) or thyroid stimulating hormone (TSH) and the corticotrophins, such as ACTH and beta-endorphin, are involved in basic body processes such as breathing, digestion, and blood pressure. In the HPA cascade, the pituitary gland responds to the CRF from the hypothalamus and releases ACTH, already manufactured and at the ready.

The Papez Circuit

According to Shah and colleagues (2012), the Papez circuit begins in the hippocampus, and works its way to the mammillary bodies through the fornix. From the mammillary bodies, it circuits to the thalamus and then to the corpus callosum, which contains many dense fibers connecting to the parietal lobe and much of the default mode and reward network areas. It then cycles through the entorhinal cortex (a main memory connector between the hippocampus and the cortex) and back to the hippocampus.

The presence of cortisol advises that the body is looking to resolve the stress response. When the body remains in chronic stress, cortisol, as well as other stress hormones, persist and most body systems become overshadowed and challenged by them. The presence of excessive cortisol makes fat and muscle cells resistant to insulin and encourages the production of glucose. With dysregulation, these unstable systems become powerfully influential. Cortisol or other HPA dysregulation is found in many modern disorders, including type 2 diabetes (Chiodini et al., 2007), childhood allergies (Stenius et al., 2011), rheumatoid issues (Cutolo et al., 2005), and irritable bowel syndrome (Taché & Brunnhuber, 2008).

In the late 1930s, James Papez originally described the circuit as indicated in emotion because of the interconnections from the hippocampus to other limbic and cortical areas. He judged this based on the multiple connections the hippocampus also has to the autonomic nervous system. In fact, he believed all of the circuitry originated within the hippocampus.

Papez may not have realized how important memory is to emotional construct. More current investigation shows that the structures involved in the circuit also involve memory processes, specifically episodic memory (Markowitsch, 1997), which is the basis of trauma (Guez et al., 2011).

A recent study (Yun et al., 2011) investigating event-related potentials in PTSD subjects found that the parahippocampal gyrus and posterior cingulate were more activated when subliminally presented with words that elicited memories related to the trauma (in this study, an earthquake). These areas are within the Papez circuit and also within reach when training posteriorly with neurofeedback through EEG networks and neuropathways (see below).

The Polyvagal Theory

Stephen Porges developed the polyvagal theory over the course of three decades (Porges, 2001; Porges, 2011). His premise is primarily based on the deep interrelationship of other cranial nerves with the vagal nerves (which are the 10th cranial nerves—one on the right and one on the left—the two-way messaging that occurs between the brainstem and the heart, and the fact that there are two vagal motor systems. He postulates that part of this evolutionary system developed more recently along with other modern systems, including the HPA axis and the brain's cortex.

It makes sense that the heart would be so closely associated with the impulses received by the eyes, nose, ears, skin, etc., considering the close proximity of the cranial nerves and their interrelatedness within the brain stem. The fast processing of the sight of something beautiful also includes a cardiac reflex. Conversely, the flat affect often seen in traumatized individuals, and Porges includes autistic individuals in this observation, is due to the heart's involvement with the striated muscles that regulate facial tone.

The vagus nerves have two branches. Porges posits that evolutionarily, only one vagus branch developed myelination. The two vagal motor branches prompt either the flight/fight or an immobilization response to stressors. The newer, myelinated one involves immediate and sometimes lingering physiological responses such as increased heart rate, dilated pupils, decreased gut mobilization and digestion, and sweaty palms and forehead – all to boost the functions of either fighting or fleeing a distressing event. This branch did not evolve in many species, but can be found in mammals and other vertebrates. The original, unmyelinated branch invokes reduced metabolism and immobilization to hide or act dead. Thus, the defense is either the very precise flight/fight or the much slower immobilization. In early stages of trauma, the faster, myelinated response occurs and in the more advanced stages, the unmyelinated actions take effect. This can be witnessed in depression, as the patient loses affect and interest in life. Porges considers this activity of the unmyelinated branch as a last attempt when the newer system seemingly fails, and it is highly correlated with vagal tone.

Porges also demonstrated that there is two-way messaging between the brain and heart, that in fact, the heart informs the brain stem as much as the brain, through the brain stem, informs the heart.

The brain stem, where the cranial nerves mitigate their inputs, is involved in auditory and visual actions through networks linking it and frontal cortical areas, including the right orbitofrontal cortex (Walz et al., 2013). In general, neurofeedback involves auditory and visual networks through its reward structure, albeit only audio for A/T training since this training is facilitated with eyes closed. Thus, the involvement of the auditory network during operant conditioning may strengthen interrelations within the brainstem and between the brainstem and the other cranial nerves, including the vagal nerves, and A/T training may have an inadvertent positive effect on the vagal tone of the individual.

Theta Origins

Brain wave frequencies generate from within different areas of the brain. Much can be reported about the full brain wave spectra, but for our purposes, we will focus on theta and alpha.

Throughout this book, we are generally discussing the theta that is cortically driven and falls in the range of 4–7 Hz. This theta is associated with creativity, intuition, and cognitive action as well as introspection.

However, another theta type is generated in the limbic, subcortical area known as the medial septal nuclei (O'Keefe & Nadel, 1978). Once generated, this theta travels through the hippocampus and parahippocampal regions. It has been shown to be counter-balanced with faster desynchronized activity (beta) in the cortex (O'Keefe & Nadel, 1978). Importantly, however, this theta is generally in the range of 6–10 Hz and has a slightly different morphology than the cortical theta to which we typically refer. Also, we should keep in mind that the beta we see cortically may well be a participant of the hippocampal theta system, making the hippocampal theta relevant in this discussion because often we observe high beta amplitude in the client base we see for A/T training. The beta may be a dysregulation of the hippocampal memory system and A/T training may regulate it because if we quiet the beta, we up-train the hippocampal theta, helping the hippocampus to manage and reprocess the memories that are the underpinnings of the PTSD or alcoholic tendencies (see chapter 14, on A/T training and memory reconsolidation).

Alpha Origins

A small range of the alpha frequency (~10 Hz) is generated predominantly from within the thalamus (Isaichev, Derevyankin, Koptelov, & Sokolov, 2011), and a wider range (8–12 Hz) is generated due to thalamocortical loops (Schreckenberger et al., 2004; see chapter 1). Alpha is associated with spirituality, introspection, simultaneous calm and alertness, physical relaxation, inattention to external stimuli, and meditation. Basically, when it is predominant, there is cortical deactivation (Tenke et al., 2013).

Networks

The cortex is highly intra-networked to cortical areas close and further as well as inter-networked to subcortical areas. Each functional network is deeply graded with multiple tasks to facilitate specific end-goals. These functional networks rely on very specialized and integrated behaviors of distinct and constant anatomical areas, each network sharing a small part of the complete and complex process. Because of the properties of networks, with any form of neuromodulation, we affect more than one area of the brain. When one area of a network is altered, whether by bioelectrical conditioning, electromagnetic shift, or electrical stimulation, the entire network is affected and also the whole brain to a degree.

The posterior areas typically trained with A/T training preside over two of these important networks–the default mode network (DMN) and reward network. In general, posterior training sites affect the frontal areas greatly because of the natural flow of the networks in general. The DMN is involved in mind wandering, inward focus, self-referential thinking, and relating self to experience. It is activated when the brain is minimally attending to outside stimuli, and is related most closely to the arguable "resting state" phenomenon.

Recent PET and fMRI studies have revealed the DMN network locations (Raichle et al., 2001). It resides in the bilateral medial temporal lobes (much of the limbic areas rests in these and they are also indicated in memory), inferior parietal lobes (language and integration of sensory, visual, and auditory information), precuneus (visuospatial imagery, episodic memory retrieval, and self-processing), posterior cingulate cortex (emotion and self-relevance), anterior cingulate cortex (emotion and cognition) and medial prefrontal cortex (emotion, cognition, and arousal).

The DMN and reward circuits are closely correlated (de Greck, 2008). The reward network contains the ventral tegmental area (dopamine production, cognition, motivation, and addiction) and the ventral striatum (which contains the nucleus accumbens—pleasure, reward, reinforcement learning—is involved in olfactory processes, and is part of the basal ganglia), the insula (consciousness, emotion, motor control, and self-awareness), the amygdala (emotional learning, memory, LTP, memory consolidation, and fear conditioning) and the prefrontal cortex (representational understanding of self, working memory, social inhibition, goal modulation, and top-down cognitive processing).

The reward network is associated with motivation, incentive, addiction, and decision-making, as well as learning and reinforcement, such as operant conditioning. Humans strive to maximize reward and logically, feeling self-relevant (a DMN task) increases feelings of connection to one's self, which lead to feelings of satisfaction and reduced fear. It makes sense that useful learning and motivation contribute to the development of reward and satisfaction. Recall our earlier discussion of prediction and expectation; the reward system's learning and motivation tasks are intrinsically coupled with prediction and expectation behaviors as well. The culmination of these network dynamics generally initiates a cascade of dopamine, the catecholamine that is involved in satiation, pleasure, and reward as long as the predicted outcome materializes.

Incidentally, the Brodmann areas (BA) related to the default mode network are: BA 21, bilaterally in medial temporal lobes, BA 7, in the parietal lobes and the precuneus, BA 23, in the posterior cingulate cortex, BA 24 and 32 in the anterior cingulate cortex, and BA 9, in the medial prefrontal cortex. On the other hand, the Brodmann areas related to the reward network areas are: BA 21 (subcortical), near the ventral tegmental area, BA 10, 11, 14, 25, 32 (BA 25; sub-cortical), in the ventral striatum (nucleus accumbens), BA 13, in the insular cortex, BA 25 in the subgenual cortex and amygdala, and BA 8, 9, 10, 11, 44, 45, 46, 47 in the frontal cortex.

Conveniently for trainers of alpha theta, the alpha rhythm is most indicated in activation of the DMN. This, of course, makes sense, since alpha is considered the "idle" or resting rhythm, seen prominently in the posterior regions in the eyes-closed rest state. Chen and colleagues (2008) showed that the most affected frequency bands when shifting from resting (EC) to active (EO) states are the alpha (7–12 Hz) and low beta bands (13–23 Hz), projecting from posterior regions. (Interestingly, delta (.5–3.5 Hz) and theta (4–7 Hz), as well as higher beta and gamma (over 23 Hz), remained fairly constant when shifting from EC to EO states, emanating from more frontal and central brain areas. Citing Scheeringa et al. (2008), Chen's group conclude that it may be that the theta activity that is seen in the frontal EEG after a shift from active to DMN state may well occur because the theta that is generated in the frontal cortices "hops on board" the DMN once its flow reaches these areas.)

While it should be noted that when people are being trained with neurofeedback, regardless of the protocol, they are not in the default or resting state because they are engaged in something – specifically, neurofeedback. As well, the DMN has been shown to be less efficient after trauma, in childhood trauma (Daniels et al., 2010), ADHD adults (Cannon, Kerson, Hampshire, & Garner, 2012) and Alzheimer's disease (Mevel, Chételat, Eustache, & Desgranges, 2011), for example. It can then be speculated that if there is alteration in the DMN as a consequence of dysregulation, it would also be altered due to neurofeedback training, and specifically during A/T training, since the training sites are specific to areas within it and at the forefront of the flow and because any change in networks that are activated during task must also affect the DMN.

How do we affect systems outside the scope of our sensor sites? We train at posterior sites with A/T training. Peniston trained at O_1; Norris and Fahrion at the Menninger Foundation trained at O2. Yet we modulate behaviors that are mostly regulated in the frontal areas, such as decision-making, attention, inhibition, memory, and encoding (Kamarajan et al., 2005). Also, in trauma, we are affecting the stress response that is consequential to the interactions within the Papez circuit, the HPA (hypothalamic-pituitary-adrenal) axis and the polyvagal systems described below, which involve subcortical structures.

Thus, this section provides a basis for the physiological response to A/T training. This is important to understanding why A/T training on parietal or occipital sites, with sensors that immediately affect only about 5cm/2 of cortex, manages to deconstruct the dysregulated reaction throughout the brain, which in turn will reorganize the emotion/cognition structure of the individual.

References

Cannon, R., Kerson, C., Hampshire, A., & Garner, C. L. (2012). Pilot data assessing the functional integrity of the default network in adult ADHD with fMRI and sLORETA. *Journal of Neurotherapy*, 16(4), 246–263.

Chen, A. C. N., Feng, W., Zhao, H., Yin, Y., & Wang, P. (2008). EEG default mode network in the human brain: Spectral regional field powers. *NeuroImage*, 41(2), 561–574. https://doi.org/10.1016/j.neuroimage.2007.12.064

Chiodini, I., Adda, G., Scillitani, A., Coletti, F., Morelli, V., Di Lembo, S., ... Arosio, M. (2007). Cortisol secretion in patients with type 2 diabetes: relationship with chronic complications. *Diabetes Care*, 30(1), 83–88. https://doi.org/10.2337/dc06-1267

Cutolo, M., Maestroni, G. J. M., Otsa, K., Aakre, O., Villaggio, B., Capellino, S., ... Sulli, A. (2005). Circadian melatonin and cortisol levels in rheumatoid arthritis patients in winter time: A north and south Europe comparison. *Annals of the Rheumatic Diseases*, 64(2), 212–216. https://doi.org/10.1136/ard.2004.023416

Daniels, J. K., Frewen, P., McKinnon, M. C., & Lanius, R. A. (2011).

Default mode alterations in posttraumatic stress disorder related to early-life trauma: A developmental perspective. *Journal of Psychiatry & Neuroscience, 36*(1), 56–59. https://doi.org/10.1503/jpn.100050

de Greck, M., Rotte, M., Paus, R., Moritz, D., Thiemann, R., Proesch, U., ... Northoff, G. (2008). Is our self based on reward? Self-relatedness recruits neural activity in the reward system. *NeuroImage, 39*(4), 2066–2075. https://doi.org/10.1016/j.neuroimage.2007.11.006

De Ridder, D. (2013). *The function of specific brain areas and brain networks.* [Webinar]. Brain Science International. Retrieved from https://www.bsiwebinars.com/index.php/2-uncategorised/51-brdm3deridder

Guez, J., Naveh-Benjamin, M., Yankovsky, Y., Cohen, J., Shiber, A., & Shalev, H. (2011). Traumatic stress is linked to a deficit in associative episodic memory. *Journal of Traumatic Stress, 24*(3), 260–267.

Isaichev, S., Derevyankin, V., Koptelov, Y. M., & Sokolov, E. (2001). Rhythmic alpha-activity generators in the human EEG. *Neuroscience and Behavioral Physiology, 31*(1), 49–53.

Kamarajan, C., Porjesz, B., Jones, K. A., Chorlian, D. B., Padmanabhapillai, A., Rangaswamy, M., ... Begleiter, H. (2005). Spatial-anatomical mapping of NoGo-P3 in the offspring of alcoholics: evidence of cognitive and neural disinhibition as a risk for alcoholism. *Clinical Neurophysiology, 116*(5), 1049–1061.

LeDoux, J. (1996). *The emotional brain: The mysterious underpinnings of emotional life* (1st Edition). New York: Simon & Schuster.

Markowitsch, H. J. (1997). Varieties of memory: Systems, structures, mechanisms of disturbance. *Neurology, Psychiatry and Brain Research, 5*(1).

Mevel, K., Chételat, G., Eustache, F., & Desgranges, B. (2011). The default mode network in healthy aging and Alzheimer's disease. *International Journal of Alzheimer's Disease*, 2011.

O'Keefe, J., & Nadel, L. (1978). *The hippocampus as a cognitive map.* New York, NY: Oxford University Press. Retrieved from http://www.cognitivemap.net/HCMpdf/HCMComplete.pdf

Porges, S. W. (2001). The polyvagal theory: Phylogenetic substrates of a social nervous system. *International Journal of Psychophysiology*, 42(2), 123–146.

Porges, S. W. (2011). *The polyvagal theory: Neurophysiological foundations of emotions, attachment, communication, and self-regulation (Norton series on interpersonal neurobiology)*. WW Norton & Company.

Raichle, M. E., MacLeod, A. M., Snyder, A. Z., Powers, W. J., Gusnard, D. A., & Shulman, G. L. (2001). A default mode of brain function. *Proceedings of the National Academy of Sciences*, 98(2), 676–682.

Scheeringa, R., Bastiaansen, M. C., Petersson, K. M., Oostenveld, R., Norris, D. G., & Hagoort, P. (2008). Frontal theta EEG activity correlates negatively with the default mode network in resting state. *International Journal of Psychophysiology*, 67(3), 242–251.

Schreckenberger, M., Lange-Asschenfeld, C., Lochmann, M., Mann, K., Siessmeier, T., Buchholz, H.-G., ... Gründer, G. (2004). The thalamus as the generator and modulator of EEG alpha rhythm: A combined PET/EEG study with lorazepam challenge in humans. *Neuroimage*, 22(2), 637–644.

Selye, H. (1950). *The physiology and pathology of exposure to stress*. Oxford, England: Acta.

Shah, A., Jhawar, S. S., & Goel, A. (2012). Analysis of the anatomy of the Papez circuit and adjoining limbic system by fiber dissection techniques. *Journal of Clinical Neuroscience*, 19(2), 289–298.

Stenius, F., Borres, M., Bottai, M., Lilja, G., Lindblad, F., Pershagen, G., ... Alm, J. (2011). Salivary cortisol levels and allergy in children: The ALADDIN birth cohort. *Journal of Allergy and Clinical Immunology*, 128(6), 1335–1339.

Taché, Y., & Brunnhuber, S. (2008). From Hans Selye's discovery of biological stress to the identification of corticotropin-releasing factor signaling pathways. *Annals of the New York Academy of Sciences*, 1148(1), 29–41. https://doi.org/10.1196/annals.1410.007

Tenke, C. E., Kayser, J., Miller, L., Warner, V., Wickramaratne, P., Weissman, M. M., & Bruder, G. E. (2013). Neuronal generators of posterior EEG alpha reflect individual differences in prioritizing personal spirituality. *Biological Psychology*, 94(2), 426–432.

Walz, J. M., Goldman, R. I., Carapezza, M., Muraskin, J., Brown, T. R., & Sajda, P. (2013). Simultaneous EEG-fMRI reveals temporal evolution of coupling between supramodal cortical attention networks and the brainstem. *Journal of Neuroscience*, 33(49), 19212–19222. https://doi.org/10.1523/JNEUROSCI.2649-13.2013

Yun, X., Li, W., Qiu, J., Jou, J., Wei, D., Tu, S., & Zhang, Q. (2011). Neural mechanisms of subliminal priming for traumatic episodic memory: An ERP study. *Neuroscience Letters*, 498(1), 10–14.

6

The Therapeutic Crossover in A/T Training Neurofeedback:
Temporal and Spectral Components of Access to Levels of Consciousness

Mark Johnson, PhD
Eugenia Bodenhamer-Davis, PhD

Several studies have demonstrated the remarkable effectiveness of the Peniston Protocol (Peniston & Kulkosky, 1989, 1990, 1991; Peniston, Marrinan, Deming, & Kulkosky, 1993; Saxby & Peniston, 1995) and its modifications (Scott, Kaiser, Othmer & Sideroff, 2005) for treating disorders such as substance abuse and PTSD. The original protocol developed by Eugene Peniston involved multiple components, beginning with pretraining in temperature biofeedback; up to 30 A/T training sessions at International 10-20 Site O1; incorporation of "scripted" guided imagery for subject relaxation induction, desired behavioral changes such as alcohol-rejection or anger-management responses, and suggestions for visualizing one's alpha and theta brainwave amplitudes increasing in amplitude (Peniston & Kulkosky, 1989, 1999; Saxby & Peniston, 1995).

The multi-modal nature of Peniston's model of A/T training made it difficult to identify which component(s) contribute most to its therapeutic outcomes. Peniston proposed that a phenomenon known to occur during A/T training neurofeedback, termed by earlier practitioners the alpha/theta crossover (Green, Green, & Walters, 1970), was a major contributor to the therapeutic outcomes obtained in this form of treatment. More accurately termed a theta/alpha crossover, this event occurs after about 10 sessions of EEG biofeedback in which amplitude increases in posterior alpha (8–12 Hz) and theta (4–7 Hz) frequency bands are rewarded. The crossover event occurs when the normally dominant alpha amplitude produced in the early stages of the training drops temporarily, and the amplitude of the theta frequency increases above that of the alpha. Figure 6.1 shows an amplitude line graph depicting a general example of this theta-over-alpha crossover event.

This crossover was considered therapeutically significant because, as Peniston observed, the event often coincided with end-of-session reports by treatment participants experiencing some form of spontaneous imagery, memory, or other sensory phenomena during the session. Peniston stated that this intra-session subjective content, produced in what he termed the "theta" or "reverie" state, often held strong personal meaning for participants and therefore could be applied psychotherapeutically toward their treatment goals (Peniston & Kulkosky, 1999). For example, some of Peniston's original treatment subjects who were military veterans recalled traumatic events from prior combat-related experiences and received emotional relief from mentally processing the events in a calmer psychophysiological state following their session (Peniston & Kulkosky, 1991; Peniston, personal communication, 1993).

Several early practitioners of Peniston's A/T training protocol also referred to the therapeutic importance of this theta-dominant state, likening it to a "deep meditative" or "altered state" (Cowan, 1993; Kelley, 1997). As early as 1992, Wuttke described it as an "awakening" state associated with greater personal insight and integration. However, not all A/T training participants report recalling subjective imagery or memory experiences during

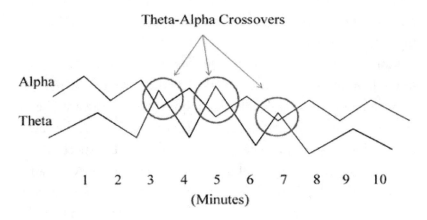

Figure 6.1. Theta-alpha crossover (broadly defined).

treatment, even though visual monitoring of their session recordings may indicate the occurrence of increasing theta amplitude and at least one theta-over-alpha crossover event. Peniston's clinical observations led him to speculate that subject recall of content emerging during an A/T training session was probably influenced by amplitude elevation in the low beta frequency range (13–26 Hz) concurrent with the theta-over-alpha crossover (Peniston & Kulkosky, 1999).

Following Peniston's early research publications and descriptions of his protocol, at least one research group examined whether an actual correspondence existed between crossovers and subjective reports of imagery. In 2000, Moore and colleagues found no relationship between A/T training participant reports of recalled sensory events and theta/alpha crossovers (Moore et al., 2000). However, their study addressed only the relationship of theta-over-alpha crossover events and subject visualization reports and did not include information on beta band activity during the crossover events sampled. In more than a decade since the Moore et al. study, no additional research has examined the crossover phenomenon assumed by Peniston and others to be so significant to therapeutic outcomes in A/T training neurofeedback.

Considering the continuing clinical interest in A/T training in the field of neurofeedback, as well as the advent of technical improvements in neurofeedback equipment and software, the authors of this chapter decided to take a closer look at the theta-over-alpha crossover, its specific temporal and EEG spectral characteristics, and its possible role in the efficacy of A/T training therapy. One of our goals was to gain a better understanding of how EEG frequency band activity may interact to produce the fertile circumstances necessary for access to imagery and memory during A/T training therapy. To accomplish this objective, we needed to explore relationships of frequency bands to imagery and memory from a wider spectral perspective than was possible during the early developmental years of A/T training neurofeedback. Very early A/T training studies were limited by neurofeedback technology that permitted monitoring and recording of only two or three frequency bands during a session. Sufficient electrophysiological research evidence exists to date to speculate that certain frequency band combinations (i.e., alpha, theta and beta; or alpha, theta, and delta) can facilitate access to different types of sensory or memory experiences.

Our initial exploration of the EEG literature on memory, imagery and states of consciousness led to a hypothetical conceptualization of how each frequency and combinations of frequencies active during a crossover event may provide "gating functions" that allow spontaneous subjective memories and sensory (especially visual imagery) content to emerge and become accessible to conscious awareness. Alpha brainwave activity can shift attention inward to a state of visual system arousal and is related to internal mental activity involving mental imagery and free-floating associations (von Stein & Sarnthein, 2000). Beta activity can enable a shift to a state capable of carrying visual attention (Wrobel, 2000). Theta can produce a shift that activates hippocampal, emotional memory processes (Tesche & Karhu, 2000); and delta may enable a shift to internal processing of cortical output and limit extraneous stimuli (Harmony et al., 1996). Since the EEG activity seen during crossover states can resemble onset of drowsiness and stage 1 sleep (drop in alpha amplitude and increase in theta and delta), A/T training is designed to promote this liminal state bordering wake and sleep that would normally be unconscious to the individual.

Subjective experiences associated with crossover dynamics could be interpreted as resembling lucid dreaming, a dream state in which the dreamer becomes consciously aware that he or she is dreaming. It has been found that dreaming is not specific to any single stage of sleep, and sleep stages that include increased beta activity are more likely to contain vivid story like imagery than stages characterized only by theta and delta (Williamson, Csima, Galin & Mamelak, 1986). Delta and beta combined can create a functional stage shift that might account for dream recall (Itil, Gannon, Hsu, Klingenberg, 1970), and increased amplitude in delta and theta has been associated with transformations in conscious experience that can involve insight, creativity, problem solving or mystical experience (Don, 1977), a fact holding relevance to some of our findings discussed later in this chapter. (For a more thorough review by the authors of research literature on the role of various frequency bands and brain areas in consciousness, imagery, dream states, memory, and recall, see Johnson, Bodenhamer-Davis, Bailey & Gates, 2013). Table 6.1 provides a summary of research related to the possible role of frequency dynamics during crossover events.

Therapeutic Crossover

Given the research literature briefly summarized above, it appears that a broader conceptualization of the theta/alpha crossover is warranted, one that recognizes the complex nature of this event. Başar, Başar-Eroglu, Karakas & Schürmann (2001) defined complex brain functions as being characterized by several superimposed brainwave oscillations that vary in their degrees of amplitude, duration, and timing. We chose the term therapeutic crossover for the type of phenomenon Peniston and others described as occurring during A/T training neurofeedback and related to therapeutic outcomes. However, our definition refines the earlier descriptions of crossovers to include theta-over-alpha crossovers that conform to specific temporal and spectral parameters and that render therapeutically useful subjective reports from participants. In a preliminary visual inspection of crossover events obtained from a sample of 182 clinical A/T training sessions (further description of this sample and methodology provided later in this chapter), the authors identified specific amplitude and duration criteria that distinguish such therapeutic crossovers from theta/alpha crossovers that do not yield personally relevant material.

The specific amplitude and temporal criteria were then evaluated with exploratory modeling analysis, and a model of best fit for mean amplitude within the superimposed beta range was defined. This analysis indicated that a therapeutic crossover likely to accompany emergent imagery would be distinguished as a theta-over-alpha amplitude crossover in which theta rises at least 1 microvolt or more in amplitude above alpha and remains dominant over alpha amplitude for 3–10 minutes or longer. Also, this crossover has superimposed 15–20 Hz beta brainwave frequency components (Table 6.2). This definition provides quantifiable and heuristic criteria that may describe the type of crossover that Peniston and others identified as a significant contributor to therapeutic success in A/T training neurotherapy.

Categories of Subjective Content in Crossover Reports

Our investigation of crossover events also led us to examine the types of sensory and memory experiences reported by participants in A/T training neurofeedback. Demos (2005) and other practicing A/T training clinicians have noted that different patterns of content may be experienced and reported by treatment participants. Previous studies of the theta/alpha crossover state do not provide specific descriptions of the kinds of visual imagery that subjects reported, although Moore et al., (2000) noted variability in the nature and complexity of self-reported imagery provided by their subjects. A/T training participant reports of spontaneous emergence of sensory experiences, especially visual imagery, can range in content from light hypnagogic imagery, such as colors and geometric shapes, to much deeper states of consciousness containing biographical memories and more personally relevant material, sometimes of a spiritual, symbolic, or transcendental nature (Brown, 1970).

Another important therapeutic aspect of the theta/alpha crossover phenomenon may involve the nature or content of subjective experiences reported by A/T training participants, especially when content emerges that can be processed and applied by participant and therapist toward treatment goals. Therefore, as part of our investigation, we undertook an analysis of the content of subjective reports taken from crossover sessions sampled from our case files and explored how categories of content might be associated with specific crossover frequency configurations. Our goal in this aspect of our study was to gain not only better understanding of the brainwave frequency and

Table 6.1

Gating Functions of Frequency Bands

Freq Band	Measures in Hz	Corresponding State of Consciousness	Gating Function
Alpha	8–12	Idling state: Internal mental activity driven by mental imagery[a]	Shifts attention inward to a state of visual system arousal.
Beta	15–20	Alert, outward focus of mental concentration[b]	Shifts to a state capable of carrying visual attention.
Theta	4–7	Pre-sleep, hypnagogic[c]	Shifts may activate hippocampal processes.
Delta	1–3	Sleeping, dreaming[d]	Shifts to internal processing of cortical output & limits extraneous stimuli
Delta and Beta	1–3 with beta 2 superimposed	Present during greater dream recall[e]	Functional state shift that might explain dream recall.

[a]von Stein & Sarnthein, 2000. [b]Wróbel, 2000. [c]Tesche & Karhu, 2000. [d]Harmony, et al. 1996. [e]Itil, 1970.

Table 6.2

Amplitudinal and Temporal Features of Therapeutic Crossover

Amplitude (Theta-over-Alpha)	Duration of the crossover	Additional Spectral Activity
1 microvolt or more	3 minutes or more	Beta (15–20 Hz) 3.75 microvolts+ versus insufficient beta amplitude

subjective consciousness dynamics involved in crossover states, but also to inform neurotherapists of the types of participant reports that might be expected to emerge during A/T training sessions when certain frequency configurations appeared in the session record.

Data used for our study were obtained through retrospective review of archived case files of individuals who completed A/T training neurofeedback as part of their treatment for substance abuse, depression, or posttraumatic stress disorder (PTSD) between 2002 and 2008. Files were obtained from a university-based clinic and a private practice, both specializing in neurofeedback. Ten files were selected that contained sufficient session data and therapist notes for the study. All subjects were Caucasian, 5 male and 5 female, ranging in age from 22 to 58 years (M = 41). The mean session length was 32.97 minutes. Although A/T training was to last 30 sessions, the actual number of sessions varied from 11 to 29, except one subject who completed only three sessions but had a crossover with biographical imagery. Case files provided all session graphs as well as neurotherapist session notes that included detailed written records of subjects' reports of any recalled imagery/memories from their sessions. The 10 case files selected provided a total of 182 theta/alpha crossover events recorded on either BrainMaster Atlantis version 3.0 software (n = 8) or Lexicor Biolex software (n = 2). A/T training protocols followed either the original Peniston Protocol (Peniston & Kulkosky, 1989, 1990) or a QEEG-based modification of the Peniston Protocol (see chapter 8 in this book).

Any study of psychological correlates of states of consciousness must depend on subjective reports of research participants. Our study accessed the content of imagery experienced by the A/T training neurofeedback participants through their reports as recorded in their case files. The investigators treated these subjective reports as qualitative observational data derived from carefully recorded neurotherapist session notes. The reports were elicited by questions routinely posed by therapists toward the end of a session after EEG biofeedback was completed. Questions might be worded as "Did anything come up for you in this session?" or "Did you have any images or memories this time?" Therapists were careful not to imply that participants should have any images or memory experiences or what form they should take. Any reports provided were received neutrally and recorded as closely as possible to the participant's own words.

Two raters independently reviewed and categorized the content of the imagery/memory reports from our subjects using a modified version of subjective experience classification systems developed by earlier neurofeedback investigators. The following descriptive groupings are our adaptation of the categories or cartographies of subjective experience provided by early practitioners of EEG alpha and theta biofeedback (Brown, 1974; Crane, 1992; Tansey, Tansey, & Tachiki, 1994) as well as descriptions of levels of subjective experience provided by other consciousness investigators (Grof, 1976).

Using this classification system, our two reviewers obtained 100% agreement in categorizing all subjective imagery reports sampled. Table 6.3 lists the category levels with their associated frequency ranges and content characteristics, along with examples of the kinds of subject reports from our study that were included in each category.

These categories covering abstract, biographical, perinatal, and transpersonal content domains provided a framework for further examining relationships between the graph configurations of A/T training neurofeedback sessions, brainwave frequency ratios, and different types of subjective reports. We statistically tested several hypotheses about temporal and spectral features of crossovers that were associated both with and without subject recall of images/memories, as well as the spectral dynamics associated with the various consciousness categories of imagery/memory contained in subject reports. In addition to the activity in alpha and theta frequencies, we traced activity in the beta and delta ranges. A/T training session graphs (N = 32) and therapist session notes were analyzed for quantitative crossover characteristics, reports of associated imagery content, and treatment outcomes.

First, we used a crosstab analysis to examine crossover activity in which theta brainwave frequency rose in amplitude above alpha brainwave frequency activity. This analysis indicated that 27.9% of the A/T training neurofeedback session graphs contained no crossover activity, 34.1% contained crossover activity without reports of spontaneous imagery or memory events, and 37.9% contained crossover activity followed by subject reports of spontaneous sensory experiences or memories. Further crosstab analysis revealed no imagery/memory reports in 67.4% of sessions and only hypnogogic imagery in 14.7% of sessions. Biographical imagery reports occurred in 7.1% of sessions, perinatal imagery in 2.1%, and imagery categorized as transpersonal in nature in 6% of the sessions, $\chi^2(df\text{-}8, n = 182) = 47.4$, $p < .001$.

Additional crosstab analyses assessed changes in the data when only therapeutically significant events (spontaneous biological, perinatal, transpersonal imagery or experiences) were reported by subjects, and to test whether increases in the mean amplitudes of slower brainwave activity correlated with progression into deeper states of consciousness, as defined by the category of imagery/memory reported. Because amorphous hypnagogic activity was more frequently observed in sessions with

Table 6.3

Categories of Imagery/Memory

I. Abstract/Aesthetic[a] (10–15 Hz, SMR/Alpha)	
Characteristics	Visual (intense colors, geometric shapes, afterimages, geometric/ abstract designs, etc.), acoustic (hypersensitivity to sound, acoustical illusions, and synesthesia), and emotional experiences (interpretation of the environment as beautiful, comical, or magical)
Examples	"There was swirly imagery and sounds that were like voices." "Pleasant imagery; rivers, crystal caves."
II. Biographical (5–10 Hz, Alpha/Theta)	
Characteristics	Important memories, emotional problems, and unresolved conflicts, guilt/moral failure, endangered survival/health/body integrity, and abandonment/separation; possible physical/motor responses such as nausea/vomiting, breathing difficulties, cardiovascular
Examples	"I re-experienced being molested by my stepfather when I was 7 years old." "Grandfather chased me and my sisters, trying to hit us with a belt."
III. Perinatal or Birth Matrix[b] (5–10 Hz, Alpha/Theta)	
Characteristics	Basic Perinatal Matrices (BPMs)
	BPM I. Intrauterine experiences
	BPM II. Contractions in closed womb (separation, meaninglessness)
	BPM III. Propulsion through birth canal (death-rebirth struggle, power struggles, aggressive and sexual energies)
	BPM IV. Release, expulsion into new mode of existence (overcoming hardship, victory)
	BPM I-IV. Separation from mother (circular, not linear)

(continued)

Examples	"I saw myself being born. A nurse kept throwing towels of blood. I was drenched in blood. It felt like it was my actual birth." "Following an umbilical cord and being the fetus..."
	IV. Transpersonal[c] (0–4 Hz, Delta/Theta)
Characteristics	Unconscious, expanded beyond ego boundaries, time and space limitations, identification with ancestral, archetypal, past-life, animal/plant, collective/racial, oneness with all life/creation, out of body experiences, encounters with deceased persons
Examples	"At first, it was like I was in a submarine exploring my body and traveling through my arteries. Then there was a spiritual being that was doing healing work with its hands over my heart, with glowing blue light.'

[a]Brown, 1974. [b]Grof, 1976. [c]Ring, 1976; Jovanov, 1998.

no crossover activity, it was decided to focus only on reports of biographical, perinatal, and transpersonal imagery in sessions where therapeutic crossover activity was observed (Table 6.4).

These three types of potentially personally meaningful and therapeutically useful imagery were reported 85.7% of the time in the therapeutic crossover condition defined above, with 71.4% of reports conveyed when the beta amplitude was sufficient (3.75 μv > alpha; see Figure 6.2). Increases in the mean amplitudes of slower brainwave activity correlated with progression into deeper states of consciousness, as defined by the category of imagery/memory reported. Table 6.4 presents a summary of imagery reports according to crossover type in both sufficient 15–20 Hz beta and insufficient 15–20 Hz beta conditions.

With the findings thus far in our exploration of the therapeutic crossover, we developed a multinomial regression model to

Table 6.4

Crossover Activity as a Percentage of Sessions by Category of Reported Imagery Content and Presence of Beta (15–20 Hz)

Category	Crossover Activity (n = 0)	Non-Therapeutic Crossover Activity (n = 4)		Therapeutic Crossover Activity (n = 24)	
		No Beta	Beta	No Beta	Beta
Biographic	0.0	7.7	7.1	3.6	28.6
Perinatal	0.0	0.0	0.0	3.6	10.7
Transpersonal	0.0	0.0	0.0	7.1	32.1
Total	0.0	7.7	7.1	14.3	71.4

describe and further evaluate the relationships emerging between spectral, temporal, and subjective report content variables related to crossover events in our study. This type of regression model was chosen for its predictive value and capability to evaluate the association of covariates with mutually exclusive patterns of dependence as well as its ability to accurately describe relationships among the variables of interest in the study. Figure 6.3 depicts a flow chart representing the hierarchical and multivariable predictive pathway that was investigated using the multinomial regression analysis procedure to evaluate the likelihood of occurrences of imagery.

For a detailed description of the multinomial regression analysis used in our study and the specific statistical outcomes, see Johnson et al. (2013).

Our multinomial regression results showed that the odds ratios for the occurrence of biographical, perinatal, or transpersonal imagery were higher for individuals experiencing a rise in 15–20 Hz beta than for those experiencing a rise in delta (1–3 Hz). For instance, individuals who experienced a rise in beta

The Therapeutic Crossover in A/T Training Neurofeedback

were 2.8 times more likely to report biographical imagery than those who reported no imagery. Participants who experienced a therapeutic crossover were 3.4 times more likely to experience biographical imagery compared with those who did not report imagery during a therapeutic crossover. Similarly, the odds of reporting perinatal or transpersonal imagery were increased when there was also a rise in amplitude and presence of therapeutic crossover activity.

Participants who experienced a rise in delta during a session and reported imagery were over 9 times more likely to report perinatal or transpersonal imagery, and those who experienced a rise in beta along with delta were almost 16 times more likely

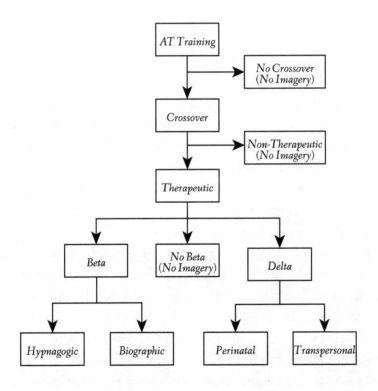

Figure 6.2. Design of the study.

Table 6.5

Mean Amplitudes (μV) for Each Frequency Range

	Category of Reported Imagery/Memory			
	Hypnogogic	Biographic	Perinatal	Transpersonal
Beta (15–20 Hz)	3.63	4.14	4.45	4.52
Alpha (8–12 Hz)	5.87	6.82	10.65	8.62
Theta (4–7 Hz)	5.30	6.91	11.02	9.75
Delta (1–3 Hz)	5.93	6.59	7.92	9.15

to report perinatal or transpersonal imagery than individuals that reported no imagery. Therapeutic crossover notwithstanding, the rise in beta together with a rise in delta provided strong evidence that participants who experience concurrent amplitude increases in these two frequency bands during a session are much more likely to experience perinatal or transpersonal imagery than participants that report no imagery during treatment. Table 6.5 contains mean frequency amplitudes associated with each category of visualization).

An analysis of category level of imagery content by mean amplitude of each frequency (beta, alpha, theta, and delta) indicated that increased amplitude across all frequency bandwidths was associated with transitions to deeper states of consciousness.

Crosstabs analysis showed that participants who achieved higher amplitudes of progressively slower brainwaves (i.e., alpha < theta < delta) were more likely to progress along the continuum of hypnagogic to biographical to perinatal/transpersonal category experiences. The A/T training sessions sampled showed that the treatment was successful in increasing the amplitude of all of these frequencies, and the imagery type was dependent upon which frequencies were dominant. For example, the hypnagogic imagery category was comprised of beta (3.63 μv [microvolts]), alpha (5.87 μv), theta (5.3 μv) and delta (5.93 μv) mean amplitudes.

The transpersonal imagery category, at the other side of the spectrum, consisted of beta (4.52 μv), alpha (8.62 μv), theta (9.75 μv) and delta (9.15 μv) mean amplitudes. Analysis of Variance (ANOVA) indicated significantly higher mean amplitudes in microvolts of delta as the level of imagery increased ($F = 3.429$, $p = .011$). It could be concluded that higher amplitude in the delta frequency range was associated with greater access to deeper levels of consciousness. Therefore, our analyses confirmed a clear relationship between the content category of subjective reports and the specific combination of EEG frequencies that have amplitude increases during the crossover events. Several A/T training session graphs recorded on BrainMaster Atlantis 3.0 provide clinical examples of this finding.

Relationship of Crossovers to Therapeutic Outcomes

Finally, we targeted what may be the most clinically important question of our investigation of the crossover phenomenon: Is there a significant relationship between crossover events and therapeutic outcomes in A/T training neurotherapy? Though hampered by our small available sample for addressing this question, we nevertheless wanted to see if our data might suggest a direct relationship between the type of crossover event and pre- and post-treatment outcome measures for our A/T training subjects. We had established that relationships and ratios of specific bandwidths were related to the type of imagery content that emerged in subject reports, but we wondered if there might be differences in therapeutic outcomes relative to therapeutic versus non-therapeutic crossovers.

An analysis of variance (ANOVA) was performed to assess whether treatment outcomes showed greater improvement when therapeutic crossover conditions were present. Pre- and post-treatment assessments were available for 8 of the 10 subjects whose case files were used for the previous analyses. Outcome measures were not available for two participants who terminated treatment prematurely.

Pre- and post-measures for the eight participants included the Beck Anxiety Inventory (BAI), Beck Depression Inventory (BDI), Beck Hopelessness Scale (BHS), Pittsburgh Sleep Quality Index (PSQI) and Minnesota Multiphasic Personality Inventory (MMPI). Because we had such a small sample for this aspect of our study, our repeated measures analysis of the number of crossovers to treatment outcomes yielded no statistically significant differences. Therefore, we decided to perform a descriptive analysis comparing their therapeutic outcome measures to conditions of no crossover, therapeutic crossover without sufficient beta, and therapeutic crossover with sufficient beta (Table 6.6 & Figure 6.7).

The largest improvements in therapeutic scores across most treatment measures occurred for four subjects in the condition of therapeutic crossover with sufficient beta. This group of four were then separated into high count number of crossovers with sufficient beta versus low count number of crossovers with sufficient beta. The subject in the high-count category showed greatest improvements on BAI, BDI, BHS, PSQI and MMPI Scales 1 (hypochondriasis), 2 (depression), 3 (hysteria), and 6 (paranoia) and 7 (psychasthenia). The 3 subjects in the low count category showed the next greatest improvements among all subjects on

The Therapeutic Crossover in A/T Training Neurofeedback

BAI, PSQI and MMPI scales 3 (hysteria), 4 (psychopathic deviance), 7 (psychasthenia) and 8 (schizophrenia). This latter group reversed on scale 5 (male/female) and scale 6 (paranoia).

Our results showed that therapeutic crossovers with sufficient beta amplitude were associated with the best improvements on posttreatment assessment measures for the subjects in this small sample. Of note was the fact that the subject who had the most therapeutic crossovers during her A/T training showed the greatest improvements in post-treatment measures. While the 3 subjects in the low count of therapeutic crossovers with sufficient beta condition showed clinical improvement, their post-treatment scores did not improve to the same extent

Table 6.6

Outcome Means and Standard Deviations

Psychometric Instrument	No Crossover		Crossover with Beta < 3.75 µV		Crossover with Beta > 37.75 µV	
	M	SD	M	SD	M	SD
BAI						
Pretest	8.0	2.8	17.5	6.4	18.8	12.3
Posttest	6.0	1.4	3.5	0.7	16.5	6.7
BDI						
Pretest	9.0	5.7	13.5	14.8	10.5	8.4
Posttest	2.5	3.5	5.0	0.0	11.3	3.8
BHS						
Pretest	1.5	2.1	4.5	0.7	7.0	2.4
Posttest	1.0	1.4	3.5	0.7	4.3	1.7
PSQI						
Pretest	11.5	2.1	8.0	5.7	7.3	4.2
Posttest	9.0	5.7	5.5	4.9	7.8	4.1

Note. BAI = Beck Anxiety Inventory; BDI = Beck Depression Inventory; BHS Beck Hopelessness Scale; PSQI = Pittsburg Sleep Quality Inventory.

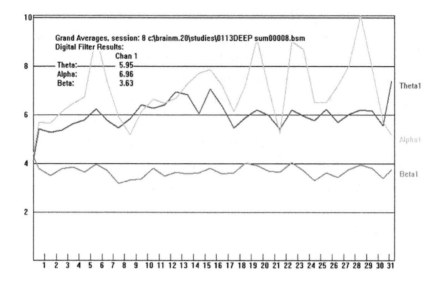

Figure 6.3. Example of a session in which the subject reported hypnagogic imagery was characterized primarily by elevated alpha activity.

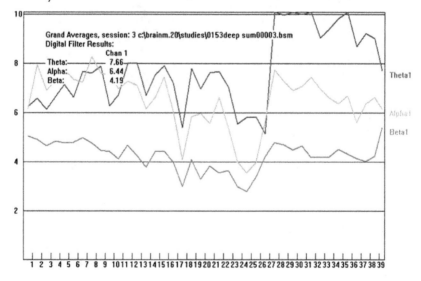

Figure 6.4. Example of a session in which the subject reported perinatal imagery was characterized by therapeutic crossover with sufficient beta, marked by higher amplitudes of alpha and theta, and increasingly elevated delta amplitude activity.

The Therapeutic Crossover in A/T Training Neurofeedback

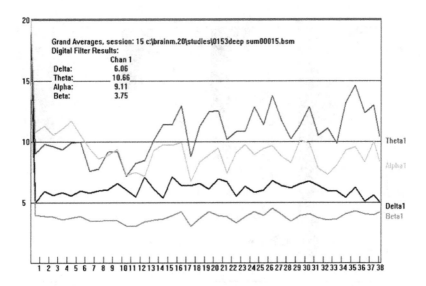

Figure 6.5. Example of a session in which the subject reported biographical imagery was characterized primarily by therapeutic crossover with sufcient beta.

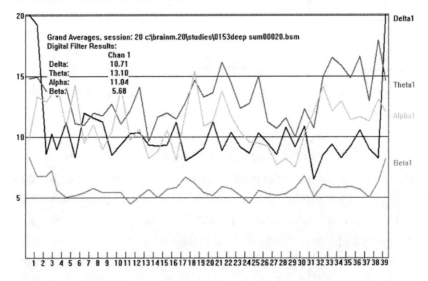

Figure 6.6. Example of a session in which the subject reported transpersonal imagery was characterized primarily by therapeutic crossover with sufcient beta, and highest amplitudes in alpha, theta, and delta activity.

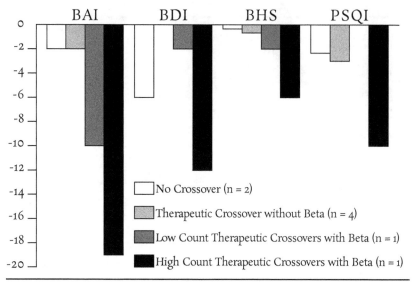

Figure 6.7. Outcome measures by crossover type. Mean difference comparison scores of pre- and post-outcome measures.
BAI = Beck Anxiety Inventory; BDI = Beck Depression Inventory; BHS Beck Hopelessness Scale; PSQI = Pittsburg Sleep Quality Inventory.

as the subject who had the highest count of therapeutic crossovers with sufficient beta amplitude. However, the subject with the highest crossover count also presented with higher baseline scores, indicating greater initial pathology.

Of further interest, the subject who showed the greatest overall improvements on post-treatment measures also achieved the highest incidence of access to transpersonal (categories III and IV) imagery. The other subject who accessed transpersonal (category IV) imagery showed post-treatment score reductions on the BAI and MMPI Scales 1, 2, 3, 4, 5, 7, and 8. A third subject accessed transpersonal imagery, but only completed three A/T training sessions. Three subjects with few or no therapeutic crossovers and who reported either hypnagogic or no imagery showed no improvement, with elevations on some pre- to post-measure scores.

Summary, Conclusions, and Clinical Implications

This chapter provided an empirically-derived description of some key components of the theta-over-alpha crossover, considered by Eugene Peniston and other A/T training clinicians to be an important contributor to the therapeutic outcome of A/T training neurofeedback. Our investigation revealed that defined spectral dynamics, including specific combinations of frequency interactions and time durations, appear to influence the recall, nature and therapeutic value of spontaneous sensory and memory experiences emerging from crossover events. Our findings led us to define a therapeutic crossover as one associated with the recall of spontaneous imagery or memories that provide potential value to the therapeutic process and can be defined quantitatively by its temporal and amplitude characteristics. Specifically, subject recall of sensory or memory experiences during crossover events can be more frequently anticipated when (1) theta amplitude elevates within a session by 1 microvolt or more over alpha amplitude, (2) theta remains dominant over the alpha for 3–10 minutes or longer, and (3) the crossover includes a 15–20 Hz beta amplitude increase that tracks the theta elevation. Therefore, as Peniston and others have speculated, low beta range activity appears to play a significant role in the ability of an A/T training participant to transfer to an alert consciousness state the content of spontaneous imagery or memory events that may emerge as subjects acquire greater elevations of alpha, theta, and delta brainwaves during their training.

The neurophysiological underpinnings of such observed clinical events associated with therapeutic crossovers have been amply described by basic EEG research summarized above. Further evaluation of low beta (15–20 Hz) amplitudes occurring during theta-over-alpha crossover events in our study revealed that 3.75 μv of low beta was the most dependable threshold for predicting reports of imagery. Also, our crosstab analyses revealed that most of the reports of imagery that can be categorized as biographical, perinatal, or transpersonal in nature occurred in the defined therapeutic crossover condition. Thus, theta-over-alpha amplitude crossovers conforming to the stipulated therapeutic crossover parameters were more likely to correlate with therapy participant access to personally meaningful imagery and memories.

Although the majority of reported biographical, perinatal and transpersonal imagery occurred in the therapeutic crossover condition, in which 15–20 Hz beta amplitude was at least 3.75 μv, a small percentage of reported imagery occurred when beta activity was less than 3.75 μv. Based on visual inspection of A/T training session reports prior to the study, 3.5 μv was initially identified as the cut-off, which should still be considered the minimum amplitude for the recall of subjective experiences from a crossover session. However, follow-up exploratory analysis found 3.75 μv to be an even more reliable predictor of recall. This finding of the importance of sufficient 15–20 Hz amplitude is also consistent with clinical observations in which some subjects that experience therapeutic crossover activity, but with insufficient beta amplitude, sometimes report limited access to the mental contents of their sessions, as evidenced by statements such as, "It seemed like a lot was going on in my mind, but I just can't recall it." The overall conclusion from our study is that a subject with sufficiently elevated (3.75 μv or more) 15–20 Hz beta amplitude occurring along with a theta/alpha crossover is more likely to recall and retain imagery and memories than a subject with insufficient beta amplitude in this range (see Figure 6.2). This fact holds true even when delta is the dominant frequency in the crossover condition. Finally, our study supported Peniston's contention that crossovers are significantly related to therapeutic outcomes for A/T training. Subjects in our study that had the most therapeutic crossovers during their treatment had the best clinical outcomes on pre-to-post treatment psychometric measures.

Since our empirical investigation of the A/T training crossover and related events involved a relatively small clinical sample of A/T training subjects, our findings must be considered suggestive only, pending further research. Nevertheless, we believe some clinical implications and recommendations may be warranted from our results as well as from our clinical experience.

Since most individuals treated with A/T training neurofeedback in recent years have dual diagnoses and/or polysubstance abuse, many with prior trauma as well as head injuries (Sokhadze, Cannon & Trudeau, 2008), we strongly recommend using a QEEG-guided protocol to eliminate excessive fast and/or slow EEG activity in frontal and/or central brain areas prior to initiating posterior A/T training. Anecdotal evidence indicates that treating frontal and central sites first tends to significantly reduce the number of A/T training sessions required to achieve crossovers and resolve symptoms (see Davis, chapter 10hapter 8).

Some neurotherapists have described modifications to the Peniston Protocol to prevent participant sleep during sessions, such as inhibiting delta under certain conditions (Scott et al, 2005). Our study showed that therapeutically significant imagery experiences can be recalled even when the participant appears by both EEG and behavioral observation to be in an unresponsive sleep state.

Our literature search on the EEG of lucid dreaming, briefly

summarized above, as well as results from our study, suggest that a major determining variable for the recall of spontaneous memories or imagery during these apparent sleep states is the presence in the subject's EEG spectral mix of around 3.75 microvolts of low beta. The disadvantage of arousing an individual from a deeper reverie state during an A/T training session to determine whether they are in unresponsive sleep is the risk of disrupting a possibly helpful subjective experience. Consequently, we recommend using the presence or absence of sufficient 15–20 Hz beta in the EEG recording as the criterion for deciding whether it is advisable to add a delta inhibit to the protocol. More research can help confirm whether participant unresponsiveness to an external prompt during a session necessarily precludes their ability to benefit from the session or to recall imagery/memories derived from the deeper states of increased delta amplitude activity.

Since the ultimate value of A/T training may derive from its capacity to help individuals develop greater self-awareness and better communication between their normal waking consciousness and previously unrecognized aspects/contents of their inner life, the A/T training therapist's role could be described as facilitating a treatment process that enables relatively unhindered personal inner exploration and self-understanding. For this reason, we strongly recommend allowing A/T training neurofeedback therapy to proceed using as closely as possible the original, empirically validated components of the Peniston Protocol, including the multi-modal breathing and relaxation pre-training and scripted auto-suggestion/guided imagery elements that Peniston used at the beginning of each session. However, we recommend routinely adding to the Peniston Protocol a higher beta range (20–30Hz) inhibit, since this frequency range is associated with the muscle tension, anxiety and rumination, symptoms common to A/T training target populations.

In their 1999 description of the A/T training protocol, Peniston & Kulkosky report using a "beta rhythm" contingency (frequency range unspecified) to prevent or relieve strong emotional abreactions during treatment. Based on our investigation of crossover events, we now consider adding a 20–30% reward contingency in the 15–18 Hz beta range when a participant's EEG during crossovers consistently lacks more than 3.5 microvolts of this low beta activity and the participant is consistently unable to recall any personally relevant material after crossover sessions.

This addition to the alpha (50–70%) and theta (20–30%) rewards at site O1 can increase the probability of participant recall of any spontaneous images/memories/insights occurring during crossovers, while making available to them a rational, dual state of awareness for therapeutic processing of accessed material from any level of consciousness. Some of our A/T training participants who experience imagery or memories of past trauma describe the event as a combination of visceral experience ("as if it were happening") combined with a sense of being an impartial witness to their own experience. This dual state of consciousness not only assists therapeutic processing of such experiences but also seems to afford the participant a sense of safety and willingness to move forward with sessions. However, questions regarding various beta range modifications to the Peniston Protocol warrant more research.

For example, a controlled study might demonstrate that it could be as effective, if not more so, to allow each A/T training participant's own individual therapeutic processing needs to dictate how much information/memory must be transferred from one level of subjective consciousness to another. This conjecture is presented in light of anecdotal clinical reports, supported by our study's findings, that some subjects derive therapeutic benefit from A/T training neurofeedback even if they never report recalling spontaneous subjective experiences from their sessions.

Because of the sometimes unconventional symbolic or dreamlike forms of imagery experiences that can emerge from crossover states involving the slower brainwave frequencies in theta and delta, it is important that A/T training neurotherapists have training in therapeutically responding to this kind of participant experience. As with any other material that emerges in a psychotherapeutic situation, the A/T training neurotherapist needs to be able to calmly and impartially receive hypnogogic, biographical, perinatal or transpersonal imagery reports from their therapy participants, as well as, according to Dr. Peniston, allow participants to interpret the contents of their own subjective experiences (Peniston, personal communication, 1993).

This more restrained role for the neurotherapist in responding to participants' subjective reports differs from the kind of therapist role traditionally assumed, for example, in psychoanalysis. Our study provides some support to long-standing A/T training clinical observations that some of the most therapeutically useful spontaneous imagery, especially from patients with histories of trauma, can come from the deeper consciousness states involving transpersonal imagery which are often of a spiritual nature and involve themes such as forgiveness and inner peace (Wuttke, 1992).

Consequently, both our research as well as our clinical findings lead us to generally discourage the use of A/T training protocol modifications intended to prevent emotional abreactions by inhibiting slower frequencies, unless the therapist is employing Peniston's recommended method of helping a participant move through a strong abreaction in progress (Peniston & Kulkosky, 1999). None of the subjects in our crossover research

The Therapeutic Crossover in A/T Training Neurofeedback

sample experienced what could be termed a strong emotional abreaction during A/T training, and we have found dissociative abreactions or emotional flooding events to be relatively rare in our clinical experience. However, we believe that neurotherapists electing to do A/T training therapy need to have both the temperament and the psychotherapy training required to recognize the potential benefits of therapeutically managed abreactions.

We find that in addition to inserting, when indicated, a 15–18 Hz reward to the protocol, as described above, the inclusion of other treatment program elements already discussed can help inoculate A/T training participants against serious emotional abreactions. These elements include improving participant executive and self-regulation functions by reducing frontal and central slow wave activity found to be excessive in QEEG pre-assessment; pre-training in self-directed stress management methods such as relaxation and breathing; and therapist monitoring of the amount of 15–18 Hz beta in the participant's EEG spectral mix during crossovers once A/T training begins. Pre-training in breathing, temperature biofeedback and relaxation techniques, such as those routinely used by Peniston and later modified by others using such methods as SMR pretraining sessions or pre-training in HRV biofeedback, serve both preparatory and stabilizing functions for the A/T training process.

Finally, due to the nature of the types of imagery/memories and levels of consciousness processing that may occur in A/T training therapy, it is important that practitioners determine if and when to structure A/T training sessions with greater frequency and allot extended pre- and post-session time to adequately address emotional content arising between or within sessions that may play a vital role in bridging inner exploration and self-understanding.

References

Başar, E., Başar-Eroglu, C., Karakaş, S., & Schürmann, M. (2001). Gamma, alpha, delta, and theta oscillations govern cognitive processes. International Journal of Psychophysiology, 39(2–3), 241–248. https://doi.org/10.1016/S0167-8760(00)00145-8

Brown, B. B. (1970). Recognition of aspects of consciousness through association with EEG alpha activity represented by a light signal. Psychophysiology, 6(4), 442–452. https://doi.org/10.1111/j.1469-8986.1970.tb01754.x

Brown, B. B. (1974). New mind, new body: Bio-feedback: New directions for the mind (Vol. xiii). Oxford, England: Harper & Row.

Cowan, J. D. (1993). Alpha-theta brainwave biofeedback: The many possible theoretical reasons for its success. Biofeedback, 21(2), 11–16.

Crane, R. A. (1992). Mind compass: A neurofeedback tool for the cartography of consciousness. Ossining, NY: American Biotech Corp.

Demos, J. N. (2005). Getting started with neurofeedback. New York: W. W. Norton & Company.

Don, N. S. (1977). The transformation of conscious experience and its EEG correlates. Journal of Altered States of Consciousness, 3(2), 147–168.

Green, E. E., Green, A. M., & Walters, E. D. (1970). Voluntary control of internal states: Psychological and physiological. The Journal of Transpersonal Psychology, 2(1), 1.

Grof, S. (1976). Realms of the human unconscious: Observations from LSD research. New York: Dutton.

Harmony, T., Fernández, T., Silva, J., Bernal, J., Díaz-Comas, L., Reyes, A., ... Rodríguez, M. (1996). EEG delta activity: An indicator of attention to internal processing during performance of mental tasks. International Journal of Psychophysiology, 24(1), 161–171.

Holzinger, B., LaBerge, S., & Levitan, L. (2006). Psychophysiological correlates of lucid dreaming. Dreaming,

16(2), 88.

Itil, T. M., Gannon, P., Hsu, W., & Klingenberg, H. (1970). Digital computer analyzed sleep and resting EEG during haloperidol treatment. American Journal of Psychiatry, 127(4), 462–471.

Johnson, M. L., Bodenhamer-Davis, E., Bailey, L. J., & Gates, M. S. (2013). Spectral dynamics and therapeutic implications of the theta/alpha crossover in alpha-theta neurofeedback. Journal of Neurotherapy, 17(1), 3–34.

Kelley, M. J. (1997). Native Americans, neurofeedback, and substance abuse theory: Three year outcome of alpha/theta neurofeedback training in the treatment of problem drinking among Dine' (Navajo) people. Journal of Neurotherapy, 2(3), 24–60.

Moore, J. P., Trudeau, D. L., Thuras, P. D., Rubin, Y., Stockley, H., & Dimond, T. (2000). Comparison of alpha-theta, alpha and EMG neurofeedback in the production of alpha-theta crossover and the occurrence of visualizations. Journal of Neurotherapy, 4(1), 29–42.

Peniston, E. G., & Kulkosky, P. J. (1989). Alpha-theta brainwave training and beta-endorphin levels in alcoholics. Alcoholism: Clinical and Experimental Research, 13(2), 271–279.

Peniston, E. G., & Kulkosky, P. J. (1990). Alcoholic personality and alpha-theta brainwave training. Medical Psychotherapy, 3, 37–55.

Peniston, E. G., & Kulkosky, P. J. (1991). Alpha-theta brainwave neurofeedback for Vietnam veterans with combat-related post-traumatic stress disorder. Medical Psychotherapy, 4(1), 47–60.

Peniston, E. G., & Kulkosky, P. J. (1999). Neurofeedback in the treatment of addictive disorders. In J. R. Evans & A. Abarbanel (Eds.), Introduction to quantitative EEG and neurofeedback. Academic Press.

Peniston, E. G., Marrinan, D. A., Deming, W. A., & Kulkosky, P. J. (1993). EEG alpha-theta synchronization in Vietnam theater veterans with combat-related PTSD and alcohol abuse. Medical Psychotherapy, 6, 37–50.

Ring, K. (1976). Mapping the regions of consciousness: A conceptual reformulation. The Journal of Transpersonal Psychology,

8(2), 77.

Saxby, E., & Peniston, E. G. (1995). Alpha-theta brainwave neurofeedback training: An effective treatment for male and female alcoholics with depressive symptoms. Journal of Clinical Psychology, 51(5), 685–693.

Scott, W. C., Kaiser, D., Othmer, S., & Sideroff, S. I. (2005). Effects of an EEG biofeedback protocol on a mixed substance abusing population. The American Journal of Drug and Alcohol Abuse, 31(3), 455–469.

Sokhadze, T. M., Cannon, R. L., & Trudeau, D. L. (2008). EEG biofeedback as a treatment for substance use disorders: Review, rating of efficacy, and recommendations for further research. Journal of Neurotherapy, 12(1), 5–43. https://doi.org/10.1080/10874200802219855

Tansey, M. A., Tansey, J. A., & Tachiki, K. H. (1994). Electroencephalographic cartography of conscious states. International Journal of Neuroscience, 77(1–2), 89–98.

Tesche, C. D., & Karhu, J. (2000). Theta oscillations index human hippocampal activation during a working memory task. Proceedings of the National Academy of Sciences, 97(2), 919–924.

Von Stein, A., & Sarnthein, J. (2000). Different frequencies for different scales of cortical integration: From local gamma to long range alpha/theta synchronization. International Journal of Psychophysiology, 38(3), 301–313.

Williamson, P. C., Csima, A., Galin, H., & Mamelak, M. (1986). Spectral EEG correlates of dream recall. Biological Psychiatry, 21(8–9), 717–723.

Wróbel, A. (2000). Beta activity: A carrier for visual attention. Acta Neurobiologiae Experimentalis, 60(2), 247–260.

Wuttke, M. (1992). Addiction, awakening, and EEG biofeedback. Biofeedback, 20(2), 18–22.

7

Alpha/Theta Training and Phenotypes

Jay Gunkelman, PhD

In the early 1970s, I was working at North Dakota State Hospital, under an alcohol and drug program's medical director, when I co-authored a grant with Larry Woodard that funded the first applied psychophysiology lab at a state hospital. The lab had access to the full range of institutionalized patients, including alcoholics and drug-addicted clients.

In these early days, the classical signs of a "low voltage fast" (LVF) EEG pattern, or an EEG "without persistent rhythmicity" were already well established (Adrian & Matthews, 1934), so our work was not to describe the population, but to treat them. We did some early EMG relaxation and thermal feedback, but we also had EEG biofeedback, now more commonly called neurofeedback, to treat these clients.

The underlying pathophysiology of the LVF EEG was already described as an "over-aroused" central nervous system in the early EEG texts (Gibbs & Gibbs, 1952). The low voltage fast EEG pattern is associated with alcoholism and the GABA-A receptor genes (Porjesz, Almasy, Edenberg, et al., 2002).

In addition to the relaxation of the muscles and increasing of surface skin temperature—both classical lowering of arousal "relaxation" techniques—we wanted to also try the new "alpha training" popularized at UC San Francisco's famous Langley-Porter Neuropsychiatric Institute's Parnassus Street laboratory run by Joe Kamiya (Kamiya, 1969).

Training to the "alpha state" was not meant to induce a hard-focused concentrative state, but the "open focus" state of Les Fehmi's work (Fehmi, 1978). In our simplistic view, the alpha state appeared to be a good remedy for the over-aroused nervous/anxious state the low voltage fast EEG represented. We attempted some sessions with some of the chronic alcoholics in the institution's cohort and they "liked it." Our psychiatric population also had some individuals who suffered from social anxiety to the point of disability and had been institutionalized at great expense for many years. So we also approached this population with the new biofeedback techniques.

Our initial funding was "preliminary," and we had to show meaningful clinical outcomes or the funding would end. In other words, the initial success with these techniques had to show clinical efficacy and reduced recidivism, or we would simply be defunded. Luckily, our first few cases had severe clinical presentations and were well-known dramatic cases, with many return hospitalizations. Thus, when we announced that we would treat our first few clients, the hope was that they would be discharged. However, the rumor was that they would "be right back." This was especially true of "Dorothy," who was so anxious that initially she would not leave her room or go to the dining hall (where her father had died choking on food).

We treated her initially with EMG relaxation, which is easy and quick with most clients, who attain the usual relaxation response (Whatmore & Kohli, 1974). However, Dorothy's response showed us that the therapists' expectations are sometimes not the same as the outcome. She experienced "relaxation" as a state where she "let her guard down," yet this made her acutely anxious. This is exactly what we were trying to treat, and it intrigued us, so we looked at her EEG and found an LVF pattern. This was almost a "flat line," though also containing EMG and random oscillations of beta and slower content, including no background alpha with eyes open or closed.

In our simple-minded view, we thought we should try Kamiya's newly popularized alpha training because Dorothy had no apparent alpha and we thought we should "train some." That said, we know now that training any frequency at any site is much more complex than a simple linear spectral shifting up or down. This training would ultimately be better understood mechanistically over the next decade. For example, at the same time as our experiments, Sterman (Howe & Sterman, 1972) was delineating the thalamic function in his animal studies with depth electrodes and Andersen and Andersson published insights on alpha mechanisms (Andersen, Andersson, & Lomo, 1967).

Alpha is not merely a "spectral feature." It is a rhythm generated in a complex network including the thalamus and the cortex (Steriade, Gloor, Llinas, Lopes da Silva, & Mesulam, 1990). According to EEG literature, it is the thalamus that sets the frequency of the so-called "background rhythm." There are also noradrenergic inputs from the brainstem and inputs from adjacent cortex that cause increases in the frequency of alpha.

Neurology did not define alpha in the same way the neurotherapy community did: as a frequency band of 8–12 Hz (or 7–13 Hz in some labs). It defined the alpha rhythm as the posteriorly prominent rhythm that attenuates with sensory stimulation, traditionally the opening of the eye (Niedermeyer & da Silva, 2004). It could be as slow as 3–4 Hz, and as fast as 15–16 Hz, but if it went any faster, the rhythmic peaks did not "line up" in phase.

This asynchrony would start to "cancel" the ongoing rhythmic activity of the waveforms with the phase rising or falling at some location. These areas also had other waves rising and falling in the background, for example, at about 15–16 Hz. The rhythm started to "desynchronize" or, in more technical terms, the waves would "phase cancel," creating random phases of the local activity, and they did not persist synchronously to create the rhythmic frequency peaks.

As waveforms become faster, they naturally tend to drop in power. This effect is shown in the classical observation of the EEG's power as being determined by "1/f" (the inverse of the frequency). The faster the EEG frequency, the lower the power is expected to be. However, the phase canceling caused the EEG to drop to extremely lower power levels. This observation in the Fourier analysis, as well as in the raw EEG's peak-to-peak measurement, was seen by the both neurologists and electroencephalographers in their visual analysis of the waveforms.

Often the maximum power peak in the waveforms did not exceed 10–20 microvolts measured peak-to-peak across the entire raw waveform's bandwidth. This peak-to-peak measure is a grand total, and lower power is seen in the traditional EEG spectral bands (delta, theta, alpha, SMR, beta, and gamma).

For the EEG biofeedback training to be successful in slowing the rhythms from a low voltage desynchronized pattern to an EEG with an alpha rhythm, the EEG biofeedback could not merely shape the power spectra in the Fourier analysis. It had to alter the underlying synchronization of the EEG in the cortex, as well as the underlying frequency of the alpha generated by the thalamus, which sets the "speed" of the alpha frequencies.

The alpha rhythm's frequencies are set in the thalamus. This is due to the polarization in the thalamic nuclei, such as the lateral geniculate for surface occipital alpha and the pulvinar nucleus for the surface parietal alpha. These frequencies are projected to the cortex, which controls the spatial and temporal distribution of the alpha. For changes to occur in the alpha band, this entire network has to be altered, not merely treated as an analytic measurement. The low voltage fast EEG condition is achieved when the central nervous system's arousal level is so high that the brainstem produces an excess of NE and the EEG has sped up to the point of desynchronization (Steriade et al., 1990).

Unwinding these changes was the intent of the alpha training in these alpha-deficient clients. We were happy to see the initial subjects respond favorably to the alpha training, especially "Dorothy," who had had the adverse and atypical increase in anxiety with EMG "relaxation" training. In very few sessions, commonly only 10–20, clients who were initially generating no appreciable alpha power began to produce nice background alpha rhythms.

Not only did the alpha power increase as compared to the pre-training condition, but the patients also reported deeply changed levels of anxiety and nervousness. Dorothy had been at the state hospital for over 8 years without a discharge lasting longer than a few days. We told her treatment team that she was done with her training and she reported herself to be much more relaxed. Also, she began going to the dining hall, which previously caused her to panic. Though the authorities at the state hospital had some trouble finding a halfway house due to her prior history of rapidly cycling back to the hospital, they found a placement and she was discharged. Her treatment team said openly that they expected her "back in a few days; if she even lasts that long!"

She never returned, and on follow-up she had a nice routine of going to the library and walking through the small town where she had been placed. Though she was in a halfway house setting, this was a great success, and her care costs dropped precipitously compared to hospitalization.

Other alpha training clients with "just alcoholism" also had good outcomes, reporting their state as changed for the better, without the anxiety and nervousness that "drove them to drink." We thought this was a wonderful new approach for the alcoholics, so in 1974 we submitted a grant to NIMH for "alpha training in alcoholics." The field of EEG biofeedback was unfortunately dismissed by NIMH at that time, which may be because of a poorly designed study (Paskewitz & Orne, 1973) in which the researchers had done "alpha training" for anxiety but could not demonstrate a learning curve. This null finding may have been because of their on-off-on-off training methodology. They concluded that the effects of "alpha training" were not significant or even measurable.

In the intervening years since the denial of funding in 1974, there were others who also worked in this area, including Tom Budzynski with his "twilight trainer" (Budzynski, 1976), and obviously Peniston and Kulkosky in their now-famous work developing the "Peniston Protocol" (Peniston & Kulkosky, 1989). In our work, we did not do the theta portion of the training that Peniston's work incorporated. However, the approach had good clinical outcomes with the alpha-only training in these clients who presented with low voltage fast EEGs.

More recently, this author developed the "phenotype" approach for determining the NF training protocol for individual clients (Johnstone, Gunkelman, & Lunt, 2005). This approach merely matches classical neurotherapy protocols with the specific initial phenotypic EEG patterns that respond to these various protocols. A phenotype is more properly called an endophenotype, which is a genetically linked EEG feature that is an intermediate step between the genetic material of the DNA and behavior. The short list of 11 phenotypic EEG patterns predicts most of the variances of the EEG (Gunkelman, 2006). These patterns are seen in both normal and clinical cases, with the difference being the phenotypical pattern severity.

In the phenotype approach, the LVF EEG gets some initial pre-training doing SMR with beta suppression at C4 or Cz, followed by the alpha/theta work. This is much like the "Scott Protocol" developed by Dr. Bill Scott (see chapter 12) due to the observed side effects of just doing the A/T training. Three of the 11 phenotypic patterns show a CNS over-arousal as a "drive mechanism" for addiction: fast alpha, the LVF pattern, and excessive beta spindling. The LVF and beta spindle patterns get a pre-treatment before the A/T training, and the fast alpha pattern goes directly to the alpha/theta training.

Though the literature supports both the Peniston and Scott protocols as "probably efficacious" for addiction and PTSD (Sokhadze, Cannon, & Trudeau, 2008), not all clients respond to these approaches in addiction or PTSD. Any standardized approach will not fit the entire population but will help a good-sized subset. A customized, targeted approach is the only way to extend the level of success beyond helping the preponderance of the cases.

In 2008, Dr. Curtis Cripe and this author wrote a paper showing the clinical outcomes in 30 cases of addiction (Gunkelman & Cripe, 2008). In the paper, we showed that only two-thirds of the addicted clients had an over-aroused EEG, and the other third had a cingulate issue, which needs a very different approach. The alpha or A/T training are appropriate for the over-arousal, but they do not address the anterior cingulate findings. These require a more direct frontal midline approach, or possibly the use of low resolution electromagnetic tomographic analysis (LORETA) to identify and treat anterior cingulate dysfunction. In our 2008 study, we showed a 100% rate of being clean and sober at one-year follow-up, and we also showed a normalization of neurocognitive function. The Woodcock-Johnson III measured this, with approximately 20-point standard score improvement noted across the full set of subscales, and with no scale worsening (Table 7.1).

The third of the population with anterior cingulate issues requires direct frontal intervention and generally does not respond to posterior alpha or A/T training. The only exception is the beta spindle pattern, which seems to be diminished by the alpha/theta work, albeit indirectly (Gruzelier et al., 2014).

Table 7.1

Changes in Neurocognitive Abilities

Test	Pre	Post
"IQ" (Woodcock Johnson III Cognitive Abilities Test)	99	120
Thinking Ability	103	122
Cognitive Efficiency	94.7	118
Audio-Visual-Learning Ability	88	112
Delayed Recall Ability	65.8	103.6
Working Memory	93	122

Note: There is a 20-point change after alpha or A/T training protocols (Gunkelman & Cripe, 2008).

The application of NF to regulate the LVF pattern appears to be optimal when alpha or A/T training is also incorporated. The LVF pattern is not only seen in addiction but is also commonly seen in anxiety and PTSD. In addition to being included in the efficacy literature on addiction, A/T training has also been shown to be effective in PTSD, where we see over-arousal as the primary issue. PTSD is not merely the exposure to a traumatic experience. Rather, it represents the lack of resilient recovery following the exposure. Treating PTSD requires the lowering of arousal as an initial step, similar to treating phobias with systematic desensitization.

Without the initial dropping of arousal level, further treatment with desensitization is not likely to be fruitful. In our experience with the U.S. military, the LVF pattern, faster alpha, and faster beta spindles load heavily into the PTSD population. All these patterns indicate a CNS over-arousal. Without dealing with the over-arousal, commonly by using NF, the other treatments seem to be relatively less effective. Once the arousal level is dropped, the abreactions seem to wane with time and life "exposure," almost like a systematic desensitization.

I encourage NF therapists who are not familiar with or trained in A/T work to become more familiar with this specialized area of NF. I would recommend getting trained by experienced master clinicians and setting up a mentoring/supervision process. A/T training is not as easy as beta or SMR uptraining, especially due to the need to deal with abreactions. The alpha/theta approach requires additional training and supervision, but the clinical yield is well worth the added efforts, as the very high success rate with the addicted and PTSD populations suggests.

References

Adrian, E. D., & Matthews, B. H. C. (1934). The Berger rhythm: Potential changes from the occipital lobes in man. *Brain, 57*(4), 355–385. https://doi.org/10.1093/brain/57.4.355

Andersen, P., Andersson, S. A., & Lømo, T. (1967). Some factors involved in the thalamic control of spontaneous barbiturate spindles. *The Journal of Physiology, 192*(2), 257–281. https://doi.org/10.1113/jphysiol.1967.sp008299

Budzynski, T. H. (1976). Biofeedback and the twilight states of consciousness. In G. E. Schwartz & D. Shapiro (Eds.), *Consciousness and Self-Regulation* (pp. 361–385). Springer US. https://doi.org/10.1007/978-1-4684-2568-0_9

Fehmi, L. G. (1978). EEG biofeedback, multi-channel synchrony training, and attention. In A. A. Sugarman & R. E. Tarter (Eds.), *Expanding dimensions of consciousness* (pp. 155–182). New York, NY: Springer.

Gibbs, F. A., & Gibbs, E. L. (1952). *Atlas of electroencephalography: Epilepsy.* Cambridge, MA: Addison-Wesley Press.

Gruzelier, J. H., Holmes, P., Hirst, L., Bulpin, K., Rahman, S., Van Run, C., & Leach, J. (2014). Replication of elite music performance enhancement following alpha/theta neurofeedback and application to novice performance and improvisation with SMR benefits. *Biological Psychology*, 95, 96–107.

Gunkelman, J. (2006). Transcend the DSM using phenotypes. *Biofeedback*, 34(3), 95–98.

Gunkelman, J., & Cripe, C. (2008). Clinical outcomes in addiction: A neurofeedback case series. *Biofeedback*, 36(4), 152–156.

Howe, R. C., & Sterman, M. B. (1972). Cortical-subcortical EEG correlates of suppressed motor behavior during sleep and waking in the cat. *Electroencephalography and Clinical Neurophysiology*, 32(6), 681–695.

Johnstone, J., Gunkelman, J., & Lunt, J. (2005). Clinical database development: characterization of EEG phenotypes. *Clinical EEG and Neuroscience*, 36(2), 99–107.

Kamiya, J. (1969). Operant control of the EEG alpha rhythm and some of its reported effects on consciousness. In C. T. Tart (Ed.), *Altered states of consciousness: A book of readings* (1st edition, pp. 507–556). New York: John Wiley & Sons.

Niedermeyer, E., & da Silva, F. L. (Eds.). (2004). *Electroencephalography: Basic principles, clinical applications, and related fields* (Fifth edition). Philadelphia: Lippincott Williams & Wilkins.

Paskewitz, D. A., & Orne, M. T. (1973). Visual effects on alpha feedback training. *Science*, 181(4097), 360–363.

Peniston, E. G., & Kulkosky, P. J. (1989). Alpha-theta brainwave training and beta-endorphin levels in alcoholics. *Alcoholism: Clinical and Experimental Research*, 13(2), 271–279.

Porjesz, B., Almasy, L., Edenberg, H. J., Wang, K., Chorlian, D. B., Foroud, T., ... Rohrbaugh, J. (2002). Linkage disequilibrium between the beta frequency of the human EEG and a GABAA receptor gene locus. *Proceedings of the National Academy of Sciences*, 99(6), 3729–3733.

Sokhadze, T. M., Cannon, R. L., & Trudeau, D. L. (2008). EEG biofeedback as a treatment for substance use disorders: Review, rating of efficacy, and recommendations for further research. *Applied Psychophysiology and Biofeedback, 33*(1), 1–28. https://doi.org/10.1007/s10484-007-9047-5

Steriade, M., Gloor, P., Llinas, R. R., Lopes, de S. F., & Mesulam, M. M. (1990). Report of IFCN Committee on Basic Mechanisms. Basic mechanisms of cerebral rhythmic activities. *Electroencephalography and Clinical Neurophysiology, 76*(6), 481.

Whatmore, G. B., & Kohli, D. R. (1974). *The physiopathology and treatment of functional disorders: Including anxiety states and depression and the role of biofeedback training.* Grune & Stratton.

8

Two Case Studies in Outpatient A/T Training for Trauma

Richard Davis, MS
Eugenia Bodenhamer-Davis, PhD

The two trauma case studies discussed below were selected because they illustrate the range of A/T training applications for adults presenting with symptoms related to trauma that can be encountered in outpatient treatment settings. Eugene Peniston published a report of his 80% success rate treating Vietnam era veterans for PTSD in an inpatient hospital setting (Peniston, Marrinan, Deming, & Kulkosky, 1993). Inpatient settings provide the optimal environment for treating moderate to severe trauma and/or substance abuse with A/T training because they provide the opportunity for daily sessions that can shorten the course of treatment; because pre- and post-session counseling support is readily available to manage and process any abreactive responses; and because frequently encountered resistance behaviors, such as session cancellations or premature dropout, can be minimized. However, none of these advantages are readily available for A/T training provided in private practice or community-based outpatient clinic settings, which almost always complicates the course of treatment. The following cases represent examples of a best-case scenario and a more complicated, prolonged case. The first case, from 2002, was a successful example of a fairly typical course of outpatient treatment for adulthood trauma using a slightly modified version of the original Peniston protocol (Peniston & Kulkosky, 1989, 1999). The second, more recent (2012–2014), case employed a QEEG-guided plus A/T training protocol demonstrating the kind of complications and setbacks that can be encountered when doing outpatient treatment for individuals subjected to multiple life traumas that begin in early childhood.

Case 1

Clinical History

In 2002, J., 59-year-old retired military pilot, presented to a private neurotherapy practice for symptoms that included anxiety, racing thoughts, apathy, fatigue, increased alcohol use, depression, and poor grooming habits. J. believed that his symptoms were related to trauma he had recently experienced. He reported no trauma experiences before the recent one, which he described as follows:

J. entered his garage one evening to smoke a cigarette and watch it rain when he noticed someone at one end of the garage. Thinking it was his elderly neighbor who had a tendency to roam, J. called the man's name; but the person turned, pointed a gun at him, and told him that he was "there for the money." J. told the intruder that there was no money, and without thinking, J.'s "military training from some 20+ years earlier kicked in", and he found himself trying to disarm the intruder. A struggle for the gun ensued, a shot rang out, and J. and intruder both stepped back.

J. mentally scanned his body for a wound, found none, but realized that he had the pistol in his hand. The intruder then said that he had been shot and lunged at J. who then fired the weapon towards the approaching figure. The intruder then slumped against the garage doorjamb and died. J. called 911 and the police arrived, taking J. into custody to sort out the situation. He was later considered a hero for having thwarted a home invasion. Police informed J. that the intruder had worn surgical gloves and no mask, indicating that his intent was to kill his victims after the robbery. One thing J. found unsettling was the fact that he had never seen the face of the intruder because the garage was dark. J. had been unable to deal with the aftermath of this home invasion and shooting event and was referred for neurofeedback treatment.

Treatment Rationale

J.'s clinical presentation, symptom picture, and background story clearly indicated autonomic nervous system (ANS) hyperarousal brought on by his recent trauma. In addition, initial EEG baseline assessment indicated elevated high beta (>25 Hz) and reduced alpha and theta amplitudes, especially at posterior sites. Research literature available at the time of this case indicated that A/T training using the Peniston protocol (Peniston et al., 1993) had demonstrated success in treating adult-onset trauma and symptoms similar to those manifested by J. Since the client had experienced a traumatic event, the possibility of emotional abreaction during the course of A/T treatment had to be considered. Therefore, the treatment plan involved application of the original Peniston protocol because it allowed for protocol modification in case of significant abreaction while focusing on increasing relaxation and reducing autonomic arousal by rewarding increases in alpha and theta brainwave amplitudes at occipital site O1. The only modification to the original Peniston protocol used in this application involved substitution of an EEG biofeedback protocol for the pre-training sessions of temperature biofeedback that Peniston had used. This alternate pre-training protocol involved 10 EEG sessions at C4, inhibiting 4–7 Hz and 20–30 Hz while rewarding 12–15 Hz. This initial "calming" protocol, routinely used successfully by the authors with previous clients, was based on an early protocol advocated by Sue and Siegfried Othmer (Othmer, Othmer & Kaiser, 1999).

Treatment Methodology

Sessions with J. were conducted 3 times a week, outpatient, using Lexicor Biolex software. After 10 sessions at C4 demonstrated reduced standard deviation/variability and amplitude movement in the targeted directions at C4, A/T training began at site O1, rewarding 4–7 Hz theta and 7–12 Hz alpha. Alpha was rewarded when above threshold 70–90 % of the time, and theta was rewarded when above threshold 25–45% of the time. A guided imagery script created with J.'s input was read by the therapist at the beginning of each session, throughout treatment, to induce deep relaxation and focus on feeling safe. Sessions continued three times per week, and session length was a minimum of 30 minutes unless the client, occasionally, opened his eyes to indicate he was finished before the 30 minutes were up.

The first few sessions of A/T training were typical for initial sessions, with little or no movement in the alpha and theta amplitudes. Session 5 showed desired changes in both frequency ranges, and it was evident that the client was settling into the process. By session 8 the alpha and theta amplitudes continued to rise above baseline and were starting to show movement toward possible crossovers (when the amplitude of alpha drops and the amplitude of theta rises above that of alpha). The client also was starting to show signs of deeper relaxation, indicating he was letting go and trusting the process. He was reporting improved sleep by this point in treatment. Impressions from his feedback session were discussed following the completion of feedback at each contact session, but no relevant experiences or memories yet emerged or at least were reported by the client. A/T amplitude progress continued steadily, but slowly, until session 14 when the client canceled his session, stating that he was stopping until his insurance started paying. While insurance reimbursement issues were discussed, the therapist suspected that this abrupt change in attendance suggested resistance to moving forward in treatment. In the authors' experience employing the standard Peniston protocol, resistance behaviors commonly occur at the 10–15 session mark, as clients have achieved deeper relaxation states, higher alpha and theta amplitudes, and crossover activity is imminent or beginning. After 2 weeks of non-attendance, J. called to say that he needed to start sessions again, regardless of insurance, because he was experiencing a return of feelings he had prior to beginning neurofeedback. Sessions resumed the next day.

During sessions 16 & 17 alpha amplitude was starting to decline while theta was slightly rising, suggesting impending crossovers. In session 18 a crossover occurred for a brief period of time, followed a few minutes later by one that lasted for several minutes, after which time J.'s EEG returned to pre-crossover levels for the remainder of the session. When asked after the feedback was completed if any imagery occurred, he told of a "faceless being of white light" suddenly appearing. He felt that this being was "of unconditional love and was offering forgiveness." Asked if this image had any significance for him, the client replied that he thought it was an ex-wife offering him forgiveness. He did not equate his use of the term "faceless" to describe this image with his earlier use of the same term for the "faceless" intruder of his home invasion experience. The therapist made no mention of this coincidence since it was important to allow the client to make his own interpretations of his images (Peniston, et al., 1993).

The next session started with higher initial amplitudes of alpha and theta than in past sessions. Alpha amplitude declined very quickly to meet with theta, and within 8 minutes another crossover appeared that lasted for several minutes, followed by 2 more brief crossovers before the session ended. Afterward, when the therapist asked, "So how did it go for you this time?" J. replied that the "being" had visited him again and was "bathing him in the white light." He stated that he enjoyed this imagery and added that the being took on the role of a "guide, leading him down a street." J. said that he started negotiating with the guide to provide him with more white light in exchange for his willingness to go more distance down the street, because he realized that it was the street to his house. He stated that the imagery experience stopped before he reached the house, however.

Session 20 started again with higher alpha and theta amplitudes than his previous norm. After about 12 minutes, alpha began declining and theta rose for an extended crossover of 8 minutes. When processing the session afterward, J. stated that the guide/being had appeared again and was starting once more to take him down the street. He said that after a short period of time, he told the guide that he did not need to go further because he "knew what this was about." J. said he realized that he had been feeling "vulnerable" since the intruder shooting, which happened less than a month after the September 11 terrorist attack. He said he had felt angry after 9-11 because he had been in the military, "done his job protecting the United States," and retired "with the expectation of being protected." J. expanded his insight by stating that when he and the U.S. were attacked, he had felt that he had not been protected and was vulnerable, in the way he felt after the home invasion. This level of insight and self-awareness, frequently seen in A/T training, can take a participant beyond recalling and desensitizing to events of a past trauma into a broader perspective on his/her life patterns.

A/T training for J. continued for another 10 sessions with some crossover activity, but no imagery that the client felt was significant. The alpha and theta activity continued to strengthen in amplitude with alpha average μV increasing from 5.7 to 7.9 μV and theta from 4.3 to 6.1 μV. By the end of 30 sessions, the client's demeanor had significantly changed from his initial symptom presentation. He looked and reported being calm and relaxed, frequently smiling. His grooming was good, he had energy, reported virtually no racing thoughts, anxiety or depression, and was no longer abusing alcohol. The client called 8 months after completing treatment to discuss having his wife come in for neurofeedback: she was in the house at the time of the invasion incident. The client reported at that time that he was "doing great" and no longer had any issues from the incident. He was grateful for the A/T training work and hoped that he could get his wife to come in as well.

Case 2

Clinical History

The next outpatient case was treated intermittently between 2012 and 2014.

M. was a 66-year-old male, retired high-level business executive who initially sought help for a 26-year history of severe insomnia. He reported chronic difficulty falling asleep, awakening during the night and then being awake for the next 72 or so hours. Additional symptoms included anxiety, chronic fatigue, irritability, and obsessive and racing thought patterns. The client was somewhat obese and had been under a psychiatrist's care for his sleep problems. He had been prescribed several medications that were minimally effective for his sleep. M. reported being a Vietnam combat veteran, and his initial symptom assessment suggested the possibility of long term post-traumatic stress from the war. However, M. did not initially identify any trauma in his life, and stated that he was seeking treatment only for chronic insomnia. His pre-treatment QEEG showed a low voltage/fast pattern (low EEG strength of signal and predominately fast frequency activity above 20 Hz), particularly at vertex sites Fz, Cz and Pz, consistent with the client's family history of alcoholism and the M.'s possible PTSD (Ehlers & Schuckit, 1990; Jokić-Begić & Begić, 2003). Although the client denied any personal history of alcohol or drug abuse, he said both his father and brother were alcoholics. This vertex pattern of excessive fast (20–30 Hz) and slow (2–7 Hz) activity can be associated with such transdiagnostic symptoms as obsessiveness, compulsivity, anxiety, insomnia, and depression, and is a pattern related to overall psychophysiological hyperarousal (Johnstone, Gunkelman & Lunt, 2005).

Treatment Rationale

Since M.'s initial symptom report and QEEG results supported a tentative hypothesis that his chronic psychophysiological hyperarousal pattern contributed to his insomnia and was possibly exacerbated by symptoms of PTSD from his earlier combat experiences, an initial treatment plan to improve his sleep included a multi-modal biofeedback protocol supplemented by cognitive-behavioral counseling and coaching to teach him self-directed relaxation skills that could be used prior to bedtime. Heart rate variability (HRV) biofeedback along with EEG biofeedback training at vertex sites were chosen to teach M. better breathing and relaxation patterns and reduce autonomic arousal. The therapist delayed a diagnosis of combat-related PTSD until additional confirming evidence might be gathered from the client as treatment progressed, in which case A/T training might be considered as well.

Treatment Methodology

Treatment began with twice-weekly sessions. HRV biofeedback pre-training was attempted in the first couple of sessions, but discontinued because M. found attempts to slow his rapid, shallow breathing very difficult and frustrating. Thus, only neurofeedback was used, in addition to counseling and coaching, for the first portion of M.'s treatment. Using BrainMaster Atlantis 3.7 software, neurofeedback began at Fz, inhibiting 2–7 Hz and 20–30 Hz activity. No frequencies were rewarded in this initial EEG protocol. Rationale for this frontal vertex starting point was the predominance in the client's QEEG of fast and slow activity at this location over the anterior cingulate associated with symptoms of autonomic hyperarousal, impulsivity and anxiety. In addition, the authors have found that improving frontal lobe attention and inhibitory functions prior to initiating treatment for trauma and related disorders can, along with other strategies described later, improve client management of any emotional abreactive responses to A/T training.

Observation of initial session EEG recordings showed 15+ μV of 2–7 Hz and 12–15 μV of 20–30 Hz activity that included a large amount of EMG artifact. As sessions progressed, visual feedback in the form of bar graphs indicating changes in amplitude levels relative to thresholds were manually set by the therapist.

M. gradually began to produce reductions in both the variability and amplitudes of the three targeted frequency bands. By session 8, he was reporting that he was sleeping a little longer before awakening, but was still having difficulty going to sleep at an acceptable hour. Often he was not able to fall asleep until dawn. Since sleep was improving, training at Fz continued until session 15, when the active electrode location was moved to Cz where the previous multi-inhibit protocol continued. The 2–7 Hz activity at Cz again was 15+ μV and the 20–30 Hz activity in excess of 10 μV, with more EMG artifact than was seen at the frontal site due to jaw clenching. Instruction was given to eliminate the jaw clenching, but M. still was unable to relax these muscles. By session 16 he was reporting going to sleep at near normal bedtime hours and sleeping through most of the night. At session 18 he reported going to sleep by 11 p.m. and sleeping through the night for the past three nights. He was very happy with these changes.

However, as M.'s sleep began improving, his session attendance had become sporadic, with many cancellations and some no-shows, slowing his overall progress. Eventually he completed the targeted goal of 30 sessions for stabilizing his acquired EEG changes at frontal and central sites. Although each session during this first round of treatment included discussion of M.'s sleep adjustment and related issues, he had offered little additional information about himself beyond mentioning his recent retirement and previous work experiences.

However, 6 months later M. called and reported that he was having sleep problems again and wanted to reinitiate neurofeedback. When he arrived for the second round of sessions, his physical appearance was markedly improved from his initial intake over a year earlier. He had lost a significant amount of weight following bariatric surgery, working out regularly with a personal trainer, and playing golf regularly.

A second quantitative EEG was recorded and compared to the

previous year's QEEG. The comparison showed that although previous levels of excessive fast and slow activity in the frontal vertex at Fz and Cz had decreased, along with diffuse slow activity, elevated 2–7 Hz activity remained at these sites. Although not targeted in the earlier training sessions, previously excessive 8–9 Hz parietal alpha with eyes open had decreased as well. Increases also were seen in left frontal and occipital 20–30 Hz activity that was related primarily to EMG muscle artifact (and demonstrating the client's continuing muscle tension). Most of the changes seen in the second map could be attributed to M.'s previous neurofeedback training focused on inhibiting slow and fast activity in frontal and central regions. However, the second map, along with M.'s continuing sleep and anxiety symptoms, indicated the need for additional neurofeedback to address his symptoms.

During the first session after his return, discussion included the importance of both consistency and continuity of training to attain and sustain acceptable sleep patterns. Also, the possibility of past trauma as a continuing contributor to his insomnia was revisited, a topic he avoided during the earlier treatment period. The therapist suggested the client needed to acquire the willingness and motivation to deal with unresolved emotional issues instead of looking for a quick fix. This opened a discussion of eventually utilizing A/T training to address possible trauma experiences, after more progress was made to reduce frontocentral site elevations. Six more sessions were completed at Fz and six more at Cz. Again his attendance was sporadic, and sleep problems would wax and wane with attendance. However, over time, the frequency ranges being inhibited continued to show improvements.

He came to understand the link between EMG and his jaw tension and would work during sessions to keep his jaw relaxed, significantly decreasing the EMG and thereby decreasing the strength of the 20–30 Hz activity. He felt empowered by discovering this control over his physiology. The active electrode location was then moved to P4, inhibiting 2–7 Hz, 20–30 Hz, and enhancing 12–15 Hz to help further relax the client and to ready him for A/T treatment. (This therapist has found the P4 site to be even more effective than C4 for a calming protocol with some clients.)

During one of these return sessions M. finally began to reveal more personal information and history, stating, "I have not told very many people this..." and related that his mother had died when he was 12, after which he ran away from home to avoid beatings from his alcoholic father. His mother had deflected the beatings from the children, but after her death, the father turned to beating the client and his siblings. The client stated that after leaving home he lived in old cars at a junk yard. He met his future wife when he was 15, and her parents took him in. He lived with them until age 17, when he lied about his age and enlisted for military service in Vietnam.

During combat in Vietnam he saw much death and carnage, and those memories remained very unsettling for him. The therapist suggested that his sleep problems might be rooted in his having to be hypervigilant during the night when living in the junkyard cars, laying down an early pattern of anxious, disrupted sleep. He immediately understood the connection and added that everything in Vietnam went on at night as well, which he felt could have furthered the problem. Following a couple of sessions discussing the client's past traumatic life experiences, neurofeedback resumed for two more sessions at P4, partly to continue a protocol that was calming to him, and then moved into A/T training.

Frequency settings for the A/T training sessions were based

Two Case Studies in Outpatient A/T Training for Trauma

on QEEG findings and consisted of rewarding 5–8 Hz for theta (the default setting for theta on the BrainMaster equipment used) and 8–12 Hz for alpha, throughout the twice-weekly sessions. The program also was set to include a 2–5 Hz delta inhibit (to address sleep during sessions if necessary) and a 20–30 Hz beta inhibit (if anxiety or muscle tension artifact should interfere during sessions); but ultimately these two contingency settings were not needed and were used only for monitoring purposes. Alpha was rewarded when above threshold 70–90 % of the time, and theta was rewarded when above threshold 25–45% of the time. Because of the client's skepticism regarding guided visualizations, simple progressive and autogenic relaxation instructions were recited by the therapist at the start of each 30-minute session. The first session contained a couple of brief, low amplitude crossovers (see minutes 18–23 in Figure 8.1 graph of this session).

Note the temporary drop in alpha amplitude beginning at minute 18.5 and subsequent elevation of theta and delta at or above alpha for the remainder of the session. This crossover contains the elements of a "therapeutic crossover" described in chapter 6: an increase in theta and delta amplitudes above alpha along with an increase in beta amplitude. The dominance of delta in this crossover configuration was consistent with the

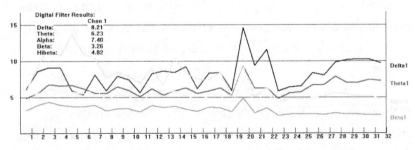

Figure 8.1. Graph of M's first A/T training session with brief crossover.

"transpersonal" category of imagery reported by the client.

When asked at the end of this session if any imagery had appeared, the client reported that he had seen a brief image: "... of a child in an old fashioned wooden row boat (like an old, high sided, life boat) that was floating/swirling in the air and the child was hanging onto one oar so as to not fall out of the boat." When the therapist inquired further, M. was unsure of any significance of the imagery other than "it was dangerous." The therapist did not challenge M.'s interpretations of his own imagery experiences during the A/t training and did not offer alternative interpretations. In this session, M. continued spontaneously, relating how as a teenager living in the junkyard car he once awakened to a rat staring at him, an event which "scared him big time." After the therapist empathized with M.'s feelings about this incident, M. started to talk about Vietnam, stating that "everything there also always went on at night." He also mentioned that when he was in school, he regularly worked the graveyard shift from midnight to 8:00 a.m., adding, "It feels safe to go to sleep when the sun comes up."

The therapist complemented M.'s insight regarding origins of his sleep pattern. Prior to starting the second A/T training session, the client reported that he had slept through the night for the last two nights and felt very good. The second A/T training session was not quite as good as the first because the client remained more alert and couldn't settle into a relaxed state. Alpha and theta amplitudes did not increase significantly during the session.

In the authors' experience this temporary backing away from a "reverie state" immediately following a session containing an emotional imagery event is a common pattern observed during the course of A/T training. This pattern may be another form of temporary resistance to confronting emotionally difficult memories, but also could be seen as serving an important self-protective pacing function for the individual, posing only a brief delay in treatment progress. By the third session, the client was more relaxed and settled quickly into alpha and theta amplitude increases. Approximately 18 minutes into the session his physiology started to shift. Respiration increased, and it appeared that his eyes were moving rapidly under the lids. There were slight head and shoulder movements as well. Alpha amplitude was starting to reduce gradually, and theta amplitude was increasing, a precursor to a crossover that occurred at the 18-minute mark, followed by another at 23 minutes (Figure 8.2).

Note: This crossover also conforms to the parameters described in chapter 6 for a "therapeutic crossover," this one producing a memory of Viet Nam combat. At 32 minutes he opened his eyes, looked at the therapist, and said he was "in Vietnam and could see the bodies." He closed his eyes and continued the feedback session for another 5 minutes. He came out of the session saying that he wasn't ready "to go there again today." Following session debriefing, the client still appeared drowsy and a bit unsettled, so 10 minutes of eyes open Fz training,

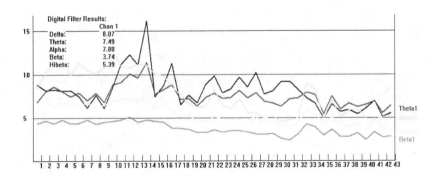

Figure 8.2. Graph of M's third A/T training session showing extended crossover (18–23 minutes).

inhibiting 2–7 Hz and 20–30 Hz, was done to help stabilize him physically and emotionally and to assure an alert state before he left the office. He departed looking forward to good sleep.

The fourth A/T training session was uneventful with amplitudes remaining steady throughout the session (the "backing away" pattern again). The fifth session showed several crossovers, and at 22 minutes a crossover began that lasted 10 minutes. As this crossover started, he opened his eyes and said, "I am back in Vietnam; this is powerful stuff." Then he closed his eyes for the remainder of the session. It is worth noting that this session took place on September 11, an anniversary of the 9-11 terrorist attack. This client's job in 2001 had involved him directly in some of the 9-11 events, adding to his history of trauma.

The sixth session was uneventful beyond a couple of short crossovers lasting less than 3 minutes. His average alpha amplitude had increased from 7.4 µV in his first A/T training session to 11.14 µV by this sixth session, demonstrating his ability to significantly increase his alpha amplitudes through the course of A/T training thus far. As well, his average theta amplitude had increased from 6.23 µV to 7.38. By this session of A/T training, M. was also going to sleep at a reasonable bedtime hour and sleeping through the night, something he was not doing consistently prior to the A/T training sessions. However, at this point in the treatment, and following last session's lengthy crossover with Vietnam memories, he informed the therapist that he needed to stop treatment for a while because his wife was having surgery. He did not return for neurotherapy for over 6 weeks.

Attempts to contact M. during this time were unsuccessful because, according to family members, he took to the road in his motor home after telling his wife that he needed to have some time to himself. Follow-up contacts with family also revealed that M. and his wife had briefly participated in marriage

Two Case Studies in Outpatient A/T Training for Trauma

counseling, and he had entered an out-of-state treatment program for PTSD, which he found unhelpful. Family reported that the client's sleep had improved over his initial baseline level of a year earlier, but his sleep problems persisted.

Six weeks later, M. contacted the therapist to report that he wanted to start neurofeedback again. He had attended a PTSD treatment program sponsored by the VA, but found it unhelpful. He stated he had prayed about what to do, and kept hearing that "he needed to return to neurofeedback."

He stated a strong commitment to remaining consistent with sessions and agreed to increase his number of sessions from two to four times a week. The therapist returned to site Fz for additional sessions, inhibiting 4–7 and 20–30 Hz, to further improve the client's attention, concentration and sleep which seemed to have deteriorated slightly since his last session 6 weeks earlier. At this time as well, each neurofeedback session was preceded by 10–20 minutes of heart rate variability (HRV) biofeedback, which M. had been unable to do when he first began treatment. This time he was able to respond more positively to the HRV training, showing steady improvement in his ability to slow his breathing and pulse rate.

However, after four sessions, M. called to say that he was having his thyroid checked due to extreme fatigue. He missed the next week of treatment while his thyroid medication was changed and his fatigue subsided. A week later, he resumed the combined HRV and Fz neurofeedback sessions, again making steady progress even though his endocrinologist had said that it would take 7 weeks to stabilize his medication. At the fourth session after his break for thyroid treatment, he achieved 89% in the high-performance category on the EmWave HRV program, after achieving a high of only 48% during previous sessions.

As mentioned above, M. had not been able to do HRV

biofeedback or control his breathing rate when he first began treatment, so this evidence of better physiological control was seen as an indication of the cumulative effects of the intermittent neurofeedback and HRV biofeedback treatment he had completed up to this point. He was again reporting improvements in all presenting symptoms, including reduced anxiety, racing thoughts, and irritability, as well as very good sleep. His physical appearance and mood were significantly improved over his initial presentation months earlier. At the time this chapter was submitted for publication, the therapist and client planned to resume alpha/ theta neurofeedback sessions that could potentially re-expose M. to emotional memories from his past.

Doubling the number of weekly sessions will permit closer monitoring of M.'s response to each treatment session. The successful reintroduction of HRV biofeedback training into his treatment regimen has provided M. greater coping skills and confidence in his ability to manage his own physiology and emotions under stressful conditions. He was urged to regularly practice his newly acquired breathing patterns at home between sessions. These modifications to the previous neurofeedback program should provide additional support for M. if and when he encounters more emotionally difficult material when A/T training sessions resume and minimize factors that could again delay his completion of A/T treatment.

This case illustrates the treatment limitations often seen in A/T training when emotional memory experiences emerge without adequate external supports to maintain client motivation to complete the treatment process. Peniston advised consistency and persistence in moving clients through the often painful abreactive process, doubling up on sessions if necessary until resolution is reached. However, this type of supportive structure is not always possible, especially in an outpatient setting. This case also demonstrates the stronger and more intractable defenses that must be dealt with in treatment programs for clients whose trauma initiated in childhood as opposed to adulthood, and for individuals with multiple and/or prolonged trauma episodes.

Recommendations for working with these types of clients include inpatient treatment if possible, or good external supports to preclude session cancellations and drop-outs. In addition, initiating treatment with QEEG-based protocols to improve overall brain regulation, as well as pre-training to a mastery criterion in psychophysiological stress coping skills, can provide additional assistance to get clients through difficult stages in the A/T training process. However, even though such precautions were taken in this case and there was good therapist-client rapport, results were nevertheless delayed because of the client's poor adherence to a regular treatment schedule, co-occurring medical condition, and reluctance to confront emerging traumatic memories.

The first author has used the QEEG-based-then-alpha-theta approach described above with consistently better results in inpatient settings. As described above, completing QEEG-based eyes-open training for 25–40 sessions (depending on severity) at frontal, central and/or parietal sites related to client symptoms, before moving to O1 for A/T training, consistently requires 10 or fewer A/T training sessions to complete overall symptom resolution. In this QEEG-based approach, crossovers and abreactions can be expected to occur within one to four A/T training sessions, and then a few more sessions can be done to insure stabilization.

As the first case discussed above suggests, traditional Peniston protocol A/T training usually required 8–15 alpha/theta sessions beyond the initial 6–10 breathing or eyes-open EEG pre-training sessions before clients began producing crossovers and to process emotional issues. The authors believe that it is during these initial sessions that the brain is learning the neurofeedback process and therapeutic trust is formed. The QEEG-supplemented approach allows the client to learn the neurophysiological self-regulation process and develop the therapeutic trust while doing eyes open training first, allowing subsequent alpha-theta work to go faster, but just as effectively.

References

Ehlers, C. L., & Schuckit, M. A. (1990). EEG fast frequency activity in the sons of alcoholics. *Biological Psychiatry, 27*(6), 631–641. https://doi.org/10.1016/0006-3223(90)90531-6

Johnstone, J., Gunkelman, J., & Lunt, J. (2005). Clinical database development: Characterization of EEG phenotypes. *Clinical EEG and Neuroscience, 36*(2), 99–107.

Jokić-Begić, N., & Begić, D. (2003). Quantitative electroencephalogram (qEEG) in combat veterans with post-traumatic stress disorder (PTSD). *Nordic Journal of Psychiatry, 57*(5), 351–355.

Othmer, S., Othmer, S. F., & Kaiser, D. A. (1999). EEG biofeedback: An emerging model for its global efficacy. In J. R. Evans & A. Abarbanel (Eds.), *Introduction to quantitative EEG and neurofeedback* (pp. 243–310). Cambridge, MA: Academic Press.

Peniston, E. G., & Kulkosky, P. J. (1989). Alpha-theta brainwave training and beta-endorphin levels in alcoholics. *Alcoholism: Clinical and Experimental Research, 13*(2), 271–279.

Peniston, E. G., & Kulkosky, P. J. (1999). Neurofeedback in the treatment of addictive disorders. In J. R. Evans & A. Abarbanel (Eds.), *Introduction to quantitative EEG and neurofeedback*. Academic Press.

Peniston, E. G., Marrinan, D. A., Deming, W. A., & Kulkosky, P. J. (1993). EEG alpha-theta synchronization in Vietnam theater veterans with combat-related PTSD and alcohol abuse. *Medical Psychotherapy, 6*, 37–50.

9

Alpha-Theta Training in the Treatment of Dissociative Identity Disorder

Dan Chartier, PhD

In the early use of alpha (8–12 Hz)-theta (4–8 Hz) band neurofeedback, the work of Peniston and Kulkosky (1989, 1990) was adapted by clinicians for treatment of patients with significant psychiatric challenges. Hardt (1978) also reported the facilitation of personality change through the development of voluntary control of alpha EEG activity. Initially, Peniston and Kulkosky reported success in treating veterans with alcoholism. A subsequent publication by Peniston and Kulkosky (1991) reported success in the use of alpha-theta training neurofeedback (A/T training) in the treatment of patients with post-traumatic stress disorder (PTSD).

Carol Manchester, a clinical psychologist in the northeastern US, published a report of her work following Peniston's and Kulkosky's lead, applying an A/T training protocol in the successful treatment of dissociative identity disorder (DID), previously identified as "multiple personality disorder" (MPD; Manchester, Allen, & Tachiki, 1998). Dr. Manchester's clinical rationale for applying an A/T training protocol was straightforward: extreme traumatic stress was an apparent key factor in the development of DID. Therefore, a treatment method that was successful in treating PTSD should be helpful in the treatment of patients diagnosed with DID. Summarizing this perspective, Manchester, Allen, & Tachiki (1998) wrote:

Peniston and co-workers (1989, 1990, 1991, 1993) report that neurofeedback is a process by which patients can be trained to remain partly conscious and still access traumatic anxiety-provoking images and thus allowing the integration of past traumatic experiences with previously unresolved conflicts within the context of anxiety-free memories of a newly learned state of consciousness. Based on these reports, we hypothesized that the integration of neurofeedback techniques with internal self-exploration could allow DID patients to utilize their mind's own naturalistic means of self-healing through an experience of reassociation and reorganization of their own experiences to bring about unification. A brain state achievable through neurofeedback (i.e., a window of opportunity) could enable patients to integrate traumatic memories while in a state of low arousal, thereby minimizing the risk of retraumatization (Kissin, 1986).

Soon after hearing Dr. Manchester present her work at a conference in 1991, I replicated her treatment methods in clinical practice. The following is a case discussion of my first experience with the use of A/T training in the treatment of a DID patient.

Case History

Ms. D was 50 years old when she was referred by her neurologist for biofeedback treatment for chronic severe headaches. In the referral note, the neurologist indicated that Ms. D's atypical response to standard treatment and her level of physical tension suggested the presence of psychophysiological factors that could be addressed with biofeedback (BFB) training.

At the intake session, Ms. D presented her history of

suffering episodic severe headaches beginning at age 16. She described herself as a former software developer who had become a "soccer mom" raising three sons. She identified multiple sources of stress and depression, including her youngest (16-year-old) son's underachieving in high school, and her two young adult sons' various misadventures (the oldest son was hitchhiking in Mexico and had been robbed of all his money and clothes). She described her husband as an alcohol-abusing workaholic who was "unsupportive" and "withdrawn from the family." The psychophysiological baseline obtained for Ms. D as a component of the intake process found elevated frontalis surface EMG (sEMG; > 5.0 uV), normal peripheral temperature (93 °F), and elevated electrodermal response (EDR). A Millon Behavioral Health Inventory (1981) completed by Ms. D identified "chronic tension" as a significant factor in her medical presentation.

In brief, the clinical impression was that of a moderately stressed middle-aged woman with a history of severe headaches exacerbated by current family stressors. She appeared to be an appropriate candidate for a course of biofeedback to assist her in reducing her tension and reactivity levels while developing appropriate coping and stress management skills.

Over the next 6 months, Ms. D completed 20 multimodal biofeedback training sessions, including sEMG (reduction), peripheral temperature (elevation), and EDR (reduction/stabilization). In brief, the goal was to assist her in improving her ability to self-regulate and reduce tension. Initially, she was seen once per week, and then tapered to bi-monthly sessions as her self-regulation skills developed. Her headache presentation showed some improvement, with decreased frequency. However, she continued to have occasional (about 2x/month) severe headaches.

Her lack of a robust response to basic BFB/self-regulation training and comments that she made during some of the training sessions revealed her significant underlying psychological distress. For example, she described her father as a "perfectionist" career military officer with a "drinking problem." She stated: "I never did enough to get his approval." She also said that when she was 10 years old her mother had a "nervous breakdown" and was hospitalized. Following the hospitalization, Ms. D's mother went to live with her mother (Ms. D's grandmother) for several years. During the time of her mother's absence, Ms. D was forced by her father into the role of housekeeper and supervisor of her two younger brothers. While not directly stated at that time, Ms. D made comments to suggest that the roles her father forced her to take on went beyond housework and child care.

Subsequent therapy sessions over the next two months included a continuation of BFB and psychotherapy utilizing methods developed by David Grove (Grove & Panzer, 1989), including a "metaphoric process" for resolving traumatic memories (RTM). In this process, any memory fragment, physical sensation, or emotion can serve as an entry point to access relevant repressed/subconscious information. As the RTM process proceeds, the focus is on the therapist's careful use of simple language to facilitate the client's staying connected to the relevant original event and moving through it. Prior experience with this method of therapy had demonstrated effectiveness in "bypassing" defensive cognitive filters to facilitate engagement at a deeper psycho-emotional level.

At this point in the process, the goal was to help Ms. D "mature" through whatever it was that she was re-experiencing by using simple encouraging phrases such as, "And what could happen next?" or "And then you might be interested in what happens next." The event "maturing" suggestions were continued with the addition of comments like, "And you might be interested in noticing how long this happens" and "And how long could it be before something else happens?" The goal was to assist Ms. D. in moving through the repressed elements of the original trauma that led to a defensive detachment from the actual flow of time, which left her in a psychically suspended state of perpetually being in an emotional space of "just before" the really bad thing happened. The next development in the treatment process for Ms. D was a therapeutic game changer and led to the use of A/T training as a central therapy process.

The change in therapy began when Ms. D came in for a session and was visibly distressed. She proceeded to describe a disturbing event from the day before. She said that on the previous morning she had agreed to meet a bowling league teammate for some practice at their local bowling alley. She recalled getting up that morning, dressing in bowling attire, loading her bag with her bowling ball and shoes into her mini-van, and heading out.

Her next "awareness" was a sense of "waking up" while still driving her minivan, but she was in a completely unfamiliar part of the city. It was now nearly noon and there were several Hispanic men in the van with her. She said that her initial response was sheer terror but she was able to maintain an appearance of calm while she listened to the men's conversation. Her fluency in Spanish was sufficient for her to understand that she had apparently stopped to help when she came upon the men at their broken-down car. She had offered to transport them to their workplace. She proceeded to drop them off, then went back to her house, confused and shaken by the bizarre experience of lost time and memory.

Upon arriving home, she found multiple messages on her home answering machine (this was prior to cell phones) from her friend, each subsequent message escalating a tone of concern: "Are you running late?" "Where are you?" "Are you OK?"

Ms. D described her experience for the rest of that day as disoriented, spacey, and exhausted—physically and emotionally. She stated that she believed she was "losing her mind—going crazy."

As we discussed the previous day's events, it was evident that Ms. D had experienced a significant dissociative experience. I provided reassurance that a number of causal factors can produce these events. She was encouraged to consult with her neurologist to rule out physical causes and she was asked to do some "homework" consisting of reflecting on any prior odd experiences that might include "significant forgetting," "lost time," or other odd occurrences. She was encouraged to talk with family members and close trusted friends to ask if they had observed her demonstrating any particularly odd behavior.

At the next treatment session, Ms. D brought in a diagram that looked like a flow chart. She handed it over, then uncharacteristically sat silently, presenting as timid/shy. When asked to explain the diagram, she haltingly began to describe the unfolding of her realization of the "people" who lived inside her and "took turns" being in charge. In the diagram, "S" represented her given first name. Then, to help S escape from/cope with the abuse from her father, Wendy (W) emerged. Over the course of multiple abusive events, her "splitting" continued, giving rise to multiple "entities/personalities" to contain and respond to the abuse in order to protect S and W. She described the solid lines as representing personalities that had endured over time while the hashed lines represented personalities that had emerged and later faded to a less active/ present position. She said, "I am Christie" (C; the person who was talking), describing herself as the "watcher," a "spirit older than she is" (referring to S) and also saying, "I am calm, peaceful and safe, able to see the good in everybody." Andy (A) was described as a "boy" personality

A/T Training in the Treatment of Dissociative Identity Disorder

who could do the physical things, e.g., sports, that Ms. D's father demanded. Wendy became the older caretaker of a "group" of children, including more prominent personalities of Karen (K), Vickie (V), and Veronica (V).

The following is an excerpt from Mrs. D's psychological record and reveals the type of revelations that occurred in subsequent therapy sessions. This example is offered to provide context regarding the personality splitting process and the resultant creation of her alternate personalities.

> Ms. D came in for an unscheduled "emergency" session saying that she was feeling significant anxiety and agitation and believed "something" was "connecting." In that session, the Grove RTM method was used. Ms. D was sitting in a reclining chair, relaxed (as much as possible given her agitated state), with her eyes closed. She was asked to stay with and focus on the feelings of anxiousness and agitation that she was experiencing instead of trying to stop or escape from them. As she followed the simple focusing suggestions, she began crying and started to move in the chair in a spasmodic/twitching manner. Then, as if she were melting, she began to slide out of the chair onto the floor until she was on her side in a fetal position sobbing uncontrollably; she clearly had engaged in a significant emotional process. Continuing to sob in what appeared to be an emotionally and physically distressed, altered state, Ms. D began to use her legs to push herself along the floor in a large circle. As the intensity of her experience continued, she began a spontaneous nosebleed, leaving a copious blood trail in a circle on the carpet (this method of therapy is not for the fainthearted).
>
> As Ms. D progressed through the event, her sliding (and bleeding) across the carpet slowed, then stopped. She

collected herself, clearly appearing to be back in the present. She got up from the floor and resumed sitting in the chair, pulling out multiple tissues from a nearby box to wipe the tears from her face. As she wiped her face she seemed surprised but not distressed by the blood on the tissues. She then commented, "Wow, that was amazing." Her anxious, agitated mood had resolved. She then proceeded to describe the event she had just worked through. As she spoke, her voice tone, posture, and gestures took on a distinctly masculine quality. She said that she had just relived an event from her childhood. When she was 10 years old, her father had taken her to a community swimming pool to teach her to do dives from the highest diving board. She climbed up the ladder and walked out onto the board. Then, realizing how high up she was, she became frightened.

Despite her father's angry insistence that she jump, she refused and climbed back down the ladder. When she got to the bottom of the ladder her father punched her in the face, bloodying her nose and knocking her down. He then continued to verbally assault her, telling her she was weak like her mother, a wimp, etc. Ms. D said that in the midst of her father's diatribe, Andy appeared.

This "boy" took over, climbed the ladder, and did the dive. Thereafter Andy would come forward in situations requiring athletic skill or masculine strength.

A/T Training

It was a logical next step to offer A/T training in the treatment of Ms. D. She met the diagnostic criteria for DID. We discussed the A/T training option and she agreed to begin neurofeedback. Because Ms. D had completed multiple biofeedback training sessions as described above, we were able to proceed directly to NFB.

The course of NFB treatment began with daily (Monday–Friday) sessions. Each session included 30 minutes of eyes-closed alpha (8–12 Hz) and theta (4–8 Hz) feedback with an audio tone indicating band magnitude > threshold. Per Peniston and Manchester, the active sensor was placed at O1 referenced to the right earlobe with the ground sensor on the left earlobe. The equipment used was a Lexicor Biolex with v200 software (1995). The Lexicor-Biolex system provided a flexible feedback experience including the setting of multiple thresholds with unique tones indicating when band magnitude had exceeded a threshold. For example, a basic audio feedback command would be: "if (alpha > threshold); Frq = 220," meaning a frequency tone at 220 Hz would occur when alpha band magnitude exceeded a set microvolt threshold. The ability to set multiple thresholds, each with a unique tonal frequency, provided a pleasant, compelling reinforcement for increasing alpha and theta activation.

The feedback segment of each session was followed by a 15–20-minute debriefing/discussion of her experience. She was already familiar with verbal processing of emerging psychoemotional awareness and was thus able to understand and work with the request that she also make notes after each session using the following topics (per the Manchester-Peniston A/T training Protocol):

- Images/recollections/what came up
- Meaning of the images/recollections
- I learned/became aware that
- Actions—I will
- Affirmation (repeated 200x/day)

These focusing/cognitive processing exercises were particularly helpful for Ms. D. The following are excerpts from some key A/T training post-session notes. Early on she noted:

> That sound [audio feedback for alpha > threshold] was present when I wasn't going anywhere. It would stop if I started going off into some thought pattern or memory. There was a sense of choice about what I thought about. Also a feeling of everybody (personalities) looking out for everybody else.

She was beginning to experience the "neutral observer state" typically associated with increasing alpha amplitude and duration. Alpha EEG activity has been referred to as the brain's idling rhythm—what the brain does when it is not engaged in more active cognitive processes. In this state of consciousness, patients report a comfortable, detached awareness in which they can "watch" an unfolding memory without experiencing the reactions that occurred in the original event. There is a sense of "I" that exists as the observer of an experience instead of the "I" immersed in the turmoil of the experience.

clearly shows the emergence of an ability to selectively increase band magnitude levels of alpha and theta, a pattern that continued throughout the treatment protocol. As treatment progressed, she noted:

> Sometimes I feel present but totally disconnected from my body, from my mind. I feel like a pair of eyes without a face, without a head. Other times I feel like I'm in another's body and mind and it's a good comfortable fit, but doesn't really belong to me, it's just borrowed. Yet it's warm and snug and fine for now. I feel a gentle tug like a gravitational pull, which I seem to want to follow, to explore. I have no idea where it wants to lead me, to take me... but it feels safe. I feel the

absence of desperation. But I don't remember ever really feeling the desperation being present.

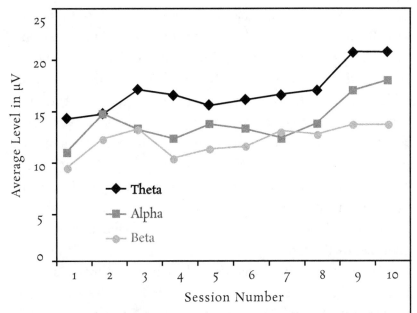

Figure 9.1. Within the first ten A/T training NFB sessions, successful increasing of average microvolt levels of the target frequencies (Alpha: 8–12 Hz, Theta: 4–8 Hz) is seen. Beta (16–20 Hz) was periodically included.

These comments suggest that she was beginning to appreciate a sense of safety within the exploration/observation of her inner landscape. Thus, continued her subjective experience as typically described by individuals who learn to increase 4–8 Hz and 8–12 Hz activation.

Therapeutic progress is rarely without challenge. For Ms. D there were some rougher, more challenging developments during A/T training. For example, there were occasions when, at the end of the feedback portion of the session, Ms. D would be unresponsive—not appearing to be "normally" asleep but in a deep trance state. On those occasions, 10 minutes of beta (16–20 Hz) enhancement feedback would be provided to support conscious re-activation.

There were also some manifestations of resistance to the process. Some early sessions led to her noting in her post-session journal, "Going back to something. Fear, fear that was always there" and "I am Andy and Andy is me." Initially, the resistance took the form of her showing up late for her appointments and wanting to "just talk" to avoid doing the feedback process. She then expressed a direct desire to stop the protocol. These expressions of resistance were discussed as a normal occurrence of the fear of change. It seemed they were the expression of the more dominant controlling personalities like "Andy." Ultimately Ms. D, with the encouragement of her best friend, agreed to continue treatment.

Therapeutically her behavior and comments were consistent with the psycho-emotional manifestation of "resistance on the verge of change." After 4 weeks of daily (Monday–Friday) treatment sessions, to soften the intensity of the process, the frequency of treatment sessions was reduced to two to three sessions per week.

At this time, a consultation with Dr. Manchester also proved helpful in assisting Ms. D in continuing the protocol. Dr. Manchester suggested the inclusion of photic-stimulation at 14 Hz (via LED goggles) to help diminish anxiety by modulating the depth of immersion in traumatic experiences while facilitating a more "present" awareness during the feedback process.

Following the first session during which the 14 Hz photo-stimulation was used, Ms. D stated, "You made Judy cry. Judy is remembering things that hurt her." The use of the photo-stimulation was continued and subsequently Ms. D reported that she found it to be helpful, an assertion that was supported by higher alpha band magnitude levels.

As treatment continued, resistance periodically re-emerged. In retrospect, it appeared to intensify just before there was a resolution (absorption) of one or more of the personalities. It was as if the resistance were a last attempt at maintaining existence before relinquishing the protective role the personality had served.

A poignant example of the personality absorption process was expressed during a debriefing session in which she shared the following story. The personality identified as Wendy had been in the role of caretaker/protector of a group of child personalities. During the feedback session, in her subjective experience, a scene developed in which Wendy and the children were in a sunlit meadow playing a game of Ring-Around-the-Rosie. As the game concluded each child, one by one, came up to Wendy hugged her, then moved past her. When the last child had hugged her and moved past her, Wendy turned to see that they had all disappeared and she knew they were now all happy and safe, no longer needing her care.

In the final weeks of her A/T training, Ms. D continued to report a sense of integration of self and a deeper understanding of her trauma history. In one of her post-session notes, she expressed a significant insight regarding her father. In all her previous comments, written or spoken, she had been consistent in her expression of hurt and hatred toward him. Then she wrote the following:

> I feel like for the first time I can feel or sense or understand some of what Dad has inside of him. It's strange, but I also sense that somehow today I became more aware of some of his true feelings that he is not or ever has been aware of, and that makes me sad. It's kind of like I was allowed to "see"

something that he can't even begin to see. The respect that he demands and feels entitled to is a very poor substitute for the love he so desperately desires but feels so totally undeserving of. He is full of self-hate, guilt, shame, doubt and confusion, but only seems to be aware of a strong need to be in control, to see himself as not only better than others but as perfect, and to believe others should strive to match that perfection. It seems like at one level he sees himself as totally worthless, but in the "reality" level he lives in, he can only see everyone else is to blame, everyone else is inferior.

She went on to express a very clear insight regarding her father's returning home from his Vietnam war experience with a "last chance desperation" of needing to be cared for but feeling rejected, turning self-contempt into critical judgment toward others, especially his children, and striving to make the children be perfect.

This shift from feelings of fear and loathing for her father to compassionate understanding reflected the psycho-emotional maturity of an emerging integrated healthy personality capable of insight and reasoned appraisal of a larger context beyond the moments of traumatic wounding. As we neared the end of the neurofeedback sessions, there were clear indications of the profound changes Ms. D had accomplished. The neurofeedback sessions were conducted in a dedicated training room and the post-NFB debriefing sessions occurred in a consulting room. In one of her last sessions, after completing the NFB portion of the appointment, she went to the restroom before coming to the debriefing session. When Ms. D came into the consulting room for the post-feedback debriefing, she was smiling and appeared to be very calm and happy. When asked about her feedback experience she said that after the feedback session when she had

A/T Training in the Treatment of Dissociative Identity Disorder

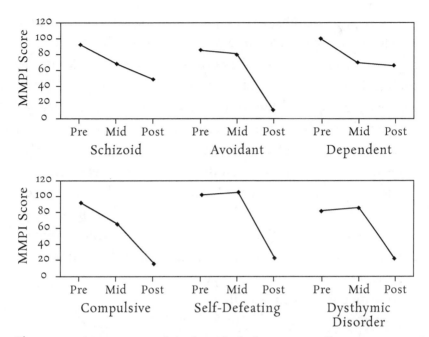

Figure 9.2. The MCMI scales identified above were all, at pre-treatment, above a raw score of 75, which is significant according to the MCMI manual. The relative "distress" of the treatment process is revealed in the mid-treatment scores for the "self-defeating" and "dysthymic disorder" scales. All scales had normalized by end of treatment.

looked at her reflection in the bathroom mirror she had a recognition of just seeing "herself" in contrast to her previous experience of never being sure who was going to be looking back at her from the mirror. Her post-session notes from those final sessions include the comment:

> My fears, traumas, conflicts, doubts, anger, confusion, dissociation, loneliness, and even memories are not a true part of my real identity and can have no power over me except the power I give them by my thoughts—my own self-judgments of good and bad.

These positive outcomes are not to say that Ms. D was completely psychologically healthy in every aspect of her being. Figure 9.2 presents the results of three Millon Clinical Multiaxial Inventories (1991) completed by Ms. D: before she began the A/T training protocol, mid-treatment, and after completion of the program. As can be seen, significant positive change occurred on multiple scales. Essentially, she moved from being an extremely distressed DID patient to a non-dissociating adult who continued to struggle with episodes of depression. She has continued to benefit from periodic psychotherapy to assist her in managing psychosocial stressors (e.g., the alcoholism of her youngest son, the death of a close friend); however, in each of these situations, she has remained an integrated personality coping with the typical adjustment challenges of life.

Conceptual Discussion

In the experience of this author, the central therapeutic power of the A/T training process in this case and in other patients suffering with DID and PTSD, is the cultivation and strengthening of an alert, neutral observer perspective. From this point of view, the patient can observe and emotionally reprocess the experience of a past trauma without being retraumatized. In this process, the sense of Self is experienced as "greater than" the original trauma that led to the defensive splitting off of the personality fragment or sub-personality to isolate and contain the trauma. In the neutral observer state, the central nervous system (CNS) and autonomic responses are not traumatically reactivated, providing an opportunity for release of the previously established defense of fragmentation or "splitting."

Neuroplasticity studies (Doidge, 2007) provide compelling support for the idea that we can self-regulate our CNS activity, thus fundamentally altering the way we experience the world. For a psychotherapy clinician, the therapeutic tool of A/T training provides a potent method for assisting clients in resolving the wounding of past trauma. In the psychotherapy process, the clinician establishes a calm, safe, accepting environment in which the client can explore the most troubling aspects of his or her history. A/T training can be conceptualized as a means for extending that environment into the deepest intra-psychic spaces maintained in the immensity of the brain's neural networks. In this process, healing truly emerges from the inside out.

References

Doidge, N. (2007). *The brain that changes itself: Stories of personal triumph from the frontiers of brain science.* New York: Penguin.

Grove, D. J., & Panzer, B. I. (1989). *Resolving traumatic memories: Metaphors and symbols in psychotherapy.* New York: Irvington Publishers.

Hardt, J. V. (1978). Personality change through control of EEG alpha activity. In *Proceedings of the Biofeedback Society of America* (pp. 215–218). Biofeedback Society of America.

Kissin, B. (1986). *Conscious and unconscious programs in the brain* (1 edition). New York: Springer.

Lexicor Medical Technology, Inc. (1995). *NRS-2D User's Manual.* Boulder, CO.

Manchester, C. F., Allen, T., & Tachiki, K. H. (1998). Treatment of dissociative identity disorder with neurotherapy and group self-exploration. *Journal of Neurotherapy,* 2(4), 40–53.

Millon, T. (1981). *Millon behavioral medicine diagnostic manual.* Minneapolis, MN: NCS Assessments.

Millon, T. (1991). *Millon clinical multiaxial inventory-III.* Minneapolis, MN: NCS Assessments.

Peniston, E. G., & Kulkosky, P. J. (1989). Alpha-theta brainwave training and beta-endorphin levels in alcoholics. *Alcoholism: Clinical and Experimental Research,* 13(2), 271–279.

Peniston, E. G., & Kulkosky, P. J. (1990). Alcoholic personality and alpha-theta brainwave training. *Medical Psychotherapy, 3*, 37–55.

Peniston, E. G., & Kulkosky, P. J. (1991). Alpha-theta brainwave neurofeedback for Vietnam veterans with combat-related post-traumatic stress disorder. *Medical Psychotherapy, 4*(1), 47–60.

Peniston, E. G., Marrinan, D. A., Deming, W. A., & Kulkosky, P. J. (1993). EEG alpha-theta synchronization in Vietnam theater veterans with combat-related PTSD and alcohol abuse. *Medical Psychotherapy, 6*, 37–50.

Peniston, E., & Kulkosky, P. (1992). Alpha-theta EEG biofeedback training in alcoholism and posttraumatic stress disorder. *The International Society for the Study of Subtle Energies and Energy Medicines, 2*, 5–7.

10

Peniston Protocol as an Integrated, Stand-Alone Therapeutic Modality

Nancy E. White, PhD
Leonard M. Richards, MBA

When Peniston and Kulkosky (1989) wrote their research, little did they know that they were skimming over a lake as deep as the universe itself, full of unspoken aspects of quantum theory and factors unseen behind neurochemical processes. They were guiding patients into the deep void we call the unconscious available for whatever the patient would choose to make of it. A process was developed that could engage the deep unconscious to rewrite traumatic experiences. This was not a neurofeedback training, but a therapeutic modality using neurofeedback to hold open brain-space for change. When the patient relaxes into the session, takes in and accepts some number of his or her desired outcome repetitions spoken in the brain's language of feeling, emotion, and sensuality, the desired outcome tends to become so. Recent research is just beginning to give us a glimmer as to how this may occur.

Commentary Illustrated With Case Studies

When Sarah came in for her first appointment, it was evident that she would be a difficult—if not impossible—case for more traditional psychotherapy. She had been sober for several years, "had fallen off the wagon" and was now craving alcohol. Her sponsor referred her to us because she did not know what more to do for Sarah and she hoped that we could help. Sarah had an eating disorder and was obese; she was experiencing frequent panic attacks; she was self-mutilating, depressed and often had suicidal ideation. She also had migraine headaches and trichotillomania. She pulled out her eyebrows, eyelashes and pubic hair.

The most difficult aspect of her case was that she was emotionally phobic. She was unable to express any feelings and would panic, become immobilized, dissociate or leave and get drunk when pressed to face any situation that was emotional. This situation offered us an opportunity to try our new protocol without the concern that we needed to do a more traditional intervention. She was a gift that offered us the opportunity to experience multiple levels of this new—and strange—therapeutic protocol.

Sarah came from an alcoholic family. Her sister was an alcoholic; her mother, a nurse, died of alcoholism; her father, a doctor, who was senile at death, was also an alcoholic. Her maternal uncle froze to death on the porch at age 19 when he came home drunk and his parents would not let him in the house. She knew that her paternal grandfather was alcoholic and believed that her mother's father may have been alcoholic also. Our assumption was that there was a genetic component to her alcoholism researched and written many times by Dr. Kenneth Blum (Blum et al., 2011).

Her initial testing with the MMPI-2 (Graham, 1990) showed anxiety and dysthymic disorders within a schizoid personality, which fit our clinical impression of her. Her testing also showed a possible schizophrenic disorder. The results of the testing with Millon II (1991) revealed her be quite elevated on the borderline personality, compulsive and dependent scales, all of which also fit our impression of her. She agreed to treatment using A/T training. After the sixth session, she experienced abreactions during the session and was having auditory hallucinations but desired to continue with the feedback sessions. She began having flashbacks and on the fifteenth session, she experienced a flashback and realized that she had been sexually abused in the crib, presumably by her father. In her flashback, the abuser had no face but wore a bow tie, which was typical for her father. She recognized this as the probable core of her lifelong problems (Rossi, 1993; Grof, 1985). During her treatments, she experienced many flashbacks of incest and physical abuse by her alcoholic mother and father. She had lived her life as a victim (of herself and others), yet when she had a flashback of the crib abuse, her adult self appeared in the room and said in a booming voice, "How dare you!" and she took the baby from the abuser. A "Resource Self" emerged and rescued her. That part of herself had not appeared in her life before.

Using the A/T training, we have found that this phenomenon of the Resource Self may occur in the deep theta state with many female cases who have experienced sexual abuse. The adult self will enter the flashback and say such things as, "How dare you!" or "Don't you ever do that again." An inner resource is reclaimed. The patient is never fully the victim again. This has been a spontaneous occurrence emerging from some part of the self and not programmed by us.

Sarah completed the treatment in 30 sessions. She was re-tested (see Figures 10.1 and 10.2). The MMPI-2 showed no clinical diagnosis on Axis I and personality disorder NOS on Axis II. There was a major drop in the depression scale from 81 to 53. She was no longer suicidal and showed the same shifts on the Millon II with the dysthymia scale dropping from 102 to 34. Borderline dropped from 86 to 70, which also fit our impression of her. Perhaps most noteworthy was her pre-treatment Millon II

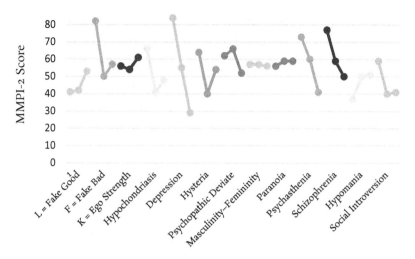

Figure 10.1. Pre– (1990), post– (1991), and follow-up (1998) testing graph of the MMPI-2 of Sarah.
Note: Scores are converted to normalized "T scores" on a scale ranging from 30 to 120. The "normal" range of T scores is from 50 to 65. Anything above 65 or below 50 is considered clinically significant and open for interpretation by the psychologist.

score of 71 on the schizoid scale perhaps denoting her unwillingness to process any emotional content. Her post-treatment score of zero on this scale suggested that she could be emotionally available for further treatment. The elevation of histrionic on the post-Millon II may be perceived as a positive developmental step also suggesting she was now not so blocked to her emotions. She was still slightly high in psychopathic deviance on the MMPI-2 scale. We often see this scale remaining slightly high after EEG feedback training and think it might reflect moving toward individuation on a test that is primarily diagnosing pathology and assumes this type of deviance to be pathological. She came in for five booster sessions during the first year when she felt stressed and sensed that she was losing some of her inner peace and connection to herself.

Peniston Protocol as an Integrated, Stand-Alone Therapeutic Modality

After completion of the program, she had no craving for alcohol and was able to face her emotions. At her closing appointment, she said she had not had to stop and get a box of doughnuts to come in for this final appointment (as she had done before her first appointment) but she proudly said she had not even thought about stopping. She was no longer binge eating but said she was not ready to lose her extra weight. She no longer had trichotillomania, and her migraine headaches were gone. The MMPI-2 and Millon II confirmed our impression of her as a relatively healthy person.

She then went through our Relationship Program which was an intense 120-hour group program extending over 5 months, attended by couples and singles. The focus was predominantly on the relationship with one's self. It was a very emotional experience for Sarah, and our belief was that she could not have gone through this kind of program if she had not completed the A/T training.

At her 3-year follow-up, Sarah was still doing well. She was seen at a lecture and she came up to speak to us. She was still overweight but said she was not bingeing and that she had remained sober. She reported she had a good relationship with her husband and was doing well at her job. She thanked us again and said, "I owe it all to you." The credit went not only to us but to her willingness to do this training and to the late Dr. Eugene Peniston and the Menninger Clinic who developed this protocol.

At our request, she came in for follow-up testing. This was 8 years later. Sarah had undergone no further formal therapy but had regularly attended AA meetings and developed a good support system in that venue. On most scales in her follow-up testing, Sarah showed further positive movement and growth (Figures 10.1 and 10.2). While attribution may be difficult so far removed in time and much of this improvement probably is due

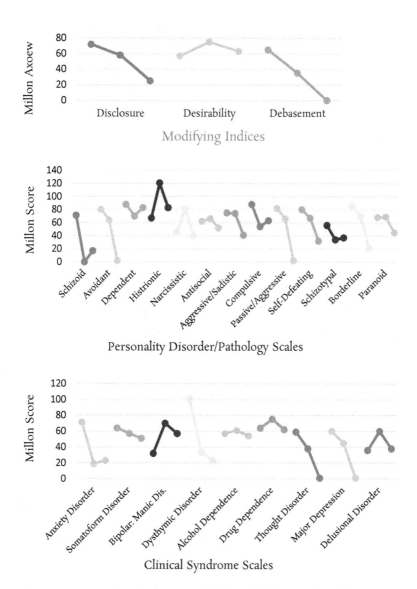

Figure 10.2. Pre- (1990), post- (1991), and follow-up (1998) testing graph of the Millon II of Sarah.

Note: Base rate scores are essentially where each score fits on a scale of 1–115 with 60 being the median score. Scores of 75–84 are taken to indicate the presence of a personality trait or clinical syndrome. Scores of 85 or above indicate the persistence of a personality trait or clinical syndrome.

to Sarah maintaining a good support system, the rest, we believe, can be attributed to the earlier healing that now allows her to take it in.

The Therapist is the Facilitator

It has now been 27 years since Eugene Peniston (1989) published his first research with his successful outcome. In this time, his powerful protocol has not reached its promised potential. The results of subsequent research have been mixed. In our opinion, there is a specific reason for these relatively disappointing results. As we have stated in the past, the A/T training protocol is a multilevel matrix that is difficult to be subdivided and studied with a standard research format. The best we can hope for is to get an appropriate perception of the results with tests (the MMPI and the Millon) similar to the pre- and post-testing that Peniston and Kulkosky originally administered.

This is because as we look at the different aspects of this protocol, it is the deeply altered state that the client accesses along with the intention set for a desired outcome, coupled with a therapist that has gained the trust, rapport and confidence of the patient that fosters the deep change.

Also, we believe that the self of the therapist is a very important element in the success of this powerful therapy, which is lost in a true research setting. The therapist's empathy and sensitivity to the patient's emotional healing experience during the highly charged, vulnerable experience of the theta state are important to create the atmosphere of trust needed for the patient's willingness to "let go."

The therapist's own level of personal involvement in the psychological, mental and spiritual domains, his or her trust of the healing process that is taking place, and his or her comfort with the possibility of abreactions are sensed by the patient and become a critical component of the therapy. In their inner healing journey together, the patient will be able to face and heal only what the therapist can hold open the space for. The patient is more likely to block or reject any spiritual or transpersonal experience around which they sense a lack of acceptance from the therapist. A/T training is a compassionate heart therapy. In our opinion, the patient's psyche will sense the level of the therapist's transpersonal comfort and will not go further.

"The art of psychotherapy... insists that what goes on inside the therapist, the artist, is crucial to the whole enterprise," Bugental (1987) states. Others, such as Dr. Edgar Wilson, have found brainwave synchrony between healer and patient at the time of peak effectiveness (Cowan, 1993). Fahrion, Wirkus, and Pooley (1993) found that interpersonal synchrony was highest during healing, especially in alpha frequencies between left occipital areas of the practitioner and the patient. In a deeply altered state, the patient seems to be more sensitized to the environment and, we assume, to the energy and attitudes of the therapist. A nonlocal connection seems to be formed; a rapport is created, and trust of the therapist is crucial.

With this in mind, we might move into a quantum view of reality, where all is connected. This view has been presented to us, for more years than we know, by the mystics and more recently by the physicists. We can see this world as one where there is no time and no space and reality emerges from the empty void—the world where all is connected, keeping in synchrony with the way the unconscious operates.

Dr. Larry Dossey (1993), speaking about the nonlocal reality, refers to the void that is encountered in the deep theta state as follows: "Paradoxically, this void becomes the fullness that gives rise to everything in the visible, phenomenal world. Modern physics seems to echo this vision. For example, in devices called cloud chambers, we can easily see subatomic particles appearing out of the void and disappearing back into it—the mysterious transformation of energy into visible matter and matter into invisible energy. Science, therefore, clearly shows us that the void, whatever else it may be, is not nothing."

Science's void, as Dossey sees it, relates to quantum physics' nonlocal reality, a transcendent space in which one may get a sense of being open to infinite potential. This view is more encompassing than Jung's Collective Unconscious and its archetypes, including one's personal archetypal figures (De Coster, 2010). Jung's view of the Collective Unconscious is distinguished from the personal unconscious "by the fact that it does not, like the latter [i.e., personal unconscious] owe its existence to personal experience and consequently is not a personal acquisition" (De Coster, p. 2). Stated either way, the patient, resting in the alpha-theta neurofeedback state, can enter a space in which he or she may draw on resources not necessarily arising from their personal experience.

The existence of a personal electromagnetic field is well-known, and in this very open and sensitive state the patient conceivably may sense much that is beyond the physical senses, meaning that he or she conceivably may gain an intuitive "sixth sense" of the therapist. If this is true, there is no such thing as an "objective" therapist able to avoid inclusion in this transpersonal world of the patient, sharing in the intentions of their desired outcome. The patients will likely be supported in their ability to heal the past and expand or extend their consciousness.

Chronic emotions affect our lives and begin prenatally. Recent research tells us that the chronic emotions held by the mother send chemical messages to the fetus and to receptor sites on the cells of the fetus by which the fetus accommodates to an expected environment, one that would cause these emotions in the mother. We might say a "Head Start" course for adaptation[1] is created. The same thing happens in our daily life as adults if we harbor chronic negative emotions or attitudes. It affects our chemistry, our energy, our noticing and our expectations, conscious or unconscious. We then attract from our negative attitudes those things that we do not want. The same thing is true when we are positive. We attract what we do want if we focus on the positive.

People who have had negative adaptations in prenatal and early childhood resulting in maladaptations in adulthood need psychological work. The historical programming must be cleared. Many therapies can facilitate this, but we think that the A/T training stands at the front of the list. This process can create the cellular reformatting and reverse the negative processes learned in prenatal and infantile periods as well as those taken on and habituated in later periods of life. Therapies which do not target this kind of training are likely to be superficially effective since they do not address this cellular and energetic level.

Whether the patient is presenting for healing a symptom or for optimal performance, we all have our woundings from the past at a time when we were little people in a world of giants that controlled us and upon whom we were dependent. The psyche has its attractors—its woundings. Any significant memory can become an attractor if it is reinforced or has sufficient initial impact that the occurrence makes an imprint on the psyche. The stability of the system will determine how the impact will play out in the life of the person, influenced by prior experience and the person's worldview.

Our lives revolve around attractors, both functional and dysfunctional. It may be said that a purpose of therapy is to resolve these dysfunctional attractors. Many patients, especially those experiencing childhood abuse, usually require many years of traditional therapy to gain reasonable functionality and a measure of well-being. Frequently the scars never fully heal, and a considerable number may require lifetime medication.

Many of these wounded exhibit attractors or symptoms arising from family patterns that have existed for generations. Using the Peniston protocol of A/T training and approaching the brain-mind psyche system with a transpersonal and open focus, the system is encouraged to resolve dysfunctional attractors which were originally developed to assure survival. This protocol could be transforming multigenerational patterns. The psyche, not being restricted by space and time, can go back to past generations and re-experience the woundings from the state of the "observer." With this training, one can eventually develop the ability to consciously observe and witness internal and external stimuli, without judging or thinking (Wuttke, 1992).

It is not unusual for some of our patients to experience an "inner guidance." This takes many forms, on a continuum from deep insight to the sense of another being or animal appearing to them. One middle-aged professional man, who had not had any prior experience of the transpersonal realm, experienced a guide that he referred to as his "Higher Power" which appeared in different guises. Initially, his guide appeared as a hawk and then as a snake. Frequently, the guide appeared as a Native American who said he was the patient's great, great, great grandfather (who was known to have been an American Indian). The hawk took him on his wings and soared out into the cosmos.

From there, the hawk pointed out the earth to him and then the pinpoint that was his home. He explained to him the insignificance of his local reality in comparison to the vastness of the cosmos. No sooner than he had absorbed this idea, he was quickly propelled to the Earth where he was taken to the microcosm world of the earthworm. It was then explained to him the significance and importance of all things. Truth is often found in paradox.

This same man had had a difficult relationship with his father for most of his life. They were not close and he didn't understand his father and his coldness. During one session, he was taken back to a time before his birth where he was shown the conditions of his father's childhood and the conditions of his father's relationship with his father (the patient's grandfather). He returned to normal waking consciousness with a new understanding and compassion for his father.

A female patient was taken by an angel to her father's deathbed where she was able to heal old wounds and say several things she had not been able to say to him when he was living. She returned with a deeper sense of inner peace.

For those who experience an "inner guidance," they express a major shift in perception about their lives and the environment.

Stanislav Grof (1985) tells us, "Sometimes the regression appears to go even further and the individual has a convinced feeling of reliving memories from the lives of his or her ancestors, or even drawing on the racial and collective unconscious." Green and Green (1977) describe theta training as a path by which to access planetary consciousness.

Sarah opened to a part of herself hitherto in slumber that forever freed her from being a victim. She truly was a victim as an infant, but she no longer had to remain a victim as an adult. The man who had problems with his father gained a sense of compassion, perhaps even empathy, from which he could recognize that much of what affected him really was not about him. He would now be able to see himself, not as a bad person, but as a worthy person to whom bad things happened.

A third, quite dramatic example may help to develop this

point further. In her alpha-theta sessions, a female who had been chronically sexually abused by her father would find herself in a library, one that was indicated in the therapist's narrative. She wrote in her journal:

> It is not an ordinary library, but the library of all souls' lives. I see my book of this lifetime open on the library table, but I cannot read it. A bright white light is emanating from the pages. I am greeted by my guardian angel who says, "You are loved. You have always been loved. You can rewrite the pages of your book." We hug.
>
> I feel like I am in Hitchcock's Spellbound, and like Gregory Peck, I am trying to make sense of flashbacks and feelings. I feel like I am dying. Everything I thought I knew and believed about my childhood is dying. It is being replaced with some very ugly truths. The truth shall set me free. And like the Phoenix, I am being reborn.

In a session toward the end of her program she was taken up to a high place from which, in panoply, she saw five generations of her family in which the fathers had abused the children. On viewing this, a deep, resonant voice rose from within her and declared: "This stops with me." In effect, she redirected her family history in an instant.

This person used the support of a personal archetype—her guardian angel—to help reframe the traumas of her past; and then, when repetition of the desired outcome reached a critical point, her psyche seemed to draw on a multigenerational family pattern of which she believed she had no conscious knowledge. From where this resource arose to facilitate healing we can only speculate, but it seems to bear out Grof's (1985) experience.

Components of the Alpha-Theta Training Protocol

State Dependent/Context Learning and Retrieval

The predominant brainwave frequency of children under the age of six is in the 0.5 to 8 Hz range which is associated with delta/theta in adults. As we mature, our average brainwave frequencies increase. In adulthood, these lower frequency waves are usually associated with reverie—hypnogogic imagery. Highly emotional experiences of childhood are learned and stored in the slower frequencies of that time. The brainwave pattern of A/T training resembles the pattern of early childhood when it is likely these original traumatic memories were stored. As the subconscious appears to become more accessible in this deeply altered state, traumatic memories of the past are released and available for reprogramming.

Imagery of Desired Outcome—Programming the Unconscious

In Peniston's original research with alcoholics, he worked with the patients to create an image of their desired outcome. With his original addicted population, he helped them create an alcohol rejection scene which they rehearsed either internally to themselves or had the therapist read their script to them as they dropped into their deeper state of alpha and then theta. This served to clarify and organize their intention for how they wished to see and experience themselves in the future. In his original work at Menninger's, Dr. Elmer Green (Green & Green, 1977) would quote an ancient Yoga Sutra: "Hold the image of change firmly in mind as you quiet down both physiology and thought processes, then release it without attachment." As they go deeper into this altered state of alpha and then theta to a place of what might be called suspended animation, most begin to dis-identify with the ego. The ego with its fear and linearity cannot seem to hold its judgments in this low frequency brainwave state, and the ego's blocking seems to move out of the way. The unconscious woundings become more available for healing. From the viewpoint of learning and memory, the repetition of intentional images or visualizations is quite different from a series of guided imagery experiences. Because the alpha-theta visualization is spoken and experienced as if it was already there, in a language of feeling and desire, it is much more likely to reinforce learning and produce the overlearning of the particular response that is important in creating personal change. Chopra tells us that it is in the silence between the thoughts where one can contact the hidden blueprint of intelligence and change it. He further states that in this deep state "the process of transcending, or 'going beyond,' detaches the mind from its fixed level and allows it to exist, if only for a moment, without any level at all. It simply experiences silence, devoid of thought, emotions, drives, wishes, fears or anything at all. Afterward, when the mind returns to its usual pitch (level of consciousness), it has acquired a little freedom to move." The imagery creates intention and intention automatically seeks fulfillment (Chopra, 1993).

Role of the Therapist

Who the therapist is energetically in the treatment setting partly determines the outcome. Every word, action, and thought in the treatment arena must come from conscious intent that affirms growth of the Self and enhancement of life for the organism. This modality's effectiveness is affected by the state of the therapist. In the quantum sense, it is impossible that he or she be an observer. There is no independent observer; the therapist is always part of the treatment equation.

Development of the Witness Consciousness

The ability of the individual consciousness to develop the "fair witness" aids in the process of healing. Deepak Chopra (1989) offers a verse from an ancient Indian Upanishad: "A man is like two doves sitting in a cherry tree. One bird is eating of the fruit while the other silently looks on." The bird, who is the silent witness, stands for that deep silence in everyone, which appears to be nothing at all when in reality it is the origin of intelligence.

This "fair witness" is the neutral observer state that appears and is often associated with increasing alpha and theta amplitudes and duration. "The brain is not engaged in more active cognitive processes. In this state of consciousness, there can be a comfortable detached awareness in which they can 'watch' an unfolding memory without experiencing the reactions that occurred in the original event. There is a sense of 'I' that exists as the observer of an experience instead of the 'I' immersed in the turmoil of the experience" (Chartier, chapter 9).

Resource Self

In this deep state of low brainwave frequency, when the patient has been traumatized as a child, a personal adult self can enter the vision of the relived original trauma and rescue the child. This part of the self becomes his or her champion and rescuer. In essence, the individual incorporates the "inner parent" for re-parenting and re-scripting his or her life. The person is never fully a victim again. In many patients, the Resource Self appears spontaneously at the appropriate timing for the patient and is not programmed by us (the therapist).

Inner Healer (Targets Somatic Complaints)

This aspect of the self will often appear to be reorganizing the physiology during immersion in the theta state. The body relaxes and lets go of resistances during theta consciousness and, we hypothesize, then has the opportunity to move toward health and homeostasis.

More on Language of the Brain

Recent research is giving us a glimmer into what we mean—in a literal sense—by the notion of addressing the brain in its own language. These researchers, observing from disparate fields of inquiry, are helping us to decipher the electrical "language" by which the brain exchanges information within and among its networks. What can be seen is still preliminary—and the proper subject for another paper elsewhere. So, we will get only a little bit technical as we mention in a general way what may be happening in "brain language" when the therapist speaks the narrative of desired outcome in the Now with feeling, emotion, and sensuality.

Song, Meng, Chen, Zhou, and Luo (2014) found accumulated evidence, including their own—and there are some twelve references in their paragraph on this—suggesting that the dynamics of brain oscillations act as "an internal temporal context, based on which neural ensembles are dynamically formed and dissolved to mediate sensory processing, perception, memory, consciousness and attention" (p. 4842). Similarly, Saarimäki et al. (2015) found that specific emotional states were represented by distinct neural signatures, regardless of how the emotions were induced. In other words, the brain communicates within and among its many networks by way of a sophisticated electrical language, complete with grammar and syntax, which, like our spoken language, has specific meanings and evokes specific responses. The "phrase" for pain, for instance, is the same whether it came from Daddy or a schoolyard bully.

Continuing in our line of speculation, it follows that the disordering of these intricate neural conversations by whatever means—trauma, injury, disease, chronic stress—can give rise to problems of mood, behavior and bodily function. From this, we can speculate as well that either a severe discontinuous event or many successive instances could build up a field within the relevant signature to a level of what we call trauma.

It also follows, then, that a patient relaxing in a slow wave state, relatively close to the relevant subcortical frequencies, can enter a desired new message so repetitively that it, too, builds up a field that changes the signature. If indeed this sequence of events is even partly accurate—and we believe that research is moving more in support than denial—what can be healed in the A/T training is not just a trauma, but one's overall susceptibility to trauma.

Conclusions

In our experience, the power of the Peniston protocol is based on what is carried within it: a combination of the procedure, the therapist's empathic involvement, the intention toward a positive and healthy outcome and an ambiance of safety and support. Consequently, the hand warming, SMR training, and other modalities can be there or not. We see these as adjuncts that can affect the outcome in certain individual situations. From this same point of view, we do not see that filtering methods or equipment is critical to outcomes. Our practice has used several different computer programs with several different manufacturers' EEGs to offer this protocol over our 27 years of experience, and we do not see that the outcomes have been significantly affected by these differences.

I think that the use of the QEEG to ascertain the possibility of such prior conditions as attention deficit disorder or traumatic brain injury can strongly affect the outcomes of the therapy. The remediation of these problems does not preclude going on to the Peniston protocol as a completion of the treatment (White, 2008).

We believe that the core element of the Peniston protocol, which is the alteration of unconscious process (both the clearing of early trauma effects and dropping in a new program of behavior) leads to profound changes in attitude, emotions, and behavior (White, 1999, 2008).

Dr. Tom Budzynski (1971, Budzynski & Lubar, 1997) reported that a predominance of theta in the EEG was the ideal state for "rescripting" or "reimprinting" the brain, eliminating destructive behaviors or attitudes that are a result of "scripts" laid down in childhood (during times when the child is naturally in a theta state) and replacing them with more suitable and more positive scripts for a mature adult. Rossi (1986) states that each time we access the state-dependent memory, learning, and behavior processes that encode a problem, we have an opportunity to "reassociate and reorganize" or reframe that problem in a manner that resolves it. This reliving, releasing, and re-scripting may be one of the few ways in which an adult can modify old scripts and store new information in the subconscious. To pay homage to the grandfather of the A/T training, Elmer Green (2000), in his three-volume book The Ozawkie Book of the Dead, states:

- Theta Brainwave Training is Transcendence-of-the-gods training.
- It is soul training. It enables the soul to communicate with the Soul and helps the personality express (display,

manifest, radiate), the Light of the Soul.
- Theta training enables a person to work in the world without being trapped by the world.

References

Blum, K., Chen, A. L. C., Oscar-Berman, M., Chen, T. J. H., Lubar, J., White, N., ... Bailey, J. A. (2011). Generational association studies of dopaminergic genes in reward deficiency syndrome (RDS) subjects: Selecting appropriate phenotypes for reward dependence behaviors. *International Journal of Environmental Research and Public Health*, 8(12), 4425–4459. https://doi.org/10.3390/ijerph8124425

Budzynski, T. H. (1971). Some applications of biofeedback-produced twilight states. Presented at the Annual Meeting of the American Psychological Association, Washington, DC.

Budzynski, T. H., & Lubar, J. F. (1997). The case for alpha-theta: A dynamic hemispheric asymmetry model. Presented at the Annual Conference of the Society for the Study of Neuronal Regulation, Aspen, CO.

Bugental, J. F. T. (1987). *The art of the psychotherapist* (1st edition). New York: WW Norton & Co.

Chopra, D. (1989). *Quantum healing: Exploring the frontiers of mind/body medicine.* New York: Bantam.

Chopra, D. (1993). *Ageless body, timeless mind: The quantum alternative to growing old.* Harmony Books.

Cowan, J. D. (1993). Alpha-theta brainwave biofeedback: The many possible theoretical reasons for its success. *Biofeedback*, 21(2), 11–16.

De Coster, P. L. (2010). *The collective unconscious and its archetypes.* Gent, Belgium: Satsang Press.

Dossey, L. (1993). *Healing words: The power of prayer and the practice of medicine* (1st Ed.). San Francisco, CA: HarperCollins.

Fahrion, S., Wirkus, M., & Pooley, P. (1992). EEG amplitude, brain mapping, & synchrony in & between a bioenergy practitioner & client during healing. *Subtle Energies & Energy Medicine*, 3(1).

Graap, K., & Freides, D. (1998). Regarding the database for the Peniston alpha-theta EEG biofeedback protocol. *Applied Psychophysiology & Biofeedback, 23*(4), 265–272.

Graham, J. R. (1990). *MMPI-2: Assessing personality and psychopathology.* New York: Oxford University Press.

Green, E. (2001). *The Ozawkie book of the dead: Alzheimer's isn't what you think it is.* Philosophical Research Society.

Green, E., & Green, A. (1977). *Beyond biofeedback.* San Francisco, CA: Delacorte.

Grof, S. (1985). *Beyond the brain: Birth, death, and transcendence in psychotherapy.* Albany, N.Y: State University of New York Press.

Millon, T. (1991). *Millon clinical multiaxial inventory-III.* Minneapolis, MN: NCS Assessments.

Peniston, E. G., & Kulkosky, P. J. (1989). Alpha-theta brainwave training and beta-endorphin levels in alcoholics. *Alcoholism: Clinical and Experimental Research, 13*(2), 271–279.

Peniston, E. G., & Kulkosky, P. J. (1990). Alcoholic personality and alpha-theta brainwave training. *Medical Psychotherapy, 3,* 37–55.

Peniston, E. G., & Kulkosky, P. J. (1991). Alpha-theta brainwave neurofeedback for Vietnam veterans with combat-related post-traumatic stress disorder. *Medical Psychotherapy, 4*(1), 47–60.

Rossi, E. L. (1993). *The psychobiology of mind-body healing: New concepts of therapeutic hypnosis.* WW Norton & Company.

Saarimäki, H., Gotsopoulos, A., Jääskeläinen, I. P., Lampinen, J., Vuilleumier, P., Hari, R., ... Nummenmaa, L. (2016). Discrete neural signatures of basic emotions. *Cerebral Cortex, 26*(6), 2563–2573.

Song, K., Meng, M., Chen, L., Zhou, K., & Luo, H. (2014). Behavioral oscillations in attention: Rhythmic alpha pulses mediated through theta band. *The Journal of Neuroscience, 34*(14), 4837–4844.

White, N. (1999). Theories of effectiveness of alpha-theta training for multiple disorders. In J. R. Evans & A. Abarbanel (Eds.), *Introduction to quantitative EEG and neurofeedback* (pp. 341–367). New York, NY: Elsevier.

White, N. E. (2008). The transformational power of the Peniston protocol: A therapist's experiences. *Journal of Neurotherapy, 12*(4), 261–265.

Wuttke, M. (1992). Addiction, awakening, and EEG biofeedback. *Biofeedback, 20*(2), 18–22.

Footnote

[1] Head Start is a federally funded program for children 3 to 5 years of age of low income families, helping them to develop mentally, socially, emotionally, and physically to prepare them for school.

11

Lessons Learned From Peniston's Brainwave Training Protocol

Estate (Tato) Sokhadze, PhD

Introduction and Background:
The Peniston Protocol (A/T Training)

Electroencephalographic (EEG) biofeedback (hereafter referred to as neurofeedback) has been employed in substance use disorder (SUD) in both out- and in-patient treatment settings over the last 40 years. Substance-related disorders, also referred to as subgroups of substance abuse (drug abuse) and substance (chemical) dependence, and commonly known as "addictions," include disorders related to the taking of substances/drugs of abuse (including alcohol) despite substantial substance-related problems and negative consequences. SUDs definitely represent one of the most common psychiatric conditions resulting in significant impairments in cognition and behavior with a huge morbidity and mortality toll. Acute and chronic drug abuse results in alteration of brain activity detectable with EEG methods. Hence, neurofeedback is applicable for restoring normal EEG patterns in addicts, and there is a clear rationale that brainwave training can be considered as a feasible approach to treat SUD.

The treatment of addictive disorders with neurofeedback became popularized due to the work of Eugene Peniston and Paul Kulkosky (Peniston & Kulkosky, 1989, 1990, 1991), and is also discussed at length in other chapters of this book.

In the beginning, it was popularly known as the Peniston Brain Wave Training Protocol (Peniston BWT), then it became the Peniston alpha-theta protocol, and currently, simply the Peniston Protocol. This intervention employed auditory feedback of two slow brainwave frequencies in an eyes-closed condition to produce a "hypnagogic" state in which the patient is given suggestion in a form of guided imagery aimed at sobriety. Repeated sessions resulted in long-term abstinence and notable changes in personality testing outcomes.

The substantial amount of literature to date regarding neurofeedback application for treatment of SUD is still focused on alpha-theta neurofeedback and its derivate protocols. The technique involves the simultaneous measurement of occipital (O1) alpha (8–13 Hz) and theta (4–8 Hz) rhythms and feedback by separate auditory tones for each frequency representing amplitudes greater than pre-set training thresholds. The subject is encouraged to relax and to increase the amount of time the signal is heard, that is to say, to increase the amount of time that the amplitude of each defined bandwidth exceeds the threshold. An important and integrated part of the protocol includes skin temperature biofeedback using autogenic training (Luthe, 1963) phrases before the initiation of neurofeedback training as such, and visualization using guided imagery targeting refusal to use drugs/alcohol (see reviews in Trudeau, 2000, 2005, 2008; Trudeau, Sokhadze, & Cannon, 2009).

As noted in our reviews of neurofeedback-based treatment approaches in addiction (Sokhadze, Cannon, & Trudeau, 2008; Trudeau, Sokhadze, &Cannon, 2009; Sokhadze, Trudeau, & Cannon, 2013) and in an earlier review by Trudeau (2005), A/T feedback training was first employed and described by Elmer Green and colleagues (Green, Green, & Walters, 1974) at the Menninger Foundation Clinic. This method was based on Green's observations of single-channel EEG activity during meditative states in experienced practitioners of meditation, during which increased amplitude in the theta range was following initial increase in amplitude of alpha activity, further followed by attenuation of the amplitude of alpha resulting in the so-called "theta/alpha crossover." This state was accompanied by subjective reports of profound relaxation and reverie. The method was considered as useful in augmenting psychotherapy outcomes and for individual insight exploration similar to studies of the alpha state (Ancoli & Kamiya, 1978; Nowlis & Kamiya, 1970). The alpha-theta neurofeedback was aimed to enable a trainee to maintain an altered state of consciousness similar to a meditative or hypnotic relaxed state over a half-hour long training session. Hardt and Kamiya (1978) also reported that the alpha state was accompanied by lower anxiety in high-anxiety subjects.

Goslinga (1975) gave the first description of the use of alpha-theta feedback in a SUD treatment program. This integrated program started in 1973 at the Topeka, Kansas Veterans Administration (VA) Medical Center, and included group and individual therapies. The first published clinical reports of efficacy of alpha-theta training at the Topeka VA were by Twemlow and Bowen (1976), who explored the impact of alpha-theta training in chronic male alcoholics enrolled in an inpatient treatment program. In another study at the Topeka VA, patients with alcohol dependence were reported to exhibit within- and across-session increases in raw theta amplitudes at occipital areas bilaterally measured by single-lead EEG during the course of alpha-theta training (Twemlow, Sizemore, & Bowen, 1977). The approach that Dr. Peniston used in his studies was influenced by the Menninger Clinic's protocol, and his efforts were strongly supported by the researchers from Dr. Green's group (e.g., Dale Walters, Patricia Norris [see chapter 2], Steve Fahrion, etc.).

Historically, in the first reported randomized and controlled study of alcoholics treated with the alpha-theta protocol, Peniston and Kulkosky (1989) described positive clinical outcomes. Their subjects were inpatients in a VA hospital treatment program (Fort Lyons VA Medical Center in Texas), all males with established chronic alcoholism (most of them with co-occurring PTSD) and multiple past failed treatments. Following a temperature biofeedback pre-training phase, Peniston's experimental subjects (n = 10) completed fifteen 30-minute sessions of eyes-closed occipital alpha-theta neurofeedback. Compared to a traditionally treated alcoholic control group (n = 10), and non-alcoholic controls (n = 10), alcoholics receiving brainwave neurofeedback training showed significant increases in percentages of alpha and theta rhythms, and increased alpha rhythm amplitudes at the left occipital EEG recording site (O1).

The experimentally treated subjects showed reductions in the Beck Depression Inventory (BDI: Beck et al., 1961) scores compared to the control groups. Control subjects who received standard treatment alone showed increased levels of circulating beta-endorphin, an index of stress, whereas the neurofeedback group did not. Thirteen-month follow-up data indicated significantly more sustained prevention of relapse in alcoholics who completed alpha-theta brainwave training as compared to the control alcoholics, defining successful relapse prevention as "not using alcohol for more than 6 contiguous days" during the follow-up period.

In a further report on the same control and experimental subjects, Peniston and Kulkosky (1990) described substantial changes in personality test results in the experimental group as compared to the controls. Notably, this small sample size study employed controls and blind outcome evaluation.

Even though the above protocol described by Peniston was

in some ways similar to that initially employed by Twemlow and colleagues (Twemlow & Bowen, 1976, 1977; Twemlow et al., 1977) at the Topeka VA and by Elmer Green at the Menninger Clinic, it had several important additions and modifications. Peniston introduced skin temperature biofeedback training as a preconditioning relaxation exercise, and used an induction script, read at the start of each session. The major content of imagery was targeting refusal to use drugs and alcohol and the maintenance of sobriety. To summarize unique specifics of the protocol, subjects are first taught deep relaxation by skin temperature biofeedback using autogenic phrases in at least five sessions. They then are instructed in brainwave biofeedback and in an eyes-closed and relaxed condition, receiving auditory signals from O_1, referenced to linked ears. A standard induction script utilizing suggestions to relax and "sink down" into reverie is read. When alpha (8–12 Hz) brainwave amplitude exceeds a preset threshold, a pleasant tone is heard, and by learning to voluntarily produce this tone, the subject becomes progressively relaxed. When theta brainwaves (4–8 Hz) are produced at sufficiently high amplitude, a second tone is heard, and the subject becomes more relaxed and, according to Peniston, enters a hypnagogic state of free reverie and high suggestibility. Following the session, with the subject in a relaxed and suggestible state, a therapy session is conducted between subject and therapist where the contents of the imagery experienced is explored, and abreacted experiences are also explored (Peniston & Kulkosky, 1989, 1990, 1991).

Saxby and Peniston (1995) also reported on 14 chronically alcohol dependent and depressed outpatients using this same protocol. Following treatment, subjects showed substantial decreases in depression and psychopathology as measured by standard instruments. Twenty-one month follow-up data indicated sustained abstinence from alcohol confirmed by collateral report.

These male and female outpatients received twenty 40-minute sessions of feedback (see Trudeau et al., 2009).

Several other studies using the Peniston Protocol and its modifications reported cases with positive clinical effects (Bodenhamer-Davis & Callaway, 2004; Burkett, Cummins, Dickson, & Skolnick, 2003; Callaway & Bodenhamer-Davis, 2008; DeBeus, 2007; DeBeus, Prinzel, Ryder-Cook, & Allen, 2002; Fahrion, Walters, Coyne, & Allen, 1992; Finkelberg et al., 1996; Kelley, 1997; Skok, Shubina, Finkelberg, Shtark, & Jafarova, 1997). These studies indicate that this applied psychophysiological approach based on the alpha-theta biofeedback protocol is a valuable alternative to conventional substance abuse treatment.

A critical analysis of the Peniston Protocol is discussed at length in previous reviews (Trudeau, 2000, 2005, Trudeau et al., 2009; Sokhadze et al., 2008; Sokhadze et al., 2013).

Several condition controlled studies of the Peniston Protocol for addictions by Lowe (1999), Moore and Trudeau (1998), and Taub and Rosenfeld (1994) suggest that alpha-theta training for addictions may be non-specific in terms of effect when compared to suggestion, sham or controlled treatment, or meditational techniques. By contrast, Egner, Strawson, and Gruzelier (2002) showed that alpha-theta training results in the increase of theta/alpha ratios, as compared to a control condition. In an in-depth critical analysis that examines inconsistencies reported in the original Peniston papers, Graap and Freides (1998) raise serious issues about the reporting of original samples and procedures in these studies. They posit that the results may have been due as much to the intense therapies accompanying the biofeedback as to the biofeedback itself and that the subjects may have been comorbid for a number of conditions that were not clearly reported, particularly PTSD, which may have been the focus of the treatment.

In his reply to these criticisms, Peniston (1998) acknowledges that it "remains unknown whether the temperature training, the visualizations, the alpha-theta BWT, the therapist, the placebo, or the Hawthorne effects are responsible for the beneficial results." The criticism and concerns noted by Graap and Freides (1998) regarding Peniston's papers could also be applied to the replication studies. Neither Peniston's studies nor the replication studies provide sufficient detail regarding the specifics of the types of equipment used for alpha-theta feedback, including filtering methods for the EEG signal or other technical information, to permit exact reproduction of the feedback protocols with other equipment. Outcome criteria also vary in the replication studies, with varying measures of abstinence and improvement.

Modification of Peniston Protocol

It should be noted that psychostimulant (cocaine, methamphetamine) addictions might require approaches and neurofeedback protocols other than alpha-theta training. Cocaine-dependent persons are cortically under-aroused during protracted abstinence (Roemer, Cornwell, Dewart, Jackson, & Ercegovac, 1995). Quantitative EEG (QEEG) changes, such as decrease in high beta (18–26 Hz) power, are typical for withdrawal from cocaine (Noldy, Santos, Politzer, Blair, & Carlen, 1994). Cocaine abusers who are still taking the drug often show low levels of delta and excess levels of alpha and beta amplitude (Alper, 1999; Prichep et al., 2002), whereas chronic methamphetamine abusers usually exhibit excessive delta and theta activity (Newton et al., 2004). Thus, cocaine and methamphetamine users may need a different EEG biofeedback protocol, at least at the beginning stages of neurofeedback therapy. For opiate-dependent or abusing patients, another technical problem, usually associated with eyes closed neurofeedback training condition, is drowsiness and difficulty maintaining alertness.

Scott, Kaiser, Othmer and Sideroff (2005) describe combining a protocol for attentional training (beta and/or sensorimotor rhythm [SMR] augmentation with theta suppression) with the Peniston Protocol in a population of subjects with mixed substance abuse, mostly stimulant abusers. The beta protocol was similar to that used in ADHD and was used until measures of attention normalized, and then the standard Peniston Protocol without temperature training was applied (Scott et al., 2005, see chapter 12). The study group was substantially different than that reported in either the Peniston or replication studies. The rationale was based in part on reports of substantial alteration of QEEG seen in stimulant abusers associated with early treatment failure likely associated with marked frontal neurotoxicity and alterations in dopamine receptor mechanisms. Additionally, preexisting ADHD is associated with stimulant preference in adult substance abusers, and is independent of stimulant associated QEEG changes.

These findings of chronic EEG abnormality and high incidence of preexisting ADHD in stimulant abusers suggest that such abusers may be less able to engage in the hypnagogic and auto-suggestive Peniston Protocol. Furthermore, eyes-closed alpha feedback as a starting protocol may be deleterious in stimulant abusers because the most common EEG abnormality in crack cocaine addicts is excess frontal alpha.

Using their approach, known as the Scott-Kaiser Protocol, Scott et al. (2005) described substantial improvement in measures of attention, and also of personality, similar to those reported by Peniston and Kulkosky. Their experimental subjects underwent an average of 13 SMR-beta (12–18 Hz) neurofeedback training sessions followed by 30 alpha-theta sessions during the first 45 days of inpatient treatment. Treatment retention was significantly better in the neurofeedback group. One hundred twenty-one inpatient drug program subjects randomized to condition, followed up at 1 year, were tested and controlled for the presence of attentional and cognitive deficits and personality states and traits. The experimental group showed normalization of attentional variables following the SMR-beta portion of the neurofeedback, while the control group showed no improvement. Experimental subjects demonstrated significant changes beyond the control subjects on 5 of the 10 scales of the MMPI-2. Subjects in the experimental group were also more likely to stay in treatment longer and more likely to complete treatment as compared to the control group. Finally, the one-year sustained abstinence levels were significantly higher for the experimental group as compared to the control group.

Therefore, in certain clinical conditions there is an excess of frontal slowing (ADHD, stimulant abuse, cannabis abuse) that is suspected to result in inability to achieve focused relaxation with occipital alpha and theta feedback. In the Scott-Kaiser modification of the Peniston Protocol, the frontal SMR or low beta training, done prior to alpha-theta training, has been shown effective in stimulant abusers (Scott et al., 2005, Burkett et al., 2003, 2005).

Thus, treatment of patients with substance abuse disorder using alpha-theta neurofeedback may become more complicated when patients present various psychiatric conditions. When addiction is comorbid with ADHD it is suggested that frontal SMR or beta increase and theta decrease training should be conducted to address ADHD prior to occipital alpha-theta relaxation training. This rationale has been discussed extensively (Sokhadze et al., 2007, 2008; Trudeau, 2005; Trudeau et al., 2009).

The recent study of Keith, Rapgay, Theodore, Schwartz, & Ross (2015) evaluated the effectiveness of an automated EEG biofeedback system in recovering illicit substance users who had attention deficits upon admission to a comprehensive residential treatment facility. All participants (N = 95) received group, family, and individual counseling. Participants were randomly assigned to one of three groups that either received 15 sessions of automated EEG biofeedback (AEB), 15 sessions of clinician-guided EEG biofeedback (CEB), or 15 additional therapy sessions (AT). For the AEB and CEB groups, operant contingencies reinforced EEG frequencies in the 15–18 Hz (low beta) and 12–15 Hz (SMR) ranges and reduced low frequencies in the 1–12 Hz (delta, theta and alpha) and 22–30 Hz (high beta) ranges at C5 (for beta) and C6 (for SMR), with references to earlobes. The Test of Variables of Attention (TOVA), a "Go No Go" task, and time in treatment were used as outcome measures. Attention scores did not change on any TOVA measure in the control group. Reaction time variability and omission and commission errors improved significantly in both neurofeedback (AEB and CEB) groups. The results demonstrate that neurofeedback based on the Scott-Kaiser version of the Peniston Protocol can effectively improve attention in recovering illicit substance users in the context of a comprehensive residential substance abuse treatment facility. Furthermore, EEG biofeedback should be recognized as a feasible adjunctive therapy for substance use disorder patients with attention deficits.

Arani, Rostami, and Nostratabadi (2010) and later Dehghani-Arani, Rostami and Nadali (2013) reported that EEG biofeedback protocols like the ones used by Scott et al. (2005) significantly reduce craving in opiate-dependent individuals. The approach of beta up-training in conjunction with alpha-theta training has been applied successfully in a treatment program aimed at homeless crack cocaine abusers in Houston, as reported by Burkett et al. (2003), with impressive results. Two hundred and seventy male addicts received 30 sessions of a protocol similar to the Scott-Kaiser modification. One-year follow-ups of 94 treatment completers found that 95.7% of subjects were maintaining a regular residence; 93.6 % were employed/in school or training, and 88.3 % had no subsequent arrests. Self-report depression scores dropped by 50% and self-report anxiety scores by 66%. Furthermore, 53.2% reported no alcohol or drug use 12 months after biofeedback, and 23.4% had used drugs or alcohol one to three times after their stay, a substantial improvement from the expected 30% or less expected recovery in this group. The remaining 23.4% reported using drugs or alcohol more than 20 times over the year. Urinalysis results corroborated self-reports of drug use. The treatment program saw substantial changes in length of stay and completion. After the introduction of the neurofeedback to the mission regimen, length of stay tripled, beginning at 30 days on average and culminating at 100 days after the addition of neurotherapy.

In their later study, the authors reported follow-up results on 87 subjects after completion of the neurofeedback training (Burkett et al., 2005). The follow-up measures of drug screens, length of residence, and self-reported depression scores showed significant improvement. It should be noted that this study had limitations, since neurofeedback was positioned only as an adjunct therapy to all other faith-based treatments for crack cocaine-abusing homeless persons enrolled in this residential shelter mission.

Defining Level of Clinical Efficacy of Peniston Protocol

The Guidelines for Evaluation of Clinical Efficacy of Psychophysiological Interventions (La Vaque et al., 2002) specify five types of classification for the effectiveness of biofeedback procedures, ranging from "not empirically supported" to "efficacious and specific." In particular, Level 3, "probably efficacious," is defined as "treatment approaches that have been evaluated and shown to produce beneficial effects in multiple observational studies, clinical studies, wait list control studies, and within-subject and between-subject replication studies merit this classification."

In 2008, based on review of published clinical studies and employing efficacy criteria adapted by the International Society for Neurofeedback and Research (ISNR) and the Association for Applied Psychophysiology and Biofeedback (AAPB), we (Sokhadze, Trudeau & Cannon, 2008) concluded that the Peniston Protocol is "probably efficacious—level 3" as an adjunct in treating alcoholics in a rehabilitative treatment modality, but may not be more efficacious than other methods to achieve relaxation. The Scott-Kaiser modification was considered "possibly efficacious—level 2" in treating stimulant addicts in residential treatment programs.

Using these criteria and based on the studies reported to date, the Peniston Protocol can be classified as probably efficacious when combined with a rehabilitative treatment modality in treating subjects with long-standing alcohol dependency. This classification is based on the original randomized and controlled study of the Peniston Protocol (Peniston & Kulkosky 1989, 1990, 1991) and multiple observational and uncontrolled studies that preceded (Twemlow & Bowen, 1977; Twemlow et al., 1977) and followed that study (Burkett et al., 2003, 2005; Bodenhamer-Davis & Callaway, 2004; Callaway & Bodenhamer-Davis, 2008; DeBeus, 2007; DeBeus et al., 2002; Fahrion, 1995; Fahrion et al., 1992; Finkelberg et al., 1996; Kelley, 1997; Saxby & Peniston, 1995; Skok et al., 1997).

This assessment of efficacy is accompanied by a caveat that it has not been demonstrated that Peniston-type alpha-theta feedback is more efficacious than control conditions that involve meditation or relaxation (Lowe, 1999; Moore & Trudeau, 1998, Taub & Rosenfeld 1994; Trudeau, 2000, 2005). Using these criteria and based on reported studies to date, the Scott-Kaiser modification of the Peniston Protocol can be classified as possibly efficacious when combined with residential rehabilitation modalities in stimulant abusers. This rating was based on one controlled study (Scott &Kaiser, 1998; Scott et al., 2005) and one observational study (Burkett et al., 2003, 2005) at the time of our initial review of efficacy.

Personal History of Neurofeedback Application in Addiction Research Treatment

Our assessment of the Peniston Protocol clinical efficacy (Sokhadze et al., 2008) was critically received by some of the strong Peniston Protocol supporters. In particular, White (2008), in her commentary, outlined that we emphasized too much of the technical aspects of alpha-theta training and specifics of EEG pattern alterations in users of different drugs of abuse, claiming that "addiction is addiction" regardless of drug of choice. She stated further that, based on her experience with the Peniston Protocol, psychological healing and personality shifted as a result of the Peniston protocol. It was also proposed that using skin temperature training or SMR neurofeedback as an introduction to alpha-theta is not critical and, along with EEG pattern specificity, is secondary to success, while combination of the Peniston procedure with therapist's empathy, intention towards positive outcome, and support of patients is actually a primary determinant of success (White, 1999).The commentary was based on 18 years of the author's experience using the Peniston Protocol with different equipment and various cohorts of patients with SUD diagnosis.

It should be noted that our review (Sokhadze, Cannon, & Trudeau, 2013) was based on even more long-term familiarity and first-hand experience with the Peniston Protocol. David Trudeau had experience using the Peniston Protocol in his practice more than 20 years ago, while I started using a practically identical version of the Peniston Protocol in Russia in the early nineties on both outpatient and inpatient populations of individuals with alcohol use disorder. Rex Cannon also is an experienced specialist in neurofeedback applications for addiction treatment. The unpublished study that I am referring to was funded back in 1993 by the education and research committee of the AAPB. It was titled "Controlled Replication Study of Alpha/Theta EEG Biofeedback Effects in Addictions" and the principal investigators were Drs. Shtark and Sokhadze. The study was carried out at two sites in Siberia: in the Kemerovo Center for Psychological Rehabilitation (active group, n = 22, all of them inpatients, and 12 controls (out- and inpatient) in the treatment as usual [TAU] group), and the Rehabilitation Department of Institute of Clinical and Experimental Medicine in Novosibirsk (20 outpatients in active treatment, and 18 patients as controls using sham biofeedback with prerecorded EEG data).

The protocol of treatment in both inpatient and outpatient active treatment groups was very similar to the one used by Peniston. The study used a visual imagery script from US-based consultants (George von Bozzay, Dale Walters, and Patricia Norris) and used the same versions of validated MMPI in the Russian language. Equipment that we used in the study was provided by J & J Engineering (I-330 with USE software; Poulsbo, Washington, USA). We also used a Russian version of the autogenic training procedure for temperature training. The only difference in our protocol was the application of muscular relaxation and EMG feedback (from the left trapezius) during temperature training sessions. The outcomes of the study were very positive, both in terms of patients' ability to get into the alpha-theta state (as judged by theta/alpha ratio percentage during individual sessions), clinical outcomes (alcohol non-use, relapse rate, retention in treatment, etc.), and psychological profile post-treatment. We reported our outcomes at several AAPB annual meetings but never published the final results. Our team included two clinical psychologists (Drs. Shubina & Zakharova) and the positive psychological outcomes of the Peniston Protocol-based treatment of alcoholics in our study were obvious and statistically significant.

However, our attempts to use the Peniston Protocol in outpatient opiate addicts were not successful. The main reason, as mentioned above, was difficulty in maintaining vigilance experienced by patients in the eyes-closed biofeedback condition. Later, in 2005–2006, I tried to apply the Peniston Protocol in a group of patients with cocaine abuse and cocaine dependence at University of Louisville, Louisville. We were running a funded research study on drug cue reactivity in crack-cocaine abusers and this was our cohort. Results were not promising at all; furthermore, teaching stimulant users to relax and slow down EEG with their eyes closed seemed somewhat counter-intuitive. Results improved when we changed the training protocol and started using SMR up/theta down at central (C3 for SMR) and frontal (F3 for theta) sites, referenced to linked mastoids. This study later was funded by the ISNR Research Committee and used Motivational Interviewing (Miller & Rollnick, 2002) as a psychotherapeutic arm. The results of this study were published (Horrell et al., 2010) and were presented at several ISNR and AAPB meetings. One of the most important observations in that study was the disproportionally high rate of PTSD occurring in cocaine addicts. Later, we started using prefrontal site Fpz for

EEG recording and theta/beta ratio and relative gamma power related indices as neurofeedback targets in adolescent drug abusers (Sokhadze et al., 2010). The treatment using neurofeedback was accompanied by weekly group behavioral therapy sessions. Therefore, our study integrated biobehavioral therapy combining specialized cognitive behavioral therapy (CBT; see chapter 14 for an in-depth view on this issue) tailored for adolescents (Seven Challenges®, Schwebel, 2004) and neurofeedback in community adolescent drug and alcohol abuse treatment settings where substance use and behavioral problems often co-occur.

The results of this pilot study (Cowan & Sokhadze, 2011) of adolescent drug users helped us formulate a rationale of neurofeedback applicability for treatment of adolescent occasional drug users with comorbid disruptive behavioral disorders (e.g., conduct disorder, oppositional-defiant disorder, ADHD). I do not elaborate that rationale here, as it was explained in that paper in detail and called for more efforts for integrated addiction treatments with a neurofeedback component in this type of dual diagnosis in adolescents. Similar ideas were proposed earlier by Trudeau (2005) and further reviewed in more detail in Sokhadze et al. (2007, 2013).

This brings us to the concluding section of the chapter that is aimed to evoke further consideration of factors that made the Peniston Protocol so effective and so popular, and attempt to clarify the major components of the intervention that has remained in the focus of neurofeedback in the addiction field for more than 25 years.

One Lesson to Be Learned From the Peniston Protocol: Comorbidity and the Role of Dual Diagnosis

As was mentioned above, the studies of Peniston were criticized on several grounds, including technical aspects of methodology, difficulties in delineating the exact factors contributing to positive clinical outcomes, insufficiently described patient differences in studies, and relatively simplified interpretation of results. Despite all these critical issues and concerns, the method was recognized and still attracts the attention of researchers and clinicians, especially those in the addiction treatment research field. It is natural to ask, how could there have been such excellent results reported? What are the components of the Peniston Protocol that offer such an advantage when using this particular method of self-regulation in this population?

Actually, these were the main questions I heard from the audience after I did a grand rounds presentation at the NIDA at Johns Hopkins University in Baltimore, where I was invited to present on the topic of neurofeedback application back in 2009. I thought that I had answers to these questions both in our review published by that time (Sokhadze et al., 2007; Sokhadze et al., 2008, Trudeau et al., 2009) and in my presentation there, so I decided to explain it in a form of a joke to make it easier to comprehend. It was the middle of May, a week after Kentucky Derby and a week before the Preakness Stakes at Pimlico, so timewise, it was reasonable to give them the answer in the form of an experienced Louisville-based handicapper offering tips and selections.

I asked them to imagine a race between known methods of addiction treatment, where they needed to make a bet after considering the odds of each intervention as a runner. In short, my handicapper advice was not to place a single bet on neurofeedback, but rather to use it as an exotic bet underneath more established interventions (replacement therapy, cognitive-behavioral therapy), or box them together, and for the best possible payout to use it on an inpatient population. Do not single out neurofeedback for the win; it is better to consider it as a show or place candidate in the addiction treatment race. I asked, why does it make sense to consider neurofeedback treatment more as an adjunct therapy rather than a primary one, why try to integrate it with other interventions, why give preference to the inpatient (rehab) setting, and ultimately, how does it relate to the specifics of the Peniston Protocol?

First, as we always claimed (see Sokhadze et al., 2008; Trudeau et al., 2009), it is important to point out that in most of the published studies, neurofeedback was used as an add-on treatment to other therapies, namely 12-step programs and/or cognitive behavioral therapies or other types of psychotherapies or residential programs. Neurofeedback is not yet validated as a stand-alone therapy for addictive disorders, and we have to admit this while discussing the current state of the art.

Secondly, it is important to point out that many persons with substance use disorders have comorbid conditions that need to be considered in designing a treatment plan that incorporates neurofeedback. These may include conditions such as mTBI or PTSD in veterans with SUD, or ADHD in adolescents or young adults with drug abuse problems, which may require separate neurofeedback treatment specific to these conditions either preceding neurofeedback treatment for addiction, or incorporated into it (Trudeau et al., 2009). There are also conditions such as affective disorders and anxiety disorders that occur commonly along with substance use disorders that may respond well to neurofeedback protocols for addictive disorders. These conditions may require separate assessments during the course of therapy to determine response and the need for changing protocols or adding other treatments, i.e., including medication (e.g., methadone or suboxone in opiate addiction) or psychotherapy into the treatment plan.

Recognition of dual diagnosis as an important part of

practically every type of substance dependence should attract more attention to more comprehensive and integrated treatment approaches. The findings about comorbidities in SUD converge on the conclusion that there exists an inherited predisposition for an externalizing psychopathology that includes ADHD, conduct disorder, and substance abuse. PTSD seems to heighten the risk for progression to addiction as well. There are several conditions commonly associated with addictive disorders that have known neurophysiological aberrations, including EEG alterations. The co-occurrence of alcohol and other substance use disorders with other psychiatric disorders has been widely recognized. Co-occurrence of SUD and other psychiatric diagnosis (e.g., PTSD, antisocial personality disorder, ADHD, unipolar depression, etc.) is highly prevalent (Biederman et al., 1995; Drake & Wallach, 2000; Grant et al., 2004). Persons with other mental disorders co-occurring with SUD have a more persistent illness course, and are more refractive to treatment than those without dual diagnosis (O'Brien et al., 2004; Schubiner et al., 2000). In designing a treatment plan employing neurofeedback, it is important to consider comorbidities and other co-occurring mental or neurological conditions that may require modification of protocol and/or ongoing assessment regarding response.

For instance, depression occurs in approximately 30% of chronic alcoholics (Regier et al., 1990). In treatment settings, depressed SUD patients can be challenging to the clinician, as they may not respond to treatment as well as other patients, may have greater relapse, attrition, and readmission rates, and may manifest symptoms that are more severe, chronic, and refractory in nature (Sheehan, 1993). Several neurofeedback approaches have been described as efficacious for depression, and may be considered as part of a treatment plan. It should also be noted that alpha/theta training alone for alcoholics has been effective for associated depression. Independent of other psychiatric comorbidity, ADHD significantly increases the risk for SUD. Associated social and behavioral problems may make individuals with comorbid SUD and ADHD treatment-resistant (Wilens, Biederman, & Mick, 1998). The incidence of ADHD in clinical SUD populations has been studied, and may be as high as 50% for adults and adolescents (Downey, Stelson, Pomerleau, & Giordani, 1997). Adult residual ADHD is especially associated with abuse of cocaine and other stimulants. ADHD alone has positive treatment outcomes of just under 80% when treated by neurofeedback (Monastra et al., 2005, see review in Arns, de Ridder, Strehl, Breteler, & Coenen, 2009; Sherlin, Arns, Lubar, & Sokhadze, 2010).

Rates of PTSD occurring in persons primarily identified with or in treatment for substance abuse vary from 43–59% (Breslau, Davis, Andreski, & Peterson, 1991; Triffleman, Carroll, & Kellogg, 1999). Cocaine abusers are three times more likely to meet diagnostic criteria for PTSD compared to individuals without a SUD. Methamphetamine-dependent individuals are at greater risk to experience particular psychiatric symptoms, particularly PTSD in females (Kalechstein et al., 2000). Finally, pharmacotherapies for comorbid conditions such as ADHD, PTSD, affective disorders, anxiety disorders, and other psychiatric conditions may work better when complemented with neurofeedback therapies for addictions.

Cognitive behavioral therapies (CBT) were always a part of interventions in SUD treatment. Successful strategies for behavioral treatment in drug addiction may include interventions aimed to decrease the reward value of the drug, and simultaneously increase values of natural reinforcement, approaches aimed to change stereotype conditioned drug-seeking behaviors, and methods to train and strengthen frontal inhibitory control

(Sokhadze et al., 2007; Volkow, Fowler, & Wang, 2004). Since stressful events can result in relapse to drug-taking behavior (Koob & Le Moal, 2001), an adjunct treatment strategy such as stress management can be aimed to interfere with the negative neurobiological responses to stress. Current research with neuro-biofeedback and addictive disorders is geared toward the use of EEG feedback to enhance one component of a cognitive behavioral therapy scheme. Another important objective for future neurofeedback treatment for SUD should be to integrate neurofeedback with other well-known behavioral interventions for drug abuse, such as CBT (Crits-Christoph et al., 1999), and motivation enhancement therapy (MET; Miller & Rollnick, 2002). As a population, drug addicts are very difficult to treat, characterized by a low motivation to change and reluctance to enter treatment programs. CBT and MET are powerful psychotherapeutic interventions to bring about rapid commitment to change addictive behaviors. These behavioral therapies are especially useful to enhance compliance of drug-dependent individuals, and facilitate their neurofeedback treatment engagement.

One needs to recognize that there are significant behavioral and functional differences (including those found in the EEG and other physiological measures) that make addiction specifics dependent on drug preference, which is further complicated in the case of poly-drug abuse. Hence, different approaches using neurofeedback need to be tailored to these specifics. This, of course, does not mean that one should ignore similarities of behavioral patterns associated with chemical (and non-chemical) addictions and dependencies (e.g., sex addiction, gambling, etc.), since these typical behaviors do have commonalities with all types of addiction. Because different drugs (e.g., heroin, cocaine, alcohol, cannabis) have distinct chemical actions, their EEG effects are different, yet their habit-forming actions and the elements of their withdrawal symptoms appear to have a common denominator, namely, similar effects in "hijacking" (Hyman & Malenka, 2001) the brain mechanisms of reward.

Combination of Interventions in Outpatients: A Conceptual Approach to Treatment and Rationale of Suggested Adjunct Neurofeedback Therapy for Opiate Addicts in Suboxone Treatment

I am an advocate for integrating neurofeedback not only with other CBT and behavioral techniques, but also with pharmacotherapy in the treatment of specific types of addiction, for example, opiate addiction, and I was always openly critical of positioning neurofeedback as a non-pharmacological approach, especially in addiction treatment. Currently methadone- and suboxone-based replacement outpatient therapies are considered to be standard intervention for opiate dependence. To improve suboxone replacement therapy outcomes, it would be feasible to modify attentional, affective, and behavioral mechanisms that mediate the motivational and emotional processes involved in drug cue-reactivity response. Thus, the goal is to modify the over-learned and consolidated response to drugs and drug-associated conditioned stimuli that are accompanied by craving and negative affect. According to Volkow et al. (2004), effective monitoring and modification of cue reactivity is considered an efficient treatment strategy to lower the chance of relapse in drug-dependent addicts in treatment. A possible effective treatment approach for opioid dependence might consist of emphasizing the risk associated with exposure to drug-related stimuli and environments, and consequent cognitive behavioral and/or applied psychophysiological regulation of responses to these stimuli in a controlled and monitored environment where both subjective reports of craving and physiological responses are recorded and analyzed.

It can be predicted that there would be an attentional bias towards opiate drug-related cues in patients with opioid dependence before their enrollment in treatment, and that the extent of the attentional bias, craving, and drug cue reactivity would change depending on the current clinical conditions of the patients enrolled in suboxone treatment with adjunct neurofeedback arms. This would result from the reduction of the motivational salience of drug-related cues, although through different moderating mechanisms, either by decreasing craving (opioid substitution therapy) or by modifying behavior using neurofeedback aimed at training upregulation of positive emotions. In line with the findings of other studies, opioid substitution therapy either with methadone or buprenorphine may result in alteration of physiological reactivity to stimuli associated with drugs by reducing craving and attenuating withdrawal symptoms, most likely through a modification of the reward response. The moderating mechanism underlying the reduction of craving and negative affect in neurofeedback therapy is different because it can be ascribed to a cognitive remediation and behavioral shift towards other types of positive reward and through a discouragement of the perpetuation of maladaptive dysphoric states.

The approach of our study fits with the model of addiction and strategies of intervention proposed by Volkow et al. (2004). These authors suggested that the treatment of drug dependence should focus on decreasing the reward value of drugs while increasing saliency and motivational values for natural rewards.

The approach considers strategies to reduce conditioned drug behaviors and improve frontal executive functioning as potential moderators. Furthermore, to achieve more prolonged results, the strategy of neurofeedback intervention in the field of addiction must incorporate techniques aimed at re-educating patients to self-regulate their emotional and motivational states, and training patients to re-learn induction of positive affect in an attempt to re-establish the normal biological, cognitive, behavioral, and hedonic homeostasis that has been distorted by drug abuse (Koob & Le Moal, 2001).

In the "allostatic model of addiction," Koob and Le Moal(2001) suggested that continued drug use may gradually deteriorate natural hedonic homeostasis, and result in a higher threshold for the amount of emotionally positive stimulation needed to experience reward and positive affect states. Active drug use and withdrawal-related alterations in neural structures involved in the stress response are well known, and these neuroadaptive changes in stress circuits, according to Li and Sinha (2008), may contribute to the increased salience of drug and drug-related stimuli in a variety of challenge or "stress" contexts (Robinson & Berridge, 2001). This may contribute to reduced coping ability, poor behavioral flexibility, and deficient problem-solving capacity during increasing levels of stress or emotional challenges in chronic substance users.

As we proposed in our conceptual paper (Sokhadze et al., 2007), drug abusers may develop hypersensitivity not only to drug-related, but also to stress-related stimuli, thus presenting similar psychophysiological reactivity to both drug- and stress-related cues. This may partially explain the high rate of comorbidity between substance use and anxiety disorders such as PTSD. Proposed applied psychophysiological emotion regulation training based on neurofeedback, combined with opiate substitution therapy, is a potentially beneficial strategy to significantly change the extent of implicit reactivity to drug cues, promote resilience to stress, and increase positive emotionality during experimental exposures and real-life situations.

Summary of Factors Contributing to the Peniston Protocol's Effects in Addiction Treatment

What in particular can be considered as an integral part of the Peniston Protocol that defines this intervention as a combined treatment that should be recommended for populations of drug addicts? I would like to present at least several important factors to consider.

First of all, the population in the early studies of Peniston and Kulkosky (1989, 1990, 1991) were inpatient veterans with predominantly combat-related PTSD, and the substance of choice was mostly alcohol.

Second, the self-regulation treatment initially started with skin temperature training, a relatively easy one, especially since it was accompanied by instructed control—actually Autogenics Training, a procedure adopted by Luthe (1963) from Schultz's training that had repeating phrases, respiratory exercises, and other instructed procedure lines. There is a very high probability that similar results could be achieved with other forms of biofeedback, for instance, HRV biofeedback with pre-recorded or instructor-delivered breathing instruction.

Third, guided imagery, or in other words script aimed at maintaining sobriety and refusal of alcohol and drugs, is an important therapeutic component of the Peniston Protocol, especially considering that in the alpha-theta crossover state the trainee is more susceptible to suggestions. In some aspects, the script has similarity to the 12-step approach and other somewhat spirituality-flavored treatment approaches.

Fourth, the neurotherapist is present during alpha-theta training sessions and usually after each session has an interaction with patients, doing what can be called a remediation, an important part of psychotherapy for anxiety disorders, specifically PTSD. This part of the Peniston Protocol can be considered as a modified psychotherapy or some type of CBT (see chapter 14 for an in-depth view of CBT).

Fifth, patients in early classic studies by Peniston were inpatients, not outpatients, and therefore were not in their natural environment, rich with alcohol/drug-related cues; they were isolated from their habitual circles that predisposed them to drug-seeking and drug-taking behaviors.

Sixth, and probably the most important part, was application of alpha-theta neurofeedback from posterior EEG sites in the eyes-closed condition, with the target to up-regulate both alpha and theta activity with subsequent "crossover," the crucial focus of the method as such.

All above six factors constituting the integrated character of the intervention should be considered when searching for answers to explain why this particular neurofeedback-centered treatment was so effective and still holds fascination for its followers. Definitely more research and clinical trials are warranted to validate the method and bring this protocol to clinical practice in addiction treatment. This is an intervention that may have significant impact in the treatment of substance use disorders.

References

Alper, K. R. (1999). The EEG and cocaine sensitization. *The Journal of Neuropsychiatry and Clinical Neurosciences*, 11(2), 209–221. https://doi.org/10.1176/jnp.11.2.209

Ancoli, S., & Kamiya, J. (1978). Methodological issues in alpha biofeedback training. *Biofeedback and Self-Regulation*, 3(2), 159–183. https://doi.org/10.1007/BF00998900

Arani, F. D., Rostami, R., & Nostratabadi, M. (2010). Effectiveness of neurofeedback training as a treatment for opioid-dependent patients. *Clinical EEG and Neuroscience*, 41(3), 170–177.

Arns, M., de Ridder, S., Strehl, U., Breteler, M., & Coenen, A. (2009). Efficacy of neurofeedback treatment in ADHD: The effects on inattention, impulsivity and hyperactivity: A meta-analysis. *Clinical EEG and Neuroscience, 40*(3), 180–189. https://doi.org/10.1177/155005940904000311

Beck, A. T., Ward, C. H., Mendelson, M. M., Mock, J. J., & Erbaugh, J. J. (1961). An inventory for measuring depression. *Archives of General Psychiatry, 4*(6), 561–571. https://doi.org/10.1001/archpsyc.1961.01710120031004

Biederman, J., Wilens, T., Mick, E., Milberger, S., Spencer, T. J., & Faraone, S. V. (1995). Psychoactive substance use disorders in adults with attention deficit hyperactivity disorder (ADHD): effects of ADHD and psychiatric comorbidity. *American Journal of Psychiatry, 152*(11), 1652–1658. https://doi.org/10.1176/ajp.152.11.1652

Bodenhamer-Davis, E., & Callaway, T. (2004). Extended follow-up of Peniston protocol results with chemical dependency. *Journal of Neurotherapy, 8*(2), 135. https://doi.org/10.1300/J184v08n02_13

Breslau, N., Davis, G. C., Andreski, P., & Peterson, E. (1991). Traumatic events and posttraumatic stress disorder in an urban population of young adults. *Archives of General Psychiatry, 48*(3), 216–222. https://doi.org/10.1001/archpsyc.1991.01810270028003

Burkett, V. S., Cummins, J. M., Dickson, R. M., & Skolnick, M. (2005). An open clinical trial utilizing real-time EEG operant conditioning as an adjunctive therapy in the treatment of crack cocaine dependence. *Journal of Neurotherapy, 9*(2), 27–47. https://doi.org/10.1300/J184v09n02_03

Burkett, V. S., Cummins, J. M., Dickson, R., & Skolnick, M. H. (2003). Neurofeedback in the treatment of addiction with a homeless population. Presented at the 11th ISNR Annual Conference, Houston, TX.

Callaway, T. G., & Bodenhamer-Davis, E. (2008). Long-term follow-up of a clinical replication of the Peniston protocol for chemical dependency. *Journal of Neurotherapy, 12*(4), 243–259. https://doi.org/10.1080/10874200802502060

Cowan, J. D., & Sokhadze, E. (2011). Prefrontal gamma

neurofeedback improves emotional state and cognitive function. *Applied Psychophysiology & Biofeedback, 36*(3), 220. https://doi.org/10.1007/s10484-011-9168-8

Crits-Christoph, P., Siqueland, L., Blaine, J., Frank, A., Luborsky, L., Onken, L. S., ... Gastfriend, D. R. (1999). Psychosocial treatments for cocaine dependence: National Institute on Drug Abuse collaborative cocaine treatment study. *Archives of General Psychiatry, 56*(6), 493–502.

deBeus, R. J. (2007). Quantitative electroencephalography-guided versus Scott/Peniston neurofeedback with substance abuse outpatients: A pilot study. *Biofeedback, 35*(4), 146–151.

deBeus, R., Prinzel, H., Ryder-Cook, A., & Allen, L. (2002). QEEG-based versus research-based EEG biofeedback treatment with chemically dependent outpatients: Preliminary results. *Journal of Neurotherapy, 6*(1), 64–66.

Dehghani-Arani, F., Rostami, R., & Nadali, H. (2013). Neurofeedback training for opiate addiction: Improvement of mental health and craving. *Applied Psychophysiology & Biofeedback, 38*(2), 133–141. https://doi.org/10.1007/s10484-013-9218-5

Downey, K. K., Stelson, F. W., Pomerleau, O. F., & Giordani, B. (1997). Adult attention deficit hyperactivity disorder: Psychological test profiles in a clinical population. *The Journal of Nervous and Mental Disease, 185*(1), 32–38.

Drake, R. E., & Wallach, M. A. (2000). Dual diagnosis: 15 years of progress. *Psychiatric Services, 51*(9), 1126–1129. https://doi.org/10.1176/appi.ps.51.9.1126

Egner, T., Strawson, E., & Gruzelier, J. H. (2002). EEG signature and phenomenology of alpha/theta neurofeedback training versus mock feedback. *Applied Psychophysiology & Biofeedback, 27*(4), 261–270.

Fahrion, S. L. (1995). Human potential and personal transformation. *Subtle Energies & Energy Medicine, 6*(1).

Fahrion, S. L., Walters, E. D., Coyne, L., & Allen, T. (1992). Alterations in EEG amplitude, personality factors, and brain electrical mapping after alpha-theta brainwave training: A controlled case study of an alcoholic in recovery. *Alcoholism: Clinical and Experimental Research, 16*(3), 547–552. https://doi.org/10.1111/j.1530-0277.1992.tb01415.x

Finkelberg, A., Sokhadze, E., Lopatin, A., Shubina, O., Kokorina, N., Skok, A., & Shtark, M. (1996). The application of alpha-theta EEG biofeedback training for psychological improvement in the process of rehabilitation of the patients with pathological addictions. *Biofeedback and Self-Regulation, 21*(4), 364.4.

Goldberg, R. J., Greenwood, J. C., & Taintor, Z. (1976). Alpha conditioning as an adjunct treatment for drug dependence: Part I. *International Journal of the Addictions, 11*(6), 1085–1089. https://doi.org/10.3109/10826087609058830

Goldberg, R. J., Greenwood, J. C., & Taintor, Z. (1977). Alpha conditioning as an adjunct treatment for drug dependence: Part II. *International Journal of the Addictions, 12*(1), 195–204. https://doi.org/10.3109/10826087709027219

Goslinga, J. J. (1975). Biofeedback for chemical problem patients: A developmental process. *Journal of Biofeedback, 2*, 17–27.

Graap, K., & Freides, D. (1998). Regarding the database for the Peniston alpha-theta EEG biofeedback protocol. *Applied Psychophysiology & Biofeedback, 23*(4), 265–272.

Grant, B. F., Stinson, F. S., Dawson, D. A., Chou, S. P., Ruan, W. J., & Pickering, R. P. (2004). Co-occurrence of 12-month alcohol and drug use disorders and personality disorders in the United States: Results from the National Epidemiologic Survey on Alcohol and Related Conditions. *Archives of General Psychiatry, 61*(4), 361–368.

Green, E. E., Green, A. M., & Walters, E. D. (1974). Alpha-theta biofeedback training. *Journal of Biofeedback, 2*(7–13).

Hardt, J. V., & Kamiya, J. (1978). Anxiety change through electroencephalographic alpha feedback seen only in high anxiety subjects. *Science, 201*(4350), 79–81.

Horrell, T., El-Baz, A., Baruth, J., Tasman, A., Sokhadze, G., Stewart, C., & Sokhadze, E. (2010). Neurofeedback effects on evoked and induced EEG gamma band reactivity to drug-related cues in cocaine addiction. *Journal of Neurotherapy, 14*(3),

195–216.

Hyman, S. E., & Malenka, R. C. (2001). Addiction and the brain: The neurobiology of compulsion and its persistence. *Nature Reviews Neuroscience*, 2(10), 695–703.

Kalechstein, A. D., Newton, T. F., Longshore, D., Anglin, M. D., van Gorp, W. G., & Gawin, F. H. (2000). Psychiatric comorbidity of methamphetamine dependence in a forensic sample. *The Journal of Neuropsychiatry and Clinical Neurosciences*, 12(4), 480–484.

Keith, J. R., Rapgay, L., Theodore, D., Schwartz, J. M., & Ross, J. L. (2015). An assessment of an automated EEG biofeedback system for attention deficits in a substance use disorders residential treatment setting. *Psychology of Addictive Behaviors*, 29(1), 17.

Kelley, M. J. (1997). Native Americans, neurofeedback, and substance abuse theory: Three year outcome of alpha/theta neurofeedback training in the treatment of problem drinking among Dine' (Navajo) people. *Journal of Neurotherapy*, 2(3), 24–60.

Koob, G. F., & Le Moal, M. (2001). Drug addiction, dysregulation of reward, and allostasis. *Neuropsychopharmacology*, 24(2), 97–129.

La Vaque, T. J., Hammond, D. C., Trudeau, D., Monastra, V., Perry, J., Lehrer, P., ... Sherman, R. (2002). Template for developing guidelines for the evaluation of the clinical efficacy of psychophysiological interventions. *Applied Psychophysiology and Biofeedback*, 27(4), 273–281.

Li, C. R., & Sinha, R. (2008). Inhibitory control and emotional stress regulation: Neuroimaging evidence for frontal–limbic dysfunction in psycho-stimulant addiction. *Neuroscience & Biobehavioral Reviews*, 32(3), 581–597.

Lowe, F. (1999). How essential is the EEG component of the Peniston and Kulkosky protocol? Presented at the 30th Annual Meeting of the Association for Applied Psychophysiology and Biofeedback, Vancouver, B.C. Canada.

Luthe, W. (1963). Autogenic training: Method, research and

application in medicine. *American Journal of Psychotherapy, 17*, 174–195.

Monastra, V. J., Lynn, S., Linden, M., Lubar, J. F., Gruzelier, J., & LaVaque, T. J. (2005). Electroencephalographic biofeedback in the treatment of attention-deficit/hyperactivity disorder. *Applied Psychophysiology & Biofeedback, 30*(2), 95–114. https://doi.org/10.1007/s10484-005-4305-x

Moore, J. P., & Trudeau, D. L. (1998). Alpha theta brainwave biofeedback is not specific to the production of theta/alpha crossover and visualizations. *Journal of Neurotherapy, 3*(1), 63.

Newton, T. F., Kalechstein, A. D., Hardy, D. J., Cook, I. A., Nestor, L., Ling, W., & Leuchter, A. F. (2004). Association between quantitative EEG and neurocognition in methamphetamine-dependent volunteers. *Clinical Neurophysiology, 115*(1), 194–198.

Noldy, N. E., Santos, C. V., Politzer, N., Blair, R. D. G., & Carlen, P. L. (1994). Quantitative EEG changes in cocaine withdrawal: Evidence for long-term CNS effects. *Neuropsychobiology, 30*(4), 189–196.

Nowlis, D. P., & Kamiya, J. (1970). The control of electroencephalographic alpha rhythms through auditory feedback and the associated mental activity. *Psychophysiology, 6*(4), 476–484.

O'Brien, C. P., Charney, D. S., Lewis, L., Cornish, J. W., Post, R. M., Woody, G. E., ... Bowden, C. L. (2004). Priority actions to improve the care of persons with co-occurring substance abuse and other mental disorders: A call to action. *Biological Psychiatry, 56*(10), 703–713.

Passini, F. T., Watson, C. G., Dehnel, L., Herder, J., & Watkins, B. (1977). Alpha wave biofeedback training therapy in alcoholics. *Journal of Clinical Psychology, 33*(S1), 292–299.

Peniston, E. G. (1998). Comments by Peniston. *Applied Psychophysiology and Biofeedback, 23*(4), 273–275. https://doi.org/10.1023/A:1022217900096

Peniston, E. G., & Kulkosky, P. J. (1989). Alpha-theta brainwave training and beta-endorphin levels in alcoholics. *Alcoholism: Clinical and Experimental Research, 13*(2), 271–279.

Peniston, E. G., & Kulkosky, P. J. (1990). Alcoholic personality and alpha-theta brainwave training. *Medical Psychotherapy, 3*, 37–55.

Peniston, E. G., & Kulkosky, P. J. (1991). Alpha-theta brainwave neurofeedback for Vietnam veterans with combat-related post-traumatic stress disorder. *Medical Psychotherapy, 4*(1), 47–60.

Peniston, E. G., Marrinan, D. A., Deming, W. A., & Kulkosky, P. J. (1993). EEG alpha-theta synchronization in Vietnam theater veterans with combat-related PTSD and alcohol abuse. *Medical Psychotherapy, 6*, 37–50.

Prichep, L. S., Alper, K. R., Sverdlov, L., Kowalik, S. C., John, E. R., Merkin, H., ... Rosenthal, M. S. (2002). Outcome related electrophysiological subtypes of cocaine dependence. *Clinical EEG and Neuroscience, 33*(1), 8–20.

Regier, D. A., Farmer, M. E., Rae, D. S., Locke, B. Z., Keith, S. J., Judd, L. L., & Goodwin, F. K. (1990). Comorbidity of mental disorders with alcohol and other drug abuse: Results from the Epidemiologic Catchment Area (ECA) study. *JAMA, 264*(19), 2511–2518.

Robinson, T. E., & Berridge, K. C. (2001). Incentive-sensitization and addiction. *Addiction, 96*(1), 103–114.

Roemer, R. A., Cornwell, A., Dewart, D., Jackson, P., & Ercegovac, D. V. (1995). Quantitative electroencephalographic analyses in cocaine-preferring polysubstance abusers during abstinence. *Psychiatry Research, 58*(3), 247–257.

Saxby, E., & Peniston, E. G. (1995). Alpha-theta brainwave neurofeedback training: An effective treatment for male and female alcoholics with depressive symptoms. *Journal of Clinical Psychology, 51*(5), 685–693.

Schneider, F., Elbert, T., Heimann, H., Welker, A., Stetter, F., Mattes, R., ... Mann, K. (1993). Self-regulation of slow cortical potentials in psychiatric patients: Alcohol dependency. *Biofeedback and Self-Regulation, 18*(1), 23–32.

Schubiner, H., Tzelepis, A., Milberger, S., Lockhart, N., Kruger, M., Kelley, B. J., & Schoener, E. P. (2000). Prevalence of attention-deficit/hyperactivity disorder and conduct disorder among substance abusers. *The Journal of Clinical Psychiatry, 61*(4), 244–

251.

Schwebel, R. (2004). *The seven challenges manual.* Tucson, AZ: Viva Press.

Scott, W. C., Kaiser, D., Othmer, S., & Sideroff, S. I. (2005). Effects of an EEG biofeedback protocol on a mixed substance abusing population. *The American Journal of Drug and Alcohol Abuse, 31*(3), 455–469.

Sheehan, M. F. (1993). Dual diagnosis. *Psychiatric Quarterly, 64*(2), 107–134.

Sherlin, L., Arns, M., Lubar, J., & Sokhadze, E. (2010). A position paper on neurofeedback for the treatment of ADHD. *Journal of Neurotherapy, 14*(2), 66–78.

Skok, A., Shubina, O., Finkelberg, A., Shtark, M., & Jafarova, O. (1997). EEG training in the treatment of addictive disorders. *Applied Psychophysiology and Biofeedback, 22*(2), 130. https://doi.org/10.1023/A:1026228312902

Sokhadze, E., Cowan, J., Tasman, A., Sokhadze, G., Horrell, T., & Stewart, C. (2010). Effects of gamma neurofeedback training on perceived positive emotional state and cognitive functions. *Journal of Neurotherapy, 14,* 343–345.

Sokhadze, E. M., Trudeau, D. L., & Cannon, R. L. (2013). Treating addiction disorders in clinical neurotherapy—Applications of techniques for treatment. In D. Cantor & J. Evans (Eds.), *Clinical neurotherapy.* San Diego: Elsevier.

Sokhadze, E., Singh, S., Stewart, C., Hollifield, M., El-Baz, A., & Tasman, A. (2008). Attentional bias to drug-and stress-related pictorial cues in cocaine addiction comorbid with posttraumatic stress disorder. *Journal of Neurotherapy, 12*(4), 205–225.

Sokhadze, E., Stewart, C., Hollifield, M., & Tasman, A. (2008). Event-related potential study of executive dysfunctions in a speeded reaction task in cocaine addiction. *Journal of Neurotherapy, 12*(4), 185–204.

Sokhadze, T. M., Cannon, R. L., & Trudeau, D. L. (2008). EEG biofeedback as a treatment for substance use disorders: Review, rating of efficacy, and recommendations for further research.

Applied Psychophysiology and Biofeedback, 33(1), 1–28. https://doi.org/10.1007/s10484-007-9047-5

Sokhadze, T. M., Stewart, C. M., & Hollifield, M. (2007). Integrating cognitive neuroscience research and cognitive behavioral treatment with neurofeedback therapy in drug addiction comorbid with posttraumatic stress disorder: A conceptual review. *Journal of Neurotherapy, 11*(2), 13–44.

Taub, E., & Rosenfeld, J. P. (1994). Is alpha/theta training the effective component of the alpha/theta therapy package for the treatment of alcoholism? *Biofeedback, 22*(3), 12–14.

Triffleman, E., Carroll, K., & Kellogg, S. (1999). Substance dependence posttraumatic stress disorder therapy: An integrated cognitive-behavioral approach. *Journal of Substance Abuse Treatment, 17*(1), 3–14.

Trudeau, D. L. (2000). The treatment of addictive disorders by brain wave biofeedback: A review and suggestions for future research. *Clinical EEG and Neuroscience, 31*(1), 13–22.

Trudeau, D. L. (2005). Applicability of brain wave biofeedback to substance use disorder in adolescents. *Child and Adolescent Psychiatric Clinics of North America, 14*(1), 125–136.

Trudeau, D. L. (2008). Brainwave biofeedback for addictive disorder. *Journal of Neurotherapy, 12*(4), 181–183. https://doi.org/10.1080/10874200802502391

Trudeau, D. L., Sokhadze, T. M., & Cannon, R. L. (2009). Neurofeedback in alcohol and drug dependency. In T. H. Budzynski, H. K. Budzynski, J. R. Evans, & A. Abarbanel (Eds.), *Introduction to quantitative EEG and neurofeedback: Advanced theory and applications* (2nd Edition, pp. 241–268). Amsterdam: Academic Press.

Twemlow, S. W., & Bowen, W. T. (1976). EEG biofeedback induced self-actualization in alcoholics. *Journal of Biofeedback, 3*, 20–25.

Twemlow, S. W., & Bowen, W. T. (1977). Sociocultural predictors of self-actualization in EEG-biofeedback-treated alcoholics. *Psychological Reports, 40*(2), 591–598.

Twemlow, S. W., Bowen, W. T., & Sizemore, D. G. (1977). Biofeedback induced energy redistribution in the alcoholic

EEG. *Journal of Biofeedback*, 3, 14–19.

Volkow, N. D., Fowler, J. S., & Wang, G.-J. (2004). The addicted human brain viewed in the light of imaging studies: brain circuits and treatment strategies. *Neuropharmacology*, 47, 3–13.

Watson, C. G., Herder, J., & Passini, F. T. (1978). Alpha biofeedback therapy in alcoholics: An 18-month follow-up. *Journal of Clinical Psychology*, 34(3), 765–769.

White, N. (1999). Theories of effectiveness of alpha-theta training for multiple disorders. In J. R. Evans & A. Abarbanel (Eds.), *Introduction to quantitative EEG and neurofeedback* (pp. 341–367). New York, NY: Elsevier.

White, N. E. (2008). The transformational power of the Peniston protocol: A therapist's experiences. *Journal of Neurotherapy*, 12(4), 261–265.

Wilens, T. E., Biederman, J., & Mick, E. (1998). Does ADHD affect the course of substance abuse?: Findings from a sample of adults with and without ADHD. *The American Journal on Addictions*, 7(2), 156–163.

12

Alpha/Theta Training Applied to Substance Abuse and Post-Traumatic Stress Disorder

William C. Scott, BSW

This chapter explains the alpha/theta (A/T training) protocol of EEG biofeedback applied to substance use disorder (SUD) and posttraumatic stress disorder (PTSD). It highlights A/T training efficacy through discussing the original Peniston protocol (Peniston & Kulkosky, 1989) and the Scott and Kaiser modification of the Peniston protocol. We will cover the recent literature that rigorously formulates a theoretical framework of the mechanisms of change with this intervention and the evidence of successful knowledge transfer of this technique to 699 clients from 39 different clinical settings. The chapter ends with a detailed description on how we conduct A/T training sessions with an evidence-based methodology that has been used in research and clinical practice since 2001.

A/T Training

Kamiya (1962; see Foreword, this book) first reported on brain-computer interaction on conditioned discrimination of alpha in humans at the Western Psychological Association's annual conference in Portland Oregon, USA. Other pioneers who expanded upon this work include Elmer and Alyce Green (Green & Green, 1977; Green, 1993) Dale Walters and colleagues (Green, Green, & Walters, 1970), and Steven Fahrion and colleagues (Fahrion, Walters, Coyne, & Allen, 1992; Fahrion, 1995) of the

Menninger Institute as well as Barbara Brown (1970), Les Fehmi (Fehmi & Fritz, 1980), and Thomas Budzynski (1973). Since then other studies have helped develop EEG biofeedback which include the subspecialty of A/T training for SUD and PTSD (Johnson & Meyer, 1974; Paskewitz, 1975; Plotkin, 1979; Heinrich, Gevensleben, & Strehl, 2007; Scott & Kaiser, 1998; Scott, Kaiser, Othmer, & Sideroff, 2005). For a comprehensive literature review on addiction studies I direct the interested reader to chapter 11, Sokhadze, Cannon, and Trudeau (2008) and other chapters in this handbook for other authors' discussion of this procedure.

Peniston and Kulkosky (1989) suggested that the alpha rhythm (8–13 Hz) is correlated with feelings of well-being, and the theta rhythm (4–8 Hz) is associated with day dreaming and the emotional release of repressed past trauma in an alcoholic population with PTSD. While this is an oversimplified notion, based upon what we know today, aspects of it can be used in a working hypothesis. The methodology in this study was difficult to interpret. I will briefly summarize the clearest outcomes.

The clinicians at the Sam Rayburn Veterans Hospital randomly placed recovering alcoholics in the 12-step based treatment program into an experimental group receiving 15 sessions of A/T training or a control group receiving more conventional treatment during the time the experimental subjects were receiving their A/T training sessions. These groups were homogeneous in terms of PTSD, alcoholism severity, combat theater, and age.

The researchers compared pre- vs. post-measures of the alcoholic groups to a third group of age-matched normals, which consisted of hospital staff. They acquired and compared pre- vs. post-six channels of EEG from C3, C4, P3, P4, O1 and O2 per the 10-20 international standard of electrode placement and found significant increases in alpha power over P3, P4, O1 and O2.

Pre- vs. post-serum beta-endorphin levels of the three groups were compared and the researchers found a significant increase in the alcoholic control group, which was interpreted as being an increased stress response to the control treatment. The two control groups received all pre and post measures at the same intervals as the experimental group. The experimental feedback consisted of training to increase peak-to-peak alpha amplitudes at O1 referenced to A1 (left ear) with the ground at A2 (right ear).

In personal communications with Peniston in 1993 about difficulty I had interpreting aspects of the team's methodology—specifically regarding the use of skin prep for sensor paste—Peniston advised he had research assistants write the methodology section of the paper and he caught and corrected numerous mistakes, but an older draft of the paper was accidentally submitted and accepted for publication. He also said impedances were kept at or below 5 kOhm which is not mentioned in the paper. The team reported that 5-minute pre- vs. post-feedback baseline recordings revealed significant increases in alpha percent power.

The equipment for this measure only produced data for alpha (8–13), theta (4–8Hz) and beta (13–26Hz). So the team reported percent power measures with the formula alpha / (alpha + theta + beta). They also compared percent power of theta and reported a significant 12 times baseline increase. Unfortunately, their described methodology to assess theta increase was not possible to interpret. Between the years 1993 and 1995 Peniston and I completed a small study (n = 24) with Native American alcoholics with PTSD at the Northland Recovery Center addiction treatment facility in Grand Rapids, MN. The mechanisms of A/T training were highly speculative and I was most curious about the theoretical underpinnings of this work. The treatment center was a small 10-bed facility so we didn't have a large enough population to conduct a randomized trial. My primary goals were to replicate earlier A/T training studies and formulate a hypothesis on mechanisms that could be tested in a subsequent randomized controlled trial.

We initially rewarded an increase in O1 alpha and theta amplitude with the same montage, impedances, alpha and theta bandwidths as Peniston and Kulkosky reported in 1989. However, clients with alpha amplitudes that started above 12 microvolts peak to peak reported feeling more anxious as their alpha increased and calmer as it decreased. This wasn't our expectation however we couldn't ignore their reports. We also found that all clients' alpha amplitude dropped as they entered crossover (the point when one's theta amplitude crosses above alpha).

A number of clients were becoming sleepy during sessions so we began to inhibit 2–5 Hz delta (the delta rhythm is known to increase in amplitude with slow wave sleep; Rechtschaffen & Kales, 1968). We also noticed that during sessions when a startle response was induced, the O1 alpha initially attenuated with the orienting response and then increased to levels higher than the average of the first 5 minutes. Alpha was also elevated when subjects came from intense confrontational groups. Being that alpha is the idling rhythm of the cortex (Adrian, 1935; Kawabata, 1974; Goldman, Stern, Engel, & Cohen, 2002), I speculated that its peak-to-peak amplitude was elevating because the paleomammalian brain was overpowering the higher functioning neocortex. Similarly, I noticed abreactions were happening with elevated levels of alpha amplitude. So we began rewarding for a decrease in alpha amplitudes for clients with alpha above 12 microvolts peak-to-peak and started inhibiting delta in an attempt to decrease sleep. These changes in procedure happened after the first eight subjects and seemed to correlate with the elimination of the intense abreactions every client previously exhibited.

Alpha/Theta Training Applied to Substance Abuse and PTSD

I initially speculated that the elimination of abreactions resulted from the delta inhibit. Though in hindsight, I suspect it was primarily related to sensitivity to my insecurities with this new procedure and the expectations I had. This is because Peniston explained that everyone had negative reactions as a part of their healing process. This phenomenon is something I still see happen in EEG biofeedback provider's practices where the provider fears abreactions, seems uncomfortable accessing calm or idle states within themselves, and/or is avoiding their own A/T sessions because they fear they may have a panic episode during a session. If the clinician's comfort level is threatened they may disconnect from the client, which could trigger the client's abandonment issues before the sensors are even placed on the head. Hysteria can be contagious and providers should be aware that this seems to be a large contributing factor in reported negative side effects. Thus, further in this chapter, I discuss the use of the panic procedure.

Every subject in our unpublished outcome study at the Northland Recovery Center completed treatment. We performed a thorough follow up with subjects for an accumulated 1.5 years post treatment verifying their abstinence with self-report and collateral confirmations for every subject. For the first few years of recovery, addicts typically have numerous moments per day where they experience intense negative emotions. The core of these emotions seems to stem from misinterpreted gestures or motives of others, overblown reactions to mistakes, easily triggered shame, and obsessions around events going their way. If a boss had a frown from a headache the addict would instantly have a projected a story about something he or the boss did wrong, how extensive the ramifications would be and what actions are required to remedy the situation. Addicts are bombarded with negative self-talk that is usually magnitudes more critical than anyone has been to them.

There is a disproportionate amount of abuse among addicted family systems, though I don't believe that abuse is a significant reason they abuse chemicals. In my 30 years of working with addicts, about 50% seem to have been born with this restlessness, irritability and discontentment. For them, their initial exposure to substances usually creates an instant addiction. "I want to do this as much as I can as often as I can," is a common report.

Substances bring on immediate relief and get ranked as important as air, water and food. It's not surprising how resistant to a treatment someone is when the treatment is perceived as separating her from substances, when there is only a hope they will eventually feel better without them. We would all become defensive if someone covered our nose and mouth. They don't use substances because they love getting high; they get high to stop feeling negative emotions.

The other half of addicts seem to have been born with an ability to self-soothe, feel a part of groups, would be curious why a boss is frowning, take in compliments, constructively use criticism, admit mistakes, maintain or elevate standards, accept accountability, and know their limitations. But after months or decades of using, they acquire identical negative states as those who were born with them. Their initial exposure to substances is indistinguishable from those who don't develop addictions.

Even after months or years of abstinence they don't return to feeling normal without some form of community support networks, even after receiving EEG biofeedback. By adding EEG biofeedback to addiction treatment we noticed their locus of control was externalizing within weeks rather than years of post-treatment recovery work. This relief would otherwise typically occur as they immerse themselves in service to other members of addiction communities. This is also evidenced by significant improvements in psychometric testing covered later in this chapter.

We performed a thorough follow up with all subjects for an accumulated 1.5 years post treatment verifying their abstinence with self-report and collateral confirmations. We confirmed a 79% abstinence rate though the study was not publishable for obvious methodological reasons. Prior to training all subjects met DSM III criteria for PTSD. One subject continued to have PTSD after 30 sessions of training. He remained symptomatic until it became resolved at 60 sessions. He had been slowly tapering from benzodiazepines across his first 30 sessions.

Saxby & Peniston (1995) reported alpha attenuation during the client's deeper states in their research and practice. People suffering from PTSD have been found to have decreased alpha power over the posterior cingulate cortex, which suggests cortical hyperarousal (Jokić-Begić & Begić, 2003; Wahbeh & Oken (2013). This likely reflects an underactivated default mode network, which is related to excessive self-reference, intrusive thoughts and hypervigilance. Phasic theta (4–7 Hz) oscillations (during active tasks) can be more complicated seeing that a decrease in variability would indicate more stable "locking" into a particular brain state, which may or may not facilitate task performance (Stam, van Walsum, & Micheloyannis, 2002; Deco & Hugues, 2012). An excellent example of this is how stronger theta, but weaker alpha synchronization variability is associated with better performance during a working memory task (Stam et al., 2002).

Studies utilizing both EEG and fMRI are beginning to find correlations between alpha amplitudes and functional brain networks including the default mode and salience networks, both of which are found to be abnormal in substance abuse and PTSD populations (Kluetsch et al., 2014; Hlinka, Alexakis, Diukova,

Liddle, & Auer, 2010; Daniels, Frewen, McKinnon, & Lanius, 2011; Lanius et al., 2010). Pre- vs. post-fMRI scans revealed that a single 30-minute alpha amplitude suppression session at Pz led to increased activation of the default mode and salience networks. Pz is over the precuneus, which is a functional core of the default mode network (Utevsky, Smith, & Huettel, 2014). This may explain why we see such large shifts in addicts' externalization of their locus of control. The fMRI scans were approximately 30 minutes prior to and 30 minutes after the EEG biofeedback session (Kluetsch et al., 2014).

Alpha rhythm (8–12 Hz) desynchronization (decrease in amplitude) occurs during directed attention in the sensory cortex (Haegens, Handel, & Jensen, 2011). It has long been found to be the idling rhythm of the cortex (Adrian 1935; Pfurtscheller, Stancak, & Neuper, 1996; Goldman et al., 2002). The clearest demonstration of this phenomenon is to measure alpha over the visual cortex as one opens and closes one's eyes. As the visual cortex stops processing visual information alpha amplitude increases. It stands to reason that if we train alpha to desynchronize over brain networks that are known to be underactivated in suffering populations, these networks could be trained to reactivate and related symptoms would improve.

The Problems With Current SUD Treatments

The most common addiction treatment approaches include community support, cognitive-behavioral therapies, motivational interviewing therapy, 12-step facilitation, psychodynamic therapy, self-help manuals, behavioral self-control, brief interventions, recovery monitoring, group and/or marital therapy, drug replacement therapy, and family support. According to the National Institute of Drug Abuse (NIDA, 2012) the best predictor of abstinence is the amount of time one spends in treatment.

SUD has extremely high social costs, particularly with long-term use and the problems of relapse associated after traditional therapies (Bechara & Damasio, 2002; Bernheim & Rangel, 2004). Twenty-seven million people in the US have a history of SUD (NIDA, 2012). Estimates from the 2004 Surgeon General's report total U.S. expenditures on tobacco products, alcoholic beverages, cocaine, heroin, mood altering prescription drugs, marijuana, and methamphetamines at more than $559 billion dollars annually. Prescription drug overdose is the leading cause of death injuries and has surpassed car accidents (Centers for Disease Control and Prevention, 2014).

The risk of relapse is high among people with a family history of substance abuse, with psychiatric dual diagnosis, and with opioid use (Domino et al., 2005). A history of studies of A/T training (Peniston & Kulkosky, 1989, 1990, 1991; Scott et al., 2005; Dehghani-Arani, Rostami, & Nadali, 2013; Keith, Rapgay, Theodore, Schwartz, & Ross, 2015; Rostami & Dehghani-Arani, 2015) have addressed problems of relapse, finding long-lasting abstinence, increased traditional treatment retention, and reduced psychiatric and attention symptomology after EEG biofeedback.

Peniston and the Scott-Kaiser Modification

The Peniston Protocol

As a reminder, in Peniston and Kulkosky's first trial, they divided the 30 subjects into three equal groups of 10 subjects: an experimental group treated with A/T training, an alcoholic control group undergoing traditional therapy, and a nonalcoholic control group. The A/T training group had significant reductions in the Beck Depression Inventory (BDI) scores, lower levels of stress serum beta-endorphins, and less relapse 13 months post treatment compared to controls. They also showed reduction on 13 scales of the Millon Clinical Multiaxial Inventory: schizoid, avoidant, dependent, histrionic, passive aggression, schizotypal, borderline, anxiety, somatoform, hypomanic, dysthymic, alcohol abuse, psychotic thinking, and psychotic depression; while controls only showed improvement on two scales.

On the 16-PF personality inventory (Cattell, 1946, 1957), the A/T training group demonstrated improvement on seven scales, compared to only one scale among the traditional treatment group. This study, with appropriate controls, found 80% abstinence for A/T training compared to 20% abstinence in the traditional treatment control at 4-year follow up.

The Peniston protocol introduced the use of complementary biofeedback autogenic training with a relaxation script to be read at the start of each session. Subjects used skin temperature biofeedback and rhythmic breathing until the temperature read at least 94 degrees in two consecutive sessions. During these eyes closed hand warming sessions they were instructed to imagine their extremities warming and relaxing in what was referred to as an autogenic script. Participants then used A/T training in an eyes-closed relaxed condition, receiving auditory signals from an EEG apparatus recording at O1. Following the A/T training sessions, a clinical interview was conducted assessing any dreamlike imagery experiences and/or abreactions (Peniston & Kulkosky, 1989, 1990, 1991).

Several other controlled studies of the Peniston protocol for addictions suggest that A/T training for alcoholism is an efficacious supplementary treatment. Using this same A/T training, Saxby and Peniston's (1995) subjects had a reduction in depression symptoms, maintained abstinence and reduced psychopathology per the Beck Depression Inventory and Millon Clinical Multiaxial Inventory-I.

Bodenhamer-Davis and Callaway (2004) conducted a study on participants mostly at high risk for re-arrests, finding at 74–98 months that 81.3% of the treatment subjects were abstinent. Kelley (1997) found, in their culturally sensitive study, using A/T training with Navajo Indians, that the majority of participants showed significant decreased levels of generalized anxiety disorder with 16 out of 19 of the patients experiencing partial or full remission.

Graap and Freides (1998) critiqued the Peniston protocol, raising significant issues about sampling; that the results could potentially be attributed to other therapies accompanying the biofeedback; that there was not enough technical detail for replication; and that the subjects may have had comorbid psychiatric conditions, particularly PTSD, that were not controlled for. These authors also noted that outcome criteria vary in replication studies, with a great degree of variance among abstinence and improvement. They critiqued that the treatment may only be useful with alcoholism as compared to all other SUDs. Peniston's neglect to mention that he combined EEG biofeedback with an inpatient 12-step treatment program was a significant oversight.

Upon my initial review of his 1989 publication, I thought it was impossible to achieve an 80% success rate so I dismissed it as a possibility. In personal communications, Ken Graap revealed his team failed to replicate Peniston's work without combining the protocol with a 12-step based treatment. Peniston's hypotheses should have encompassed how his temperature training, autogenic phrases and A/T training improves the effectiveness of a hospital based 12-step treatment program. That's what we did in our 2005 publication, The Effectiveness of an EEG Biofeedback Protocol on a Mixed Substance Abusing Population (Scott et al., 2005).

The Scott–Kaiser Modification of the Peniston Protocol

Upon review of the anomalies in the posterior cingulate cortex (over what is now known to be an important hub within the default mode network; Raichle et al. 2001), Scott and colleagues (2005) sought to address the underlying brain states related to cognition, mood and resistance to SUD treatments.

The study consisted of 121 mixed substance abuse volunteers in an inpatient substance abuse program undergoing biofeedback compared to treatment as usual controls. EEG biofeedback included training in beta and SMR to address attentional variables, followed by an A/T training protocol. Subjects received a total of 40 to 50 biofeedback sessions. The control group received additional time in 12-step treatment groups and lectures equivalent in time to the experimental procedure.

The Test of Variables of Attention (T.O.V.A.; Greenberg & Waldmant, 1993) and Minnesota Multiphasic Personality Inventory (MMPI) were administered with both tester and subject blind to group placement to obtain unbiased baseline data. There was no significant difference between groups in initial baseline TOVA scores, $F(1,303) = 1.333$, $p > .05$. A univariate, mixed-design ANOVA was used to compare the two groups on four dependent measures of the TOVA: inattention (% omission), impulsivity (% commission), response time, and response variability. Low scores were truncated at four standard deviations below normal. The experimental group exhibited significant improvement in impulsivity and variability measures in response to beta-SMR training, $F(1, 68) = 18.749$; $p < .005$, whereas no comparable change was found for the control group, $F(1, 68) = 19.405$; $p > 0.05$. The experimental group exhibited significant improvement in impulsivity and variability measures in response to beta-SMR training $F(1, 68) = 18.749$; $p < .005$ whereas no comparable change was found for the control group $F(1, 68) = 19.405; p > 0.05$ (Figure 12.1).

Experimental subjects also demonstrated significant improvement in inattention; however, the score only marginally differed from that of the control group, $F(1, 68) = 5.549$ ($p < .05$). T.O.V.A. scores were not further enhanced by either the A/T training or 30 additional sessions of treatment.

Treatment retention and abstinence rates as well as psychometric and cognitive measures were compared. Experimental subjects remained in treatment significantly longer than the control group. Of the experimental subjects completing the protocol, 77% were abstinent at 12 months, compared to 44% for the controls. Experimental subjects demonstrated significant improvement on the T.O.V.A. after an average of 13 beta-SMR sessions. Following A/T training, significant differences were noted on seven of the 10 MMPI-2 scales (see Table 12.1 and Figure 12.2). Thus, the Scott-Kaiser protocol enhanced treatment retention, variables of attention and abstinence rates at an accumulative 1.5 years post treatment. Follow-ups included self-reports with collateral confirmations. Only two controls and one experimental subject were unable to be contacted during the follow up period. However, several years after the study, the missing experimental subject referred a client to the CRI-Help treatment center and reported ongoing abstinence.

A successful 100 subject randomized controlled trial has replicated our results on opiate addictions (Dehghani-Arani et al. 2013). Another successful replication of our work (Rostami & Dehghani-Arani, 2015) occurred in a 100 subject study on methamphetamine addicts. However, while A/T training studies need further attention, Sokhadze et al. (2008) noted that it is probably an efficacious supplement to standard treatment for SUD. Finally, Hashemian (2015) completed a double blind placebo

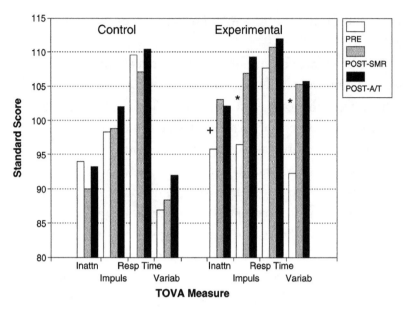

Figure 12.1. T.O.V.A. standard scores for experimental and control groups for pre-training, post-SMR, and post-AT assessments (+ p < .05, * p < .005).

controlled trial of alpha and theta enhancement at Pz for twenty 30 minute sessions and found significant reductions in cravings post treatment in the treated group. They did not report any significant EEG changes post study.

Issues With SUD Comorbidities for Individualized Treatment

Comorbidities to SUD, including major depressive disorder, antisocial personality disorder, ADHD, and PTSD are well documented (Jacobsen, Southwick, & Kosten, 2001). It is important for addiction treatment clinicians to realize that psychological disorders associated with SUD have their own neurophysiological aberrations. For example, patients with dual-diagnoses have more chronic illness and are more resistant to treatments (Brown, Recupero, & Stout, 1995).

Depression occurs in approximately 30% of chronic alcoholics seeking treatment presenting particular challenges to traditional therapies: they may have greater relapse, higher numbers of attrition, and/or readmission rates, manifest symptoms that are more chronic and severe, and tend to not respond as well to treatment (Regier et al., 1990).

As well, ADHD significantly increases the risk for substance use (Biederman, Wilens, Mick, Faraone, & Spencer, 1998). Associated social and behavioral problems may make individuals with comorbid SUD and ADHD treatment resistant (Wilens, Biederman, & Mick, 1998). Childhood ADHD associated with conduct disorder in males is an antecedent for adult substance use as well as anti-social personality disorder (Gittelman, Mannuzza, Shenker, & Bonagura, 1985). The incidence of ADHD in clinical SUD populations has been studied and may be as high as 50% (Downey, Stelson, Pomerleau, & Giordani, 1997). Adult residual ADHD is especially associated with cocaine and

Table 12.1

The Experimental Group Exhibited Significant Improvements Compared With the Changes in the Control Subjects.

Significance	Scale	F
$P < 0.005$	Hs (Hypochondriasis	$F(1, 81) = 14.08$
$P < 0.005$	D (Depression)	$F(1, 81) = 48.13$
$P < 0.005$	Hy (Conversion Hysteria)	$F(1, 81) = 32.68$
$P < 0.005$	Sc (Schizophrenia)	$F(1, 81) = 15.24$
$P < 0.005$	Si (Social Introversion)	$F(1, 81) = 24.65$
$P < 0.05$	Pt (Psychasthenia)	$F(1, 81) = 1.73$
$P < 0.05$	Pd (Psychopathic Deviate)	$F(1, 81) = 29.02$
$P < 0.05$	Ma (Mania)	
$P < 0.05$	Pa (Paranoia)	

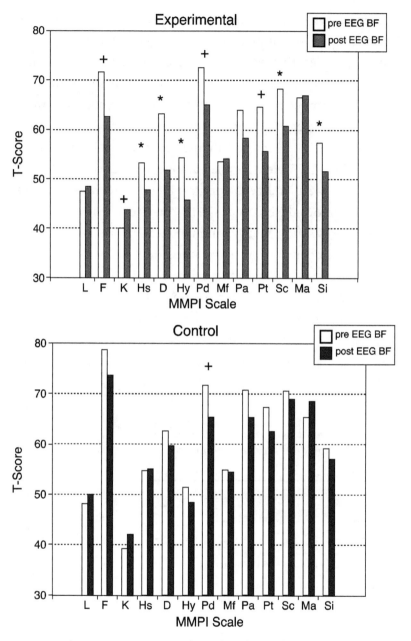

Figure 12.2. Changes in 10 MMPI clinical scales and three validity scales for the experimental and control groups (+ $p < .05$, * $p < .005$).

stimulant abuse (Levin & Kleber, 1995). Research has shown that EEG biofeedback outcomes compare favorably to those of stimulant medication. Scott and Kaiser (1998) describe combining a protocol for attention training (beta reward) with A/T training in a polysubstance abusing population whose primary drugs of abuse were cocaine, methamphetamine, and heroin.

Rates of PTSD occurring in persons identified with or in treatment for substance abuse are approximately 50% (Brady, Killeen, Brewerton, Tim, & Lucerini, 2000). These high rates of comorbidity suggest that PTSD and SUDs are functionally related, with PTSD comorbidity preceding substance usage and dependence (Jacobsen, Southwick, & Kosten, 2001). Cottler and Mager (1992) reported that cocaine abusers were three times more likely to meet diagnostic criteria for PTSD in the general population compared to individuals without a SUD. Kalechstein, Newton, and Green (2003) found that methamphetamine-dependent individuals are at greater risk to experience particular psychiatric symptoms. There was also a reported significant dependence-by-gender; methamphetamine-dependent females report more PTSD symptomatology compared to females without dependence, whereas males differed only with respect to depression.

Employing this A/T method in our clinics, we have had a high success rate for the PTSD population. When there is not an SUD comorbidity, this is an easier population to train with A/T training simply because necessary adjunct forms of therapy, such as 12-step and faith-based community models, are not confounding the outcomes. Yet the PTSD population is often in extreme stress-producing environments while undergoing treatment, and the majority report benefits within 3–5 sessions.

Addicts appear to require ongoing psycho-social treatments and community support, and EEG biofeedback may reduce resistance to these treatments. We have found with substance abusers, a high number of people continued with ongoing recovery work following our training. In the Scott-Kaiser UCLA study, we found less treatment resistance as evidenced by higher patient retention and consistent 12-step involvement during the accumulated 18 months of follow-up. There was only one subject among the entire 121 cohort who was maintaining abstinence without a scheduled routine of weekly 12-step meetings and some form of regular contact with a 12-step sponsor. While the research results with this method are impressive, how might this translate into clinical practice?

Metadata Analysis

As of the time of this publication, Steven Lowen, PhD of Harvard School of Medicine analyzed outcome metadata from 699 clients with PTSD symptoms who received A/T training (in press). The large sample was accumulated from 39 clinics between April 2010 and March 2014 using the Scott-Kaiser modification of the Peniston training. The population consisted of 450 females and 249 males with ages ranging from 11 to 85. Their median age was 39 (SD 13.82). The clinicians operating and overseeing the sessions were licensed psychologists, social workers, and psychiatrists in private or group practice, inpatient and outpatient mental health hospitals, addiction and eating disorder clinics who were trained and supervised via live webinar by Bill Scott. Their experience using EEG biofeedback averaged 3.26 years and ranged between 2 weeks to 4.2 years. During each session, de-identified metadata regarding, gender, age, artifacts, impedance quality, numbers of crossovers, longest period of crossover, training desires, training desire outcomes, diagnostic categories, positive and negative effects on mood, energy, sleep, nightmares, attention, and

Table 12.2

The Significance and Correlation of Comparisons of Normalized Alpha, Number of Crossovers, Length of Crossover, Relative Improvement, and Absolute Improvement

	Normalized Alpha		Number of Crossovers		Length of Crossover	
	Cor	Sig	Cor	Sig	Cor	Sig
Absolute Improvement	0.38	0.55	0.000009	0.99	-0.07	0.27
Relative Improvement	0.05	0.39	-0.007	0.91	-0.12	0.056
Length of Crossover	-0.66	9.13e-37	0.28	5.51e-06		
Number of Crossovers	-0.61	4.43e-29				

organization, were stored on an Amazon Web Services server for training purposes and quality control.

Lowen analyzed self-reports of the frequency of occurrences of PTSD symptoms (flashbacks, intrusive thoughts, hypervigilance, depersonalization) as being the same or worse, and then compared to being resolved or better across sessions. Clients training desires are referred to as growth areas and are selected from a list of approximately 250. One example is, "PTSD: I have at least three flashbacks per day that result in my cringing like I'm about to be hit." Lowen states, "After seven sessions, 84% report improvement in their symptoms. As this method is effective, relatively inexpensive and with a negligible side-effect profile, it represents an important, innovative intervention for symptoms of PTSD" (personal communication, 2014). After 20 sessions, 93% reported improvements of PTSD symptoms. Figure 12.3 shows the trends of EEG changes across sessions by these clients. These significant reductions, which we trained at Pz alpha, were similar to those found by Kluetsch et al. (2014) where the fMRI revealed significant activation in the default mode and salience networks. Unfortunately, in our analysis post session alpha amplitude measures were not taken where we may have seen the alpha amplitude rebound as found by Kluetsch and his colleagues.

Theta-over-alpha amplitude crossover had been reported by Green, Green and Walters (1970) to be associated with a hypnagogic state in which spontaneous imagery and recovery of repressed personal memories may occur. Crossover was thought to represent a state of consciousness in which the individual may access imagery representative of issues in one's life.

Lowen analyzed crossover from 250 clients for whom crossover data were available from the original cohort (n = 699). On a group level there was a strong negative correlation of alpha attenuation with session number ($p < .001$). There was not a significant correlation between clients' reported progress with the incidence of crossover. He found a tendency toward shorter crossovers showing better future progress at the group level, but this did not achieve significance ($p > 0.05$). He also found that at the group level, longer periods of crossover had a tendency to negatively correlate with progress. This is likely related to people falling asleep during sessions. Anecdotally, they don't seem to make progress. These data may suggest a marginally significant negative correlation between length of crossover and relative improvements on the group level. This analysis suggests one cannot predict progress or the lack thereof based on the occurrence of crossover by an individual. However, as a group, there is a trend that suggests that those with longer lengths of crossover may not progress as well as those with shorter durations.

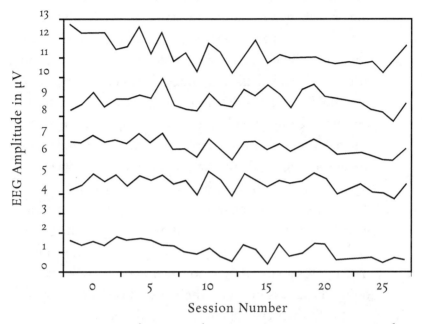

Figure 12.3. EEG grand average changes across 30 sessions reveals significant reductions in alpha (8–11 Hz) and beta (15–30 Hz) bands in the direction of training. No significant changes were found in theta (5–8 Hz) or delta (2–5 Hz).

The Protocol:

1. Prep the skin, attach sensors and create a low impedance hook-up. We attach the active sensor at Pz, which is over the precuneus with left ear referenced and grounded on the right ear. Impedances were kept below 10 kOhm and balanced within 1 kOhm of each other. It is strongly recommended that the clinician use an amplifier with continuous impedance monitoring or software indicators to simplify this procedure.
2. Throughout every session we inhibit 2–5 Hz and 15–30

Hz and reward 5–8 Hz theta. Prior to one's theta amplitude crossing over alpha (the crossover) we inhibit 8–11 Hz. All inhibit percentages are kept at between 10–20% above threshold; theta is rewarded between 40–60%, and after crossovers alpha is rewarded between 50–70% above threshold. The rewards and inhibits are adjusted after 1 minute of being outside these ranges. Specific and distinguishable sounds for the alpha and theta play while they are above threshold and the inhibit sounds are played when the amplitudes are below their thresholds.

3. The client sits back at about a 45-degree angle in a recliner, asked to close their eyes and begin reading the guided visualization script during the first 5 minutes of feedback in every session. If they report being too uncomfortable doing these sessions with their eyes closed, do not proceed with their eyes open. Rather process this as a therapeutic issue, and consider resuming the sessions when they are able to do them with their eyes closed.

4. Once the feedback sounds are heard, begin reading the guided visualization script, which contains these four aspects, (1) ideal personality, (2) behavior or reaction change scene, (3) subconscious instruction and (4) imagery of safety and well-being.

Ideal Personality;
(i) Go ahead now and sit back at about a 45 degree angle and close your eyes."
(ii) "Bring to mind an idea of you in more of your ideal world. Think through a list of qualities you would like to further enhance" (some examples could be feeling calmer, having more inner peace, improved access to intuition, increased freedom with

Alpha/Theta Training Applied to Substance Abuse and PTSD

self-expression etc.).

(iii) "Just tell me 'OK' out loud after you've gone through some of these in your mind."

Behavior or Reaction Change:

(iv) "Now bring to mind a specific future event that could be somewhat stressful for you; one you would like to move through with more grace and freedom. Again, tell me 'OK' when that event comes to mind."

(v) "Now think to yourself as if this event was over and the thought occurs to you, 'That was easy.' And again just say 'OK' out loud here after you've gone through that as well."

Subconscious Instruction:

(vi) Next think to yourself, "Subconscious, do whatever you can to make that happen. Your subconscious mind is the part of you where your motives, dreams, ambitions and desires come from. It can work on your intentions, independent of thought, both in and out of these sessions. Just tell me 'OK' after you've told your subconscious to internalize your intention."

Imagery of Safety and Wellbeing:

(vii) "Finally, for about a minute, bring to mind a time you have felt better than you're feeling at this moment or an event that was fun. Perhaps you were enjoying yourself or the company you were with."

(viii) "And after about a minute of this (neutral or positive) thought just let your mind wander onto or into any places of consciousness it happens to. Don't try to rehearse these intentions, direct your mind with thoughts or use meditative techniques beyond this next minute. These instructions were an attempt

to seed your subconscious mind with your change intentions so the feedback can assist you in working through obstacles both in and out of these sessions. After a period of time I will invite you back from where ever you happen to be but until then, you just enjoy!"
5. Inviting the client back after the 24 minutes of feedback completes, you might say, "Slowly start bringing yourself back now. Whenever you are ready feel free to describe your experience."

Stay in the room with them for at least the first 2–3 sessions. If they have an issue with your presence in the room, consider having a bell they can ring if they need you.

We do not instruct the clients to focus on one sound over another. Doing so seems to increase anxiety and frustration, making the client more anxious while trying to regulate psychological mechanisms that they have not yet had success with. Some strategies employed by EEG biofeedback participants may lead to cognitive overload and prevent EEG biofeedback learning. For example, Kober, Witte, Ninaus, Neuper, & Wood (2013) repeated attempts to get control over fMRI feedback, called efforting, might impede progress by trying too hard. If the client has previously done beta/SMR or other brain training with specific goals to remain attentive, advise that this training is the opposite of that. Here one's self-organizing brain can instantaneously hear when it's moving into states that are more or less activated. It can learn to balance these states of arousal in a similar way it learns how to balance on a bicycle. This doesn't require thought after one is done going through each of the four parts of the guided visualization script.

Alpha/Theta Training Applied to Substance Abuse and PTSD

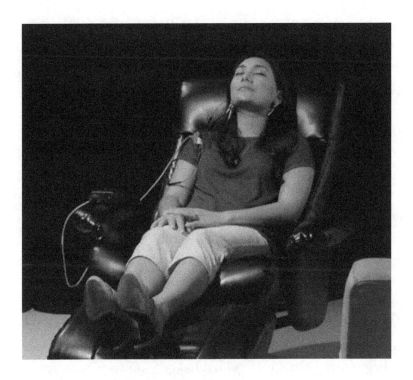

Figure 12.4. Patient during A/T training.
Image courtesy of BrainPaint, Inc., Los Angeles, CA

If a client falls asleep during a session, pause the feedback, and consider having her do the remainder of the session in a straight back chair without a headrest. Avoid simply trying to wake them up each time. Doing so may create reliance upon external factors and failure to learn self-regulation and being more present. For clients with a propensity for panic or extreme anxiety we suggest our progressive muscle relaxation technique we use in the first 3–4 sessions. The same A/T training mentioned in the previous section is used here. Clients with a recent history of panic often have intrusive thoughts or flashbacks during idle moments. Many of them become overcome with anxiety when asked to sit anywhere for 24 minutes with their eyes closed. This appears to be the most frequent cause of abreactions Peniston referred to in his A/T training courses and I have seen this clinically over the years. We induce calming and openness to experience in the client and we combine progressive muscle relaxation and with the EEG biofeedback. Behavioral research suggests that distraction (see further discussion) can be effective at temporarily relieving rumination and improving mood (Kross & Ayduk, 2008).

It seems that when this population has a negative first experience they become conditioned to anxiety in subsequent sessions. This exercise increases the likelihood of having a neutral or pleasant introduction to A/T training. In our clinics the first three sessions are 7, 15, and 24 minutes long respectively. We consider doing an additional 15-minute session when they present panic symptoms or heightened arousal at the end of the second session. After 3–4 of these exercises for clients with panic, we begin using the 4-part guided imagery protocol described above.

Further Research

Like other scholars, we believe finding causal effects of EEG biofeedback on brain plasticity would improve recognition of A/T training and afford it as a veritable, safe, and inexpensive treatment. A future consideration for A/T training may be through fMRI research to capture causal neuromodulatory effects on various brain functional networks and behaviors as a result of the training.

In general, EEG biofeedback studies need improved and clearly defined outcome measures to establish greater reliability and validity as well as control for nonspecific effects. The essential components, protocols, session and treatment durations need to be researched. For example in the Scott-Kaiser UCLA addiction study, participants were administered an average of 43 EEG biofeedback sessions, while results may likely appear quicker than 43 sessions.

Keith (personal communication, 2015) replicated Scott & Kaiser's (2005) average length of stay in treatment and reduction of those leaving against medical advice following just 15 sessions of beta/SMR training on an ADHD subset of an inpatient addicted population. However, the reviewers disallowed this finding in their 2015 (Keith et al., 2015) publication.

Longitudinal studies with long follow up data are needed to determine the permanence of the A/T training effects as well as the most effective number of sessions. Finally, other physiological effects, such as heart rate, breath rate, electrodermal activity and psychological effects, such as changes in depression and anxiety symptoms and changes in perceived fear associated with A/T training in SUD need greater investigation. Thus, these, among other factors, are important to determine specificity and efficacy.

Furthermore, we recommend assessing executive functions and cue reactivity implicated in SUD, possibly through the Balloon Analog Risk Task, Wisconsin Card Sorting Task, and/or Stroop test.

In personalized medicine, the gold standard is to look at the whole, individual patient. Thus, clinicians need to consider common comorbidities (major depressive disorder, generalized anxiety disorder, ADHD, etc.) before administering A/T training to improve diagnostic assessment is highly recommended (Duric, Assmus, Gundersen, & Elgen, 2012; Mann, Lubar, Zimmerman, Miller, & Muenchen, 1992).

As we have seen, EEG biofeedback improves compliance, especially with people with SUD, who are conventionally treatment-resistant. It is therefore recommended to study the effects of a combined A/T training/CBT protocol to CBT treatment alone. This may ascertain a heightened combined effect of A/T training in tandem with one of the current efficacious behavioral treatment for SUDs. Finally, I would most like to see a large n replication of Peniston's 1989 study on serum beta-endorphins with PTSD subjects with pre- vs. post-MRIs.

Acknowledgements

I wish to thank Marcus Sola (CRI-Help, chairman of the board) and Jack Bernstein (CRI-Help, CEO) for their support and funding of the 2005 addiction study that comprised the majority of what I have learned and teach. Thanks also to Steven B. Lowen, PhD of the Harvard McLean School of Medicine, for his insights, guidance, critical review and analytics, which have brought clarity to numerous anecdotal observations discussed in our field. Thank you, Cynthia Kerson, for your commitment to this field, all the time you have put into this book endeavor and how intimately involved you've been every step of the way. My biggest thanks go to my wife Cora, who is my primary source of inspiration and who is always squeezing the absolute best out of me.

References

Adrian, E. D. (1935). Discharge frequencies in the cerebral and cerebellar cortex. In *Proc Phys Soc* (Vol. 83, pp. 32–33).

Bechara, A., & Damasio, H. (2002). Decision-making and addiction (part I): Impaired activation of somatic states in substance dependent individuals when pondering decisions with negative future consequences. *Neuropsychologia*, 40(10), 1675–1689.

Bernheim, B. D., & Rangel, A. (2004). Addiction and cue-triggered decision processes. *The American Economic Review*, 94(5), 1558–1590.

Biederman, J., Wilens, T. E., Mick, E., Faraone, S. V., & Spencer, T. (1998). Does attention-deficit hyperactivity disorder impact the developmental course of drug and alcohol abuse and dependence? *Biological Psychiatry, 44*(4), 269–273.

Bodenhamer-Davis, E., & Callaway, T. (2004). Extended follow-up of Peniston protocol results with chemical dependency. *Journal of Neurotherapy, 8*(2), 135. https://doi.org/10.1300/J184v08n02_13

Brady, K. T., Killeen, T. K., Brewerton, T., & Lucerini, S. (2000). Comorbidity of psychiatric disorders and posttraumatic stress disorder. *The Journal of Clinical Psychiatry.*

Brown, B. B. (1970). Recognition of aspects of consciousness through association with EEG alpha activity represented by a light signal. *Psychophysiology, 6*(4), 442–452. https://doi.org/10.1111/j.1469-8986.1970.tb01754.x

Brown, P. J., Recupero, P. R., & Stout, R. (1995). PTSD substance abuse comorbidity and treatment utilization. *Addictive Behaviors, 20*(2), 251–254.

Budzynski, T. H. (1973). Sonic applications of biofeedback produced twilight states. In D. Shapiro (Ed.), *Biofeedback and self-control* (pp. 145–151). Aldine.

Cattell, R. B. (1946). Description and measurement of personality.

Cattell, R. B. (1957). Personality and motivation structure and measurement.

Centers for Disease Control and Prevention. (2014). Wide-ranging online data for epidemiologic research. Retrieved from https://wonder.cdc.gov/

Cottler, L. B., Mager, D., & others. (1992). Posttraumatic stress disorder among substance users from the general population. *The American Journal of Psychiatry, 149*(5), 664.

Daniels, J. K., Frewen, P., McKinnon, M. C., & Lanius, R. A. (2011). Default mode alterations in posttraumatic stress disorder related to early-life trauma: A developmental perspective. *Journal of Psychiatry & Neuroscience, 36*(1), 56–59. https://doi.org/10.1503/jpn.100050

Deco, G., & Hugues, E. (2012). Neural network mechanisms underlying stimulus driven variability reduction. *PLoS Computational Biology, 8*(3), e1002395.

Dehghani-Arani, F., Rostami, R., & Nadali, H. (2013). Neurofeedback training for opiate addiction: Improvement of mental health and craving. *Applied Psychophysiology & Biofeedback*, 38(2), 133–141. https://doi.org/10.1007/s10484-013-9218-5

Domino, K. B., Hornbein, T. F., Polissar, N. L., Renner, G., Johnson, J., Alberti, S., & Hankes, L. (2005). Risk factors for relapse in health care professionals with substance use disorders. *JAMA*, 293(12), 1453–1460.

Downey, K. K., Stelson, F. W., Pomerleau, O. F., & Giordani, B. (1997). Adult attention deficit hyperactivity disorder: Psychological test profiles in a clinical population. *The Journal of Nervous and Mental Disease*, 185(1), 32–38.

Duric, N. S., Assmus, J., Gundersen, D., & Elgen, I. B. (2012). Neurofeedback for the treatment of children and adolescents with ADHD: A randomized and controlled clinical trial using parental reports. *BMC Psychiatry*, 12(1), 107.

Fahrion, S. L. (2002). Group biobehavioral treatment of addiction. Presented at the 4th Meeting on the Neurobiology of Criminal and Violent Behavior, Scottsdale AZ.

Fahrion, S. L., Walters, E. D., Coyne, L., & Allen, T. (1992). Alterations in EEG amplitude, personality factors, and brain electrical mapping after alpha-theta brainwave training: A controlled case study of an alcoholic in recovery. *Alcoholism: Clinical and Experimental Research*, 16(3), 547–552. https://doi.org/10.1111/j.1530-0277.1992.tb01415.x

Fehmi, L., & Fritz, G. (1980). Open focus: The attentional foundation of health and well-being. *Somatics*, 2, 34–40.

Gittelman, R., Mannuzza, S., Shenker, R., & Bonagura, N. (1985). Hyperactive boys almost grown up: I. Psychiatric status. *Archives of General Psychiatry*, 42(10), 937–947.

Goldman, R. I., Stern, J. M., Engel Jr, J., & Cohen, M. S. (2002). Simultaneous EEG and fMRI of the alpha rhythm. *Neuroreport*, 13(18), 2487.

Graap, K., & Freides, D. (1998). Regarding the database for the Peniston alpha-theta EEG biofeedback protocol. *Applied Psychophysiology & Biofeedback*, 23(4), 265–272.

Green, E. (1993). AT brainwave training: Instrumental vipassana?

Presented at the Montreal Symposium, Montreal, Canada.

Green, E. E., Green, A. M., & Walters, E. D. (1970). Voluntary control of internal states: Psychological and physiological. *The Journal of Transpersonal Psychology, 2*(1), 1.

Green, E. E., Green, A. M., & Walters, E. D. (1974). Alpha-theta biofeedback training. *Journal of Biofeedback, 2*(7–13).

Green, E., & Green, A. (1977). *Beyond biofeedback*. San Francisco, CA: Delacorte.

Greenberg, L. M., & Waldmant, I. D. (1993). Developmental normative data on the Test of Variables of Attention (TOVA™). *Journal of Child Psychology and Psychiatry, 34*(6), 1019–1030.

Haegens, S., Händel, B. F., & Jensen, O. (2011). Top-down controlled alpha band activity in somatosensory areas determines behavioral performance in a discrimination task. *Journal of Neuroscience, 31*(14), 5197–5204.

Hashemian, P. (2015). The effectiveness of neurofeedback therapy in craving of methamphetamine use. *Open Journal of Psychiatry, 5*(02), 177.

Heinrich, H., Gevensleben, H., & Strehl, U. (2007). Annotation: Neurofeedback—Train your brain to train behaviour. *Journal of Child Psychology and Psychiatry, 48*(1), 3–16.

Hlinka, J., Alexakis, C., Diukova, A., Liddle, P. F., & Auer, D. P. (2010). Slow EEG pattern predicts reduced intrinsic functional connectivity in the default mode network: An inter-subject analysis. *Neuroimage, 53*(1), 239–246.

Jacobsen, L. K., Southwick, S. M., & Kosten, T. R. (2001). Substance use disorders in patients with posttraumatic stress disorder: A review of the literature. *American Journal of Psychiatry, 158*(8), 1184–1190.

Johnson, R. K., & Meyer, R. G. (1974). The locus of control construct in EEG alpha rhythm feedback. *Journal of Consulting and Clinical Psychology, 42*(6), 913.

Jokić-Begić, N., & Begić, D. (2003). Quantitative electroencephalogram (qEEG) in combat veterans with post-traumatic stress disorder (PTSD). *Nordic Journal of Psychiatry, 57*(5), 351–355.

Kalechstein, A. D., Newton, T. F., & Green, M. (2003). Methamphetamine dependence is associated with neurocognitive impairment in the initial phases of abstinence. *The Journal of Neuropsychiatry and Clinical Neurosciences*, 15(2), 215–220.

Kamiya, J. (1962). Conditioned discrimination of the EEG alpha rhythm in humans. Presented at the Western Psychological Association, San Francisco, CA.

Karson, S., & O'Dell, J. W. (1976). A guide to the clinical use of the 16 PF.

Kawabata, N. (1974). Dynamics of the electroencephalogram during performance of a mental task. *Biological Cybernetics*, 15(4), 237–242.

Keith, J. R., Rapgay, L., Theodore, D., Schwartz, J. M., & Ross, J. L. (2015). An assessment of an automated EEG biofeedback system for attention deficits in a substance use disorders residential treatment setting. *Psychology of Addictive Behaviors*, 29(1), 17.

Kelley, M. J. (1997). Native Americans, neurofeedback, and substance abuse theory: Three year outcome of alpha/theta neurofeedback training in the treatment of problem drinking among Dine' (Navajo) people. *Journal of Neurotherapy*, 2(3), 24–60.

Kluetsch, R. C., Ros, T., Théberge, J., Frewen, P. A., Calhoun, V. D., Schmahl, C., ... Lanius, R. A. (2014). Plastic modulation of PTSD resting-state networks and subjective wellbeing by EEG neurofeedback. *Acta Psychiatrica Scandinavica*, 130(2), 123–136.

Kober, S. E., Witte, M., Ninaus, M., Neuper, C., & Wood, G. (2013). Learning to modulate one's own brain activity: The effect of spontaneous mental strategies. *Frontiers in Human Neuroscience*, 7.

Kross, E., & Ayduk, O. (2008). Facilitating adaptive emotional analysis: Distinguishing distanced-analysis of depressive experiences from immersed-analysis and distraction. *Personality and Social Psychology Bulletin*, 34(7), 924–938.

Lanius, R., Bluhm, R., Coupland, N., Hegadoren, K., Rowe, B.,

Theberge, J., ... Brimson, M. (2010). Default mode network connectivity as a predictor of post-traumatic stress disorder symptom severity in acutely traumatized subjects. *Acta Psychiatrica Scandinavica, 121*(1), 33–40.

Levin, F. R., & Kleber, H. D. (1995). Attention-deficit hyperactivity disorder and substance abuse: Relationships and implications for treatment. *Harvard Review of Psychiatry, 2*(5), 246–258.

Mann, C. A., Lubar, J. F., Zimmerman, A. W., Miller, C. A., & Muenchen, R. A. (1992). Quantitative analysis of EEG in boys with attention-deficit-hyperactivity disorder: Controlled study with clinical implications. *Pediatric Neurology, 8*(1), 30–36.

NIDA. (2012). Principles of drug addiction treatment: A research-based guide (3rd Ed). Retrieved from https://www.drugabuse.gov/publications/principles-drug-addiction-treatment-research-based-guide-third-edition

Paskewitz, D. A. (1975). Biofeedback instrumentation: Soldering closed the loop. *American Psychologist, 30*(3), 371.

Peniston, E. G., & Kulkosky, P. J. (1989). Alpha-theta brainwave training and beta-endorphin levels in alcoholics. *Alcoholism: Clinical and Experimental Research, 13*(2), 271–279.

Peniston, E. G., & Kulkosky, P. J. (1990). Alcoholic personality and alpha-theta brainwave training. *Medical Psychotherapy, 3*, 37–55.

Peniston, E. G., & Kulkosky, P. J. (1991). Alpha-theta brainwave neurofeedback for Vietnam veterans with combat-related post-traumatic stress disorder. *Medical Psychotherapy, 4*(1), 47–60.

Pfurtscheller, G., Stancak, A., & Neuper, C. (1996). Event-related synchronization (ERS) in the alpha band—An electrophysiological correlate of cortical idling: A review. *International Journal of Psychophysiology, 24*(1), 39–46.

Plotkin, W. B. (1979). The alpha experience revisited: Biofeedback in the transformation of psychological state. *Psychological Bulletin, 86*(5), 1132.

Raichle, M. E., MacLeod, A. M., Snyder, A. Z., Powers, W. J., Gusnard, D. A., & Shulman, G. L. (2001). A default mode of brain function. *Proceedings of the National Academy of Sciences, 98*(2), 676–682.

Rechtschaffen, A., & Kales, A. (1968). *A manual of standardized terminology, techniques and scoring system for sleep stages of human subjects*. Bethesda, Md.: U.S. Dept. of Health, Education, and Welfare, Public Health Services-National Institutes of Health, National Institute of Neurological Diseases and Blindness, Neurological Information Network.

Regier, D. A., Farmer, M. E., Rae, D. S., Locke, B. Z., Keith, S. J., Judd, L. L., & Goodwin, F. K. (1990). Comorbidity of mental disorders with alcohol and other drug abuse: Results from the Epidemiologic Catchment Area (ECA) study. *JAMA*, 264(19), 2511–2518.

Rostami, R., & Dehghani-Arani, F. (2015). Neurofeedback training as a new method in treatment of crystal methamphetamine dependent patients: A preliminary study. *Applied Psychophysiology and Biofeedback*, 40(3), 151–161.

Saxby, E., & Peniston, E. G. (1995). Alpha-theta brainwave neurofeedback training: An effective treatment for male and female alcoholics with depressive symptoms. *Journal of Clinical Psychology*, 51(5), 685–693.

Scott, W. C., Kaiser, D., Othmer, S., & Sideroff, S. I. (2005). Effects of an EEG biofeedback protocol on a mixed substance abusing population. *The American Journal of Drug and Alcohol Abuse*, 31(3), 455–469.

Scott, W., & Kaiser, D. (1998). Augmenting chemical dependency treatment with neurofeedback training. *Journal of Neurotherapy*, 3(1), 66.

Sokhadze, T. M., Cannon, R. L., & Trudeau, D. L. (2008). EEG biofeedback as a treatment for substance use disorders: Review, rating of efficacy, and recommendations for further research. *Applied Psychophysiology and Biofeedback*, 33(1), 1–28. https://doi.org/10.1007/s10484-007-9047-5

Stam, C. J., van Walsum, A.-M. van C., & Micheloyannis, S. (2002). Variability of EEG synchronization during a working memory task in healthy subjects. *International Journal of Psychophysiology*, 46(1), 53–66.

Utevsky, A. V., Smith, D. V., & Huettel, S. A. (2014). Precuneus is a functional core of the default-mode network. *Journal of Neuroscience, 34*(3), 932–940.

Wahbeh, H., & Oken, B. S. (2013). Peak high-frequency HRV and peak alpha frequency higher in PTSD. *Applied Psychophysiology and Biofeedback, 38*(1), 57–69.

Wilens, T. E., Biederman, J., & Mick, E. (1998). Does ADHD affect the course of substance abuse? Findings from a sample of adults with and without ADHD. *The American Journal on Addictions, 7*(2), 156–163.

13

Evolution of Alpha-Theta Training Over a Quarter Century

Siegfried Othmer, PhD
Susan F. Othmer, BA

In this chapter, we present what has emerged in our clinician network as a comprehensive neurofeedback strategy that incorporates alpha-theta as the essential element to resolve trauma syndromes. Preliminary stages of training are introduced in order to enhance the subsequent success of the alpha-theta experience. This chapter relates how the comprehensive strategy emerged. Some case reports and group data are presented in support of the therapeutic strategy.

Our EEG Institute staff in Los Angeles has been involved with alpha-theta training since the early nineties, after becoming acquainted with the work of Eugene Peniston. Up to that time we had been working with SMR/beta training exclusively, ever since our entry into the field in 1985. In those early days we had absorbed the prevailing wisdom of the field that alpha training had been thoroughly discredited. This sentiment was so well established that Peniston's presentation at the AAPB meeting in Washington, DC in 1990 encountered considerable resistance from the old-timers. Nevertheless, that presentation launched numerous clinical initiatives within the biofeedback community, ours among them.

The CRI-Help Study at EEG Spectrum

We developed the alpha-theta capability for our NeuroCybernetics system in 1992, and in 1994 the opportunity opened up to do a large-scale controlled study, now known as the CRI-Help study. This likely remains the largest and most extensive controlled study ever undertaken in biofeedback or neurofeedback. We had hired Bill Scott to do alpha-theta training at our clinic in Encino, California, and thus he could also supervise the clinicians who would be doing the training at CRI-Help, a large residential treatment center in North Hollywood. David Kaiser, who was also working for us at the time, was responsible for the study design. We saw this as another replication of the Peniston Protocol, but Peniston himself demurred on our insertion of SMR-beta training in place of the temperature training element. We knew what we were bringing the table. We did not know what we might be giving up by dropping the temperature training. In retrospect, we were caught in a cognitive bias, with our emphasis on taming impulsivity and enhancing pre-frontal inhibitory control. The well-regulated brain, we assumed, is better able to exercise good judgment, thus paving the way for mastery over addiction.

Indeed, we were rewarded for our efforts with a normalization of TOVA scores and improved retention in the program. And relapse prevention was successful at the 70+% level (after 1 year) for a population that was generally more impaired than Peniston's veterans had been (Scott, Kaiser, Othmer, & Othmer, 2005; see also Scott, chapter 12). But when participants were asked, at 3-year follow-up, to what factors they attributed their ongoing success in retaining sobriety, they mainly gave credit to their continued participation in group. Clearly, they still had to work at remaining abstinent, which meant that most of them were still contending with a physiological dependency at some level. We had not solved the problem of addiction categorically. The alpha-theta training had helped with the resolution of trauma syndromes where that had been an issue, but any acquired physiological drug dependency could retain its grip. Liberation from drug cravings was certainly something we observed, but we could not count on it in the general case.

Development now had to take place on another front, because the alpha-theta training was sufficiently mature technologically that it was accomplishing all that could be expected of it. Alpha-theta has an experiential purpose rather than a brain-training objective. It merely provides the entry portal to our deeper states, and gentle cueing with respect to alpha- and theta-dominant states is all that is required. Entry into deeper states is mainly a matter of removing impediments. Our central executive insists on its own priorities without reprieve. The alpha-theta process deposes the central executive for a spell; it silences the verbal scold that we carry around in our brains, the rule-maker, and the tyrannical left hemisphere. Harsh self-judgment is silenced for the moment. The result can be a wholesome encounter with the core self. There follows a healing of fractured relationships as they are simply re-envisioned. There is a healing of traumas as these are re-framed experientially by being revisited in a benign context. This experience separates the physiological response from the recall of the event, and allows it to be recommitted to memory as a historical memory like any other. There is the envisioning of a wholesome life going forward.

Alpha-theta is therefore best seen as a remedy for the grip of trauma rather than for addictions per se. Trauma memories are whole body memories, unitary phenomena in which the re-constitution of the memory trace extends into the peripheral physiology. Trauma memories are state-stamped rather than date-stamped. Recovery by alpha-theta is in essence a psychological process, but it is one that is crucially dependent on what happens at the physiological level. That aspect, however, remains somewhat obscure, and needs further clarification. Such clarity was not available to us at the time, however. It came through further development of the clinical approach, which then allowed our understanding to catch up.

The further evolution took place on the SMR-beta side of the protocol. In the CRI-Help study we had employed our first iteration beyond the then-standard "C3beta-C4SMR" protocol, which involved 15–18 Hz reinforcement on the left sensorimotor cortex and 12–15 Hz reinforcement on the right. We modified the left-hemisphere training to introduce a frontal bias, and the right-hemisphere training to introduce a parietal bias. The new placements were C3-Fpz and C4-Pz, which also implied a return to the bipolar montage we had used at the outset. The training effects were distinctly stronger than before, no doubt for reasons of both placement and montage. The state of affairs at this juncture was captured in a chapter for a psychiatry textbook on addictions treatment (Othmer, S. & Steinberg, 2010).

The Journey to Low Frequency

The discovery of high frequency-specificity of the SMR-beta training opened up exploration of the entire EEG band, eventually leading to the very lowest frequency that was accessible with a 3 Hz bandwidth, namely 0–3 Hz, with a 1.5 Hz center frequency. The clinical strategy was to start out with our standard bands of low beta and SMR and then to find the optimum response frequency (called the ORF) for each client. Clients distributed themselves over the entire spectrum, but more clients ended up preferring the lowest frequency than any other. By the time we were well along in this process, hardly anyone optimized at our old standard frequency of 15–18 Hz, where we had trained everybody over several years! The brain had been doing the best that it could with the information we provided at the standard frequencies, but that was not its own preference when we finally started paying attention to that issue.

The pile-up at the lowest frequency, which was well-established by 2004, was an invitation to explore even lower frequencies, the range below 0.1 Hz that is referred to as the infra-low frequency (ILF) region. A difficulty was that such low frequencies needed to be trained differently, in a signal-following manner, which meant the abandonment of any operant conditioning aspect of the feedback design. Thresholds lose their meaning in this context. We initiated the exploration of the frequency range down to 0.05 Hz in 2006, and it was not long before we observed the same pattern as before: clients favored the lowest frequency, and they did so by an even larger margin than before. We needed to press on to lower frequencies, and on each occasion the pattern then repeated. For a substantial fraction of our clients, the favored frequency was always the lowest available. Work at such low frequencies does present technical challenges, however, and the invasion of new frequency space posed new clinical challenges as well. In consequence, this process of development has continued systematically to the present day, more than 10 years later.

At the same time, a shift occurred in the priority being given to right-hemisphere placements. The right-parietal placement migrated from C4-Pz to T4-P4 for stronger effects, and it became a priority for nearly every client. Sometimes we never got around to the left hemisphere placements at all by the time the client was ready to graduate out of the program. The subjective experience of the right-parietal placement was a profound and pervasive sense of calm, particularly in those who were most in need of it. We had finally found a way to calm the seas of a profoundly dysregulated physiology.

With the progression deep into the ILF region, our success in re-regulating a severely dysregulated physiology mounted. The progression to lower frequencies was always driven by our most challenging clients, after all, the ones where the lowest frequency was not low enough. At the same time, however, the role of volition in the feedback process was now precluded. We had arrived at a process that could be understood purely at the neurophysiological level. This was a matter of the brain engaging with a correlate of its own behavior. How the brain responded to that signal was entirely its own affair. The process is well captured as a "dance with the brain, but the brain gets to lead."

This closely mirrors what happens in alpha-theta. Here a context is created in which the person is liberated to migrate in psychological state space toward the priorities of the core self. In ILF training, the brain is liberated to migrate in neurophysiological state space toward its own priorities, namely restored functional competence. In both undertakings, the brain merely requires information; it is not in need of instruction. Both kinds of feedback are permissive rather than prescriptive. There is a remarkable parallelism here, and the two approaches clearly complement each other.

The training of self-regulation is begun with a combination of enhancing arousal regulation with T4-P4 and of enhancing cerebral stability with T3-T4, each optimized on the basis of client response. Operating at the ORF is critical. The regulation of physiological arousal is intimately associated with the regulation of the autonomic nervous system. Both arousal regulation and autonomic regulation are in turn intimately associated with the regulation of the affective domain (Othmer, Othmer, & Legarda,

2011; Othmer S. F., 2015).

In this manner, we have encroached upon the home turf of the traditional biofeedback modalities—the regulation of the autonomic nervous system. Here affect regulation is the secondary consequence of autonomic regulation, and the same holds for arousal regulation. ILF neurofeedback goes more directly to the source of the problem. Arousal regulation, autonomic regulation, and affect regulation are simultaneously engaged at the level of the resting state networks (Othmer & Othmer, et al, 2013).

An Emerging Synthesis

Several elements of our narrative now fall into place. The ILF training covers the base that in the CRI-Help study was being targeted with the SMR-beta training. It also addresses the issues that Peniston covered with the temperature training component of his protocol. And finally, it handles the problems that Bill Scott covered with his alpha down-training. As recounted in his chapter, Bill Scott found that several clients did not respond well to the alpha-theta training at the outset, for reasons of their profound dysregulation status. His remedy was to train down elevated alpha amplitudes in a self-regulation model before initiating the usual alpha-theta protocol.

It turns out that attending to the client's general dysregulation status beforehand potentiates the alpha-theta experience when it is encountered later. It does so by removing impediments to the success of the latter. Additionally, there are the many cases where substance dependency or addiction is traceable to physiological mechanisms rather than to the trauma response or other psychological factors. And finally, there are the many cases of addiction that are seen in conjunction with antisocial personality disorder or other personality disorders.

In these cases, the underlying personality disorder needs to be addressed, for which once again ILF training is the remedy of choice.

Consider the implications of the following case vignette: an older veteran is court-referred for neurofeedback because of a violent episode. He has a 20-year history of both PTSD and schizophrenia. At the end of the first session of training, he remarks to the practitioner that—curiously—he does not feel like smoking. By this time, he has not smoked in several hours and would ordinarily need another cigarette. Coming in for session 5 some weeks later, he tells the therapist that he has not smoked since session 4. Consulting his notes, the therapist establishes that it had been 19 days.

It is well-known that nicotine is typically experienced as calming in schizophrenia, and would therefore not be given up readily. The fact that it was abandoned so easily in this case, and without any intention to do so, speaks volumes. There was no transformative moment here, no psychological involvement. There was no therapeutic mandate here, no moral suasion, not even a subtle suggestion. Smoking had even not been raised as an issue. What happened here must be understood entirely at the physiological level. The training had impacted the mechanism of nicotine dependency that had undoubtedly consolidated over many years. It had impacted the schizophrenia. And it had done so in very short order.

This was clearly a highly unusual case, unprecedented in our experience. And yet it was not unique. Sue Othmer once worked with a middle-aged woman who was well situated with an intact family and ambitious plans for her future. The roadblock was a dependency on heroin and cocaine that had a 15-year history. From the first moment the young woman experienced heroin, she was willing to move heaven and earth to have that experience again. She had undergone 25 failed addiction treatments of the conventional sort. After 14 ILF training sessions, she declared: "There has been no urge to use drugs. Pretty shocking, actually. No craving since starting the neurofeedback. I feel like a normal person." After 20 sessions: "Just getting off the drugs is such a great relief. I am much happier." "Life involved this compulsive, self-destructive drug behavior. It's gone. The desire for drugs is completely gone." Observe that the subsidence of drug cravings was not mentioned until session 15, even though it was noted already after the first session. The reason is obvious: the client was reluctant to believe that the change would persist, so it went unmentioned.

All this transpired well before any thought was given to introducing alpha-theta. The later role of alpha-theta would be the appropriate one of resolving the traumatic aspects of this woman's crushing failure in her own eyes and those of her family. Once the addiction itself was tamed, it no longer conveyed the stigma of personal failing, and recovery from the psychological trauma could proceed more benignly. The two aspects of the protocol were both critical, and they reinforced each other.

The Evolution of Addiction Treatment

Throughout the history of alpha-theta, there has been an established pattern of promoting self-regulation by one or another means prior to initiating alpha-theta training. With ILF training we now have the additional rationale of redressing the physiological mechanisms of substance dependency directly. This gives us a multi-pronged ability to target both the physiological and the psychological drivers of the addiction process. This is best done sequentially, with psychophysiological regulation preceding the initiation into the alpha-theta process.

With the maturation of the ILF training over the past decade, the major burden of the recovery process has increasingly shifted to the ILF component of the neurotherapy. The alpha-theta experience is introduced only when the person is ready for it. This makes for a more efficient training process, and the term abreactions has slipped out of the conversation entirely. At an appropriate point during the ILF training, an alpha-theta session is offered on a trial basis, and if the client is drawn into the process, then it is continued and becomes part of the mix. If not, then the ILF training is resumed exclusively for a time before the alpha-theta experience is offered once again. Sooner or later, alpha-theta training will typically be welcomed. When that occurs, it is likely to become the preferred and dominant training mode going forward. Shorn of impediments, progress in alpha-theta may then occur swiftly.

A Comprehensive Treatment Program

Taking stock of where we are presently, a comprehensive strategy toward self-regulation has emerged, one that respects the hierarchy of concerns. Core regulation is addressed at the outset, followed by more specific targeting of dysfunctions. Only after physiological regulation has been restored are the psychic wounds of trauma tended to. With respect to physiological regulation, the hierarchy we discern is also the developmental hierarchy, and this turns out to line up well with the hierarchy in the frequency domain. We have been well rewarded for our journey to the low frequencies. In view of the above correlations, this protocol can also be seen as a journey back in time to the early phases of the child's development. In this manner, patterns of dysregulation that were consolidated via early trauma become accessible to remediation.

Subsequently, the EEG range of frequencies is addressed to achieve more refined regulation of temporal relationships in cortex. Finally, we arrive at the point where our intrinsically human faculties—as opposed to our brain's operating system—can become our primary concern through the alpha-theta experience. The individuality and particularity of the response to these protocols is evident in every phase of the program. And at each stage, it is either the client's brain or the core self that is in charge of the journey. Full latitude is being given to the person's intrinsic healing resources, and these merely need to be potentiated by providing real-time information on the person's state, on the one hand, and the removal of impediments, on the other. The role of the therapist in this process is critical, but it is largely supportive rather than being directive or even prescriptive.

The natural history of PTSD, of substance dependency, and of traumatic brain injury (TBI) is that self-recovery is the predominant expectation. Most people age out of an addiction at some point in their lives, and most do so without the benefit of any therapy. The implication is that those who visit our offices with these conditions are most likely those whose nervous systems were more severely impacted by the trauma, or they were already dysregulated when they had their significant head injury, encountered their trauma, or were beguiled by their drug of choice. Their recovery potential had been compromised. We get to see the result of a cumulative history of prior traumas, minor head injuries, and chemical insults to the brain. We refer to this as the dysregulation cascade.

The key factor that made TBI so prominent an issue in the recent wars was blast injury, where no physical injury to the brain could be identified and yet service members were rendered dysfunctional. This experience supports the case for redressing physiological deficits—the functional injury—prior to dealing with the psychological aspects of trauma. The physical trauma of TBI is simultaneously also a psychological trauma, as the victim surveys his uncertain prospects in the face of the precipitous loss of functionality.

Clinical experience with both EMDR and exposure therapy is supportive of the above proposition. EMDR procedures frequently lead people into distress, just as exposure therapy does. In all such cases, one surmises, the causal chain involves responses triggered by dysregulation. Recovery from PTSD must therefore be seen firstly in a physiological rather than a psychological frame. Indeed, once the physiological aspects of PTSD are resolved, PTSD can no longer be diagnosed. This is in consequence of the dominant role of physiological symptoms in the diagnostic criteria for PTSD, which belies the larger reality of the trauma response. We are happy to have the tools to resolve the physiological dysregulation in ILF training, but that merely prepares the ground for the alpha-theta experience to assume its intended role, the healing of the psyche and the unbinding of the soul. This is an intensely personal and essentially spiritual journey.

The most critical test of the above propositions is provided by our military veterans. The Vietnam era veterans have lived for 40 years with the condition (some amalgam of PTSD and TBI), and have witnessed the progressive deterioration of their physiological integrity over that time. Veterans of the recent and ongoing wars give us a chance to work with PTSD and TBI in its early post-trauma status.

Clinical Validation

Franklin came to us in 2009 from Bell Shelter, a Salvation Army shelter for formerly homeless veterans, offering them transitional housing until they can be rehabilitated. He was one of their most challenging residents. His family had cut off contact years ago. He had had a very checkered history with drug use and with the criminal justice system. By now he was diabetic, obese, and had sleep apnea. In consequence of poor sleep, it was difficult for him to stay awake during the early sessions of ILF training. Our symptom tracking program was used to record symptom severity every three sessions. Tracking the symptoms most closely associated with PTSD revealed the following: suicidal thoughts, flashbacks of trauma, nightmares and vivid dreams, and binging and purging were no longer listed as problem areas by the third session, and were never a problem again thereafter. Other rapidly resolving symptoms included irritability, anxiety, anger, and emotional reactivity, all of which essentially resolved in 18 sessions. By session 18, all the above categories were listed as zero on a 10-point scale, whereas they had been key issues at the outset.

In line with the presumption that his extended history with PTSD had shaped Franklin's total dysregulation status, symptoms of dysregulation were tracked comprehensively. These included (in addition to those already mentioned) peripheral neuropathy pain, chronic nerve pain, nausea, high blood pressure, fatigue, difficulty walking or moving, chronic constipation, lack of appetite awareness, tinnitus, sleep apnea, restless sleep, and difficulty maintaining sleep. Many of these are not expected to yield quickly to neurofeedback, yet collectively these symptoms exhibited more than 80% reduction in severity in 18 sessions. Symptom severity largely plateaued at that point for the subsequent 40 sessions, except for a transient increase in emotional reactivity as Franklin reconnected with his family at session 42.

At the point of graduating from the training at session 60, residual symptoms related to his obesity (difficulty walking, although he was now mostly out of his wheelchair); lack of appetite awareness; and the emotional reactivity already mentioned. Sleep apnea had ceased to be an issue, apparently. There were no more complaints of pain. The 23 medications he was supposed to be taking were down to one: insulin. Franklin became the happy and joyful man that he had once been, and he now lives independently.

With regard to PTSD and TBI relative to recent and ongoing conflicts, we have the extraordinary opportunity to work with the Department of Deployment Health at Camp Pendleton. The staff there had heard my talk at the Navy and Marine Corps Combat Stress Management Conference in 2008, and invited me to give a presentation at Camp Pendleton. When the commander of the Department heard that we were talking about nothing more than biofeedback, and that the procedure had the necessary approvals from the FDA, she saw no further barriers to a trial. It was not long before the ILF and alpha-theta training came to dominate the work at the Department, which had to give approval to every service member planning to redeploy. The entire professional staff of the Department got trained in ILF neurofeedback. Between 2009 and the present, between one and two thousand Marines and Navy received the benefits of the ILF and alpha-theta training to qualify them for redeployment.

In essence, the findings were as follows: some 25% of the service members reduced their symptoms below clinical significance within 20 sessions, with a median of about 10 sessions. A further 50% reduced their symptoms to clinical insignificance within 40 sessions, with a median of about 20 sessions. The remaining 25% either needed more sessions or complementary therapies in addition to the neurofeedback, or they were simply non-responsive. The staff was working under difficult circumstances of inconsistent scheduling, and estimated that under more ideal conditions the intractable portion of the training cohort was likely around 5%.

In line with the above observations, most individual symptom categories distributed tightly around 75% to 80% response. Over 60 different symptoms were being systematically tracked, grouped into categories of sleep, pain, physical, psychological, psychophysiological, sensory, and cognitive function. The most responsive symptom was migraine, with 90% responding. The least responsive symptom was tinnitus, with 50% showing substantial recovery. Addictive behaviors responded at the 60% level. Suicidality, hypertension, asthma, constipation, effort fatigue, and stomach pain responded in everyone where it had been an issue (out of a cohort of over 300 being tracked by 2010). The most dramatic response was for depression and anxiety, where scores for nearly all the responders were cut in half within six sessions.

Most of the trainees did not stay around for the alpha-theta experience. This was not much of a surprise to the clinicians, as they had already experienced the reluctance of service members to engage in psychotherapy before the neurofeedback was introduced. This can be attributed to the spirit inculcated in the Marines of taking responsibility for one's issues. One reason the neurofeedback flourished as it did was that it fit the military training model. ILF neurofeedback was seen as brain fitness training.

It is possible that in view of a rushed training schedule, alpha-theta was offered too early, at which point they tended not to like it or get much out of it. The experience is very different when alpha-theta is phased in appropriately, as now occurs with the veterans being seen in private practice. They gravitate to the A-T readily, and from then on tend to prefer it to the ILF training.

Finally, we have the report on a pilot project conducted by the Swedish Red Cross, in which ILF training was offered to victims of torture among the refugees, all of whom had failed to respond to conventional therapies for from 6 months to several years. A substantial reduction in symptom severity was achieved, even though the practitioners were relatively new to the method. Also, torture victims present a challenge to our method because they don't respond well to being asked to tune into their bodies. They have learned not to attend to how their body feels as a counter-measure against the torture. In consequence, it was difficult to determine the ORF for these patients.

Clinical Strategies and Clinical Realities

The tools are now in hand with which both the physiological aspects and the psychological consequences of dysregulation in general, and of trauma specifically, can be systematically, effectively, and efficiently remediated. The problem of addiction, in its various manifestations, fits nicely within this schema. Just where remediation is to be found in a particular case is not predictable in advance. It is therefore incumbent on the clinician to have at his or her command the full panoply of remedial techniques, along with skill in their deployment.

In this section, we shed more light on the respective roles of the two tall poles in the tent, the ILF and the alpha-theta aspects of the therapy. We do so with the aid of some instructive clinical vignettes. As indicated previously, the problem of drug craving can frequently be resolved within the ILF phase of the program, and sometimes quite readily. A clinician working with a binge drinker with ILF protocols reported that he had been "thinking about" his use of alcohol as he was undergoing the training for his general condition of overwhelm at work and at home. He had five training sessions over the course of 7 weeks. Coming in after New Year's he reported that he hadn't had a drink since mid-December, despite severe year-end pressures on his job. When tempted to drink after work, he was now able to tell himself, "why blow it," and to maintain abstinence, even well before alpha-theta training was begun with him. The resolution of drug craving fits into a larger picture of relief for the compulsive aspect of various addictive tendencies such as gambling, thrill-seeking, and lying, etc. The alpha-theta training is more particularly helpful in moderating and defanging specific triggers of addictive behavior. It buffers the person against the external, environmental, and contextual drivers of the propensity to use, whereas the ILF training more directly resolves the internal drivers.

With the insertion of ILF training in preparation for alpha-theta training, the alpha-theta experience is typically more consistently positive, with the dropout of concern about the abreactions that exercised Eugene Peniston. Our professional training course environment, however, continued to present a special circumstance in which the training schedule was necessarily compressed, and alpha-theta was experienced before some attendees were ready for it. The experience of a seasoned trauma specialist who had been working with torture cases for many years is illuminating on the relationship of both aspects of the training under such unusual conditions.

Voices intruded on his first alpha-theta experience, and they were insistent and persistent. His outward demeanor was totally calm during this time, according to his partner in the training, and yet he was experiencing a lot of turmoil. This lasted about 15 minutes, at which time he removed the eye shades and headphones and ended the session. He continued with ILF for stabilization, and interestingly the thoughts were the same, but now he could manage them better.

All this came as rather a surprise to him, because as a long-time psychotherapist he thought that he had been successful in keeping himself in line with his skill set. And yet he was now confronted with all these loose ends. It was unsettling. He was confronted with self in a new way.

Here is how he described the experience.

> I just had these voices in my head; they were terrible voices... I couldn't stop it. It was quite awful... I was really in the grip of it... A lot of what my life is about is working with these systems... I started using everything I knew in terms of breathing and imagery, and it wouldn't quit... My question coming in: Is this real? Is this placebo? The reason I threw myself at this in this way... I wanted to see whether something was going to happen to me without my doing anything...

That question was clearly resolved!

With the shift back to ILF after 15 minutes in the boat, he said:

> My relationship to these thoughts changed. There was a qualitative shift in my experience of my own thoughts... The ILF allowed me to have the thoughts rather than the thoughts having me... From a psychotherapist point of view, it was about the absolute intra-subjective shift in my reaction to my own thoughts... [The experience] was great, but it was also "oh, shit"... "More work to do..."

In the grip of the moment, he consoled himself with the realization that "I have lots of ways to get back to normal..."

Most unusual here is that his alpha-theta experience was so intensely verbal. And yet it had the qualities of an alpha-theta experience—it came out of another part of himself that he had not yet tamed with his left-brain consciousness. From beginning to end his reaction to the new phenomenology was that of a psychotherapist—restoring control to the cognitive domain. Scariest was the loss of top-down control of his own thoughts, and the realization that the part of himself he had succeeded in mastering was only a part of the whole. The cauldron of his own collective trauma experience was in fact still bubbling.

The more generalizable aspect of this report is that people in general—but mental health professionals in particular—tend to react more strongly to both ILF and alpha-theta than they expect. Both kinds of training take them out of the comfort zone of their cognitively ordered self-perception. "I was not prepared for this. I did not think I had a problem," is a typical response. A further observation, however, is that in retrospect the journey is almost never regretted.

Sometimes the alert-state training has a transformational quality itself. Before the era of ILF training, Sebern Fisher worked with a CEO-type over an extended period with neurofeedback alone—no psychotherapy, as he was not there for that. At one session he became overtly emotional, and when Sebern inquired, said that "I have never known what love is. I don't know why my wife has stuck with me all these years." Obviously, the connection had just been made in his internal circuitry. With ILF training we now have the key to the personality disorders. This work takes a long time, and progress is largely accomplished in the ILF phase of the training, but at least this is now doable.

At issue here is the entire spectrum of attachment disorder, of which personality disorders are a manifestation. Sebern Fisher reported on yet another case in which extensive alert-state training had been done (at low EEG frequencies, but before the ILF era) with a young adult with an extreme case of attachment disorder. When alpha-theta training was finally initiated, the girl regressed, stopped coming to therapy, and even neglected the feeding of her dog. The conditions for successful alpha-theta training had not yet been met. There was no core self to come home to; the girl instead encountered a black hole, a total emptiness, without means of support. Matters might well have gone differently with ILF to shore up the scaffolding for the project of constructing a self. This cautionary tale remains a singular event in memory (and a good outcome was ultimately achieved). With ILF having priority in the training, nothing remotely similar has been observed since.

Transformational experiences are much more commonplace in the alpha-theta portion of the therapy. One middle-aged man reported that his journey took him back the New Jersey beaches where his father used to walk with him. At one point the father dropped his hand, and the 8-year old boy interpreted that as the loss of the love of his father, with long-term adverse consequences for their relationship. Revisiting that event in his adult consciousness, the man now realized the innocuous nature of that event, and in that moment repaired the relationship with his father. This was not a matter of mere cognitive reframing. It was affective, and it was visceral. The bond of filial affection had been restored.

A middle-aged woman reported on her remarkable alpha-theta journey as follows. She was an eagle flying in the vicinity of her home. She flew higher and higher, with her home becoming ever smaller, until she was among the stars. Eventually she retraced her flight, ending back at her former family home. Nothing more happened than that she had re-constructed her relationship to her mother and to her siblings in the course of that flight. This had occurred entirely non-verbally and essentially beneath consciousness. The negatives in each of these relationships from childhood times had simply shrunk to insignificance along with the house during that singular journey into space.

Another middle-aged woman, one with a history of early trauma, found herself walking the beach until she came upon an infant girl sitting alone on the wet sand. "I picked her up and realized that that was me." She would now get the caring that she herself had not had.

These are healing journeys that appear to be so totally inner-directed that one might readily ask just what the role of a therapist needs to be in this aspect of the work. One voiced his frustration as follows: "Personally, I am getting a little glum seeing people have amazing experiences, resolving intense trauma, and blossoming while I sit on the sidelines entering notes...." It is imperative, first of all, that clinicians have their own house in order. One M.D. who had transitioned to neurofeedback practice after burning out as an emergency room doctor never had good results with alpha-theta work among her patients—by self-report. Her own unresolved PTSD may well have been an issue.

One explanation for the lack of abreactions in our alpha-theta work could be that in connection with the CRI-Help study back in the mid-nineties we increased the center frequency of the theta band from what Eugene Peniston had relied on, from 4–7 Hz to 5–8 Hz. This may have kept clients from going too deep into theta dominance. In our present realization in Cygnet, the standard center frequency of the theta band is 7 Hz. There appears to be a relationship between the theta target frequency and early trauma: lower theta frequencies may target traumas that occurred earlier in the child's history or had more pervasive impact. This relationship became quite evident in one case of alert-state training in which Sue Othmer walked down the target frequency toward the delta band in one session and the client (with dissociative identity disorder) transiently regressed to ever younger ages, eventually speaking in the high voice of a child. Walking the frequency back up restored her to her adult self.

The conjectured frequency dependence motivates a clinical strategy in which clients who are well along in their alpha-theta experience could be invited to venture into the lower frequency range for a deeper experience by gradually lowering the theta-band center frequency from session to session. This progression can be fine-tuned as necessary. One clinician recently reported on her results with this approach:

> I started off slowly on the theta band, going from 7 to 6.5 and eventually to 5. [Clients] would come back with so much information and resolution of trauma that at times they themselves were overwhelmed with how much they achieved from alpha-theta versus years of talk therapy. It really digs deep and I think the client needs to be fully prepared in terms many sessions of awake state and regular alpha-theta...

The reader acquainted with EMDR will recognize the point of contact here between the two methods. EMDR was an early method of accessing traumas with a frequency-based stimulation technique in the delta range of frequencies. This allowed them to be dealt with cognitively. In our current perspective, the difficulties encountered in such work can be readily identified. In first instance, traumas can be stirred up that the client is not ready to handle either psychologically or physiologically. And the role assigned to the cognitive domain is more than it can bear. A proper sequencing of the process of trauma recovery (and of addiction recovery) is easier on the client and the clinician, as well as being much more successful.

Early on, Tom Allen turned alpha-theta sessions into something like EMDR. Armed with the physiological measures of finger temperature and galvanic skin response, he would seize moments of excursion in the measures to rouse the client from his journey and to engage him with whatever might have prompted that turmoil. He talked so proudly of his tactics, utterly persuaded of their merit. We now know better.

What holds for EMDR holds even more for exposure therapy, which is surely the therapy from hell. It is simply perverse to think that exposing people to traumatic material ought to help them, particularly when the evidence is so strongly against it. Unfortunately, established belief is difficult to dislodge even with solid evidence. Doctrine readily trumps experience. Trauma is not lodged in the cognitive realm, and the solution is not to be found there. The evidence for this is very clear. Once trauma is resolved by methods described here, previously traumatic material can be readily revisited without dramatic consequence. The trauma no longer has the person in its grip.

In one memorable instance from many years ago, we were working with a person recovering from rape. She was also seeing a psychotherapist, who in her wisdom decided at one point that flooding would be a good idea. The client completely cratered. She went straight home, took to her bed, remained in seclusion for many days, and stopped all therapies. This is supposed to be helpful? (Once again, the story ended well. Eventually, she came back for neurofeedback, where she also resolved her PMS, a major issue in her life. Years later, upon a reporter's inquiry, we asked whether she would be willing to talk to him. "Well, yes" she said, "but why are you asking me about PMS?" It had all been forgotten.)

Even worse than exposure therapy is the insult to the integrity of the human body that is represented by detox. In all instances of drug dependency, from anxiolytics to anticonvulsants to neuroleptics, the watchword is to insist on slow titration downward whenever that is called for. The singular exception appears to be alcohol. Why the infernal haste? Is this just the residue of the moral opprobrium we have historically attached to alcoholism? The physiological ravages attributable to detox are so unnecessary. Even the risk of seizure is tolerated. We can now train the brain away from its dependence on alcohol and it will be very clear when one has succeeded. Moreover, it will be the client's own victory over his condition. Success does not lie in the client clutching onto abstinence by sheer force of will. It lies in a life transformed… a brain restored to functional integrity and a psyche liberated from its traumas.

A common thread running through the above narrative is that historically the clinician has sought to install himself as the central persona in the healing journey out of trauma and addiction, to place himself in charge of the process and to micro-manage it. This was justified because the pathway to healing was thought to be via the cognitive domain. This has been a monumental blunder on all counts. With core dysregulation at issue, there is no alternative but to facilitate the path to self-healing; it cannot be mandated or willed. The project cannot be outsourced—to a clinician or even to an instrumental process. Cognition plays a minor role. Instead, our role is to remove impediments to the intrinsic healing process, and to empower both the brain and the core self with guidance on its own journey rather than instruction. The desired process of transformation must ultimately be self-directed. One therapist said:

> I have seen multiple sessions with nothing more than a good relaxed feeling and one 22 min session where someone goes back to Iraq, has a coherent conversation with dead comrades in the middle of battle, gets chewed out for having little to no insight, and returns with a more profound understanding of life than I could offer up in a century of therapy. I feel like a damn porter in a cosmic

train station.

Perhaps it's time to board the train.

Optimum Functioning

Alpha-theta training has been utilized and researched in an optimum functioning context for many years. The most prominent such study was undertaken at the Royal College of Music in London, where music students were offered beta and SMR training along with alpha-theta training, using our protocols and our NeuroCybernetics instrumentation. No benefits of the SMR and beta training were identified among these highly selected and highly functional students. The alpha-theta component, on the other hand, made a substantial difference in their musical performance. Gains were the equivalent of 2 years' progress in musical maturity, as established in blinded testing by professional musicians (Egner & Gruzelier, 2003). And yet the students had only experienced 10 sessions for 20 minutes each. In this study, one has the chance to observe the positive contribution that the alpha-theta experience can make in a context where no obvious impediments to functionality exist. In consequence of this finding, Egner and Gruzelier then studied the temporal dynamics of alpha and theta in more detail (Egner & Gruzelier, 2004).

It would be preferable if no distinction were made at all between clinical applications and training toward optimal functioning. That would be entirely appropriate to the methods under discussion here. These are all function-focused rather than dysfunction-focused. Irrespective of the specific objectives, the ILF training is always individualized with respect to placements and target frequency, and always uses standard placements. Orientation is toward generality rather than specificity. Dysfunction subsides by virtue of the enhancement of function.

Alpha-theta utilizes standard bands and standard placements throughout. It is appropriate for the entire range of functionality from dysfunction to optimum functioning, and ultimately to the frontier of anomalous experience. This is also in line with the self-perception of our clients, who generally choose to see themselves as functional rather than as being defined by their condition. The optimum functioning perspective takes us beyond a narrow focus on symptoms and on functional shortcomings. It is the common ground that should be the point of departure for our therapeutic adventure.

Summary and Conclusion

Surveying the history of alpha-theta from the early days at the Menninger Foundation to the present day, it appears that we have come full circle. The primary interest of the Menninger group early on was not in remediating addiction or any other condition. It was in exploring the dimensions of our human condition more fully, aided now with instrumental conditioning. Realization of the therapeutic potential emerged over time. In the Peniston era, the late eighties and early nineties, alpha-theta became identified with recovery from addiction and PTSD. Even in our CRI-Help study, we saw alpha-theta as the essential core of the overall program, with the SMR-beta component playing a supporting role.

The ILF neurofeedback now alters the landscape substantially. The burden of recovery has shifted toward alert-state training from the deep-state training of alpha-theta as the clinical priority. This follows straight-forwardly from the regulatory hierarchy: physiological self-regulation must come first. Further, whereas the domains of physiological self-regulation and of psychological and spiritual healing are now procedurally more distinct, they serve a common purpose. This brings us much closer to the objectives that the Menninger group had for alpha-theta training at the outset. Already during the ILF training at Camp Pendleton the trainees often complained that the focus was entirely on their symptom status: "Why don't you ask about what is going well in my life?" They had moved on toward an optimum functioning orientation, and were no longer tied up with their earlier symptoms.

Liberated from the conceptual burden of being tied up with "recovery," alpha-theta needs to be seen more in the positive frame of facilitating the journey toward wholeness, toward acceptance, toward integration of the fragmented self, toward personal integrity, and toward enlarging one's affective depth and scope. It speaks to the yearning for transcendence. Alpha-theta opens the door to an encounter with self that is likely to be welcomed by most people. It should be offered to all adolescents when issues of personal identity first arise for them. It should be available to all elderly as they approach the end of life's journey.

But there is more. Ultimately one cannot make transpersonal phenomenology go away. It exists, and if that is the case, does it not make our universe richer and more interesting? Does it not testify to our being in relationship in the larger sense? Does it not contradict the materialist hypothesis, and thus give us grounds to believe that we live in a "warm" universe rather than a "cold" one? This is the reality in which Elmer Green lived his entire life, and which inspired his work. We honor him by continuing his work in that same inquisitive and open spirit.

References

Egner, T., & Gruzelier, J. H. (2003). Ecological validity of neurofeedback: Modulation of slow-wave EEG enhances musical performance. *Neuroreport, 14*(9), 1221–1224.

Egner, T., & Gruzelier, J. H. (2004). The temporal dynamics of electroencephalographic responses to alpha/theta neurofeedback training in healthy subjects. *Journal of Neurotherapy, 8*(1), 43–57.

Othmer, S., Othmer, S. F., Kaiser, D. A., & Putman, J. (2013). Endogenous neuromodulation at infra-low frequencies. *Seminars in Pediatric Neurology, 20*(4), 246–260.

Othmer, S., Othmer, S. F., & Legarda, S. B. (2011). Clinical neurofeedback: Training brain behavior. Treatment strategies. *Pediatric Neurology and Psychiatry, 2*, 67–73.

Othmer, S. F. (2015). *Protocol guide for neurofeedback clinicians* (5th Ed.). Los Angeles: EEG Info Publications.

Othmer, S., & Steinberg, M. (2010). EEG Neurofeedback therapy. In D. Brizer & R. Castaneda (Eds.), *Clinical addiction psychiatry* (pp. 169–187). Cambridge University Press. http://www.eeginfo.com/research/pdfs/Addictions.pdf

Peniston, E. G., & Kulkosky, P. J. (1995). *The Peniston/Kulkosky brainwave neurofeedback therapy for alcoholism and posttraumatic stress disorders: Medical psychotherapist manual.* Certificate of Copyright Office. The Library of Congress, 1–25. http://www.aaets.org/article47.htm.

Scott, W. C., Kaiser, D. A., Othmer, S., & Sideroff, S. I. (2005). Effects of an EEG biofeedback protocol on a mixed substance abusing population. *American Journal of Drug and Alcohol Abuse, 31*(3), 455–469.

14

The Integration of the Peniston Protocol:
A Tool for Neurotherapists and Psychotherapists

Antonio Martins-Mourao, PhD

Peniston and Kulkosky's (1991) evidence suggesting that expert manipulation of specific brain frequencies could lead to the remission of traumatic symptoms in war veterans with PTSD was revolutionary for its time. They were among the first to use *technology* to tap into the brain's ability to unlock traumatic memories, showing that unresolved emotional issues could be retrieved and potentially reprocessed in an objective and systematic way. It would take mainstream neuroscience another 20 years to finally explain this new form of neuroplasticity now known as memory reconsolidation. As the name suggests, the "re" stands for the reorganization of previously stored content.

Along with their initial results showing improved health outcomes as well as positive personality shifts for the majority of the participants in their studies, Peniston and Kulkosky also described a *replicable* method that has since been validated for the treatment of a range of conditions (Gruzelier & Egner, 2005; Scott & Kaiser, 1998; Sokhadze, Cannon, & Trudeau, 2008; White & Richards, 2009) and further refined by different clinical groups (Scott, Kaiser, Othmer, & Sideroff, 2005; see also the Johnson & Bodenhamer-Davis study, chapter 6). The net result has been positive and the above studies have helped consolidate the evidence-based therapeutic value of the Peniston protocol, which has been listed by the British Royal College of

Psychiatrists (National Institute for Health and Care Excellence, NICE Guideline 26, 2005) as an effective treatment, thus earning a respected place among a select group of innovative therapies currently used for the rehabilitation of deep trauma in children and adults.

The Peniston protocol offers a replicable technique to tap into the brain's ability to modify unwanted traumatic memories, and a method to explore specific empirical questions that may facilitate potential progress in the field of trauma rehabilitation. Yet, it remains virtually unknown to a significant majority of trauma rehabilitation therapists and psychotherapists currently working outside the neurofeedback field (the term neurofeedback and neurotherapy will be used interchangeably in this chapter). This limits its potential as a therapeutic tool for those who need it.

This chapter reviews some of the issues and obstacles that may have justified the relative isolation of alpha-theta training (A/T training) from other therapeutic approaches and proposes a way to support its active dissemination as a powerful technique that may be used by psychotherapists. The following analysis is intended to facilitate useful cross-fertilizations between neurotherapy (or neurofeedback) and allied areas for the benefit of patients with a range of mental health conditions.

Summarizing the Current Relevance of the Peniston Protocol

The A/T (or Peniston) protocol is a bio-behavioral therapeutic approach that sits between the areas of clinical neuroscience, psychotherapy, and psychoanalysis. This field is currently known as neuropsychoanalysis (see, for example, Panksepp & Solms, 2012). Differently from traditional psychotherapy and psychoanalysis, A/T training uses specific neurofeedback equipment to inform clients about their brainwave patterns.

During a typical session, the therapist monitors the client's brainwave frequencies (eyes closed) using specific 10-20 system placements such as O1 or Pz, while providing feedback (e.g., the sound of waves and the sound of a gong) to enable the client to increase alpha and theta frequencies. Ideally, the alpha frequency will eventually drop (due to early sleep stages), and the increase of the theta over the alpha amplitude may, at that point initiate a state of reverie. This state is known as the "crossover," alluding to the higher amplitude of theta (4–7 Hz) over alpha (8–12 Hz). Chapter 8 by Johnson & Bodenhamer-Davis discusses how other factors such as the concurrent amplitude of the beta frequencies may further facilitate the "therapeutic crossover."

A/T training shares common ground with some old-school psychotherapeutic methods by addressing and facilitating the expression of subconscious content. However, and quite crucially, it differs by avoiding the traditional analytical tools and associated limitations. Most experienced therapists will recognize the truth of the saying, "You cannot think your way out of trauma" (van der Kolk, 2014).

The cutting-edge concepts introduced by Peniston and Kulkosky (1989, 1991) involved using brain feedback technology to gradually train patients to remain *partly conscious* as their EEG entered a long-enough crossover period to enable access to, and expression of, highly emotional and traumatic anxiety-provoking images and feelings. Successive training sessions then led patients to benefit from a "newly learned state of consciousness, which is close enough to a waking alpha state, to facilitate transfer of these images" into conscious awareness (Peniston, Marrinan, Deming, & Kulkosky, 1993, p. 46).

So, instead of facilitating intellectual awareness of the traumatic experiences, as typically expected in the traditional analytic therapies, A/T training participants are invited to reprocess and ultimately free their traumatic contents by allowing their expression—as if these were being witnessed again, albeit (very importantly) from a safe distance (an der Kolk, 2014).

It follows that the Peniston protocol has two main parts. During the brainwave session (first part), the client is likely to experience the crossover and often becomes aware of relevant trauma-related contents. Scenes from the past may jump into the patient's awareness, often causing surprise, which in itself has considerable therapeutic power. Then, during the second segment of the A/T training session (i.e., after the brainwave session), the patient expresses these contents and interprets them with the help of the therapist, who must be careful not to influence the patient's interpretation.

Crucially, the second part is about creating meaning and context for the emerged contents. I take the view that both parts of the protocol are essential for a faster and more effective promotion of better health outcomes, although many may not share this view.

In fact, the second part of the Peniston protocol is still controversial and is practiced only by a minority of therapists. The majority puts more emphasis on the brainwave session and the facilitation of the crossover. The actual steps used during the second part are unclear and only rarely have descriptions of this process been made available within very small groups—to the point that its practice has attained near-mystical status. Consequently, no agreement has been reached regarding the steps used to facilitate client interpretation of subconscious contents that may emerge during the crossover. Such lack of clarity compromises good practice standards and may have also created subtle divisions between practitioners, likely to hamper the progression of the field as a whole.

Regarding known limitations, it should be noted that the diagnosis of PTSD—the focus of this chapter—can be fraught with pre-existing comorbidities including mood disorders, learning difficulties and personality disorders, as well as coexisting mTBI (mild traumatic brain injury) often acquired during combat. This understanding is missing from Peniston's work and the several attempts to reproduce it. The lack of the appropriate controls for these confounding factors is likely to limit the conclusions of future A/T training studies.

David Trudeau, also an author in this book, brought this point home while president of the ISNR Research Foundation (ISNR-RF, now the FNNR). Accordingly, the board included the assessment of mTBI, along with an array of other screening tests in the protocol used in a research proposal presented by the foundation for a study to be conducted at a residential veteran's home-based PTSD program. This study still awaits funding, perhaps reflecting how little A/T training is known by other health care and mental health professionals.

In a nutshell, the therapeutic merit of the Peniston protocol resides in its capacity to create a neurophysiological "window of opportunity" to:

- facilitate systematic access to traumatic memories within a limited number of sessions;

- reveal the developmental origin of the abreactive anxiety-provoking imageries (note that the term developmental refers to a life-span perspective);

- support the reorganization and reprocessing of traumatic contents into a meaningful narrative; and, thus,

- enable the long-term prevention of PTSD relapse (for example) and associated symptoms.

The Peniston protocol represents a powerful, systematic, and relatively fast technique ready to be applied to hundreds of thousands of patients in clear need of urgent intervention such as soldiers with war-related PTSD. Recent data estimates 22 daily suicides amongst war veterans with war-related PTSD (Kemp & Bossarte, 2012). Additional evidence that both traditional psychotherapeutic—often CBT-oriented—and pharmacological treatments (see report by the IOM, 2007, for a review of 170 studies dating back to the 1980s) have had limited success with this population

A/T is rarely used outside the field of neurotherapy, so this chapter will argue for creating the right conditions to facilitate its dissemination amongst therapists from other orientations. For that to happen, however, we must first recognize and resolve some issues of identity and theoretical jurisdiction that seem to have affected the dissemination of the A/T training since its early days. The discussion turns to this issue in the next section.

Issues of Theoretical Jurisdiction:

Where Does the Peniston Protocol Sit?

Eugene Peniston affiliated his work within an (at the time) alternative tradition that hadn't yet made its mark in neuroscientific circles. This discipline was based on the autogenics training (i.e., self-regulation; Schultz & Luthe, 1959) and emerging biofeedback school developed and practiced at the Menninger Clinic in Kansas (Green & Green, 1977).

Unfortunately, however, the mainstream psychotherapeutic circles of the time may have not been acquainted with methods such as thermal biofeedback (or hand warming) to help participants down-regulate sympathetic overactivation (i.e., hypervigilance) and other symptoms of sympathetic overarousal

The Integration of the Peniston Protocol

(Greenhalgh, Dickson, & Dundar, 2010; Lehrer & Gevirtz, 2014). Thirty years on, current psychotherapists are comparatively more familiar with these techniques, which signals an important shift showing renewed interest in psychophysiology, and A/T training.

Still, a crucial issue with direct impact on affiliation and dissemination has been that Peniston (himself an educational psychologist) decided, from the outset, to omit clear theoretical and conceptual connections between the A/T training protocol and either neuroscience or psychotherapy in his writings. This decision may have created issues of theoretical jurisdiction affecting the scope of A/T training, which may have turned out to be a major factor in its isolation from other disciplines.

Peniston probably had valid reasons for such a decision. Firstly, Peniston and Kulkosky's (1989, 1991) studies were ahead of their day and emerged before the advent of two significant revolutions that were to change the direction of clinical neuroscience. The first one was the shift towards the study of the emotions in the brain, initiated by influential works such as Joseph LeDoux's (1999) *The Emotional Brain*, among others. Up until then, this area of research had been neglected by neuroscientists.

In other words, Peniston had presented a brain-based technique to process repressed emotions in the early 1990s, when most influential neuroscientists did not believe this was possible or indeed an effort worth pursuing. Peniston's publications emerged a decade before mainstream science understood the role of the amygdala in the processing of fear-related stimuli (LeDoux, 2015). This was also a time when the developmental effects of trauma in the brain were unclear.

The second revolution relates to the neuroscientific discovery that traumatic memories could be revised in the *brain* (Ecker,

Ticic, & Hulley, 2012). This finding is supported by new evidence suggesting that traumatic memories may be modified by a newly discovered type of neuroplasticity, or synaptic change, that became known as "memory reconsolidation" (Ecker et al., 2012; McGaugh, 2000). I will return to memory reconsolidation later in the chapter.

Unfortunately, Peniston and Kulkosky's suggestion that traumatic memories could be rehabilitated emerged at a time when most influential neuroscientists still believed that the neural circuits of trauma, once physically installed—or consolidated—in long-term memory remained unchangeable and therefore permanent for the lifetime of the individual (see McGaugh, 2000).

The memory consolidation lobby proved hard to shift and, in some way, continues to dominate mainstream psychotherapy. Its power stemmed from Pavlov's seminal studies suggesting that conditioned responses could only be temporarily suppressed but not eliminated from memory (Bouton, 2004; Milner, Squire, & Kandel, 1998), for which he was awarded the 1904 Nobel Prize in physiology and medicine. This notion had been supported by earlier suggestions that extinction training and the initial target learning would be separate events, believed to be stored in physically separate memory systems, so no relation between such events could be hypothesized.

The "suppression concept," as Ecker et al. (2012) have named it, has had a dramatic impact on psychotherapeutic thinking. It supports the rather dogmatic view that extinction learning (i.e., treatment) would have to compete against target learning (i.e., traumatic content) instead of replacing it (Bouton, 2004; Foa & McNally, 1996; Milner, Squire & Kandel, 1998). These assumptions are in direct opposition to Peniston's findings.

Concepts such as suppression and competition had been anchored in seminal studies suggesting the "indelibility of subcortical emotional memories" (LeDoux, Romanski, & Xagoraris, 1989), and on van der Kolk's (1994) influential clinical perspective strategically subtitled "Emotional Memories Are Forever." This authoritative paper, in particular, published in the *Harvard Review of Psychiatry*, introduced clinicians to an understanding of implicit emotional memory as the basis of symptom production, a significant (albeit now dated) advance for its time. Meanwhile, compared to the academic elite of his era, Peniston was a relatively unknown innovator working from the fringes with limited research resources and connections.

Incidentally, Bessel van der Kolk, a respected trauma author, later discovered and integrated neurofeedback in his research agenda with positive results. In the results of a randomized control study (N = 52) he has reported that neurofeedback had improved PTSD symptoms and affect regulation capacities in individuals with chronic PTSD (van der Kolk et al., 2016).

Thirdly, Peniston's work may have been obscured by the fact that the Peniston and Kulkosky studies were published at the beginning of the "decade of the brain" in the 1990s, when, to be accepted, innovative thinking had to be supported either by the latest brain imaging technologies or brain-based experimental data. LeDoux's (1999) groundbreaking data about the "emotional brain," for example, was supported by a series of animal experiments that highlighted the relevance of specific neuronal networks involved in emotional processing. Eugene Peniston's reality was rather different. As a clinician working at VA Medical Center, he obviously could not offer an explanation for the neurobiological circuitry involved in the revision of traumatic memories, nor complex imagery, to support his findings, which may have further reduced the impact of his proposals among neuroscientists of this time.

Incidentally, it was only recently that some neurotherapists, or neurofeedback practitioners, have become equipped with QEEG (quantitative electroencephalography) technology, which may now enable the investigation of changes in biomarkers pre- and post-A/T training, which is likely to offer significant advances in our understanding of brain changes following this type of intervention (see also chapters 1 and 3).

Finally, Peniston's ideas found no relevant echo among the cognitive-behavioral therapy (CBT) movement that dominated the memory "consolidation" era of psychotherapy in the 1990s. CBT's indifference towards the role of the subconscious in trauma rehabilitation is widely documented, which may have led Peniston to take his ideas "underground" and affiliate his work with an alternative group affiliated with the autogenics training tradition, led by Elmer and Alyce Green at the Menninger Clinic. I am grateful to Pat Norris (chapter 2), for clarifying that Elmer and Alyce started their work in biofeedback with the intention of demonstrating the unconscious mind, and of making the unconscious conscious.

From the beginning, it was a natural fit for Eugene Peniston, who studied with the Voluntary Controls Group in consecutive workshops. It was from this data that he would eventually derive his protocol, as Pat explained. With the benefit of hindsight, it is now possible to see that Peniston's decision to affiliate his work with the Menninger tradition was also ahead of its time.

It seems therefore that Peniston's isolation may have resulted from his lack of "recognizable" theoretical affiliation, to which other psychotherapeutic groups could not relate. But this is not all. The issue of theoretical jurisdiction seems to have been compounded by an apparent mismatch between Peniston's low-key writings, as explained, and what he actually said during personal communications, as discussed in the next sections.

Consequences of the Myth of Indelibility for Psychotherapeutic Practice

The myth of indelibility, arguably disseminated by the memory consolidation lobby, has had important consequences by shaping psychotherapeutic thinking around the core idea that there is no option other than to *suppress* unwanted emotional memories. As elegantly explained by Ecker et al. (2012), "Indelibility implied also that the only possible psychotherapeutic strategy for preventing symptoms based in emotional memory was the use of *counteractive* methods—the class of methods (including extinction training prototypically) that *compete* against unwanted learning by building up a preferred learning and response intended to override and suppress the unwanted response. The unwanted response remains relatively free to recur, so an *ongoing counteractive* effort is typically required indefinitely" (pp. 16–17, my italics).

The above suggests two essential consequences for trauma rehabilitation and, ultimately, the Peniston protocol. On the one hand, it establishes that implicit (or subconscious) emotional memories last a lifetime, and that the hope that clients may become free from traumatic emotional conditionings is unrealistic. On the other, it follows that the only possible hope would be for psychotherapists to engage their clients in the active learning of counteractive methods, such as extinction training, designed "to compete against unwanted learning by building up a preferred learning and response intended to override and suppress the unwanted response" (Ecker et al., pp. 16–17).

The idea behind counteracting a response, is to prevent the expression of the relevant symptom by teaching the client to choose a more desired state to occur, instead of the symptom. Authors interested in the cognitive-behavioral therapy approach have championed the above concept.

However, what many may not realize is that the counteracting concept also includes other strategies such as learning relaxation techniques to counteract anxiety or building positive thoughts to counteract depression, or using oxytocin to enhance feelings of emotional connection and empathy. Although helpful, these are unlikely to facilitate the expression of repressed emotional memories, the crux of the matter (Freud, 1895). Such level of emotional expression requires a *transformational* method (Ecker et al., 2012).

Interestingly, it is now possible to see that the Peniston protocol defied the indelibility myth in the late 1980s before mainstream psychotherapy was aware that there were alternatives to the *counteractive* school of thought. Yet, and with the benefit of hindsight, Peniston's transformational protocol now deserves a place among other cutting-edge treatments for trauma rehabilitation with the proviso that we, as neurotherapists, agree to embrace, elaborate, and disseminate the concept of *transformational* therapy as the epistemological basis for the Peniston protocol. (For a discussion of counteractive vs. transformational change, see Toomey and Ecker, 2009). It is perhaps useful at this point to review the Peniston protocol's often-forgotten psychodynamic roots.

The Peniston Protocol's Unacknowledged Psychodynamic Roots

In writing, Peniston was very sparse with clinical terminology and psychodynamic expressions. In the discussion section of their second paper, for example, Peniston & Kulkosky (1991) wrote that "the combat veterans' recurring anxiety-provoking nightmares/flashbacks are *symbolic* expressions of survival guilt feelings reflective of those traumatic combat events that had been repressed and displaced by guilt-ridden emotions" (p. 56, emphasis added).

He offers no psychologically framed interpretation for his findings. The only written reference (of affiliation) to Freudian concepts, or the unconscious, is brief and tangential. Further, Peniston and Kulkosky (1991) seem to have ignored classic psychodynamic literature on issues such as repression and displacement—both known Freudian mechanisms of defense—and to have chosen to frame their findings as an "unexpected development [that] has been referred to in the past decade as Breuer and Freud's Abreaction concept" (p. 56, emphasis added).

This statement is at least contradictory. Then, rather cryptically for a potential audience of mainstream psychotherapists, they preferred to suggest that A/T training might have facilitated "greater inter-hemispheric synchrony" (Peniston et al., 1993, p. 46).

In later papers, Peniston et al. (1993) do mention Freud, albeit quite briefly and in the context of other PTSD-related authors, steering away from direct references to a psychodynamic approach or affiliation. They wrote: "Freud (1953), Kardiner and Spiegel (1947), and Kolb and Mutalipassi (1982) postulated that traumatic anxiety-provoking imageries might be due to long-standing amnesias, shorter-term defenses against remembering, or the patient's inability to convey his internal experience" (p. 46).

The above excerpt contains an important point that requires some tentative translation. Were the authors alluding to the need to construct a meaningful emotional narrative? Crucially, Peniston makes no mention (in writing, that is) of the actual psychotherapeutic process he used after the brainwave sessions to help patients "convey [their] internal experience."

Fortunately, other neurotherapists seem to have no doubts in their interpretation of Peniston and Kulkosky's work as psychodynamic, highlighting its relation to the unconscious, although many A/T training practitioners may not agree with this interpretation. As stated by White and Richards (2009), "The late Eugene Peniston may have given us an elegant process, increasingly supported by neurobehavioral research, to unlock the unconscious and alter perceptions, *rewrite personal history,* heal the self and enhance one's life" (p. 143, emphasis added).

Note that White and Richards (2009) use the expression "rewrite personal history," which arguably means constructing a meaningful emotional narrative. However, in *contrast* to his written work, where he mainly described the steps used during the brainwave section of his protocol, Peniston's personal communications were filled with detail and recognition for the role of the therapist in facilitating the interpretation of contents revealed during the crossover, and their *integration* into a meaningful narrative. All authors in this book who met Eugene Peniston personally have confirmed this account.

Unfortunately, these crucial accounts were lost to a wider audience. The resulting lack of clarity has apparently led to a silent rift amongst A/T training practitioners, who can now be divided into those who favor the "technical approach"—as "printed"—and those who have incorporated the second part of the protocol—as "told."

Consequently, the psychotherapeutic community is less likely to co-opt a purely technical protocol, which does not incorporate the second part dedicated to finding meaning (it should be noted that the only exception to this would be in cases where A/T training is used for peak-performance enhancement). The result has perhaps led to a situation akin to the metaphor of a genie reluctant to leave the bottle, alluding to some of the Peniston protocol's untapped potential as a therapeutic tool.

The good news, however, is that recent developments in neuroscience have changed the landscape of psychotherapy, which in turn may have helped reframe the relevance of the Peniston protocol to a new generation of brain-savvy psychotherapists who now search brain-based methodologies (or tools) to enable them to work with patients with trauma. It seems that the Peniston protocol is now having a second lease on life that may lead to its active dissemination to a wider audience. I turn to a brief review of these developments in the next section.

Recent Developments in Neuroscience and Reframing the Relevance of the Peniston Protocol

The first key development has been the discovery of memory reconsolidation, which has finally unveiled the cellular mechanisms underlying a new form of neuroplasticity capable of revising or even deleting traumatic memories (Dudai & Eisenberg, 2004; Duvarci & Nader, 2004; Nader, Schafe, & LeDoux, 2000; Pedreira & Maldonado, 2003; Przybyslawski & Sara, 1997; Przybyslawski, Roullet, & Sara, 1999; Roullet & Sara, 1998; Sara, 2000; Schiller et al., 2010; Walker, Brakefield, Hobson, & Stickgold, 2003). The surprising advance lies in the identification of the brain synapses and processes involved in the storing of implicit memories and the evidence suggesting that the brain circuits involved in the storing of long-standing implicit memories are, after all, more *unstable* than previously thought.

Data supporting the memory reconsolidation process has been replicated by several laboratories. These studies show that unstable and unconsolidated synapses (as well as well-learned consolidated responses) could be destroyed by specific chemical agents and no longer be evoked (Nader et al., 2000; Przybyslawski et al., 1999; Przybyslawski & Sara, 1997; Roullet & Sara, 1998; Sara, 2000).

So, following decades dominated by the myth of indelibility, the new brain science of memory reconsolidation centers on surprising evidence that the brain has the ability to revise specific, unwanted emotional learning (including core, non-conscious beliefs, and schemas) at the level of the physiological, neural synapses that encode it in emotional memory (Ecker et al., 2012).

The above implies that the once-believed stability of memories is merely illusory. In reality, any reactivation presupposes a window of destabilization that, if not used therapeutically, simply returns to stability until a new reactivation occurs again. This process seems to correspond to Peniston and Kulkosky's crossover. If this hypothesis is true, then particular attention and guidance should be given to patients in the immediate moments after the occurrence of the crossover (i.e., destabilization) so that the process of memory reconsolidation may be maximized and the emotional content released, via a powerful re-interpretation and re-integration of its meaning. This is a process that one of my clients has described as her "light-bulb moments." The development of such guidelines is still work in progress.

Repercussions for Psychotherapy

The emergence of the neuroscience of memory reconsolidation has initiated a revolution in psychotherapeutic thinking leading to changes in key terminology used in trauma rehabilitation. For further reading about this theme, see a fascinating book by Ecker and colleagues (2012) titled *Unlocking the Emotional Brain, Eliminating Symptoms at Their Roots Using Memory Reconsolidation*.

An important consequence of the above is that a significant number of psychotherapists now have access to brain-based, and somewhat theory-independent terminology to deal with the dynamics of trauma rehabilitation (Ecker et al., 2012) without the traditional stigma associated with the "old-school" psychodynamic approaches. Genie Bodenhamer-Davis, also an author in this book (chapters 6 & 8) who worked with Eugene Peniston in the early 90's, told me that he would refer to the post-crossover therapeutic process as "there, there therapy" without the need to impose a theoretical lens on the spontaneous contents being offered by the patients.

The term emotional learning refers to contents that are stored in memory during experiences involving strong emotion and a sense of being under inescapable threat (McGaugh & Roozendaal, 2002; Roozendaal, McEwen, & Chattarji, 2009). The former "unconscious," has been reformulated as "emotional memories," which, according to the above-mentioned evidence can be reprocessed via psychotherapeutic work.

Emotional memories typically include "implicit" or procedural knowledge, consisting of schemas, patterns, and templates that have been extracted from experience and are stored in memory systems that are different from those dedicated to autobiographical, "episodic" knowledge of past events (Siegel, 1999; Toomey & Ecker, 2007).

Although emotional memories typically remain out of awareness, they still generate and modulate thoughts, behaviors, and emotions in response to everyday-life experiences (Ecker et al., 2012). A specific feature of emotional memories is that they are stored in specialized subcortical implicit memory circuits that typically become exceptionally durable and active decades *after* the initial incidents (McGaugh, 1989; McGaugh & Roozendaal, 2002; Roozendaal, McEwen, & Chattarji, 2009). In extreme cases of trauma, emotional memories are responsible for impairments of cognitive neurobiological function that create a negative feedback loop that amplifies the effects of subsequent (and unrelated) stressful events, leading sufferers to have frequent traumatic flashbacks and a perpetual cycle of fear, depression, anxiety, and insomnia that will need to be addressed so they may heal.

In Table 1, we attempt to match these steps reflecting recent findings in neuroscience with Peniston's "full" protocol, suggesting that both lines of thought address the steps mentioned above.

The procedural steps involved in the process of memory reconsolidation and the subsequent transformation of existing emotional memories are now clear. Such knowledge has changed therapeutic dynamics by enabling a "first-person," client-centered," "brain-based" approach to deal with trauma.

According to Hupbach (2011), for example, the steps used to replace the target learning (trauma) effectively with new learning depend on "the degree with which the newly presented information [within the consolidation window] competes [i.e., is incompatible] with the previously encoded information." (p. 33) Hence, the brain-based rules for unlearning and erasing a target memory include three fundamental steps: reactivation, mismatching (or unblocking), and erasure or revision via new learning.

Eugene Peniston seems to have known this intuitively as he asked his alcoholic participants (as they were referred to in those days) to focus, with as much detail as possible, on the image of the desired outcome, as their brainwave patterns began to drop into the lower frequencies. As reported by White and Richards (chapter 10), an important element of this exercise was the invitation for the patients to feel their desired outcome as real and already accomplished, using the language of feeling and desire. This step, said White and Richards, "served to clarify and organize their intention for how they wished to see and experience themselves in the future," a concept that is today documented by a series of studies showing how meditation may affect brain net-

Table 1

Comparing the Memory Consolidation Process to A/T Training

Memory Consolidation Process	A/T Training
	Patient relaxation and focus on the issues to be addressed (target learning); i.e., visualization of the desired outcome.
Step 1. Reactivation: the therapist re-triggers or re-evokes the target content by presenting salient cues or contexts from the original learning.	Step 1. Crossover (brainwave session): reverie state during which traumatic contents may come to the patient's awareness.
Step 2. Mismatching or unblocking: concurrent with the reactivation, the therapist creates an experience that is significantly at variance with the target memory's model and patient expectations of how the world functions. This step unblocks synapses and renders memory circuits labile, i.e., susceptible to being updated by new learning.	Step 2. Integration: therapist facilitates the patient's re-interpretation and integration of traumatic contents (target learning) revealed during crossover into a meaningful narrative, without influencing their comments. This process is likely to suggest experiences and interpretations that are significantly at variance with the target memory's model and the patient expectations of how the world functions.
Step 3. Deletion or revision via new learning: During a window of about five hours before synapses have relocked, the client and therapist create a new learning experience that contradicts (for erasing) or supplements (for revising) the labile target knowledge. (The new learning experience may be the same as or different from the experience used for mismatch in Step 2; if it is the same, Step 3 consists of repetitions of Step 2.)	Step 3. Post session brief: a post-session brief orients the patient towards learning experiences that will continue to contradict or supplement the (now) unstable target learning (or traumatic content).

works and volitional changes in attention (King et al., 2006) as well as changes in structure (Hözel et al., 2011; Kang et al., 2012; Lazar et al., 2005; Vestergaard-Poulsen et al., 2009), ultimately supporting changes in behavior.

Conclusion

The Peniston protocol offers a reliable technique to tap into the brain's ability to modify and heal traumatic memories within a relatively low number of sessions. A/T training effectiveness has been recognized by the British Royal College of Psychiatrists (NICE guideline 26, 2005). It is the only neurotherapy protocol to have received such official recognition.

The Peniston protocol is also in sync with the most recent developments in neuroscience and their influence in modern psychotherapeutic thinking. Yet, it remains unknown to the significant majority of trauma rehabilitation therapists and psychotherapists currently working outside the field of neurotherapy.

Lo and behold, both brain-oriented psychotherapists and neurotherapists alike now find themselves exploring the intriguing relation between biomarkers, emotional learning, and the mechanisms of repression. As hypothesized a century earlier in a "project for a scientific psychology" (Freud, 1895), the Peniston protocol has come a step closer to solving the "heart of the riddle," which has invaluable worth for everyday psychotherapeutic practice.

A/T training offers a unique platform for collaboration between neurotherapists and psychotherapists interested in using a brain-based technique to access emotional memories and traumatic content. The full spectrum of professionals would include trauma rehabilitation specialists, addiction counselors, and life coaches at one end of the spectrum, and psychologists, psychiatrists, and neuropsychoanalysts at the other end, under the understanding that A/T training does not represent a conceptual field in itself nor should be the property of any of the above professions or professional services. Looking ahead, we suggest that this points to a new and fruitful collaboration between allied areas.

We have also proposed that neurotherapy, as a field, could benefit from the rethinking of A/T training epistemological roots and aim at reconnecting it with its original home: psychotherapy and (neuro) psychoanalysis.

This suggestion is based on evidence that Peniston's initial work did include crucial psychotherapeutic and psychodynamic elements that were reported by the author himself (personal communication, 1993) but were never included in the published papers. At the time, Peniston may have feared the stigmatization of the A/T training protocol as psychodynamic and, perhaps, unscientific.

This may have caused a silent rift among A/T neurotherapists. Those concerned with the protocol's scientific status opted for excluding the psychotherapeutic (or psychodynamic) segment and focused on its technical aspects, as reported in the Peniston and Kulkosky's papers. On the other hand, those interested in its psychodynamic dimension—more in tune with the initial Menninger school's teachings—may have become progressively isolated. Unfortunately, this informal rift may have affected the dissemination and scientific recognition of the Peniston protocol beyond the field of neurotherapy

However, recent developments in neuroscience have changed the landscape initially found by Peniston. New evidence has revealed the procedural steps necessary to support memory reconsolidation, a new form of neuroplasticity capable of revising traumatic memories. The advantage of hindsight suggests may have already understood memory reconsolidation as a process Peniston but could not explain it (at the cellular level) in the late 1980s. On the other hand, memory reconsolidation was discredited by mainstream neuroscience in those days.

Meanwhile, the discovery of memory reconsolidation has reframed the clinical and scientific relevance of the Peniston protocol and influenced a new generation of brainsavvy psychotherapists interested in theory independent (Ecker et al., 2012) terminology to deal with the dynamics of emotional memories and trauma rehabilitation, without the stigma associated with traditional psychodynamic theory.

In concrete terms, a fundamental step used to facilitate the process of memory reconsolidation is the mismatch: a process that unblocks synapses and renders memory circuits labile, i.e., susceptible to being updated by new learning. Interestingly, the mismatch loosely describes the psychotherapeutic steps taught by Peniston during his personal communications (see "integration" in table 1; Peniston, personal communication, 1993), where therapists were instructed to avoid influencing the patient's responses. However, although the above suggests that both methods (i.e., memory reconsolidation and A/T training) are compatible, the psychotherapeutic procedures used during "integration" in the Peniston protocol still need further clarification and perhaps harmonization amongst neurotherapists.

Predictably, many psychotherapists will now be looking for effective and innovative methods for accessing traumatic memories, and this is likely to drive the curiosity of a significantly larger audience for the A/T training protocol. Hence, a fruitful conceptual and methodological cross-fertilization between neurotherapy and memory reconsolidation psychotherapists, including neuropsychoanalysts, now seems not only possible but also imminent, for the benefit of hundreds of thousands of patients across the world.

As a final note, A/T practitioners should also focus on the development of clear guidelines for the application of the second part—i.e., the psychodynamic part—of the Peniston protocol. Such harmonization is likely to have a direct impact on the training of future clinicians, so that this powerful technique may be useful to many other psychotherapists interested in the field of trauma rehabilitation.

References

Bouton, M. E. (2004). Context and behavioral processes in extinction. *Learning and Memory, 11,* 485–494.

Dudai, Y., & Eisenberg, M. (2004). Rites of passage of the engram: Reconsolidation and the lingering consolidation hypothesis. *Neuron, 44,* 93–100.

Duvarci, S., & Nader, K. (2004). Characterization of fear memory reconsolidation. *Journal of Neuroscience, 24,* 9269–9275.

Ecker, B., Ticic, R., & Hulley, L. (2012). *Unlocking the emotional brain: Eliminating symptoms at their roots using memory reconsolidation.* New York, NY: Rutledge.

Foa, E. B. & McNally, R. J. (1996). Mechanisms of change in exposure therapy. In R. M. Rapee (Ed.), *Current controversies in the anxiety disorders* (pp. 329–343). New York, NY: Guilford Press.

Freud, S. (1895). A project for scientific psychology. In *The Standard Edition of the Complete Psychological Works of Sigmund Freud, 1950;* Vol. 1: 283–397. London: Hogarth Press, 1966.

Green, E. E., & Green, A. (1977). *Beyond biofeedback.* San Francisco, CA: Delacorte.

Greenhalgh, J., Dickson, R., & Dundar, Y. (2010). Biofeedback for hypertension: A systematic review. *Journal of Hypertension, 28*(4), 644–52.

Gruzelier, J., & Egner, T. (2005). Critical validation studies of neurofeedback. *Child and Adolescent Psychiatric Clinics of North*

America, 14, 83–104.

Hölzel, B. K., Carmody, J., Vangel, M., Congleton, C., Yerramsetti, S. M., Gard, T., & Lazar, S. W. (2011). Mindfulness practice leads to increases in regional brain gray matter density. *Psychiatry Research: Neuroimaging, 191*(1), 36–43. doi: 10.1016/j.pscychresns.2010.08.006.

Hupbach, A. (2011). The specific outcomes of reactivation-induced memory changes depend on the degree of competition between old and new information. *Frontiers of Behavioral Neuroscience, 5*, 33.

Institute of Medicine (IOM, 2008). *Treatment of posttraumatic stress disorder: An assessment of the evidence.* Washington, DC: The National Academies Press.

Kang, D. H., Jo, H. J., Jung, W. H., Kim, S. H., Jung, Y. H., Choi, C. H., ... & Kwon, J. S. (2012). The effect of meditation on brain structure: cortical thickness mapping and diffusion tensor imaging. *Social cognitive and affective neuroscience, 8*(1), 27–33.

Kardiner, A., & Spiegel, H. (1947). *War stress and neurotic illness.* Oxford, England: Hoeber.

Kolb, L. C. & Mutalipassi, L. R. (1982). The conditioned emotional response: A sub-class of the chronic and delayed post-traumatic stress disorder. *Psychiatric Annals, 12*(11), 979–987.

Kemp, J., & Bossarte, R. (2012). *Suicide data report. Suicide Prevention Program, Mental Health Services.* Department of Veterans Affairs.

King, A. P., Block, S. R., Sripada, R. K., Rauch, S., Giardino, N., Favorite, T., ... & Liberzon, I. (2016). Altered Default Mode Network (DMN) Resting State Functional Connectivity Following a Mindfulness-Based Exposure Therapy for Posttraumatic Stress Disorder (PTSD) in Combat Veterans of Afghanistan and Iraq. *Depression and Anxiety, 33*(4), 289–299.

Lazar, S. W., Kerr, C. E., Wasserman, R. H., Gray, J. R., Greve, D. N., Treadway, M. T., ... & Rauch, S. L. (2005). Meditation experience is associated with increased cortical thickness. *Neuroreport, 16*(17), 1893.

LeDoux, J. E., Romanski, L., & Xagoraris, A. (1989). Indelibility of subcortical emotional memories. *Journal of Cognitive*

Neuroscience, 1, 238–243.

Le Doux, J. (1999). *The emotional brain.* London: Weidenfeld & Nicholson.

Le Doux, J. (2015). *Anxious: Using the brain to understand and treat fear and anxiety.* New York, NY: Viking.

Lehrer, P. M., & Gevirtz, R. (2014). Heart rate variability biofeedback: How and why does it work? *Frontiers in Psychology, 5,* 756.

McGaugh, J. L. (1989). Involvement of hormonal and neuromodulatory systems in the regulation of memory storage. *Annual Review of Neuroscience, 2,* 255–287.

McGaugh, J. L. (2000). Memory—A century of consolidation. *Science, 287,* 248–251.

McGaugh, J. L., & Roozendaal, B. (2002). Role of adrenal stress hormones in forming lasting memories in the brain. *Current Opinion in Neurobiology, 12*(2), 205–210.

Milner, B., Squire, L. R., & Kandel, E. R. (1998). Cognitive neuroscience and the study of memory. *Neuron, 20,* 445–468.

Nader, K., Schafe, G. E., & Ledoux, J. E. (2000). Fear memories require protein synthesis in the amygdala for reconsolidation after retrieval. *Nature, 406,* 722–726.

National Institute for Health and Care Excellence (UK, 2005), *NICE Guideline 26.*

Panksepp, J., & Solms, M. (2012). What is neuropsychoanalysis? Clinically relevant studies of the minded brain. *Trends in Cognitive Sciences, 16*(1), 6–8.

Pedreira, M. E., & Maldonado, H. (2003). Protein synthesis subserves reconsolidation or extinction depending on the reminder duration. *Neuron, 38,* 863–869.

Peniston, E., & Kulkosky, P. (1989). Brainwave training and b-endorphin levels in alcoholics. *Alcoholism: Clinical and Experimental Research, 13*(2), 271–279.

Peniston, E., & Kulkosky, P. (1991). A/T brainwave neurofeedback therapy for Vietnam veterans with combat related post-traumatic stress disorder. *Medical Psychotherapy: An International Journal, 4,* 47–60.

Peniston, E. G., Marrinan, D. A., Deming, W. A., & Kulkosky. P. (1993). EEG A/T brainwave synchronization in Vietnam theater veteran with combat-related posttraumatic stress disorder and alcohol abuse. *Advances in Medical Psychotherapy: An International Journal, 6,* 37–50.

Przybyslawski, J., & Sara, S. J. (1997). Reconsolidation of memory after its reactivation. *Behavior and Brain Research, 84,* 241–246.

Przybyslawski, J., Roullet, P., & Sara, S. J. (1999). Attenuation of emotional and nonemotional memories after reactivation: Role of beta adrenergic receptors. *Journal of Neuroscience, 19,* 6623–6628.

Roozendaal, B., McEwen, B. S. & Chattarji, S. (2009). Stress, memory and the amygdala. *Nature Reviews Neuroscience, 10,* 423–433.

Roullet, P., & Sara, S. J. (1998). Consolidation of memory after its reactivation: Involvement of beta noradrenergic receptors in the late phase. *Neural Plasticity, 6,* 63–68.

Sara, S. J. (2000). Retrieval and reconsolidation: Toward a neurobiology of remembering. *Learning & Memory, 7,* 73–84.

Schiller, D., Monfils, M. H., Raio, C. M., Johnson, D. C., Ledoux, J. E. & Phelps, E. A. (2010). Preventing the return of fear in humans using reconsolidation update mechanisms. *Nature, 463,* 49–53.

Scott, W., & Kaiser, D. (1998). Augmenting chemical dependency treatment with neurofeedback training. *Journal of Neurotherapy, 3*(1), 66.

Scott, W. C., Kaiser, D., Othmer, S., & Sideroff, S. I. (2005). Effects of an EEG protocol on a mixed substance abusing population. *American Journal of Drug and Alcohol Abuse, 31,* 455–469.

Siegel, D. J. (1999). *The developing mind: Toward a neurobiology of interpersonal experience.* New York, NY: Guildford Press.

Sokhadze, T., Cannon, R., & Trudeau, D. (2008). EEG biofeedback as a treatment for substance use disorders: Review, rating of efficacy, and recommendations for further research. *Applied Psychophysiology and Biofeedback, 33,* 1–28.

Schultz, J. H., & Luthe, W. (1959). *Autogenic training: A*

psychophysiologic approach in psychotherapy. New York: Grune and Stratton.

Toomey, B., & Ecker, B. (2007). Of neurons and knowings: Constructivism, coherence psychology and their neurodynamic substrates. *Journal of Constructivist Psychology, 20*, 201–245.

Toomey, B., & Ecker, B. (2009). Competing visions of the implications of neuroscience for psychotherapy. *Journal of Constructivist Psychology, 22*, 95–140.

van der Kolk, B. (1994). The body keeps the score: Memory and the evolving psychobiology of post traumatic stress. *Harvard Review of Psychiatry, 1*(5), 253–265.

van der Kolk, B. (2014). *The body keeps the score: Mind, brain and body in the transformation of trauma*. London: Penguin Books.

van der Kolk, B. A., Hodgdon, H., Gapen, M., Musicaro, R., Suvak, M. K., Hamlin, E., & Spinazzola, J. (2016). A randomized controlled study of neurofeedback for chronic PTSD. *PLoS One, 11*(12), e0166752. https://doi.org/10.1371/journal.pone.0166752

Vestergaard-Poulsen, P., van Beek, M., Skewes, J., Bjarkam, C. R., Stubberup, M., Bertelsen, J., & Roepstorff, A. (2009). Long-term meditation is associated with increased gray matter density in the brain stem. *Neuroreport, 20*(2), 170–174.

Walker, M. P., Brakefield, T., Hobson, J. A., & Stickgold, R. (2003). Dissociable stages of human memory consolidation and reconsolidation. *Nature, 425*, 616–620.

White, N. E., & Richards, L. M. (2009). Alpha theta neurotherapy and the neurobehavioral treatment of addictions, mood disorders and trauma. In T. H. Budzynski, H. K. Budzynski, J. R. Evans, & A. Abarbanel (Eds.), *Introduction to Quantitative EEG and Neurofeedback, Second Edition: Advanced Theory and Applications* (2nd edition). Amsterdam: Academic Press.

15

Equipment, Training and Ethical Issues

Antonio Martins-Mourao, PhD
Cynthia Kerson, PhD

Issues Related to Equipment

Most equipment with 1- and 2-channel ability, that can be used for neurofeedback training, can provide the platform for A/T training. Because this is eyes-closed training, the salient requirements are soothing sounds and a different and distinct sound for each frequency bin, whether delta, alpha, theta or beta. Sounds should be able to modulate louder or softer or in tone along with the amplitude of the band. Preferably, nature-type tones should be available, such as a babbling brook, the ocean, rain, or birds. There can also be beats, such as that of Tibetan drums or other beat that in itself could help to entrain to the specific and appropriate frequency. Individual client preferences should be considered as they will be constantly reacting to the stimuli provided during the sessions. Thus, at the beginning of the first session a few minutes of acclimation and fine-tuning should be performed. In clinical practice, your author (CRK) always makes sure the client can tell the difference between each tone to be sure the client is training to the appropriate tones. She will also check in at the beginning of each A/T session to be sure the client remembers which tone is which.

While most alpha training described in this handbook considers alpha to be 8–12 Hz and theta 4–7 Hz, practitioners should be able to alter the frequency bins to accommodate the specific electrophysiological needs of the client. For example, if an assessment shows that the client has excessive high alpha (10–12 Hz) suggesting sympathetic over-arousal, the clinician may choose to train only 8–10 Hz and possibly inhibit the alpha faster frequency bin.

Additionally, as suggested in this handbook, training other pathologies prior to the A/T training would necessitate that the equipment be flexible to accommodate these training needs, which is generally the case in the more recent neurofeedback amplifier and software packages. This would include being able to change thresholds and length of time for sustained reward within each training paradigm, such as relative power, phase, or connectivity paradigms.

On the other hand, and as expected, the field has several challenges and opportunities ahead, as neurofeedback practice considers 19-channel amplifiers capable of deploying multi-channel neurofeedback, in some cases based on Independent Component Analysis (ICA) technology, capable of estimating deeper cortical sources of activity in the brain. This could represent another historical milestone for A/T training, which could clarify and transform the problem of scalp location. The more recent search for biomarkers may further establish scalp location for A/T training. Each biomarker may well correlate with a different location for A/T training.

So far, A/T practitioners have been divided into two main schools of thought; i.e. those applying electrodes in parietal locations, such as Pz, and those preferring to use occipital locations such as O1, as originally suggested by Eugene Peniston. However, Peniston's preference for the use of the occipital locations was never explained, other than by relying on the well-known notion, backed by electrophysiological data, that the occipital lobes are involved in the cortical expression of alpha oscillations.

Fresh 19-channel recordings and the subsequent 3-D tomographies offered by LORETA and sLORETA (Pascual-Marqui, Michel, & Lehmann, 1994; Pascual-Marqui, 2002) as well as studies from MRI, PET and MEG data, may well clarify issues of sensor location and help explore and categorize individual differences in A/T training candidates. The hope is that via a thorough assessment and the comparison of pre- and post A/T training interventions, practitioners will be able to understand individual EEG-phenotypes (see chapter 7) and which location will best serve individual cases, thus predicting greater intervention success.

Training Requirements

While A/T training can be performed with clients who have sleep issues, mild anxiety, and/or stress issues, it often involves patients with complex fear-based psychological difficulties. As discussed throughout the book, most often this includes PTSD, addictions and other forms of severe anxiety and personality disorders.

It is, for this reason, an advisable requisite that the clinician be trained in psychotherapy and competent in providing immediate attention to the client should an abreaction occur either during the session or afterwards. Practitioners should be prepared to join the client immediately and formulate an emergency plan that may be followed through by other health care parties and immediate family. A/T training brings the client into deep states that can be interrupted by the sudden emergency of the very memories the client has avoided for years, thus putting them in a vulnerable and unstable state whilst attempting to manage the emotional and cognitive resurgence specific to their particular issues.

The BCIA (Biofeedback Certification International Alliance, bcia.org) notes in its current blueprint for certification in neurofeedback that "psychotherapeutic skills and additional training beyond the introductory level course [is] required for Alpha-Theta practitioners."

Ethical Principles in A/T Training

A/T training, like any other form of neurofeedback practice, requires the application of ethical principles and best practice guidelines applicable to psychotherapeutic work and/or medical intervention. Many ethical issues encountered by A/T practitioners are the same as those encountered by psychotherapists and medical professionals, and relate to the obligation to maintain client confidentiality, offer informed consent, the need for clinical and research support and the clarification of issues relating to fees and billing.

It is assumed that the readers are familiar with the standards of practice and ethical principles disseminated by their own discipline such as those published by the American Psychological Association (APA) in the US, the British Psychological Society (BPS) in the UK, those offered by the Biofeedback Certification International Alliance (BCIA), and with those offered by professional associations such as the Association of Applied Psychophysiology and Biofeedback (AAPB) and the International Society for Neurofeedback Research (ISNR), for example.

Ensuring Good Standards of Care

Generally, A/T practitioners must adhere to all relevant ethical principles and standards of practice suggested by the professional bodies under which they are covered. This includes the obligation to protect their clients' rights and welfare by doing no harm through acts of omission or commission. For example, A/T practitioners should not, in any circumstance, falsify any diagnostic or procedural codes. They should not discriminate against any client on the basis of age, race, gender, nationality, sexual preference, religion, disability or socioeconomic status. Nor should they make false statements or complaints about clients or other practitioners and should not intentionally or unintentionally influence clients inappropriately.

Exaggerated claims for A/T training should be expressly avoided and practitioners should always strive to be honest and clear in the dealings with their clients and with those under their supervision or mentorship. A/T practitioners should not engage in problematic relationships with clients, supervisees, students, members of staff at their practice or research participants. They should also know the boundaries of their areas of competence and practice.

Further, A/T practitioners must be prepared to demonstrate that they are licensed and competent to work with particular populations and recognize different and co-morbid diagnostic categories and their associated behavioral symptoms. They should engage in ongoing continuing education to maintain and expand their areas of expertise, and strive to improve their credentials by seeking certification in specialties relevant to their area of practice. Whenever necessary, they should be prepared to refer clients for treatment to another practitioner if they believe they are not competent to meet the expected minimum standard of care with supervision and/or consultation available. They should also be prepared to seek competent supervision when clients present problems or when in doubt about how to proceed.

A/T practitioners should only supervise or mentor others in areas in which they are competent and exercise judgment when delegating work to supervisees; i.e. they should only perform procedures they are competent to perform. They should not attempt to treat every client with A/T training and should always make sure that treatments are appropriate and justified according to the client's needs in terms of efficacy and cost.

A/T training practitioners should monitor their own mental states, physical health and behaviors for signs of fatigue burn out and personal and emotional problems that may impact negatively on their clients. A/T practitioners are responsible for their treatments, actions and those whom they supervise or mentor (Striefel, 1995, 1999, 2006; Zuckerman, 2003) and should not abandon a client in need, making sure they may be referred to further competent treatment. A/T practitioners must keep good clinical records that adhere to the local regulations and offer support in after-hour emergencies.

Client Engagement and Decision-making

In more specific terms, A/T practitioners must have clear decision-making processes in place to support judgments about whether they should accept particular clients for treatment. Such judgments are likely to include several aspects such as potential diagnostic difficulties, the client's symptoms and their level of risk, any previous treatments followed and their reported effectiveness, likely side effects such as the risk of abreactions and the client's ability to finance their treatment.

Further, practitioners must give considerable thought to their own demonstrated and certified competence to treat the range of issues expected in clients seeking A/T training, whether they feel they would require supervision or even are legally authorized to treat these patients. A/T practitioners must ponder if their client's clinical needs may be better met if referred to other, more experienced, practitioners.

In some cases, practitioners should work collaboratively with other professionals. In any case, these considerations are likely to produce ethical dilemmas and "may require the integration of healthy personal experiences and values, positive emotions and good judgments to support and establish an ethical practice" (Striefel, 1999).

Striefel (1999) and Fowers (2005) have suggested that good, ethical practice should be based on a range of character traits including confidence (the ability to do what is seen as right, proper and effective), compassion (awareness and warmth towards another distress), commitment (accepting the responsibility to carry out competent service to a client), and ethical competence (good ethical judgment; i.e. knowing what to do and how to do it, despite potential negative repercussions).

A/T practitioners should be familiar with the current literature so that they may be capable of explaining the efficacy status of their intervention avoiding misleading clients or third-party treatment funders. "The ethical clinician never promises a cure and always makes it clear from the start that not everyone responds" (Demos, 2005; p. 8).

Informed Consent

To protect both client and practitioner, informed consent should be well documented stating what was—and was not—explained about the procedure used. The client should also be made aware of other treatment options available to them. Informed consent should be obtained in written form for all procedures included in the intervention, should the client, a competitor, or a licensing board raise questions, doubts or potential reasons for conflict at some point during or after the intervention.

The informed consent process should:
- provide the client with all the information necessary to make the required decisions before engaging in the treatment;
- make sure that the information is provided in a way that it is understood by the client, as verified by having the client answer questions about the information provided;
- ensure that the client has the capacity to give consent, which is assumed unless evidence to the contrary is presented; i.e. the client has diagnosed mental disability;
- inform the client about the limits of confidentiality (e.g. risk of self harm or harm of other) and not violate confidentiality except for the reasons stated;
- be given voluntarily without coercion;
- be given in written formed and signed;
- include written forms that are identical for all clients, explaining details of the intervention, risks, rules of confidentiality and details about fees, billings and cancellation policies.

Boundary Issues

Practitioners must pay careful attention to potential boundary issues with other professional groups. Obvious examples include making diagnoses in areas outside the scope of the practitioner's license, or suggest changes in the prescription of medications without the required license.

References

Demos, J. N. (2005). *Getting started with neurofeedback*. New York: W. W. Norton & Company.

Fowers, B. J. (2005). *Virtue and psychology: Pursuing excellence in ordinary practices* (Vol. xii). Washington, DC, US: American Psychological Association.

Pascual-Marqui, R. D. (2002). Standardized low-resolution brain electromagnetic tomography (sLORETA): Technical details. *Methods Find Exp Clin Pharmacol, 24*(Suppl D), 5–12.

Pascual-Marqui, R. D., Michel, C. M., & Lehmann, D. (1994). Low resolution electromagnetic tomography: A new method for localizing electrical activity in the brain. *International Journal of Psychophysiology, 18*(1), 49–65.

Striefel, S. (1995). Professional ethical behavior for providers of biofeedback. In M. S. Schwartz (Ed.), *Biofeedback: A practitioner's guide* (pp. 685–705). New York, NY: The Guilford Press.

Striefel, S. (1999). Ethical, legal, and professional pitfalls associated with neurofeedback services. In J. R. Evans & A. Abarbanel (Eds.), *Introduction to Quantitative EEG and Neurofeedback* (1st Edition, pp. 371–400). San Diego, California: Elsevier.

Striefel, S. (2006). Ethical responsibility and professional socialization. *Biofeedback, 34*(2), 43–47.

Striefel, S. (2009). Ethics in neurofeedback practice. In T. H. Budzynski, H. K. Budzynski, J. R. Evans, & A. Abarbanel (Eds.), *Introduction to Quantitative EEG and Neurofeedback, Second Edition: Advanced Theory and Applications* (2nd edition, pp. 475–492). Amsterdam: Academic Press.

Zuckerman, E. L. (2003). *The paper office: Forms, guidelines, and resources to make your practice work ethically, legally, and profitably* (3rd edition). New York: The Guilford Press.

Afterword

The collection of chapters included in this handbook represent the first attempt, nearly 30 years on, at binding together some of the best work in the field. We have included direct accounts given by a pioneering generation of practitioners who met Eugene Peniston personally and learned the technique directly from him, as well as those who experimented outside the box and devised training unique paradigms.

We have also discussed the required methods and strategies necessary for the application of A/T training and suggested that the field should benefit from an in-depth discussion around core theoretical issues that may facilitate a reconnection with clinical neuroscience and psychotherapy.

The above chapters suggest that A/T training has become a mature and cohesive therapeutic modality that offers a replicable and tried-and-tested technique to tap into the brain's ability to modify unwanted traumatic memories. The British Royal College of Psychiatrists and the UK's National Institute for Health and Care Excellence (NICE) have already recognized the relevance of this technique, as an effective treatment for the rehabilitation of deep trauma in children and adults.

As discussed in the book, A/T training offers a systematic method to explore specific empirical questions that may facilitate future progress in the fields of trauma and substance abuse rehabilitation. Finally, and quite crucially, A/T training also sits at the core of an ongoing NIMH-backed change in paradigm that has signaled a shift from the traditional DSM-based observation of symptoms on to biomarker-based diagnoses in mental health.

The Editors

Index

Abreaction, 119, 167–169, 181, 187, 202–203, 284–285, 306, 326, 333, 337, 375, 378

Addiction, see Substance use disorder (SUD)

Alcohol, see Substance use disorder (SUD)

Alpha rhythms (brainwaves), 5–6, 8, 10–11

Alpha-theta training

    Contraindications, 35–36

    Peniston protocol, 1, 346–350

    Scott-Kaiser modification, 252–257, 281–315

Amplitude, 5–6

Amygdala, 125, 134, 351

Anxiety, 92, 174, 177–178, 180, 247, 255, 262, 264, 268–269, 291, 305–307, 329, 331, 347, 356, 362

Artifact, 8–9, 12, 25, 193–195, 197, 298

Attention-deficit/hyperactivity disorder (ADHD), 15–16, 19–20, 32, 91–92, 109, 135, 252–254, 260, 262–264, 294–297, 307

Autism spectrum disorder, 16, 31–32, 130

Beck inventories and scales, 158–159, 162, 248, 290–291

Beta rhythms (brainwaves), 5, 8, 11–12

Biomarker, 10, 12, 21–22, 24, 27, 30–31, 354, 364, 374, 383

Bipolar Disorder (formerly manic depression), 320

Borderline Personality Disorder (BPD), 224–225, 290

Brain default network (BDN), 25

British Royal College of Psychiatrists, 364, 383

Cigarettes, see Tobacco

Contingent negative variation (CNV), 14–15

Index

Crossover, Therapeutic, 35, 84, 95–96, 141–169, 300, 348, 358, 360

Debriefing, 95, 108, 199, 213, 217–218

Delta rhythms (brainwaves), 5–8

Depression, 88, 149, 159, 162, 186, 191–192, 225, 248–249, 255, 263–264, 290–291, 295, 331, 356

Desensitization, 180, 191

Dissociative identity disorder, 205, 207, 209, 211, 213, 215, 217, 219, 337

Dopamine, 21, 133–134, 252

Drug Abuse/Addiction, see Substance use disorder (SUD)

DSM, 16, 22, 26–27, 30–31, 287, 383

Electroencephalogram (EEG), xxi, 2–3, 7, 23, 63, 76, 176, 245, 354

Electromyogram (EMG), 9, 62, 79, 91, 173–174, 177, 193–196, 207, 258

EMDR, 328, 338–339

Epilepsy, 3, 16, 22, 31–32

Equipment, 373–374

Ethical principles, 376, 379

Fatigue, 186, 191, 201, 329, 331, 378

Frequency, 5

Gamma rhythms (brainwaves), 5, 8–9, 12–13

Heart rate variability (HRV), 33, 169, 192–193, 201–202, 269

Heroin, see Opioid (heroin and prescriptions)

Hippocampus, 128–129, 132, 145, 148

HPA-axis, 126–130, 136

Hypertension, 64, 331

Imagery, 56, 59, 115, 142–169, 236–237, 303

Impedance, 9, 79, 85, 283–284, 298, 301

Independent component analysis (ICA), 25–26, 28–29, 31, 374

Index

Induction, 81, 141, 249, 268

Informed consent, 376, 379

Infra-low frequency (ILF), 8, 321–326, 328–336, 341–343

Insomnia, 191–192, 195, 362

Jurisdiction, theoretical, 350–351, 354

Learning theory, 17–20

Limbic, 1, 32, 125, 129, 131, 133

LORETA, 26, 28–29, 93, 96–98, 179, 375

Low voltage fast (LVF), 173–174, 178–180

Marijuana, see Substance use disorder (SUD)

Meditation, xxvii, 7, 75–87, 89–98, 132, 142, 247, 250, 257, 303, 362

Memory reconsolidation, 132, 345, 352, 359–360, 362, 365–366

Methamphetamine, see Substance use disorder (SUD)

Millon Clinical Multiaxial Inventories, 219–220, 225–228, 290–291

Minnesota Multiphasic Personality Inventory (MMPI), 58, 158–159, 162, 219, 224–227, 253, 258, 292, 296

Narrative, 33, 78, 95–96, 235, 239, 349, 357–358, 363

National Institute for Health and Care Excellence (NICE), 346, 383

National Institute of Mental Health (NIMH), 27, 30–31, 383

Neurometric, 23–24, 26, 31

Neuromodulation, 30–31, 133

Neuroscience, 1, 17, 21–22, 32, 36, 345–346, 351, 359–360, 362, 365, 383

Nightmares, 118, 299, 329, 356

Oscillation, 5, 7, 10, 13, 146, 174, 239, 287, 374

Pain, 63, 126, 240, 329–331

Phase, 6

Phenotype, EEG, 11, 24, 30, 91, 173, 175, 177–179, 375

Index

Phobias, 180, 224

Pittsburgh Sleep Quality Index (PSQI), 158–159, 162

Placebo, 89, 97, 251, 294, 334

Post-reinforcement synchronization, 18–20

Post-traumatic stress disorder (PTSD), see Trauma and post-traumatic stress disorder (PTSD)

Power, 6

Psychometric, 23, 35, 80, 90, 159, 165, 287, 293

Psychotherapy, 87–92, 95, 98, 169, 220–221, 223, 230, 247, 262, 269–270, 331, 335, 351–365, 375, 383

PTSD, see Trauma and post-traumatic stress disorder (PTSD)

Schizoid, 219, 224, 226, 290

Schizophrenia, 23, 58, 159, 224, 295, 324

Standards of care, 376–378

Stimulants (cocaine, methamphetamines), see Substance use disorder (SUD)

Suboxone, 262, 266–267

Substance use disorder (SUD)

    Alcohol, 62–73, 80, 115–120, 174, 177–179, 186–196, 223–229, 245–270, 281–308, 332–335, 339–340, 362

    Cannabis (marijuana), 253, 265

    Opioid (heroin and prescriptions), 251–252, 254–255, 259, 262, 265–268, 289, 293, 297, 324–325, 356

    Stimulants (cocaine, methamphetamines), 62–63, 69–73, 92, 251–260, 264–266, 297, 324–325

    Tobacco, 116, 289

Suicide, 224–225, 329, 331, 350

Test of Variables of Attention (TOVA), 254, 292, 318

Thalamus, 11, 125, 128, 132, 175–176

Therapist, role of, 166, 168, 237, 327, 337, 358

Theta rhythms (brainwaves), 5, 8–10

Tinnitus, 329, 331

Tomography, 26, 28–29, 93, 375

Training for practitioners, 26, 375–376

Trauma and post-traumatic stress disorder (PTSD), 32, 77, 79, 95, 119–120, 180, 264, 281, 297

Traumatic Brain Injury (TBI and mTBI), 76, 87, 262, 327–328, 330, 349

Trichotillomania, 224, 227

Unipolar, 263

Yoga, 78, 85, 87, 94–95, 109, 236